Video Production Handbook

Fifth Edition

Jim Owens
Asbury University

Gerald Millerson

NEW YORK AND LONDON

First published 2012 by Focal Press
70 Blanchard Road, Suite 402, Burlington, MA 01803

Simultaneously published in the UK by Focal Press
2 Park Square, Milton Park, Abingdon, Oxon OX14 4RN

Focal Press is an imprint of the Taylor & Francis Group, an informa business

Notices
Practitioners and researchers must always rely on their own experience and knowledge in evaluating and using any information, methods, compounds, or experiments described herein.

Product or corporate names may be trademarks or registered trademarks, and are used only for identification and explanation without intent to infringe.

Library of Congress Cataloging-in-Publication Data
Owens, Jim, 1957–
Video production handbook / Jim Owens, Gerald Millerson.–5th ed.
p. cm.
Rev. ed. of: Video production handbook / Gerald Millerson, Jim Owens. 2008.
Includes index.
ISBN: 978-0-240-52220-3 (pbk.)
1. Video recording. 2. Video recordings–Production and direction. I. Millerson, Gerald. II. Title.
TK6655.V5M55 2011
778.59—dc22
2011013098

ISBN 13: 978-0-240-52220-3 (pbk)

Contents

Acknowledgments

Many people and organizations contributed greatly to this project. I have listed many of these people below. Of special note is Asbury University, my school, which has allowed me the flexibility to stay involved in professional television production around the world.

The editors at Focal Press have been encouraging and helpful in many ways:

Elinor Actipis and Michele Cronin.

The reviewers spent a significant amount of time reviewing the manuscripts and providing guidance:

For the Fifth Edition: Cory Byers (Southern Illinois University-Edwardsville), Thomas Caputi (St. John's University), John Caro (University of Portsmouth), Matthew J. Cupach (North Central State College), Steve Keeler (Cayuga Community College-SUNY), Leah B. Mangrum (Angelo State University), Mik Parsons (Bournemouth University), Roger Paskvan (Bemidji State University), David Sholl (Miami University of Ohio).

For the Fourth Edition: Osabuohien P. Amienyi (Arkansas State University), Thomas E. Caputi (St. John's University), Tony Grant (BBC-trained Lighting Cameraman and Consultant), Roy Hanney (University of Chichester), Phil Hoffman (University of Akron), Paul Kaspar (Lytchett Minster School, Dorset), Steven Keeler (Cayuga Community College-SUNY), Tom Kingdon (Emerson College), Sarah Lewison (Southern Illinois University), Larry Scher (Rio Hondo College) and Doug Smart (Asbury University).

A number of video/television professionals agreed to be interviewed for this book:

Brock Smith, Robin Sjogren.

Contributors of photographs, illustrations, and advice:

Will Adams, Alfacam, Asbury University, Audio-Technica, Avanti Group, BandPro, Dennis Baxter, BBC, K. Brown, Canon, Chyron, Chad Crouch, Compix, Countryman Associates, Doremi, Paul Dupree, Firestore, Focus Enhancements, FX Group: www.fxgroup.tv, Grass Valley/Thomson, Jon Greenhoe, David Grosz, Holophone, Imagine Products, Russ Jennisch, JVC, Hank Levine, Litepanels, Lowell, LPG, Manfrotto, Don Mink, Shannon Mizell, MobiTV, Mole-Richardson, Brady Nasfell, NBC, Lynn Owens, Sarah Owens, Panasonic, Steve Rehner, Kristin Ross, Sarah Seaton, Shure, Doug Smart, Sony, Steadicam, Mark Stokl, Ben Taber, Josh Taber, Tektronix, Tiffen, Uni-Set,

Vortex Media, VFGadgets, Videosmith, Taylor Vincent, Nathan Waggoner, Wescott, WLEX-TV, WOOD-TV, YouTube, Tyler Young, Adam Wilson, and Zeiss.

Some illustrations were created using StoryBoard Quick software.

The unwavering support of my wife, Lynn, and daughter, Sarah, has been incredible throughout the writing process.

Introduction

The digital revolution in television and video has changed the way we create and distribute projects. In many ways it has levelled the playing field between a recent college graduate and the CEO of a network. If your project is good, you can draw millions to it online. However, the basic production principles have stayed the same. For over 50 years, Gerald Millerson's books on television and video production have been highly regarded for their clarity of explanation and emphasis on techniques to enhance storytelling. This fifth edition of *Video Production Handbook* continues that tradition while embracing the new technologies that are now around us. Again, the book has been completely updated with the latest changes in technology and production strategies. Highlights include the following:

- A visual presentation of the material with updated full-color illustrations *throughout*
- Interviews featuring professionals working in video and television
- Up-to-date information on new equipment (DSLRs, 3D, cell phones, and flash memory) and techniques
- Valuable material on new distribution outlets (the web, cell phones)
- Detailed teaching resources for instructors

WHAT IS THIS BOOK ALL ABOUT?

This book was designed to provide you with the basics of video production in an easily digested format. It covers the production process and techniques involved in transforming ideas in your head into an effective presentation on a screen.

The knowledge you develop by reading this book will provide a solid foundation for video projects and future studies. We have concentrated on the practical features of video production so that you can achieve worthwhile results right from the start, whether you are using a simple consumer camcorder or professional equipment. This book will help you get the best out of your equipment. When the highest level of equipment is shown, adapt the concepts to the level you are working at.

WHO IS THIS BOOK WRITTEN FOR?

We designed this book for anyone who wants high-quality videos on a modest budget. The book was developed to help the beginner in video production learn the right way to create a video, whether in a class or working on your own. It is especially helpful for entry-level and medium-level television production courses and workshops. This text does not assume that you have any type of technical background or any previous experience—or that you are really interested in the nuts and bolts of equipment.

DO I HAVE THE RIGHT EQUIPMENT?

The equipment available today at the lowest consumer level, even some mobile phones, is good enough. The emphasis is on how to create a quality video program, and that requires a knowledge of how to effectively use the equipment and how to tell a story. Today the equipment is not a big issue.

WHY IS IT IMPORTANT TO LEARN "TECHNIQUES"?

Great ideas do not automatically make great programs. It is not enough to simply show what is going on. The way you present your subject will influence how your audience responds. You need know how to create quality video and audio, to convey your ideas in interesting ways to impact your audience.

TERMINOLOGY

We have tried to apply the most commonly used video production terminology in this book. However, terminology sometimes differs from country to country, and even company to company within a country. You will notice that some expressions have a term in parentheses next to them. The terms in the parentheses are usually words from the United Kingdom or Europe.

TEACHING WITH THIS BOOK

The book has been designed with numbers that refer to each topic area. This makes assigning reading areas much simpler. Instead of being limited to just page numbers, teachers can assign specific section numbers. While we have written this material in what we consider to be a logical sequence, we understand that every teacher has an order that he or she likes to use when covering the different subjects. The section numbering system allows the teacher to simply assign the material in any order. For more specific suggestions on reordering the sequence of material, please consult the instructor's manual.

INSTRUCTOR'S MATERIAL

We have also created instructor's material to aid in using this book in a classroom setting. Qualified instructors may access the material by contacting their Focal Press textbook representative or registering at
www.focalpress.com/9780240522203.

The instructor's material includes the following:

- PowerPoint/Keynote slides and images that match the illustrations in the text
- Exam questions for each chapter
- Video demonstrations
- Instruction recommendations

SUMMARY

We are mainly concerned with principles and practices, since these are the timeless essentials of video productions that effectively communicate. We have updated this edition to cover the latest technology and distribution media in order to help your programs have greater audience appeal and to help you with the problems you may encounter while working in video production. Keep in mind that in the end, what really matters is what you have to say and how effective you are at saying it. Wayne Freedman, from KGO-TV, summarizes it well: "When you present your story, try to think of the television as a window or conveyance … because if you can break through the din of everything else going on … viewers are going to look, listen, and perhaps even go on a journey with you."

Jim Owens
November 2010

CHAPTER 1

Overview of Video Production

Please answer the TV set. I am watching the phone.
—Stefan Kurten, Director of Operations, European Broadcast Union

1.1 WHAT IS VIDEO PRODUCTION?

The differences between "video production" and "television production" have become increasingly blurred over the past few years. Most video production is concerned with nonbroadcast program making. Video productions are generally distributed via DVDs, online, or mobile phones. Although video productions are generally made with a lower budget, it does not mean that fewer people see them. A simple tour of YouTube will show that millions of people are looking at video productions every day (Figure 1.1).

Television productions, on the other hand, are usually shown to a large public audience by broadcast or cable transmission, either "live" (during the performance) or "recorded" (carefully edited video recordings). Television broadcast transmissions are required to conform to closely controlled technical standards. However, television productions may be considered to be a type of video production once they are distributed in a nonbroadcast method (DVD, Internet, etc.).

With the high quality of today's consumer and prosumer equipment, video productions can be made with equipment ranging from the most sophisticated professional broadcast standards to low-cost consumer items (Figure 1.2). There is no intrinsic reason, though, why the final video productions should differ in quality, style, or effectiveness as far as the audience is concerned. Video programs range from ambitious presentations intended for mass distribution to economically budgeted programs designed for a specific audience. This book will help you, whatever the scale of your production.

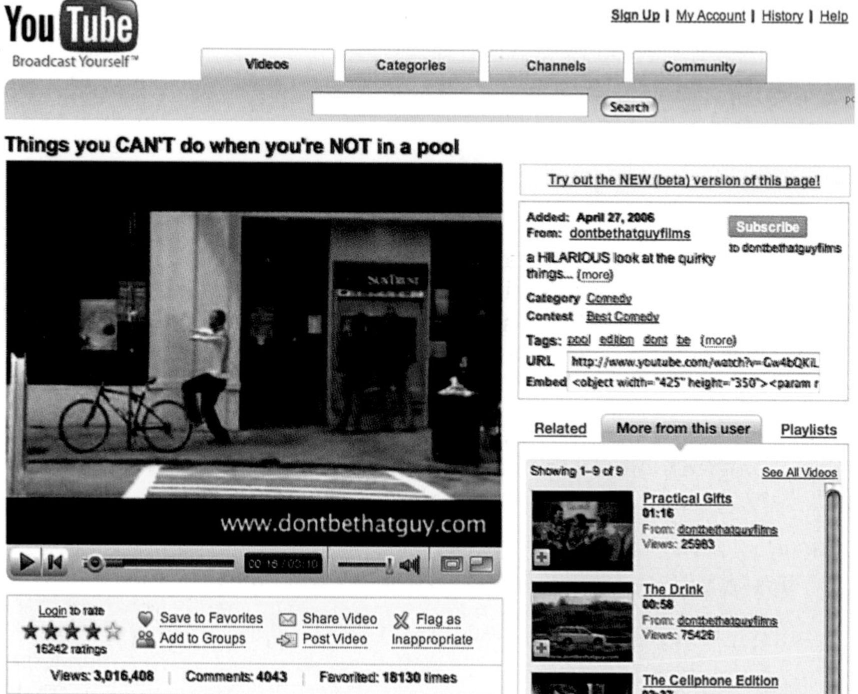

FIGURE 1.1
YouTube is a collection of both high-budget and low-budget video productions that millions of viewers watch online. Note that the video shown has been seen by more than 3 million viewers.

FIGURE 1.2
Today's high-quality consumer equipment allows professional results—if you understand how to use it effectively.
(Photo courtesy of Vortex Media.)

1.2 DEFINING THE NEW MEDIA

There is always a question about what "new media" is. It is a term we hear frequently. When the European Broadcast Union recognized that its members did not understand the definitions, it worked with those members to define the term. The organization's basic question was, how can we distinguish television from the new media? The organization adopted two basic terms: *linear service* and *nonlinear service*.

Television is considered a linear service—that is, the broadcasting of a program where the network or station decides when the program will be offered, no matter what distribution platform is used. Although there are many new distribution platforms (satellite, broadband Internet, iPod/PDA, and the cell phone), if television uses the platform, it is a linear service.

On the other hand, the nonlinear services equal the new media, which means making programs available for on-demand delivery. For instance, video-on-demand can use any platform. It is the *demand* that makes the difference.

> Most people's experience of web video is characterized by the tiny, pixilated windows familiar to YouTube users. But tomorrow's web users will expect service quality much closer to television, and major content owners like Disney recognize that they will have to step up to this mark to win and retain web viewers.
>
> **—David Mercer, Principal Analyst, Strategy Analytics**

FIGURE 1.3
Mobile phones, computer tablets, and computers are changing the way the audience watches television.

1.3 DISTRIBUTION

As mentioned earlier, the traditional means of distribution have been limited to DVD, satellite, cable, and broadcast. The whole concept of television is changing. In the past, viewers watched by appointment, at the time designated by the networks. Today, viewers want to be able to watch any program they want, on any viewing device that may be nearby, at any time. Online, DVRs, and mobile phones have stepped up to the demand … allowing it to happen (Figure 1.3).

FIRST STEP IN VIDEO PRODUCTION

1.4 UNDERSTANDING THE FIELD OF VIDEO PRODUCTION

Video production appears deceptively simple. After all, the video camera gives us an immediate picture of the scene before us, and the microphone picks up the sound of the action. Most of us start by pointing our camera and microphone at the subject but find the results unsatisfying. Why? Is it the equipment or us? It may be a little of both. But the odds are that *we* are the problem.

As you may have already discovered, there is no magic recipe for creating attractive and interesting programs. All successful production springs from a foundation of knowing the equipment, production techniques, and video production process:

1. Knowing how to handle the equipment properly and the effects of the various controls.
2. Knowing how to use the equipment effectively. Developing the skills underlying good camerawork and sound production.
3. Knowing how to convey ideas convincingly and how to use the medium persuasively.
4. Knowing how to organize systematically. Applying practical planning, preparation, and production.

As you work through this book, the knowledge you develop will soon become a natural part of your approach to creating a production. Knowing what the equipment can do will enable you to select the right tools for the job and use them the right way. In the end, sloppy production reduces the effectiveness of a program.

1.5 IT'S DESIGNED FOR YOU

Most production equipment has been designed for quick, uncomplicated handling. After all, it is there for one fundamental purpose—*to enable users to communicate their ideas to an audience.* Video equipment is as much a communication tool as a computer or a cell phone.

1.6 LEARNING BASICS

It is not important to know *how* every function of the equipment works, but it is important to know its capabilities in order to get reliable results. Even with the most sophisticated video and audio equipment, you need to answer only a handful of basic questions to use it successfully:

- What is the equipment *for*?
- What can it *do*?
- What are its *limitations*?
- Where are the *controls* and *indicators* (menus, buttons, etc.)?
- How and when should they be *adjusted*?
- When adjusted, what will the *result* be?

1.7 REMEMBER THE PURPOSE

There is no shortcut to experience. As you handle equipment, you grow familiar with its use. But don't let the latest trendy camera handling preoccupy you.

Many new camera operators have tried to show how good they are by quick moves, fast zooms, and attention-getting composition—where an experienced camera operator would have avoided these distractions and held a steady shot, letting the subject work to the camera instead. Smooth, accurate operation is important, but *appropriateness* is even more desirable. In the end, it is *audience impact* that really counts—the effect the chosen camera treatment has on the viewer.

1.8 EQUIPMENT

Don't get too enamored with the hardware. You do not need elaborate or extensive facilities to produce successful productions. Even the simplest equipment may provide the needed essentials. It really depends on the type of production you are creating. For some purposes, one camera is ideal. For others, a dozen may be insufficient.

What is done is more important than *how* it is done. If it is possible to get an effective moving shot along a hospital corridor by shooting from a wheelchair rather than a special camera dolly, the audience will never know—or care.

Sometimes extra effects on equipment can tempt the camera operator to use them *because they are there* rather than because they are needed. On broadcast television, for example, wipes, star filters, or diffused shots are sometimes used in the wrong place, at the wrong time, just for the sake of variety and because they are readily available. What appears at first sight to be a sophisticated, stylish presentation may have far less impact on the audience than a single still shot that lingers to show someone's expression.

> It's funny to me that I'm pretty against auto-settings, but I'm going to be working on a piece soon that's going to be 75% iPhone video. Videography seems to be going two ways: super-fast and easy (iPhones, flip cameras), and high-quality HD cinematography (Red cameras, D-SLR). The audience seems fine with both, depending on the situation. Being able to adapt is key right now.
>
> **—Nathan White, Videographer**

VERSATILITY OF VIDEO

Video Medium

- The television camera provides an instant image in full color.
- Cameras may be automated and can be remotely controlled (Figure 1.3).
- Images can span from the microscopic to the infinities of outer space.
- Video images from several sources can be combined (inset, split screen).
- The image can be modified and manipulated (color, tonal values, shape and form, sharpness, etc.).

Video Presentation

- The video picture can be shown on screens that range from pocket-sized to giant displays or from a single screen to a "videowall" (multiscreen) display.
- Videos can be shown by themselves or combined with other media such as a PowerPoint or on a website.
- The video signal can be distributed instantly by cable (wire, fiber-optic), Wi-Fi, microwave, infrared link, or satellite.
- Videos can be stored online to be downloaded whenever it is convenient for the viewer.
- Video artwork and titles can be created electronically (computer graphics).
- While historically video has been shot for a horizontal screen, the increased popularity of mobile phone video and the placement of video on websites has opened the door to vertical video images.
- See Figure 1.4.

Video Recording

- The video signal can be stored in different forms (photographic, tape, flash memory, DVD, CD, and hard drive/servers).
- Video recordings can be played back immediately and replayed many times. They can be stored indefinitely.
- Video recordings can be erased in selected parts or completely. New recordings can usually be made on the erased medium.

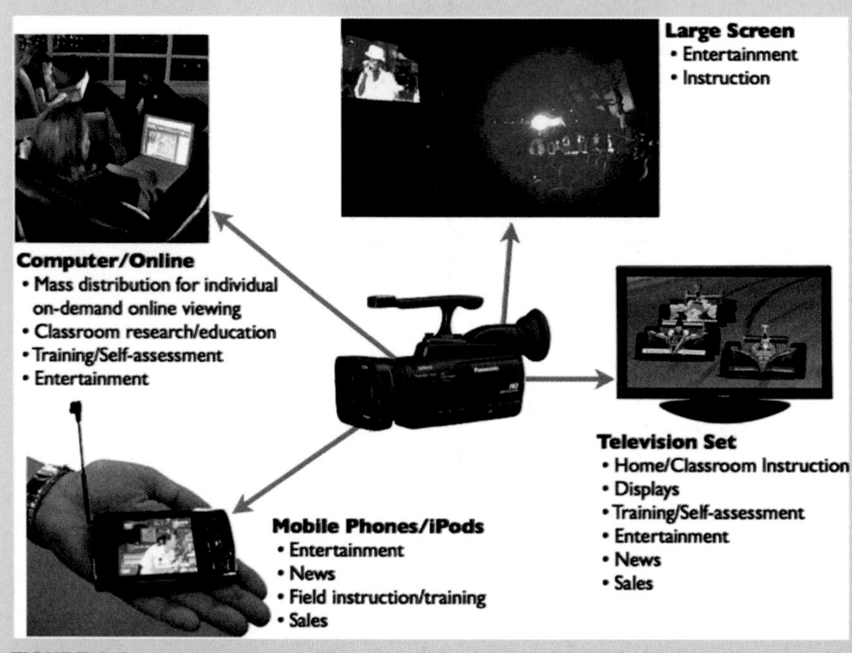

FIGURE 1.4
Video productions can be shown on many different media.

- Video recordings can be reproduced at faster or slower speeds than normal. A single moment of action can be frozen ("still frame," "freeze frame"); a day's events can be played back in a few seconds using time-lapse recording.
- Taped programs can be edited to delete faulty or irrelevant shots, enhance the presentation, adjust program duration, and so on.

Recorded Sound

- The sound normally recorded with the picture when video recording can be augmented or replaced (e.g., music, commentary).

1.9 WHAT EQUIPMENT IS NEEDED?

Let's take a look at the types of issues that affect the equipment you will need. When working with a larger production, a wide range of facilities is usually available. Extra items can be rented from a rental house or production facility. Look through any manufacturer's or supplier's catalog or a video magazine to see the endless variety of equipment available.

On the other hand, a small production may need to work within the limitations of *existing* equipment, unless it proves possible to augment it in some way. A lot is going to depend on the kind of program that you are making and on your specific approach to the subject:

- *Production style.* There is not a single way every production must be created—they can be tackled in a number of different ways. Each style will have its merits and its drawbacks. Suppose, for example, you are shooting two people talking together (an interview or general conversation). You can treat this formally, by shooting them seated at a desk, or informally, by shooting them while they are resting in easy chairs. But to create a more natural ambience, you might show one of them working at a task, such as gardening, while the other looks on. Alternatively, you might shoot them walking side by side along a pathway. Another familiar approach is to shoot them within a car as they drive to their destination.
- *Limitations.* Every production will have its own types of limitations for camera and sound treatment. In one situation, the camera may need to be held firmly on a tripod; in another, the camera will probably need a dolly; while in another, it will be necessary to carry the camera on your shoulder or even attach it to a car. Sound pickup problems will also vary. Clearly, how one shoots the action and where it takes place will affect the selection of the optimum gear for the job.
- *Shooting circumstances.* Obviously, equipment that is essential for some situations, like an underwater camera, proves unsuitable for other projects. While a robust camera mounting is necessary for continuous shooting, it can become an encumbrance if the camera constantly needs to be repositioned in crowded surroundings. At times, even a microphone may be

superfluous if the shoot does not need audio, since sound content can be added during the postproduction (Figure 1.5).

> If we simply produce a flow of TV images for mobile phones, then probably we shall simply say, "Well, this is just a gadget." But, on the contrary, if we create formats, which are specific to this new platform, then we shall be able to meet [or exceed] the consumers' expectations.
>
> **—Patrick Chene, Former Head of Sport for France Televisions, currently Chair of Sporever**

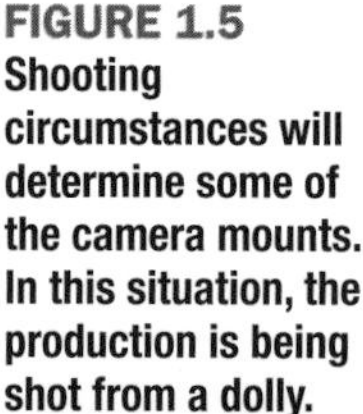

FIGURE 1.5 **Shooting circumstances will determine some of the camera mounts. In this situation, the production is being shot from a dolly.**

1.10 IS THERE A RIGHT WAY?

Creating a video production is a subjective process. It is often pretty easy to learn the basic mechanics of the equipment, but learning how to use that same equipment to persuade an audience and influence their reactions is another matter entirely. Some "creative" or "original" production styles can be a pain to watch, such as a rapid succession of unrelated shots or fast cutting between different viewpoints. Amateurs who use these techniques hope to create an illusion of excitement for a dull subject. After a while, however, these techniques only succeed in annoying, confusing, or boring the audience.

You can learn a lot by studying videos, television shows, and films, particularly those covering the topics you are interested in emulating. Review them over and over, and you will see that while some approaches are little more than stereotyped routines, others have an individuality and flow that is appropriate for the subject matter. Adjust your own approach to fit the situation rather than imitating the way things have always been done. If your production does not have the impact you are aiming for, you need to do it differently.

1.11 THE PRODUCTION APPROACH

When you are preoccupied with ideas about how the subject should be covered, it's easy to overlook a lot of issues that have to be faced at some time or other, such as budgets, availability of facilities, labor, materials, scheduling, safety issues, weather conditions, transportation, accommodations, legalities, and so on. Again, a lot is going to depend on the desired program. At the same time, the potential possibilities will inevitably be affected by the expertise and experience of the production crew, the program budget, the equipment being used, the time available, and similar factors. With a little imagination and ingenuity, you can often overcome limitations or at least leave your audience unaware that there were any. Later we will explore typical strategies that enable you to do just that.

At an early stage directors should have given a great deal of thought about the production and the audience, settling basic questions such as these:

- **What is the program's main purpose?** Is it to entertain, amuse, excite, or intrigue? Is the show educational? Are specific methods being demonstrated, such as showing how to make or repair something? Is the goal to persuade the audience—for example, to visit a specific place or to make a purchase? Or is the goal to warn them against doing so?
- **Who is the program being made for?** Is the intended audience an individual or a group? What are their ages? What production methods are most effective for the targeted group? Is it for the general public or for a specific audience?
- **How will the production be seen?** Will the production be viewed online, on a mobile phone, or on a large screen? Will it appear on commercial television or on a niche cable channel? Is it targeted at prospective customers in a store (such as an advertising display), for delivery to a student group at a school, or for an in-house corporate symposium? Perhaps it is intended for home study on an iPod?

> If content is king, then content delivery is the power behind the throne. Reaching the audience requires knowledge of not just what they are watching, but how and where.
>
> **—Chris Purse, *HD* magazine**

The style that is adopted for the production, the pace of delivery, and how much to emphasize various points are all determined by the program's ultimate purpose (Figure 1.6).

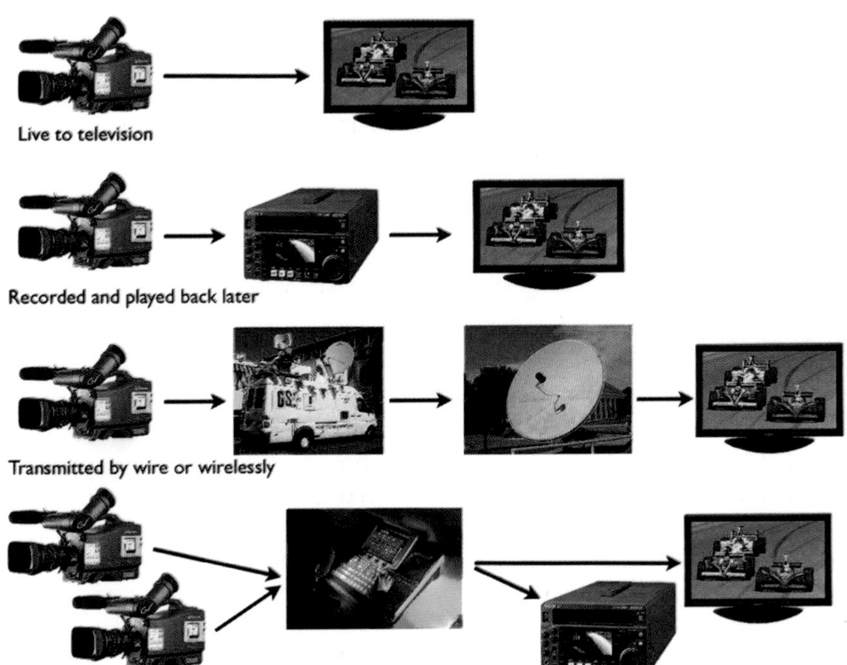

FIGURE 1.6
The flexibility of video equipment allows you to arrange it in many different ways from acquisition (the camera) to homes (the television).

TECHNICALITIES

1.12 EQUIPMENT PERFORMANCE

Thanks to good design and engineering, the majority of even the most complex television equipment will perform faultlessly for long periods of time with little attention. But it is good practice to make regular checks and carry out routine maintenance.

It is simple enough to check that parts are clean (lenses) and that controls are working correctly and ready for use. However, it is also important to study the instruction manuals that come with the equipment to know how to carry out the basic equipment checks and adjustments. If you are not an engineer, you may need the services of an experienced engineer to maintain equipment performance up to specification. But remember, don't tweak (adjust) internal controls unless you know what you are doing.

Interview with a Pro

Ben Brown, Media Executive

Ben Brown, Media Executive

Tell me about the future of video and television.
I believe we are in a transition, and the future will look much different from what we have now. With video on demand (VOD), web and multiple other sources for content, broadcasters are faced with an overall shrinking and fractionalized audience. Over-the-air stations are already struggling to stay financially viable as cable networks receive subscriber fees. However, once you get past the top five or six cable networks, the ratings plummet and the difference between the 35th and 70th place networks is less than a .5 share.

Once the economics are sorted I think the delivery method will be the biggest change. I can see more and more content coming through broadband-based sources as the next generation is already acclimating itself to watching programming they want on their schedule (my six-year-old is already proficient at navigating the cable system to select specific shows and cartoons from the kids on-demand channels).

How is video/television changing?
With fractional viewership and the emergence of more web-based content, how we receive programming is changing, and how/what is programmed is changing. As more programming moves to the web, typical half- hour and full- hour shows are no longer the norm. Episodes can be 6 minutes or 76 minutes. Additionally, programming will be more focused on specific target audiences.

Advertising will also change, as advertisers now are already moving away from the standard 30-second spot to 15- and even 10-second models. You will see more embedded advertising and more strategic placement.

In your mind, what is the difference between video and television?
Television has traditionally been thought of as coming over the air (broadcast) or via "cable." Video is content, which may be transmitted via traditional methods or over broadband, web, or other on-demand methods. However, the boundaries between television, video, and even film have eroded. Today the words "video" and "television" are often used interchangeably.

What challenges do you see for video and television in the future (or now)?
I see challenges in two areas:

1. Content: With the fractionalization of audiences, more content is needed. However, with the proliferation of inexpensive gear/edit systems, the ability to produce content has increased, but the ability to put together well-thought-out, well-written and/or well-edited products has decreased exponentially. Everyone thinks they can edit or shoot—just because they can operate the software or point the camera—but they can't answer the "why" behind what they do. And good writers are just as rare as they ever have been (and good stories even rarer!).
2. Financial: In a related corollary to the above, the proliferation of outlets for content that has led to the increased demand has also brought with it the fractionalized audiences, which means smaller share and less associated revenue. So paying for programming and content is becoming ever more difficult, as is evidenced by the number of mainstream outlets gobbling up perpetual re-air rights for reruns of older programming.

What are some of the basics that people need to know to get into this field?
Meet people. I have never been hired for a job based on just submitting my resume, and have never hired anyone just from a resume submission. Have the right attitude; no one really wants to work with a know-it-all or an "Eeyore." Once you are hired, be the best at that position that is humanly possible. Trust me—someone ***will*** take notice. Keep your eyes open. Look for opportunities to fill a niche, or apply for positions that don't even exist—yet. Resumes are well and good and can lead to getting hired, but most jobs I found, I found because I knew someone, or knew someone that knew someone. Talk with anyone willing to talk to you. They may not have a job open, or even be the person with the authority to hire, but if they are willing to talk, see what you can glean from them, and at the same time you are exposing yourself to another connection.

Ben Brown is Vice President of Wheeler Television. They create programming for television networks.

CHAPTER 2
Production Crew

I've always maintained that, with the right crew, you can make a toenail-clipping competition riveting television. With the wrong crew, you can make an international soccer championship boring.

—David Hill, CEO of Fox Sports Television

People are much more important than the coolest gear. The bottom line is that crew members who know what they are doing can make an incredible program with mediocre equipment. However, crew members who do not know what they are doing can make a mediocre program with the latest professional equipment. Because of the importance of people within a production, we are putting this chapter near the beginning of the book.

2.1 PRODUCTION CREW SIZE

Production crews come in all sizes. The crew for a documentary may consist of one person with a palm-sized camera. Many television stations are moving to one-person crews to reduce costs (see Figure 2.1). Other types of programming, such as a network dramatic production, may require a large number of people. It all comes down to what you are trying to accomplish.

VIDEO PRODUCTION CREW JOB DESCRIPTIONS

Most job descriptions for the crew have some commonalities from company to company. However, you will find that the actual duties may fluctuate based on the company, production style, and the talents of the individual crew members. In this chapter we describe some of the basic positions that may exist on a video production. Because this book focuses on smaller productions, we will limit the list to the most common positions.

2.2 PRODUCER

The producer is generally responsible for a specific production. Usually the producer is concerned with the business organization, budget, the choice of the staff

FIGURE 2.1
Many television stations, due to tight budgets, have moved to one-person news crews. In this photo, the reporter not only asks the questions and holds the microphone, but is also holding the camera on her shoulder.

and the crew; interdepartmental coordination; script acceptance; and production scheduling. The producer may select or initiate the program concepts and work with writers. He or she may assign the production's director and is responsible for meeting deadlines, production planning, location projects, rehearsals, production treatment, and other duties. Producers may also become involved in specifics such as craft or union problems, assessing postproduction treatment, and the final program format (see Figure 2.2).

FIGURE 2.2
A producer and director review the production plan with the video crew.

2.3 ASSISTANT PRODUCER OR ASSOCIATE PRODUCER

The assistant or associate producer (AP) is responsible for assisting the producer. These responsibilities, as assigned by the producer, may include coordinating appointments and production schedules, making sure contracts are completed, booking guests, creating packages, and supervising postproduction. This person may be assigned some of the same responsibilities as an associate director.

2.4 DIRECTOR

Ultimately the director is the individual responsible for creatively visualizing the script or event. This means that the director instructs the camera operators on the type of shots wanted and then selects the appropriate camera shots for the final production. The director is also responsible for running the talent through their lines and stage movements based on the script. Directors are people who can effectively communicate their vision to the crew. They are also team builders who move the crew toward that vision. This involves advising, guiding, and coordinating the various members on the production team (scenic, lighting, sound, cameras, costume, etc.) and approving their anticipated treatment. The director may choose and hire performers/talent/actors (casting), envision and plan the camera treatment (shots and camera movements) and editing, and direct/rehearse the performers during prerehearsals (Figure 2.3).

He or she also evaluates the crew's contributions (sets, camera work, lighting, sound, makeup, costume, graphics, etc.). The director's job can range in practice from being the sole individual who creates and coordinates the production to a person who directs a camera and sound crew with material organized by others.

FIGURE 2.3
The field director is reviewing the camera shot on an HD monitor (the monitor has a sun shade on it to increase visibility). The multicamera live production director (foreground of second photo) must look at multiple camera images and select the most appropriate shot.

2.5 ASSISTANT DIRECTOR OR ASSOCIATE DIRECTOR

The assistant director (AD) is responsible for assisting the director. Functions may include supervising prerehearsals and location organization. The AD may also review storyboards, implement the shooting schedule, and shield the director from interruptions, and he or she is sometimes responsible for the cast. The AD may take the director's notes on changes, retakes, performance, and other factors. For multicamera shoots, the AD may be responsible for lining up shots, graphics, and tapes. He or she may also be responsible for checking on special shots (such as chroma key), giving routine cues (tape inserts), and other duties, while the director guides the actual performance and camera(s). The AD may also check program timing and help the director with postproduction. This person may be assigned some of the same responsibilities of an associate producer. This position may be merged with the floor manager.

2.6 PRODUCTION ASSISTANT

The production assistant (PA) assists the director or producer with production needs. These may include supervising the production office (making copies, making coffee, and running errands), prerehearsals, and location organization. His or her responsibilities may also include logging tapes and taking notes during production meetings. During rehearsals and recording, this person may assist the producer/director with graphics or serve as a floor manager.

FIGURE 2.4 **The stage manager represents the director on the set or in the studio. Here, she is shown giving the actors instructions from the director on the set of a sitcom.**

2.7 FLOOR MANAGER OR STAGE MANAGER

The floor manager (FM) is the director's primary representative and contact when the director is not on the set or in the studio. He or she may be used to cue talent and direct the floor crew. During the shoot, the FM is responsible for general organization, safety, discipline (e.g., managing noise), and security. At times, the FM may be used to ensure that the talent is present. This job may be merged with the assistant director (Figure 2.4).

2.8 TECHNICAL DIRECTOR OR VISION MIXER

The technical director (TD) generally sits next to the director in the control room and is responsible for operating the television production switcher (and perhaps electronic effects). The TD may also serve as the crew chief. This person reports to the director (Figure 2.5).

2.9 MAKEUP ARTIST

The makeup artist designs, prepares, and applies makeup to the talent, aided by makeup assistants and hair stylists (Figure 2.6).

FIGURE 2.5
Technical directors "edit" a live program by utilizing a production switcher and multiple cameras.

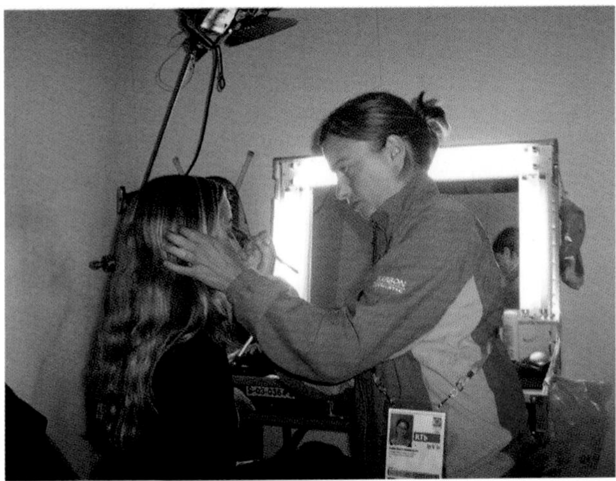

FIGURE 2.6
A makeup artist prepares talent for a production.

2.10 GRAPHIC DESIGNER/OPERATOR

The graphic designer/operator is responsible for designing and implementing the graphics for the production. This individual is responsible for organizing and typing onscreen text and titles for a production, either to be used during the production or stored for later use (Figure 2.7).

2.11 LIGHTING DIRECTOR/VISION SUPERVISOR

The lighting director is responsible for designing, arranging, and controlling all lighting treatment, both technically and artistically. This responsibility may

FIGURE 2.7
Graphic designer/operators must design, organize, and edit graphics for video productions.

include indoor or outdoor lighting situations. The lighting director supervises the electricians, or gaffers, who rig and set the lighting equipment (Figure 2.8).

FIGURE 2.8
Lighting director.
(Photo by Will Adams.)

2.12 VIDEOGRAPHER/CAMERA OPERATOR/ PHOTOGRAPHER

The camera operators are responsible for setting up their cameras (unless the cameras have already been set up, such as in a studio situation) and then operating the cameras to capture the video images as requested by the director (Figure 2.9). On small productions, the videographer may have a lot of creative control over the image. In a multicamera production, the director usually makes most of the final creative decisions about the shot. In a dramatic production, the camera videographer may be called a cinematographer.

2.13 CAMERA ASSISTANT

The camera assistant is responsible for assisting the camera operator in setting up the camera. This individual is also responsible for making sure that the camera operator is safe (by keeping the person from tripping over something or falling), keeping people from walking in front of the camera when it is on, keeping the camera cable from getting tangled or tripping others, and guiding the camera operator during moving shots. A camera assistant may also work as a grip and push a camera dolly if needed (Figure 2.10).

FIGURE 2.9
Camera operators are responsible for setting up their cameras as well as operating them.
(Photo by Will Adams.)

FIGURE 2.10
The camera assistant at the concert makes sure that the camera cables do not get tangled and protects the camera operator from falling off the platform. Camera assistants may also be required to push the camera dolly.
(Photo by Ben Tabor.)

2.14 AUDIO MIXER/SOUND MIXER/SOUND SUPERVISOR

The audio mixer is responsible for the sound balance as well as the technical and artistic quality of the program sound. This includes determining the number and placement of the microphones required for the production. He or she also makes sure that the audio cables are properly plugged into the audio mixer and is responsible for the final mix (audio levels, balance, and tonal quality) of the production. The audio mixer supervises all personnel operating microphones and audio equipment (Figure 2.11).

FIGURE 2.11
The field audio mixer is using a small portable mixer to adjust the levels on the talent's mic. Studio or remote production truck audio mixers use a larger audio mixer.

2.15 STEREOGRAPHER

The term *stereographer* is used in a number of different ways in relation to shooting 3D video. Some call a camera operator who is shooting 3D a stereographer. Others consider the stereographer's role to be someone who is there for technical support of the 3D equipment, adjusting the lenses for the desired 3D imagery.

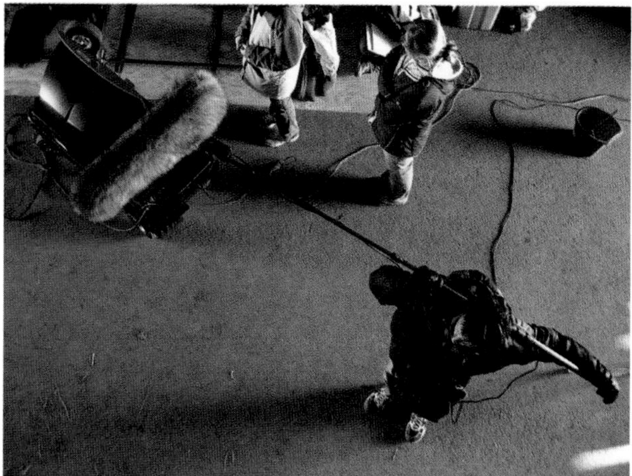

FIGURE 2.12
Boom operators are sometimes also called audio assistants.

2.16 BOOM OPERATOR OR AUDIO ASSISTANT

Supervised by the audio mixer, the boom operator is responsible for positioning the microphones, running audio cables, operating the sound boom, troubleshooting audio problems, and operating field audio equipment (Figure 2.12).

2.17 ENGINEER

Engineers are responsible for setting up, adjusting for optimal performance, maintaining, and troubleshooting all equipment used in a production.

2.18 WRITER

The writer is responsible for writing the script. Occasionally the producer or director will write material. At times, writers are assisted by a researcher, who obtains data, information, and references for the production writer.

2.19 EDITOR

The editor selects, compiles, and cuts video and audio to produce programs. He or she may assemble clips into segments and segments into programs, or this person may simply correct mistakes that occurred during the production process (Figure 2.13).

FIGURE 2.13
The editor selects, compiles, and cuts the video and audio together in order to create a television program.

THE CREW

Each studio facility is designed differently. The control room of the studio or the truck may be separate rooms or have everyone in one big room. Whatever the layout, everyone has their own area and everyone needs to be able to communicate clearly to everyone else. Communication may occur through the intercom, or crew members may be close enough to one another that they can hear what is being said (Figure 2.14).

FIGURE 2.14
While control room layouts differ from facility to facility, this is a very common layout for the crew of a large production.

FIGURE 2.15
Set designer.

2.20 SET DESIGNER

The set designer is responsible for conceiving, designing, and organizing the scenic treatment for a production (perhaps even the graphics). He or she supervises the scenic crew in erecting and dressing the sets (Figure 2.15).

PROFESSIONAL CREW

2.21 FREELANCE CREW

Many companies today have moved from a full-time professional production staff to utilizing a freelance crew. Freelancers are independent contractors who work for multiple organizations, hiring out their production skills on an as-needed basis. There are freelancers available who can fill every one of the production positions. Freelancers are generally paid on an hourly or day rate basis. If they have travelled far from their home base, freelancers usually get lodging and a per diem added to their contract. The per diem is a stipend that covers incidental costs such as laundry, meals.

2.22 BELOW-THE-LINE/ABOVE-THE-LINE

You may hear the terms "below-the-line" and "above-the-line" personnel. Although these terms may have different meanings to different companies, overall they are budgeting terms. Here are some common descriptions:

Above-the-line personnel usually refers to people who may have a fixed salary but who also will share in any profits the project generates. They are generally thought of as more artistic in nature. These positions would include producers, directors, actors, writers, and possibly graphic artists and designers.

Below-the-line personnel refers to everyone who is paid a wage and will not share in the profits. It generally refers to camera operators, editors, engineers, production designers, costume designers, and makeup artists. Below-the-line personnel may be eligible for overtime pay.

2.23 THE STRUCTURE OF A VIDEO PRODUCTION CREW

The structure of a production crew differs greatly from company to company. Even different types of productions, such as dramatic and sports productions, require different styles of hierarchy. Figures 2.16 and 2.17 show common general structures for single-camera and multicamera crews.

2.24 WHAT DO YOU WEAR?

What crew members wear differs depending on your job, who will see you, if you are indoors or out, and the event.

If you are in the studio, the public generally does not see the crew. The most common clothes are as casual as jeans. However, studios can often be cold, which means it is good to have a couple of layers so that clothing can be removed or added, depending on the temperature. Set-up days are always casual. Some inside events, such as a major awards ceremony, may dictate that the crew seen by the public actually dress well in order to fit into the overall environment during the shooting.

FIGURE 2.16
The single-camera crew.

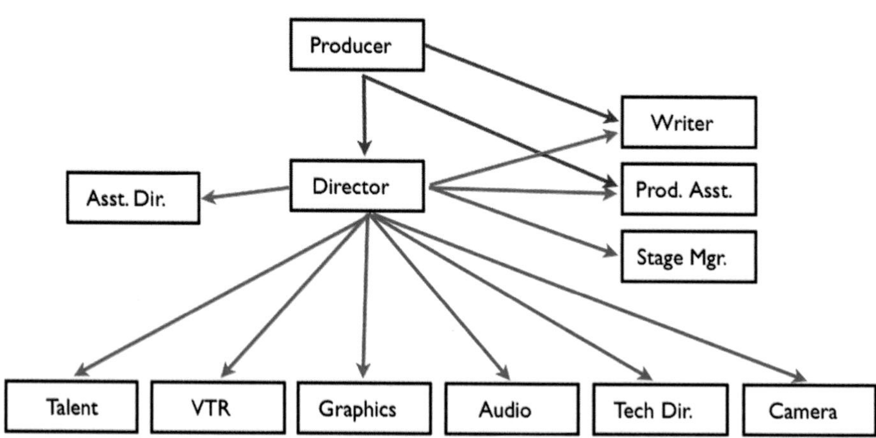

FIGURE 2.17
A fairly common multicamera television production crew organization.

Outdoor work is much more unpredictable. In the morning it may be sunny, and by afternoon it may be pouring rain and cold. That means that multiple layers and types of clothing should be carried. Depending on where you are, that may include a T-shirt and jeans if it is hot, a long-sleeve shirt and hat to project you against the sun, and a warm jacket to project you from the cold.

Whatever the situation, it is always important to look professional. You will get more respect from others, which will help you get your job done.

2.25 WHAT DO YOU BRING WITH YOU?

Bringing the right supplies with you can make all the difference in the world on a shoot. Again, it depends on where you are. It is always important to have something to write with and some paper. Here are some of the other things that should be considered:

- Hat
- Sunblock
- Bug spray
- Sunglasses
- Snacks
- Multitool (see Figure 2.18)
- Simple first-aid supplies
- Small flashlight

FIGURE 2.18
A variety of multitools are available.
(Photo courtesy of Leatherman.)

Interview with a Pro

Tommy Mitchell, Crewer

Tommy Mitchell, Crewer

What do you look for in a person when hiring?
Based on the needs of my show, experience would be the number one thing I look for before hiring. We keep detailed past histories of performance for every show that someone works for us and have a pretty extensive database of names. I generally am reluctant to hire someone who hasn't worked for us in the past unless I get a reference from someone I particularly trust.

After experience, I'm looking for reliability and versatility. I like versatility because it provides a lot of flexibility to the director or producer. A solid camera operator who's comfortable on hard camera and handheld is more valuable to me that someone who does only hard camera. An EVS replay operator who could do some editing if needed has a skill set that can make the show better.

How important is attitude when hiring?
Attitude is paramount when hiring. The freelance community is littered with fantastically talented ops that can't get big shows because their attitude holds them back. We deal with it all the time with those who are unhappy that we booked them on Delta when United is their preferred airline, or that we don't pay as much as someone else does. As crewers, we deal with so many events per day that we just don't have time for the whiners and complainers, and pretty soon, their phones stop ringing. If there's one thing I can say to a freelancer, it's "No matter how good you are and how much you think you are needed for a show, I can replace you in a heartbeat."

How important is networking?
It is all still about who you know. Most producers and directors have their favorite operators and look to take them to all their shows. You can certainly make a good living as a "gun for hire," but becoming a "core" member of a crew requires some networking. In this business, your reputation certainly precedes you, so knowing the right people will keep you busy throughout the year.

Tommy Mitchell is responsible for hiring freelance crews for ESPN productions.

CHAPTER 3

Organizing the Production

It's about people, not hardware.

—Vincenzo Natali, Director

In dramatic productions, a director has to pour it on six days a week and twelve hours a day.

—Steven Spielberg

A lot of what is covered in this chapter is obvious—so obvious that many production people overlook these essentials in their initial enthusiasm—and their product is less effective.

Key Terms

- ***Arc:*** A camera move that moves around the subject in a circle, arc, or "horseshoe" path.
- ***Empirical production method:*** The empirical method is where instinct and opportunity are the guides.
- ***Goals:*** Broad concepts of what you want to accomplish with the program.
- ***Objectives:*** Objectives are measurable goals. That means something that can be tested for, to see that the audience did understand and remember the key points of the program.
- ***Planned production method:*** The planned method, which organizes and builds a program in carefully arranged steps.
- ***Remote survey (Recce):*** A preliminary visit to a shooting location.
- ***Shot sheet (shot card):*** A sheet created by the director that lists each shot needed from each individual camera operator. The shots are listed in order so that the camera operator can move from shot to shot with little direction from the director.
- ***Site survey:*** See "remote survey."
- ***Storyboard:*** The storyboard is simply a series of rough sketches that help you to visualize and to organize your camera treatment.

3.1 ART CONCEALS CRAFT

When watching a show on television, our thoughts normally center on the program material: the story line, the message, and the argument. We become interested in what people are saying, what they are doing, what they look like, and where they are. Unless we start to get bored or the technology becomes obtrusive, we are unlikely to concern ourselves with how the production is actually *made*.

We *believe* what we see. We respond to techniques but remain unaware of them unless they happen to distract us. We even accept the drama of the hero dying of thirst in the desert without wondering why the director, camera, and sound crew do not help him.

All this is fine until you begin to make programs yourself. You soon realize the gulf between watching and enjoying from the audience's point of view, and creating the illusion by the way the equipment is used (Figure 3.1).

FIGURE 3.1
Beginning directors often find that the illusion of reality is much more difficult to create than they first imagined.

3.2 SHOT SELECTION

You cannot just point a camera at a scene and expect it to convey all the information and atmosphere that the on-the-spot observer would experience.

A camera is inherently selective. It can only show certain limited aspects of a situation at any given time. If, for instance, you provide a wide shot of the entire field at a ball game, the audience will have an excellent view of the movement patterns of teamwork, but the viewers will be unable to see for themselves who individuals are or to watch exactly how they are playing the game. A close-up shot gives details, even shows how a player is reacting to a foul, but prevents the audience from seeing the overall action at that time (Figure 3.2).

FIGURE 3.2 Shot selection at a baseball game determines whether you are showing the teamwork with a long shot or the emotions with an extreme close-up shot.

3.3 THE PROBLEM OF FAMILIARITY

There is an essential difference between the way any director looks at the program and how the audience reacts. That is not surprising when you stop to think about it. The director is completely familiar with the production and the circumstances in which it has been prepared. For example, let's say that the program is showing us a collection of priceless objects in a museum. There can be significant differences between the critical reactions of an enthusiastic viewer seeing the program for the first time and the director's own reactions:

From the audience's point of view. "There were some unusual items in the display case, but the camera continued past them. Why didn't we have a closer look at the decorated plate so that we could read the inscriptions? There seems to be elaborate ornamentation on the other side of this vase. But we don't see it. Why isn't it shown? Why aren't we looking at all the interesting things there in the background?"

The director could no doubt have explained. "The camera picked out the most important details for the topic we were discussing. There isn't time to cover everything. When shooting the vase, this was the best viewpoint we could manage. The voiceover read the inscription to us. Nearby display cases prevented a better camera position. The museum was about to close, and we were scheduled to be elsewhere the next day."

This imaginary discourse reminds us of several important points. First, there are many ways of interpreting any situation. A good director will give the subject a great deal of thought before shooting and will rationalize how best to tackle the shoot. But most productions are a matter of compromise between aesthetics and mechanics, between "what we would like to do" and "what we are able to do." Quite often, the obvious thing to do is quite impractical for some reason (it is too costly, there is insufficient time, it requires equipment beyond what is available, it is too elaborate, the light is failing, etc.). In the real world, you will discover great on-the-spot opportunities that you did not anticipate. But you shall also encounter frustrating disappointments that will require you to rethink your original plans.

Directors spend a considerable amount of time on a project and become very familiar with each facet of the production as well as the locations. Members of the audience, on the other hand, are continually finding out what the program is about; they are interpreting each shot as they see it, often with only a moment or two to respond to whatever catches their attention.

The director was not only there at the shoot but has probably seen each shot on the screen many times: when reviewing the takes, during postproduction sessions, and when assessing the final program. He or she knows what material was available and what was cut. The audience members are seeing and hearing everything for the first and probably the only time. They do not know what might have been. They cannot assess opportunities missed. For them, everything is a fresh impression.

The audience only sees as much of a situation as the camera reveals, quite unaware of things that are just a short distance outside the lens's field of view—unless something happens to move into the shot, or the camera's viewpoint changes, or there is a revealing if unexplained noise from somewhere out of shot (Figures 3.3 and 3.4). When the camera presents us with impressive shots of a world-famous scene, it may carefully avoid including crowding tourists, stalls selling souvenirs, or a waiting coach. A carefully angled shot of a scene can produce a powerful effect on screen but a disappointing reaction when one stands on the specific spot and sees its true scale and its surroundings.

FIGURE 3.3
Overfamiliarity: The director knows how interesting the location is, but is it revealed to the audience? The director has to decide whether to show the context of the shot or a close-up. Directors have to determine which shot best communicates the story.
(Photo by Josh Taber.)

At times, the director is at a disadvantage. Because the director is familiar with every moment of the production, it is not possible for the director or the production team to judge with a fresh eye. It might seem to the director that a specific point is so obvious that only a very brief "reminder" shot is needed at the moment. He or she may decide to leave it out altogether. But for viewers who are watching the scene for the first time, this omission could prove puzzling. They may even misunderstand what is going on as a result.

FIGURE 3.4
The audience only sees as much of a situation as the camera reveals. Note the large screen behind the talent showing what the camera is actually getting.

To simplify the mechanics of production, scenes are often shot in the most convenient order, irrespective of where they come in the final script. This will all be sorted out during the editing process. While this arrangement can be a practical solution when shooting, it does have its drawbacks. Not only does shooting out of sequence create continuity problems, but it can make it difficult for the director to judge the subtleties of timing, tempo, and pace that the viewer will experience when looking at the final program (Figure 3.5).

FIGURE 3.5
Shooting scenes out of sequence can create continuity, timing, and pace difficulties.

Show an intense close-up of an odd detail of your subject without revealing the complete subject and it can leave the audience puzzled, even though the director knows that the shot obviously comes from that subject over there. The opposite situation also occurs, when a director holds a shot for some time so that the audience can assimilate all the information in it, when in fact they have lost interest in the subject and their minds have wandered onto other things.

3.4 THE PROBLEM OF QUALITY

When shooting pictures for pleasure, you can be philosophical if the odd shot happens to be slightly defocused, or lopsided, or cuts off part of the subject. It is a pity, but it doesn't really matter much. You can still enjoy the results. But when you are making a program for other people, any defects of this kind are unacceptable. They will give a production the reputation of carelessness, amateurishness, and incompetence so that it loses its appeal and authority. Faulty camerawork and poor techniques will not only distract your audience, but they can turn even a serious, well-thought-out production into a complete disaster.

3.5 THE PROBLEM OF "BIGGER AND BETTER"

How you tackle any program is directly influenced by your resources (equipment, finance, crew and their experience, etc.), time, conditions, standards, intended market, and so on. While there is no one correct way to handle any subject, there are a number of bad methods.

Suppose you want to discuss the problems of growing a specific crop. You could make an impressive program using special computer graphics, an expert walking through the crops speaking of problems, aerial views of the fields, and time-lapse demonstrations. However, this treatment could be expensive and time consuming.

Alternatively, you could use a simpler approach. The camera could explore a typical field and show the program title finger-traced in the earth. It could look at typical crop features, with close-ups of specimens. A commentary could provide an explanatory voiceover to pictures. If any additional sounds are required, they could be the natural ones, such as wind, birds, or tractors, recorded as a wild track at the site.

"Bigger is better" does not necessarily translate into a better production. Sometimes it distracts viewers from the real subject itself and draws their attention to the clever techniques instead. If all the viewer remembers is the special effects, then you have not communicated your message. The treatment must be appropriate for the target audience and the program content.

3.6 COMMUNICATION CAN BE ELUSIVE

There are no absolute rules when creating a production, but there are a lot of well-established guiding principles. These principles have been discovered through years of experience. Occasionally a director can deliberately ignore these guides and create an interesting or unusual effect. However, you must be careful because the audience response may not turn out as you hoped.

The human mind is great at seeing relationships, even when there aren't any. We all spend our time interpreting the world about us, frequently seeing meanings or significance where there is none. In an experimental film made up of a random series of close-up stills from magazine covers, the disjointed fragments of buildings, foliage, and objects appeared on the screen as patches of color, progressive patterns, and geometric forms. When this film was run at 24 frames a second and accompanied by any music, from Bach to Brubeck, the audience interpreted the result as an exciting animation sequence, with the visual theme changing to the beat of the music. Yet in reality there was no theme, no editing (since the project was as shot in the camera, frame by frame). It was all in the minds of the audience. This example reminds us of how frail the process of communication really is. The audience will at times accept and interpret visual or audio garbage, for they assume that it has a valid purpose, even if they cannot understand what this purpose is.

At other times, although we select images and sound carefully, we find that the audience's attention has been taken by some irrelevant distraction in the background. They were maybe reading the book titles on a shelf and not really listening to what was being said.

> Before somebody laughs at the idea, remember that concepts like an all-news network, a food channel, and a weather channel were thought to be fallacies at the conception stage. All have developed into unquestioned broadcasting successes over the years.
>
> **—Tim Griffin, Writer**

3.7 IT ALL STARTS WITH AN IDEA (CONCEPT)

It is unlikely that you will suddenly decide, out of the blue, to make a video program on a specific subject. Something has triggered the idea. Perhaps you heard of an interesting incident that gave you the idea for a narrative. Maybe a local store asked you to make a point-of-sales video to help the home handyman. Here is how to start with the project:

You know the *subject* to be covered (in principle at least), what the program is to be *used* for, and *who* the audience for the program will be. The next question you should probably ask is "*How long* should it be?" It is important to know if the client wants a two-hour epic or a two-minute video loop.

Determine how the audience is going to relate to this program. If it is one of a series, don't go over the same material again unless it requires revision. There is also the chance that the viewer may not see the other videos in the series (Figure 3.6).

Idea

1. The Idea

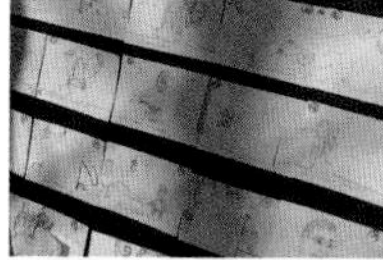

2. Organizing

3. Coordinating

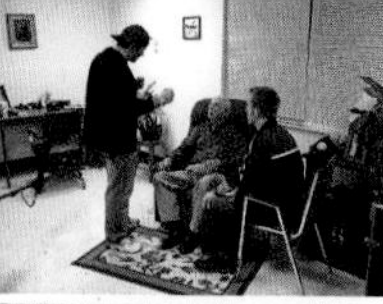

4. Rehearsing

5. Shooting

6. Postproduction

7. Viewing

FIGURE 3.6
The stages that a video production goes through, from idea (concept) to the viewing.

3.8 GOALS AND OBJECTIVES

What do you really want your audience to know after they have viewed your production? The answer to this question is essential because it guides the entire production process. The goals and objectives will determine what is used as a measuring stick throughout the production process. *Goals* are broad concepts of what you want to accomplish:

Goal: I want to explain how to field a Formula One racing team.

Objectives are measurable goals. That means something that can be tested for to see that the audience did understand and remember the key points of the program. Take the time to think through what the audience should know after seeing your program:

Objectives: When the viewers finish watching the program, they should be able to do the following:

- Identify three types of sponsorship
- Identify four crew positions
- Identify two scheduling issues

All three of these are objectives because they are measurable. The number of objectives is determined by the goals. This means that sometimes only one objective is needed, while other times five may be required.

3.9 TARGET AUDIENCE

Whether your program is a video "family album" or a lecture on nuclear physics, it is essential to determine *whom* the program is for and its chief *purpose*:

- Who is the viewing audience?
- Is it for the general public, for a specific group, or for a local group?
- What is the target age group? Is the production for children, young adults, adults, or seniors? Some age groups, such as children, have many subsets as well such as preschool, grade school, middle school, and high school. Each subset must be communicated to in a different way.
- Is any specific background, qualification, language, or group experience necessary for the audience?
- Are there specific production styles that this audience favors?

The target audience should determine your program's coverage and style. It is self-evident that the sort of program you would make for a group of content experts would differ from a program made for young children (Figure 3.7).

FIGURE 3.7
The intended audience should determine how the director covers the subject. In this situation, generally a younger crowd would favor a different style of coverage than elderly people.
(Photo by Paul Dupree.)

The conditions under which the audience is going to watch the program are important too. Most video programs are not made to be broadcast. They are viewed as DVDs, stored on flash memory or hard drives, or streamed in homes, classrooms, corporate offices, and many other locations. The wise director tries to anticipate these conditions, since they can considerably affect the way the program is produced:

- How and where is your audience going to see the program? Will they be a seated group of students watching a large screen in a darkened classroom?
- Will the viewers be watching a streamed video off of the Internet while at the office?
- Or will the program be viewed on a cell phone or player while riding in a car? (Figure 3.8).

FIGURE 3.8
With small mobile phone devices having the ability to play hours of video, as well as shoot video, they are rapidly becoming the video player of choice for many people.

If the program will be primarily viewed in direct daylight, directors may want to avoid dark or low-key scenes. The images displayed on many receivers/monitors in daylight can be poor quality, although they are continually improving in quality.

Try to anticipate the problems for an audience watching a distant picture monitor. Long shots have correspondingly little impact. Closer shots are essential since they add emotion and drama. Small lettering means nothing on a small distant screen. To improve the visibility of titles, charts, maps, etc., keep details basic, and limit the information (Figure 3.9).

If your target audience may be watching on an iPod or other very small video screen device, directors should lean toward more close-ups than usual since the long shots may not be as discernible on the small screen (Figure 3.10).

Here are a number of reminder questions that can help you to anticipate your audience's problems:

- Does the program rely on previously established knowledge? How much is known about the subject already?
- Does the program relate to other programs in a series?
- Does the audience need to be reminded of earlier programs?
- Is the audience going to see the program individually or in a group?
- Are they only watching the program once, from the beginning, or as a continuous loop?

FIGURE 3.9
Close-up shots add emotion and drama to a production and add needed detail to small-screen productions, such as those seen on an iPod-type device.

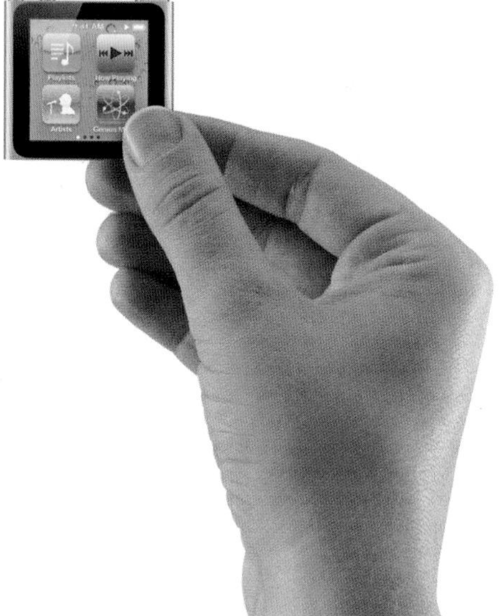

FIGURE 3.10
As viewing screens get smaller and smaller, care must be taken to create videos that can be seen with clarity.
(Photo courtesy of Apple.)

- Can they see the program as often as they want, including stopping and replaying sections?
- Will viewers watch the program straight through, or will it be stopped after sections, for discussion?
- Will there be any accompanying supporting material (maps, graphs, or statistics) to which the audience can refer?
- Will there be other competing, noisy attractions as they watch (such as might occur at an exhibition)?
- Will the program soon be out of date?
- Is the program for a formal occasion, or will a certain amount of careful humor be useful?
- Are there time limits for the program?
- Will the program need to be updated with fresh material on an ongoing basis? If so, what is the schedule?

3.10 RESEARCH

For some programs, such as documentaries, news, or interviews, the production team must conduct research in order to create the program's content or make sure the existing content is accurate. This research may be going to the library, doing online research, or contacting recognized experts in the content area. Travel may even be required.

It is important to remember that research is time consuming and may impact the production budget. This is especially true if a content expert wants an appearance fee or if flights and lodging are included for the crew or guest.

3.11 COVERING THE SUBJECT

The kind of subject that is being covered, who makes up the audience, and the content that needs to be featured will influence how the camera is utilized in the program, where it concentrates, how close the shots are, and how varied they are. Here are some of the areas that the director needs to think through:

- What content areas need to be covered?
- Is the subject (person or object) best seen from specific angles?
- Are the surroundings (context) important?
- Would the addition of graphics help the audience understand the content?
- How will I give the talent and crew the vision and goals for the production and then help them know what they can do to help us attain these goals?
- Would it help to create a shot list for each camera operator? A shot list is a description of each shot needed, listed in order, so that the operator can move from shot to shot with little instruction from the director. Other camera operator supports may include team rosters to help the operator find a specific player for the director (Figure 3.11).

FIGURE 3.11
Create shot sheets (shot card) or other support information for the camera operators as needed.

3.12 PRODUCTION METHODS

Great ideas are not enough. Ideas have to be worked out in realistic, practical terms. They have to be expressed as images and sounds. In the end, as the director, you have to decide what the camera is going to shoot and what your audience is going to hear. Where do you start?

There are two quite different methods of approaching video production:

- The *empirical* method is where instinct and opportunity are the guides.
- The *planned* method, which organizes and builds a program in carefully arranged steps.

3.13 THE EMPIRICAL APPROACH

Directors following the empirical approach get an idea, and then they look around for subjects and situations that relate to it. After shooting possible material, they later create a program from whatever they have found. Their inspiration springs from the opportunities that have arisen.

An example would be that the director decides to make a program about safety at sea. Using the empirical approach, the director might go to a marina and develop a production based on the stories heard there. Or the director might discuss the idea with the life-guards and decide to follow an entirely different plan. The director might also visit a commercial dock and discover material there of an entirely different kind.

After accumulating a collection of interesting sequences (atmospheric shots, natural sound, interviews, etc.), the director reviews the content and puts it into a meaningful order. He or she then creates a program that fits the accumulated material, probably writing a commentary as a voiceover to match the edited pictures.

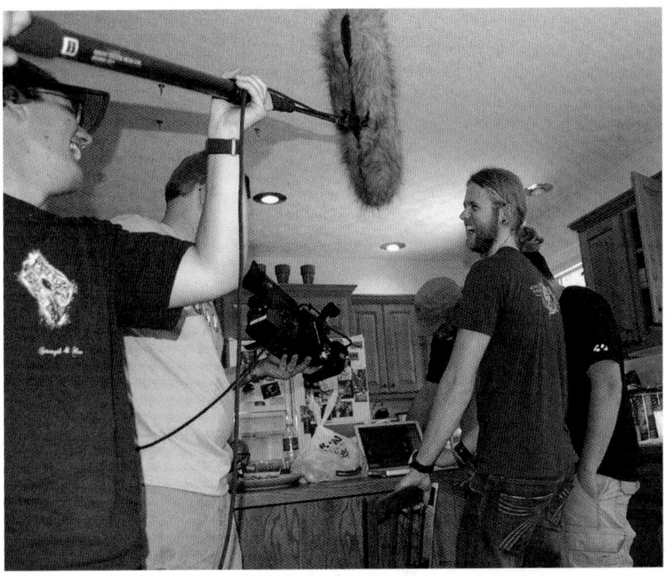

FIGURE 3.12
Some documentaries are shot using the empirical method, which is when instinct and opportunity are the guides.
(Photo by Will Adams.)

At *best*, this approach is fresh and uninhibited, improvises, makes use of the unexpected, avoids rigid discipline, and is adaptable. Shots are interestingly varied. The audience is kept alert, watching and interpreting the changing scene.

At *worst*, the result of such shot hunting is a haphazard disaster, with little cohesion or sense of purpose. Because the approach is unsystematic, gaps and overlaps abound. Good, coherent editing may be difficult. Opportunities may have been missed. The director usually relies heavily on the voiceover to try to provide any sort of relationship and continuity between the images (Figure 3.12).

3.14 THE PLANNED APPROACH

The planned method of production approaches the problem quite differently, although the results on the screen may be similar. In this situation, the director works out, in advance, the exact form he or she wants the program to take and then creates it accordingly.

Fundamentally, you can do either of the following:

- Begin with the environment or setting, and decide how the cameras can be positioned to get the most effective shots (Figure 3.13).
- Envision certain shots or effects you want to see, and create a setting that will provide those results (Figure 3.14).

A lot will depend on whether you are

- *Interpreting an existing script* (as in drama). This will involve analyzing the script, examining the story line and the main action in each scene, and visualizing individual shots.

FIGURE 3.13
Production staff review a venue for an ice hockey production using the planned approach. They began with the setting (venue) and then decided where to place the cameras.

or

- *Building a treatment framework*. This will involve considering how you are going to present a specific program subject and working out the kinds of shots you want.

At *best*, the planned approach is a method in which a crew can be coordinated to give their best. There is a sense of systematic purpose throughout the project. Problems are largely ironed out before they develop. Production is based on what is feasible. The program can have a smooth-flowing, carefully thought-out, persuasive style.

At *worst*, the production becomes bogged down in organization. The program can be stodgy, routine, and lack originality. Opportunities are ignored because they were not part of the original scheme and would modify it. The result could be a disaster.

In reality, the experienced director uses a combination of the *planned* and the *empirical* approaches, starting off with a plan and then taking advantage of any opportunities that become available.

FIGURE 3.14
Narrative directors use the planned approach to production by utilizing a storyboard. However, they create the setting to fit the story.

3.15 STORYBOARDS

> Storyboards generally save time on-set, help to avoid rushed decisions on-set, help you improve and get feedback on ideas, give you an idea about how many cameras and angles you will need, help you experiment with different angles and techniques, can help with continuity, and help orientate actors and crew members.
>
> **—Kyle Van Tonder, Director**

Before even picking up a camera, directors need to think through each scene in their minds so that they can then capture the best images that tell their story. The storyboard is simply a series of rough sketches; these sketches help the director to visualize and organize the camera treatment. Generally, the script, if you are using a script, is broken down into segments, and each segment is visualized on the storyboard—giving the director a visual interpretation of the script. The storyboard is a visual map of how the director hopes to arrange the camera shots for each scene or action sequence (Figures 3.15 and 3.16).

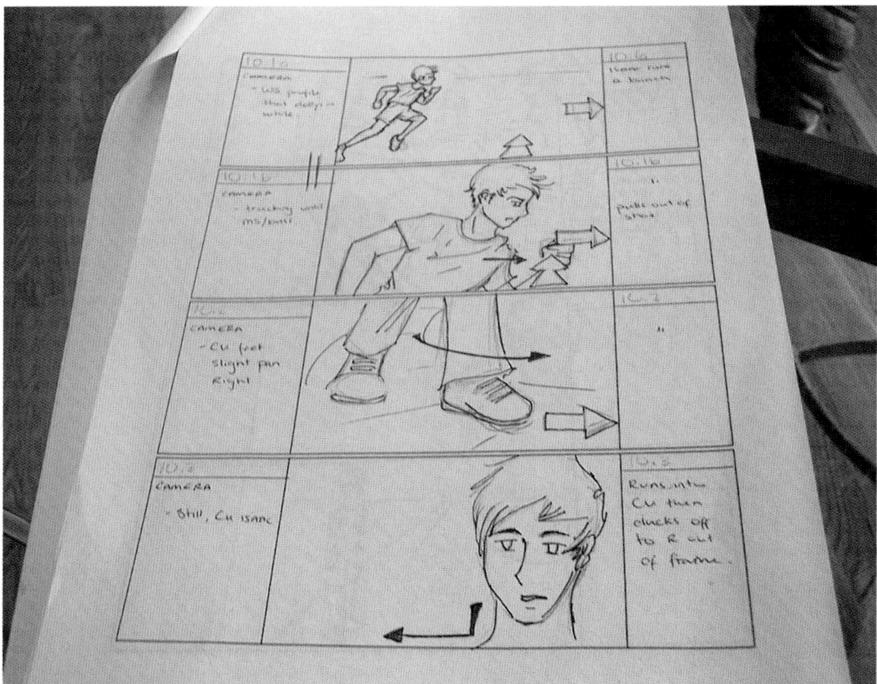

FIGURE 3.15
A storyboard on the set of a production. The storyboard roughly visualizes what the program will look like.
(Photo by Taylor Vinson.)

FIGURE 3.16
The first image is of a frame from a storyboard. The second image shows how the camera shot that specific scene.
(Photo by Taylor Vinson.)

As a director, you will find that the storyboard can be a valuable aid in whatever manner you are going to shoot the action:

- Continuously, from start to finish
- In sections or scenes (one complete action sequence at a time)
- As a series of separate shots or "action segments," each showing a part of the sequence

Storyboards can be designed a number of different ways. There are software programs that assist the director in visualizing ideas; someone can roughly sketch them out, or a storyboard artist can create detailed drawings that can even be animated to show during the fund-raising period. You don't have to be able to draw well to produce a successful storyboard. Even the crudest scribbles can help you organize your thoughts and show other people what you are trying to do (Figures 3.17 and 3.18).

Whether you choose a storyboarding software or drawing it by hand, you begin by imagining your way through the script, roughly creating the composition for each shot. If the action is complicated, you might need a couple of frames to show how a shot develops. In our example, the whole scene is summarized in five frames.

Let's look at a simple story line to see how the storyboard provides you with imaginative opportunities (see the storyboard sidebar "Analyzing Action").

The young person has been sent to buy her first postage stamp.

There are dozens of ways to shoot this brief sequence. You could simply follow her all the way from her home, watching as she crosses the road, enters the post office, goes up to the counter. The result would be totally boring.

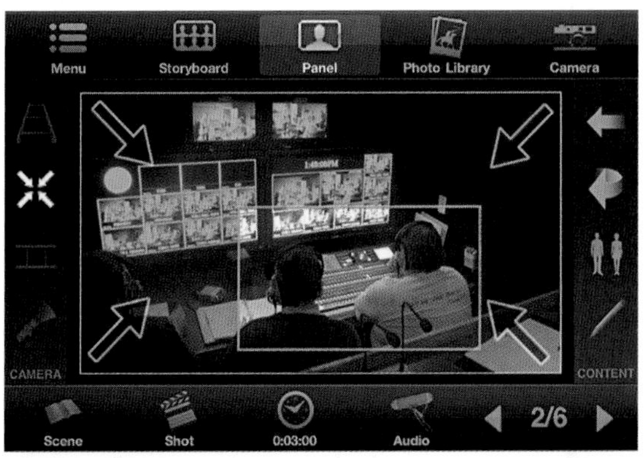

FIGURE 3.17
Storyboard programs are available on all types of devices. Both of these screenshots were taken from a storyboard program on an iPhone.
(Software by Cinemek.)

FIGURE 3.18
Computer-based storyboard programs allow the nonartist to create professional-looking storyboards.
(Software by StoryBoard Quick.)

Let's think again. We know from the previous scene where she is going and why. All we really want to register are her reactions as she buys the stamp. So let's cut out all the superfluous footage and concentrate on that moment.

1. The child arrives at the counter, and looks up at the clerk.
2. Hesitatingly, she asks for the stamp.

3. She opens her fingers to hand the money to the clerk.
4. The clerk smiles, takes the money, and pulls out the stamp book.
5. A close shot of the clerk tearing the stamp from a sheet (Figure 3.19).

ANALYZING ACTION

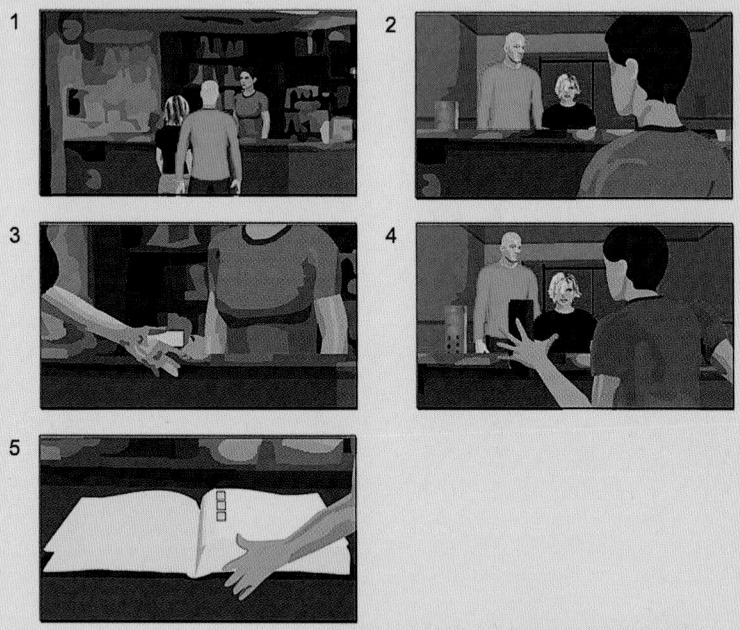

1

2

3

4

5

FIGURE 3.19
When edited together correctly, a sequence looks natural. But even a simple scene showing a person buying a stamp needs to be thought through. Note how shots 1 and 3 are taken on one side of the counter and shots 2, 4, and 5 on the other.
(Illustration created by StoryBoard Quick software.)

You now have a sequence of shots, far more interesting than a continuous "follow-shot." It stimulates the imagination. It guides the audience's thought processes. It has a greater overall impact. However, if this type of treatment is carried out badly, the effect can look disjointed, contrived, and posed. It is essential that the treatment matches the style and theme of the subject.

You could have built the whole sequence with dramatic camera angles, strong music, and effects. But would it have been *appropriate*? If the audience knows that a bomb is ticking away in a parcel beneath the counter, it might have been. It is all too easy to overdramatize or "pretty up" a situation (such as star filters producing multiray patterns around highlights, diffusion filters for misty effects). Because so much is now done in postproduction, resist the temptation.

This breakdown has not only helped you to visualize the picture treatment, but you begin to think about how one shot is going to lead into the next. You start to deal with practicalities. You see, for example, that shots 1 and 3 are taken from the front of the counter, and shots 2, 4, and 5 need to be taken from behind it. Obviously, the most logical approach is to shoot the sequence *out of order*. The storyboard becomes a shooting plan.

To practice "storyboarding," review a motion picture carefully, making a sketch of each key shot. This way, you will soon get into the habit of thinking in picture sequences rather than in isolated shots.

3.16 WHY PLAN?

Some people find the idea of planning restrictive. They want to get on with the shooting. For them, planning somehow turns the thrill of the unexpected into an organized commitment.

But many situations *must* be planned and worked out in advance. Directors need to get permission to shoot on private property, to make appointments to interview people, and to arrange access, among other tasks. They might occasionally have success if they arrive unannounced, but don't assume this. However, directors also need to be prepared to take advantage of unexpected opportunities. It is worth taking advantage of the unexpected, even if you decide not to use it later.

3.17 THE THREE STAGES OF PRODUCTION

Most programs go through three main stages:

1. *Planning and preparation*. Also known as preproduction, this phase of the production includes preparation, organization, and rehearsal before the production begins. Ninety percent of the work on a production usually goes into the planning and preparation phase.
2. *Production*. Actually shooting the production.
3. *Post-production*. Editing, additional treatment, and duplication.

The nature of the subject will influence the amount of work needed at each stage. A production that involves a series of straightforward "personality" interviews is generally a lot easier to organize than one on Arctic exploration or a historical drama. But in the end, a great deal depends on how the director decides to approach the subject.

Working at the highest quality, directors can create incredible programming by using simple methods. Treatment does not have to be elaborate to make its point. If a woman in the desert picks up her water bottle, finds it empty, and then the camera shows a patch of damp sand where it rested, the shot has told us a great deal without any need for elaboration. A single look or a gesture can often have a far stronger impact than lengthy dialog that attempts to show how two people feel about each other.

It is important to understand the complexity of the production. Some ideas seem simple enough but can be difficult or impossible to carry out. Others look very difficult or impracticable but are easily achieved on the screen. For example:

"Hurry and arc the camera around the actor." (Difficult. Movement shots are always time consuming, making it almost impossible to do quickly.)

"Make her vanish!" (Simple. Keep the camera still, have the subject exit, and edit out the walk.)

3.18 COVERAGE

What do you want to cover in the available time? How much is *reasonable* to cover in that time? If there are too many topics, it will not be possible to do justice to any of them. If there are too few, the program can seem slow and labored. There is nothing to be gained by packing the program full of facts; even though they may sound impressive, audiences rarely remember more than a fraction of them. Unlike the printed page, on video the viewer cannot refer back to check an item, unless the program is designed to be stopped and rewound or is frequently repeated.

3.19 BUILDING A PRODUCTION OUTLINE

Directors often create a production outline. This begins with a series of *headings* showing the main themes that need to be discussed.

If we use the example of an instructional video about building a wall, the topics we may cover could include tools needed, materials, foundation, making mortar, method of laying bricks, and pointing. We can now determine how much program time to devote to each topic. Some will be brief and others relatively lengthy. While we will need to emphasize some of the topics, we will skip over others to suit the purpose of the program.

The next stage is to take each of the topic headings and note the various aspects that need to be covered as a series of *subheadings*. Under "tools," for instance, each tool that must be demonstrated should be listed. Once this program structure has been designed, the director can begin to see the form the program is likely to take.

3.20 BROAD TREATMENT

The next stage in the planning process will be to decide how to approach each subheading in the outline. Remember, you are still thinking things through. At this stage, the idea may even need to be altered, further developed, shortened, or even dropped altogether.

This is a question-and-answer process. Let's imagine the situation:

What is the topic, and what is its purpose?

It is discussing "animal hibernation in winter."

How will you approach it?

It would be nice to show a bear preparing its den for hibernation and settling down. Show the hard winter weather with the animal asleep. Later, show the bear waking up in the spring and foraging. And do all of this with a commentary.

- This is a good idea, but where are the pictures coming from?
- Do you have any?
- Are you using a film library's services?
- Does the library have that sort of material?

Let's say that we cannot afford to obtain the pictures. We need to find a less expensive method.

You could have an illustrated discussion or a commentary over still photographs and drawings (graphics, artwork).

That could be boring, a little like a slide show.

Not necessarily, for you could explore the still photographs with the camera, panning or tilting the camera across the photographs. The key is to keep the shots brief and add sound effects and possibly even music.

How do you find bear photographs that you can use?

You could take the photographs yourself in the wild or at a museum or zoo. Stills can also come from books (with permission), online stock photo agencies, or the private collections of photographers (Figure 3.20).

Note how each decision leads to another development. For example, if you decide that you are going to shoot photographs at a zoo, you then have to figure out how, when, and where you are going to get these shots. You have to figure out how the zoo needs to be lit. Will the glass cage cause reflection problems? Can you get the viewpoint you need? You may not be able to decide at this point, but you will have to do some research to see how feasible each specific idea is.

FIGURE 3.20
Photographs can be purchased from an online stock photo agency for use in video productions.
(Photo by Sarah Owens.)

3.21 PRODUCTION RESEARCH

There are, in fact, several stages during the creation of a program when you will probably need more information before you can go on to the next step (Table 3.1). "Research" might amount to nothing more than hearing that Uncle David has a friend who has a

Table 3.1 Typical Research Information for the Planning and Preparation Phase of the Production Process

Lists can be daunting, but here are reminders of typical areas you may need to look into in the course of planning your production.

The Idea	The exploratory process: – Find sources of information on the subject (people, books, and publications). – Arrange to consult these sources. – Accumulate data. – Select material that is relevant and appropriate to the idea. – Determine whom the program is for. – What is the purpose of the program? – Does it have to relate to an existing program? (Are there specific levels or standards that must be adhered to?) – Does the program need to be a specific length? – Coordinate ideas into an outline with headings and subheadings. – Consider the program development, forming a rough script or a shooting script.
Practicality	Consider the ideas in practical terms: – What does the viewer actually need to see and hear at each point in the program? – Where can the program be shot? – What sort of props are needed for each sequence (items, furnishings)? – How should the scene be arranged? (Action in broad outline.) – What talent (people in front of the camera) are needed for the program?
The Equipment	What is needed to shoot the program: – Single camera or multicamera? – What equipment, beyond the camera(s), will be required to make the production a success? – Is equipment owned, can it be borrowed, or does it need to be rented?
Feasibility	Check what is really involved: – Are the ideas and treatment being developed reasonable for the available resources? – Is there another way of achieving similar results more easily, more cheaply, more quickly, or with less labor? – Can the needed items be acquired? – Are the locations available and affordable? – Is there sufficient time to do research, organize, rehearse, shoot, and edit the production? *Costs*: – What is the budget? – How will you arrange to research possible costs for a sequence before including it in the production? – Is it possible to obtain advance payment for expenses? – Are advance payments required for some services and purchases?

(*Continued*)

Table 3.1 (Continued)

	Assistance: – Will you need assistance, manpower, expert aid or advice, extra transport, etc., to do the job? – What talent is involved (amateur, professional, casual)? – Do you need professional services (to make items, service, prepare graphics, etc.)? *Facilities*: – Are there facilities available that are sufficient for the anticipated shooting requirements and the post-production work? – Will additional facilities be needed to augment the existing facilities? *Problems*: – What might be the impact of major problems, such as weather, on each sequence of the production? – Is there any obvious danger factor (shooting a cliff climbing sequence)? – Will the situation you need be available at the time the program needs to be shot (snow in summer)? *Time*: – Is there sufficient time to shoot the sequence? – What backup plans must you make to protect the production in case serious problems arise? For example, instead of taking a couple of hours to shoot a scene, it might take two days with an overnight stay if things go wrong (high wind, rain, noise, etc.).
Administration	Various business arrangements and agreements: – Obtain permission to shoot, passes, permits, fees, and so on. – Obtain copyright clearances, if using music, copying photographs, and so on. – Insurance may be necessary to cover losses, breakage, injury, and so on. – Union agreements may need to be followed. – Contractual arrangements may be needed for the talent, crew, equipment, transportation, scenery, props, costumes, and editing suite. – Arrange for transportation, accommodation, food, and storage. – Return borrowed/hired items.

stuffed bear that he would lend you for the program. Additional opportunities and problems will be discovered as research is being completed. Sometimes those opportunities and problems will even alter the outcome of the project. You may encounter an enthusiast who can supply enough material to fill a dozen programs on the subject, or you might have to really dig for program content.

3.22 REMOTE SURVEYS (RECCE)

Fundamentally, there are two types of shooting conditions: at your *base* and *on location*. Your *base* is wherever you normally shoot. It may be a studio, a theater, a room, or even a stadium. The base is where you know exactly what facilities are available (equipment, power, supplies, and scenery), where things are, the amount of room available, and so on. If you need to supplement what is there, you can usually do so easily.

A location is anywhere away from your normal shooting site. It may just be outside the building or way out in the country. It could be in a vehicle, down in a mine or in someone's home. Your main concern when shooting away from your base is to find out what you are going to deal with in advance. It is important to be prepared. The preliminary visit to a location is generally called a remote survey, site survey, or location survey. It can be anything from a quick look around to a detailed survey of the site. What you find during the survey may influence the planned production treatment. The checklist in Table 3.2 gives more remote survey specifics (Figure 3.21).

Table 3.2 Checklist: The Remote Survey

The amount of detail needed about a location varies with the type and style of the production. Information that may seem trivial at the time can prove valuable later in the production process. Location sites can be interiors, covered exteriors, or open-air sites. Each has its own problems.

Sketches	■ Prepare rough maps of the route to the site that can ultimately be distributed to the crew and talent (include distance, travel time). ■ Prepare a rough layout of the site (room plan, etc.). ■ Outline anticipated camera location(s). ■ Designate parking locations for truck (if needed) and staff vehicles.
Contact & Schedule Information	■ Get location contact information from primary and secondary location contacts, site custodian, electrician, engineer, and security; this includes office and cell phones as well as e-mail. ■ If access credentials are required for the site, obtain the procedure and contact information. ■ Obtain the event schedule (if one exists), and find out if there are rehearsals that you can attend.
Camera Locations	■ Check around the location for the best camera angles. ■ What type of camera mount will be required (tripod, Steadicam, etc.)? ■ If a multicamera production, cable runs must be measured to ensure that there is enough camera cable available. ■ What lens will be required on the camera at each location to obtain the needed shot? ■ Are there any obstructions or distractions (e.g., large signs, reflections)? ■ Do you anticipate any obvious problems in shooting? Anything dangerous?

(Continued)

Table 3.2	(Continued)
Lighting	▪ Will the production be shot in daylight? How will the light change throughout the day? Does the daylight need to be augmented with reflectors or lights? ▪ Will the production be shot in artificial light? (If so, will you use theirs, yours, or a combination of the two?) Will they be on at the time you are shooting? ▪ What are your estimates for the number of lamps, positions, power needed, supplies, and cabling required?
Audio	▪ What type of microphones will be needed? ▪ Any potential problems with acoustics (such as a strong wind rumble)? ▪ Any extraneous sounds (elevators, phones, heating/air conditioning, machinery, children, aircraft, birds, etc.)? ▪ Required microphone cable lengths must be determined.
Safety	▪ Are there any safety issues that you need to be aware of?
Power	▪ What level of power is available, and what type of power will you need? This will differ greatly between single-camera and multicamera production. ▪ What type of power connectors are required?
Communi-cations	▪ Are radios needed? How many? ▪ How many cell phones are needed? ▪ If it is a multicamera production, what type of intercom and how many headsets are required?
Logistics	▪ Is there easy access to the location? At any time, or at certain times only? Are there any traffic problems? ▪ What kind of transportation is needed for talent and crew? ▪ What kind of catering is needed? How many meals? How many people? ▪ Are accommodations needed (where, when, how many)? ▪ If the weather is bad, are there alternative positions/ locations available? ▪ Has a phone number list been prepared for police, fire, doctor, hotel, and local (delivery) restaurants? ▪ What kind of first-aid services need to be available? (Is a first-aid kit sufficient, or does an ambulance need to be on-site?) ▪ Is location access restricted? Do you need to get permission (or keys) to enter the site? From whom? ▪ What insurance is needed (against damage or injury)?
Security	▪ Are local police required to handle crowds or just the public in general? ▪ What arrangements need to be made for security of personal items, equipment, props, etc.)? ▪ Do streets need to be blocked?

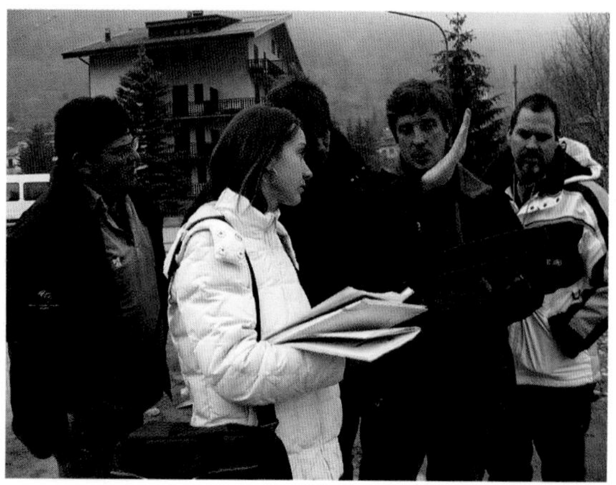

FIGURE 3.21
Site surveys allow you to check out the actual location to make sure it will meet the production needs.

3.23 FREEDOM TO PLAN

In practice, how far you can plan a production depends on how much control you have of the situation. If shooting a public event, planning may consist of finding out what is going on, deciding on the best visual opportunities, selecting camera locations, and so forth. The director may have little or no opportunity to adjust events to suit his or her production ideas.

If, on the other hand, the situation is entirely under the director's control, he or she can arrange the situation to fit the production's specific needs. Having planned the ideas, the director can then organize the elements of the production and explain the concept to the other people involved (Figure 3.22).

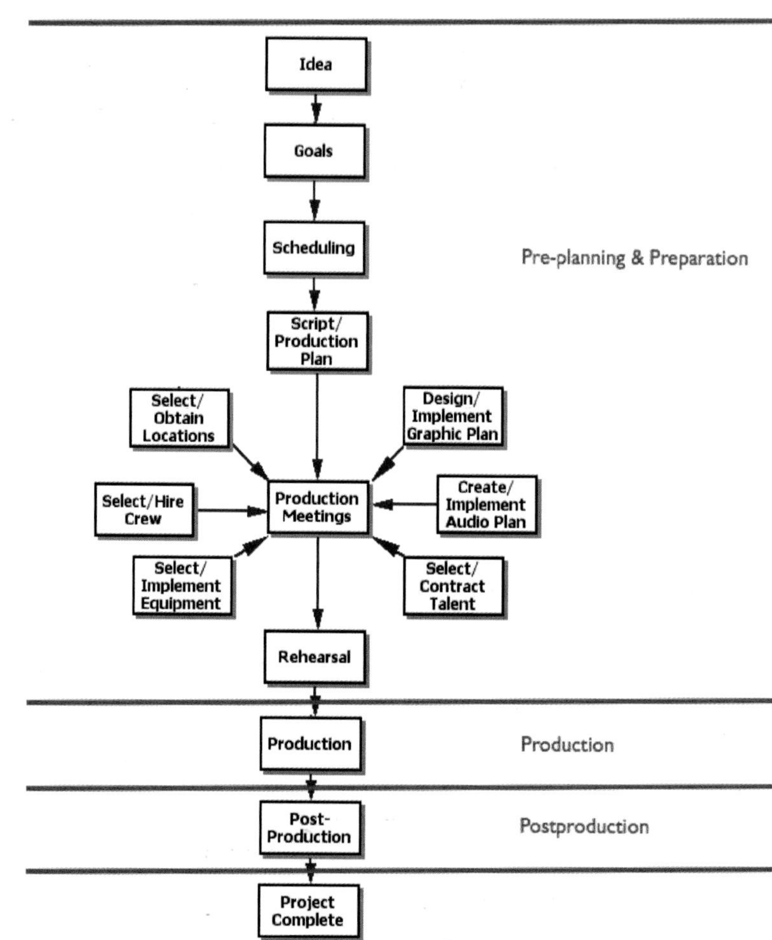

FIGURE 3.22
During the flow of the video production process, the production meetings provide a forum for all parties involved in the production to hear the vision, share ideas, and communicate issues.

3.24 SINGLE-CAMERA SHOOTING

When shooting with a *single camera*, the director is usually in one of two situations:

- *Planning in principle and shooting as opportunity allows*. For example, the director intends on taking shots of local wildlife, but what is actually shot will depend on what the crew finds at the location (Figure 3.23).

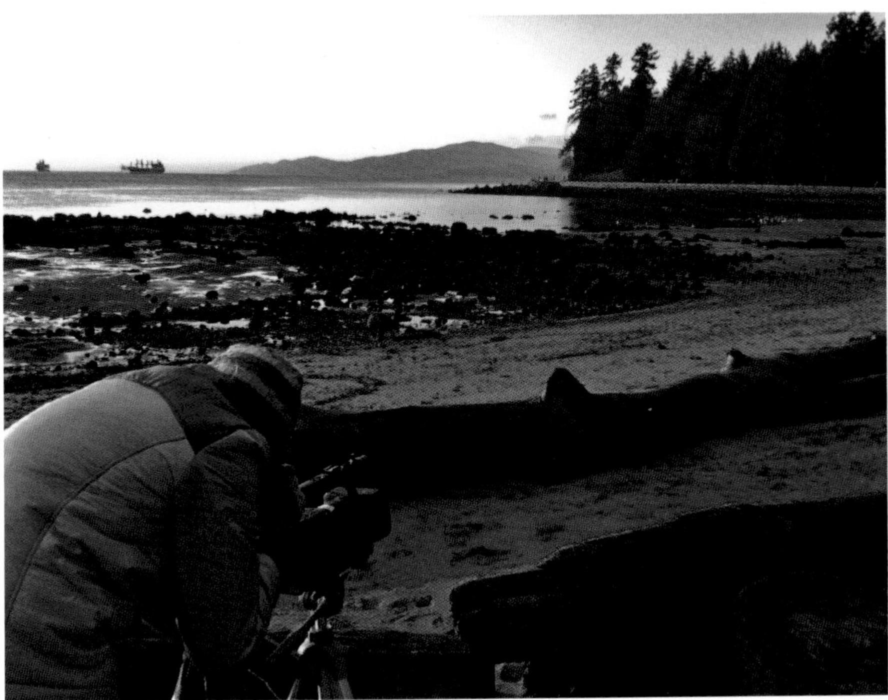

FIGURE 3.23
Single-camera shooting.

- *Detailed analysis and shot planning*. This approach is widely used in filmmaking. Here the action in a scene is reviewed and then broken down into separate shots. Each shot is rehearsed and recorded independently. Where action is continuous throughout several shots, it is *repeated* for each camera viewpoint.
- *Shot 1*. Long shot: An actor walks away from the camera toward a wall mirror.
- *Shot 2*. Medium shot: The actor repeats the action, approaching the camera located beside the mirror.
- *Shot 3*. Close-up shot: The actor repeats the walk as the camera shoots into the mirror, watching his expression as he approaches.

When edited together, the action should appear continuous. It's essential to keep the continuity of shots in mind throughout.

It is regular practice to shoot the complete action in one long shot and then take close-up shots separately. These individual shots can then be relit for maximum visual effect. Even when a person is supposedly speaking to someone else, it is quite usual to shoot the person alone, repeating a speech to the camera, to allow the camera to be placed in the best possible position.

3.25 MULTICAMERA SHOOTING

When shooting with two or more cameras, a director tends to think in terms of *effective viewpoints* as well as specific shots. Cameras need to be positioned to capture specific shots, but they also need to catch various aspects of the continuous action (Figure 3.24).

FIGURE 3.24
Multicamera shooting allows the director to think in terms of effective viewpoints rather than specific shots.
(Photo by Jon Greenhoe/WOOD TV.)

When planning a multicamera production, directors have to consider a variety of situations:

- Will one camera come into another camera's shot?
- Is there time for cameras to move to various positions?
- What kinds of shots does the script dictate?

- How will the microphones and lighting relate to the cameras' movements (visible mics or shadows cast by the boom pole, etc.)?

3.26 BUDGETING

It is understandable that most directors are more creative minded than business minded. However, you have to be financially savvy in order to stay within the budget constraints—and every production has budget constraints.

In Table 3.1, in the feasibility study, we talked a little about budgeting. It is important to understand what you have available financially at the beginning of the project. Once the total budget has been established, it needs to be broken down into categories. The categories may include but are not confined to the following:

- Transportation
- Staff/crew
- Talent/actors
- Script
- Equipment costs (rental or purchase)
- Postproduction
- Props
- Permits
- Food
- Lodging
- Supplies

An estimate needs to be made for each category. Once the estimates are completed, you can see if your project is going to fit the assigned overall budget. Most of the time you will need to trim here and there in order to fit the budget. However, occasionally you will see that you have some extra money in the budget, allowing you to increase a category or two (Figure 3.25).

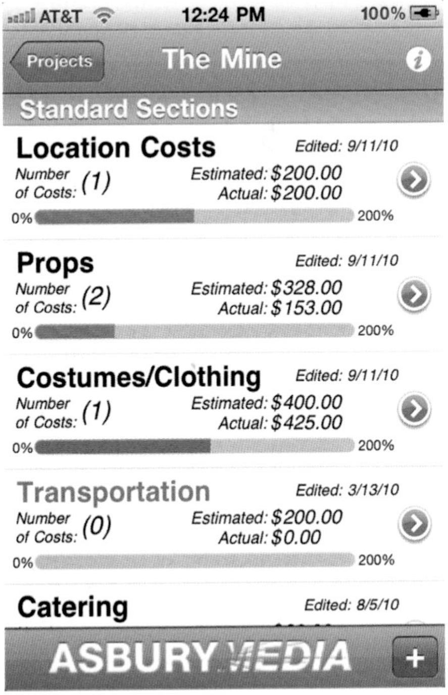

Once the budget is final, it is important to begin tracking each expenditure. This enables you to keep an eye on the categories as well as the overall budget. If you go over in one category, it means that you have to take money from a different category—or you will go over budget.

Building a track record of being able to stay within budgets will increase the trust that clients have in you, knowing that you can responsibly create productions.

FIGURE 3.25 **Budgeting software keeps track of production expenses, comparing the estimated costs to the actual costs. Computer software is available to keep a very detailed budget. Mobile software that works on a portable device is helpful when in the field. This is a screenshot from a free iPhone budgeting app for small films.** *(Software used is Film Budget.)*

3.27 COPYRIGHT

If you can't get permission from the copyright owner, you probably need to remove the item from the scene.

Whenever material prepared and created by other people is used—a piece of music, a sound recording, videotape, film, a picture in a book, labels on a jar, CD covers, a sculpture, a photograph, and so on—it must be cleared for use in your production if it will be seen beyond the educational classroom. The copyright may even include artwork and even trademarks, and it must be cleared with the appropriate copyright owner(s). Many times the producers/directors are required to pay a fee to the *copyright holders* or an appropriate organization operating on their behalf for copyright clearance. The copyright law is complex and varies among countries, but basically it protects the originators from having their work copied without permission. You cannot, for example, prepare a video program with music dubbed from a commercial recording, with inserts from television programs, magazine photographs, advertisements, and so on without the permission of the respective copyright owners. Copyright fees will depend on the purpose and use of the program. Some of the exceptions to this policy occur when the program is only to be seen within the home or used in a class assignment that will not be seen by the public. In most cases, the copyright can be traced through the source of the material needed for the production (the publisher of a book or photograph).

Agreements take various forms. They may be restricted or limited. For music and sound effects, directors are usually required to pay a royalty fee per use, or it may be possible to buy the rights to use an item or a package ("buyout method").

The largest organizations concerned with performance rights for music (copyright clearance for use of recorded music or to perform music) include the Performing Rights Society (PRS) in the United Kingdom, the American Society of Composers, Authors and Publishers (ASCAP), the Society of European Stage Authors and Composers (SESAC), and Broadcast Music Inc. (BMI). When clearing copyrights for music, both the record company and the music publishers may need to be involved.

Music in *public domain* is not subject to copyright, but any arrangement or performance is. Music and lyrics published in 1922 or earlier are in the public domain in the United States. While anyone can use a public domain song in a production, no one can "own" a public domain song. Sound recordings, however, are protected separately from musical compositions. There are no sound recordings in the public domain in the United States. If you need to use an existing sound recording, even a recording of a public domain song, you will either have to record it yourself or license a recording.

3.28 CONTRACTS

Whenever you hire talent (actors, talent, and musicians) or use services (such as a scaffolding company), contractual agreements arise. Union agreements may also be involved. So before you commit in any way, find out exactly what is entailed both financially and legally.

Apart from general shots, whenever you want to shoot in the street, it is wise to let the local police know in advance. Productions may cause an obstruction or break local laws. If you are going to be shooting footage of people, you are required to get their permission in writing (with their name and address) on a *talent release form* (Table 3.3). While terminology varies, depending on the purpose of the production and the nature of the actor's contribution, the release form generally authorizes the director to use the individual's performance—free or for a fee.

Table 3.3 Sample Talent Release Form

Video Project Title: ______________________________

I hereby consent for value received and without further consideration or compensation to the use (full or in part) of all videotapes taken of me and/or recordings made of my voice and/or written extraction, in whole or in part, of such recordings or musical performance for the purposes of broadcast, cybercast, or distribution in any manner by __________ (production company name).

Location: __________________ Date: ____________

Talent's or legal guardian's signature: __________________

Address: __________________ City: ____________

State: _____ Zip code: _________ Date: __/__/__

Interview with a Pro

DT Slouffman, Producer

DT Slouffman, Producer
DT Slouffman has worked on productions for ABC, NBC, Lifetime, and TLC.

What do you like about being a producer?

- Producing affords me the opportunity to collaborate with a team—other producers, shooters, editors, and talent—while still exercising a certain amount of creative control over the project and the process.
- I often have the opportunity to assemble and manage my own team. Putting the right people in the right roles can make or break a production.
- My favorite thing about producing is the results. Like any artist, to have a body of work that you created to be enjoyed by others, it's even more rewarding when that product can help or encourage its respective audience.

Tell me about how communication works in the organization of a production.

If the end goal of your work is to communicate with an audience, then you better be able to communicate to the team working with you. I have seen many productions implode or fizzle out because the producer at the top was super creative, maybe even a visionary, but unable to effectively communicate the vision with the production personnel. Without communication, the execution was flawed or the production rendered inferior or ineffective.

How do you deal with communicating to everyone?
In this age of post-modern technology, there are limitless choices when it comes to communicating with the team working with me and for me. I cannot count the number of e-mails, texts, phone calls, and voicemails I receive daily. From pre-production to post-production I have to make sure that schedules and scenarios are readily available for every member of the team and accurate. However, the most important document for any production, even more important than the budget, is the contact sheet. This is usually a one-page document that is compiled during pre-production and updated until the production is complete. The contact sheet contains the name, position, cell phone number, and e-mail of everyone working on the production. I keep an electronic copy on my laptop, an attached copy in my saved e-mail, and a printed copy folded in my wallet.

What challenges do you have to deal with as a producer?
The biggest challenge for me on any production is dealing with people who do not work in the business and don't automatically understand why I may be doing things a certain way.

A large part of any nonfiction production is dealing with the everyday people you are following and interviewing. They don't work in the business and often have a hard time answering questions in a way that their answer makes sense on television.

I always feel like I am teaching a small television class with the people that I am making shows about. It truly is the most challenging part of my job, but if I cannot communicate the how and why to the people my series will be about, I won't get what I need, and the finished episode will suffer.

How do you prepare for a specific assignment as a producer?
I prepare for every production that I produce by doing massive amounts of homework. I need to know everything I can know about the subject matter of the show and the people we will follow in the process of shooting. You cannot know too much about your subject because you will follow and interview people who will know the subject intimately. If you don't have a working knowledge of what you are covering, you will fail while working with them.

As well, if you bluff your way through it, your audience will know. Remember that in most cases your demographic chooses what they watch because the subject is interesting to them. If you are heading up a production and you don't truly understand the subject you are covering, the audience always knows.

Effective producing involves managing people, understanding how to tell a story, and working well with others. You can be great at all of those things, but if you haven't done your homework, when it comes to your subject matter, none of those things can save you.

CHAPTER 4

Production Techniques

You can't assume that you can take a 30-second ad and make it fit everything; put it at the end of something, put it on YouTube, get it in a banner or create a website around it. Content must be translatable and it has to be conceived to translate. Shooting with multiplatforms in mind and repurposing it for mobile, web, cinema, banners, is what companies are working toward.

—David Rolfe, Senior Vice President, DDB Chicago

The production techniques that video crew members employ vary greatly from person to person, company to company, and country to country. The goal of this chapter is to review the most common production techniques in order to broadly prepare you for the television industry.

Key Terms

- ***Camera control unit (CCU):*** Equipment that controls the camera from a remote position. The CCU includes setting up and adjusting the camera: exposure, black level, luminance, color correction, aperture, and so on.
- ***Clapboard:*** The clapboard (also known as a *clapper* or *slate*) is shot at the beginning of each take to provide information such as film title, names of the director and director of photography, scene, take, date, and time. Primarily used in dramatic productions.
- ***Continuity:*** The goal of continuity is to make sure there is consistency from one shot to the next in a scene and from scene to scene. This continuity includes the talent, objects, sets, and so on. An example of a continuity error in a production would be when one shot shows the talent's hair combed one way and the next shot shows it in perfect condition.
- ***Cut:*** An instantaneous transition between two images. This is the most common switcher transition used in production. (Also known as a "take.")
- ***Dissolve (mix):*** A gradual transition between two images. A dissolve usually signifies a change in time or location.

- ***Dolly (track):*** To move the whole camera and mount slowly toward or away from the subject.
- ***Fade in/out (up/down):*** A *fade* is a transition to or from "video black." Usually defines the beginning or end of a segment or program.
- ***ISO:*** While all the cameras are connected to the switcher as before, the ISO (or isolated) camera is also continuously recorded on a separate recorder.
- ***Multicamera production:*** When two or more cameras are used to create a television production. Usually a production switcher switches the cameras.
- ***Objective camera:*** The camera takes on the role of an onlooker who is watching the action from the best possible position at each moment.
- ***Pan:*** To pivot the camera to the left or right.
- ***Single-camera production:*** Single-camera production is when one camera is used to shoot the entire segment or show.
- ***Stand by:*** To alert the talent to stand by for a cue.
- ***Stretch:*** To tell the talent to go more slowly (there is time to spare).
- ***Subjective camera (point of view/POV):*** When the camera represents the talent's point of view, allowing the audience to see through the talent's eyes, as the camera moves through a crowd or pushes aside undergrowth.
- ***Switcher (vision mixer):*** A device used to switch between video inputs (cameras, graphics, video players, etc.).
- ***Take:*** See *Cut*.
- ***Truck (crab):*** To move the whole camera and mount left or right.
- ***Wipe:*** A special effect transition between two images. Usually shows a change of time, location, or subject. The wipe adds novelty to the transition but can easily be overused.

4.1 SINGLE- AND MULTICAMERA PRODUCTION

There are two radically different ways of shooting a video production:

- Single-camera production, in which one camera is used to shoot a segment or an entire show.
- Multicamera production, in which a production switcher (vision mixer) links two, three, or more cameras, and their outputs are selected or blended as required by the director.

Each of these techniques has its own specific advantages and limitations. Some types of programs, such as sports, cannot be shot effectively (such as recording an entire game) with a single camera; for other program types, a multicamera approach can seem overpoweringly inappropriate (such as a news interview in someone's home). From the director's point of view, the production techniques are markedly different. For a live production, a single camera would be unnecessarily inhibiting. But for a taped production, the director can adopt techniques that are similar to those of a filmmaker (Figure 4.1).

Single-Camera Production

A single lightweight camera is independent (has its own recorder), compact, and free to go anywhere (is not attached by a cable to a switcher). The director can be right there on the spot beside the camera, seeing opportunities and explaining exactly what he or she wants to the camera operator. In many cases, the person devising and organizing the project may also be operating the camera (Figure 4.2).

FIGURE 4.1
Single-camera news production.

FIGURE 4.2
Documentaries are generally shot with a single camera.

PREPARING TO RECORD A SINGLE-CAMERA SHOT (DRAMATIC STYLE)

- Review details of the next shot from the storyboard.
- Mark clapboard with scene and shot numbers (optional, primarily used with dramatic productions). (Figures 4.3 and 4.4)
- Announce "Is everyone ready?"
- Call "Quiet, please!"
- Start recording.
- Shoot clapboard.
- Call "Action!" (Cues action to begin.)
- Announce the end of action. "Cut!" (Action stops, talent waits.)
- Stop recording.
- Check recording (end only, or spot check).

FIGURE 4.3
"Slating" the beginning of a take with a clapboard.

FIGURE 4.4
Clapboards can be an actual board, as in Figure 4.3, or they can be on a mobile device such as a cell phone or tablet. This image is from the screen of an iPhone.
(Software from iSlate.)

- Note final frames for continuity, log shot details (identification, duration), and label the tape (Figure 4.5).

  One of the following is then appropriate:

  "TAKE IS OK. LET'S GO ON TO SHOT 5."

  or

  "WE NEED TO RETAKE THAT SHOT BECAUSE . . ."

- Set up for next shot.

FIGURE 4.5
A production assistant is logging the shots the camera operator is shooting. She is responsible for noting the content of shots. Loggers may also note shot durations, whether it is a good or bad shot, and any other pertinent notes.

This method offers the director incredible flexibility—both when shooting and later when editing. Directors can select and rearrange the material they have shot, trying out several versions to improve the production's impact. There is none of the feeling of instant commitment, which can typify a multicamera production. But it is slow, and patience is a necessity.

Shooting with a single camera will often involve interrupting or repeating the action in order to reposition the camera. The problems of maintaining *continuity* between setups, even the way in which shooting conditions can change between takes (such as light or weather variances), are not to be underestimated.

It has been said that, unlike multicamera production, which is a "juggling act," shooting with a single camera allows the director to concentrate on doing one thing at a time, on optimizing each individual shot. The director is free to readjust each camera position, rearrange the subject, change the lighting, adjust the sound recording, modify the decor, and make any other alterations that are necessary to suit each take. That's great. But shooting can degenerate into a self-indulgent experimental session. It is all too easy to put off problems until tomorrow with "We'll sort it out during the edit" or "Let's leave it till postproduction."

When shooting with a single camera, directors do not have to worry about coordinating several different cameras, each with its different viewpoint. Directors are relieved of the tensions of continually cueing, guiding, and switching between cameras. All production refinements and supplementary features from background music to video effects are added at a later stage, during the postproduction session. The other side of the coin is that when shooting with a single camera, you finish with a collection of recordings containing a mixture of takes (good, bad, and indifferent; mistakes and all) shot in any order, all needing to be sorted out at a later time. So compiling the final production—including titles, music, and effects—can be a lengthy process.

Multicamera Production

If you are shooting continuous action with a single camera and want to change the camera's viewpoint, you have basically two choices. You can move the camera to a new position while still shooting, or you can miss some of the action as the camera is repositioned at the next setup. A multicamera production director simply switches from one camera to another, which is a clear advantage when shooting a series of events going on at the same time or spread over a wide area (Figure 4.6).

Unlike the director on a single-camera shoot, who is close to the camera, the director of a multicamera production is located away from the action. This director watches a series of television monitors in a production control room and issues instructions to the crew over their intercom (talkback) headsets and to the floor manager who guides the talent on the director's behalf (Figures 4.7 and 4.8).

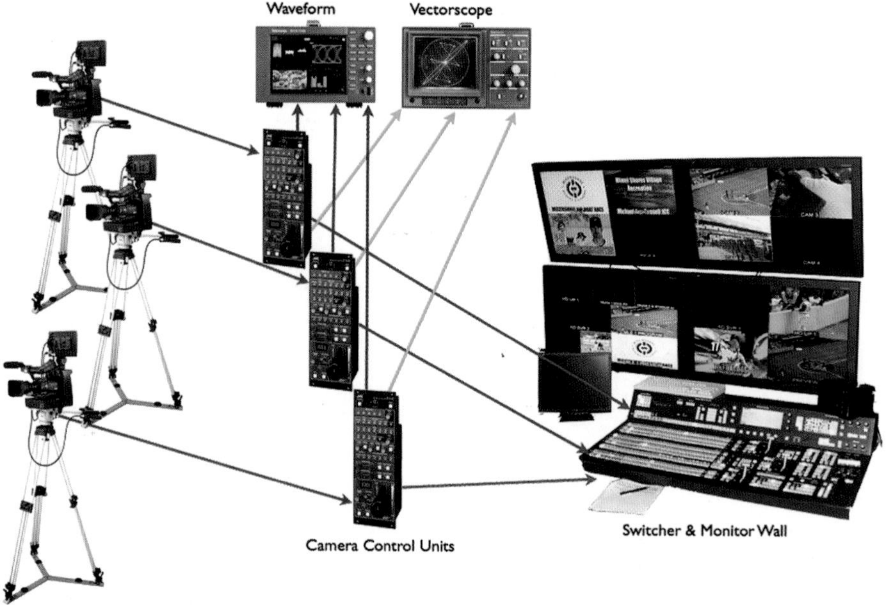

FIGURE 4.6
The basic multicamera video setup begins with the lens, moves to the camera, then to the camera control unit, is tested for quality (waveform and vectorscope), and then goes to the video switcher.
(Photos courtesy of JVC, Tektronics and Russ Jennisch.)

FIGURE 4.7
Multicamera production in a studio.
(Photo by Josh Taber.)

FIGURE 4.8
Video production switcher in the control room.

In a *live* multicamera production, most of the shot transitions (cuts, dissolves, wipes, etc.) are made on a *production switcher* (also known as a *vision mixer*) during the action. The switcher takes the outputs from various video sources (cameras, video recorders, graphics, etc.) and switches between them (Figure 4.8). There are no opportunities to correct or improve. However, the director does have the great advantage of continuously monitoring and comparing the shots (Figure 4.9). The continuity problems that can easily develop during a single-camera production disappear during the multicamera production because it is real time. An experienced multicamera crew can, after a single rehearsal, produce a polished show in just a few hours. At the end of the recording period, the show is finished.

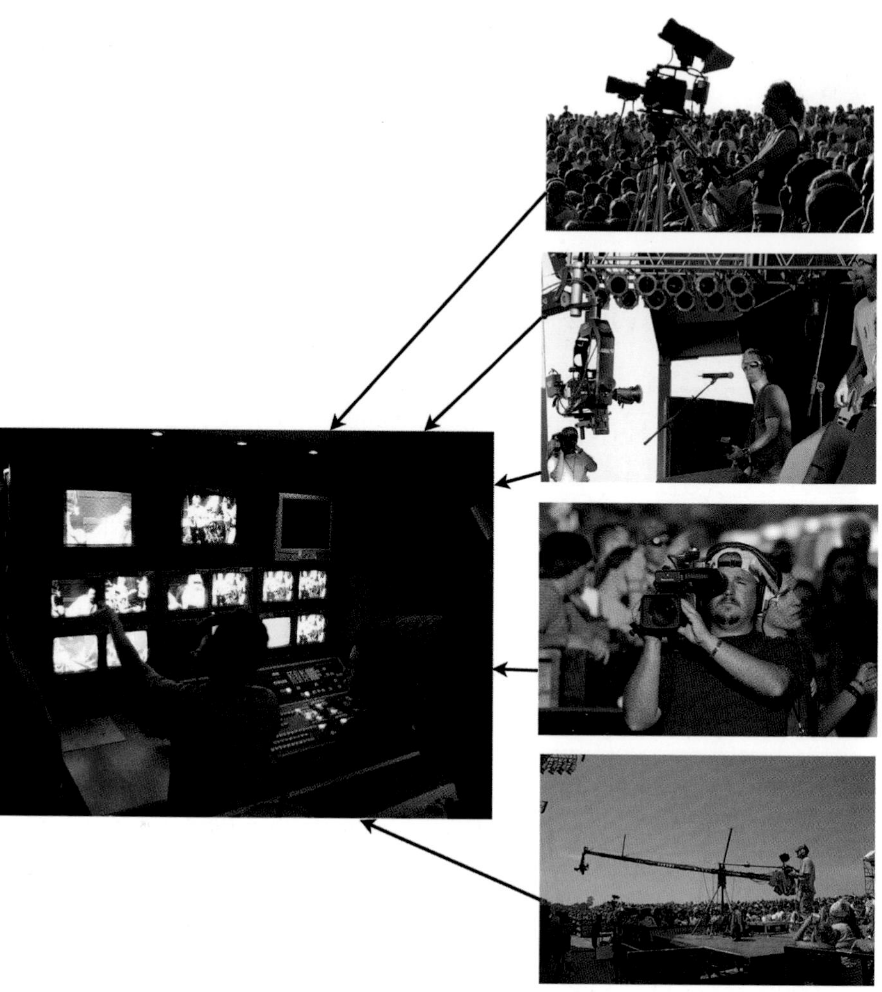

FIGURE 4.9
Multicamera production directors receive a variety of camera shots all at the same time and must choose the shot that best communicates the action.
(Photos by Josh Taber and Paul Dupree.)

Multicamera productions may be shot as follows:

- *Live*. Transmitted live to the viewing audience.
- *Live on tape*. Shot from beginning to end and recorded. This style of production allows the director to clean it up in postproduction.
- *Scene-by-scene*. Each scene or act is shot, corrected, and polished one at a time (Figure 4.10).

A multicamera production can degenerate into a shot-grabbing routine in which the director simply cuts between several camera viewpoints for the sake of variety. But for directors with imagination, the ability to plan ahead, and a skilled team, the results can be of the highest standards.

FIGURE 4.10
A sitcom is a good example of a scene-by-scene multicamera television production.
(Photo by Josh Taber.)

3D SHOT SELECTION

You have to take into account that what seems slow in 2D may be just what you want to see in 3D. There are times when your instinct tells you to cut faster in flat space, but you have to slow it down in this new dimension.

For example, we have a shot where a man is sliding down a zip line toward the camera. If this were a fast music video in 2D, I'd chop it into many individual shots. But in 3D, we locked off the camera and let the man come up to the lens and fly out of frame. It worked really cool.

—Shane Marr, Cinemarr Entertainment

4.2 MULTICAMERA ISO

When the action cannot be repeated or events are unpredictable, some directors make use of an *ISO* (isolated) camera. This simply means that, while all the cameras are connected to the switcher as before, one of them is also continuously recorded on a separate recorder. This ISO camera takes wide shots of the action (cover shots) or concentrates on watching out for the arrival of the guest, for instance, or a specific player at a sports event, so that if the director misses the needed shot "live," it is still recorded. Shots on ISO can be played back during a live show or edited in where necessary later.

4.3 MULTICAMERA PRODUCTION WITHOUT A SWITCHER

Another multicamera approach is to use camcorders. Instead of cutting between cameras with a switcher, shots from their separate recordings are edited together later during a postproduction session. It is fairly simple to sync multiple cameras together on even some of the lowest-cost nonlinear editing systems. Voiceover narration, sound effects, video effects, graphics, or music are then added in postproduction. The advantage of this type of multicamera technique is that it significantly reduces the cost of having to pay for a large crew and a control room or remote production truck/OB van. The disadvantage is that the production is not over when the event is over; it still needs to be finalized in postproduction, which can be time consuming.

TELEVISION AND ILLUSION

Roone Arledge, former president of ABC Sports, was an early innovator in television sports production. Arledge pushed his directors to "use the camera—and the microphone—to broadcast an image that approximates what the brain perceives, not merely what the eye sees. Only then can you create the illusion of reality." His example was an auto race where, even though cars may be traveling more than 200 miles per hour, the perception of speed disappears when a camera with a long shot is used. However, when a POV camera is placed much closer to the track than spectators would normally be allowed, the close camera and microphone give the television viewer the sensation of speed and the roar that a live viewer would perceive by sitting in the stands. "That way, we are not creating something phony. It is an illusion, but an illusion of reality."

4.4 THE ILLUSION OF REALITY

Some directors (and camera operators) imagine that they are using their cameras to show their audience "things as they are." However, they are not. Television is inherently *selective*. Even if the camera is simply pointed at the scene, and the rest left to the audience, the director has, whatever the intention, made a selective choice on the audience's behalf. The audience has not chosen to look at that specific aspect of the scene; the director has. The type of shot shown and the camera's viewpoint determines how much the audience sees. The audience has no way of seeing the rest of the scene. In fact, a skilled director uses camera and microphone placement to create an illusion, to give the audience the *impression of reality*. The goal is to make viewers feel as though they are there, actually experiencing the event.

Program making is a *persuasive* art—persuading the audience to look and to listen; persuading them to do something in a specific way; persuading them to buy something, whether it is an idea or a product. Directors want not only to arouse the audience's interest but also to sustain it. The goal is to direct their attention to certain features of the subject and to prevent their minds from wandering to other areas. Directors achieve this goal by the shots they select, by the way they edit those shots together, and by the way sound is used. Persuasion is not a matter of high budget and elaborate facilities but of imagination.

Directors can even take a dull, unpromising subject, such as an empty box, and influence how the audience feels about it. Imagine you are sitting in darkness when up on the screen comes a shot containing nothing more than a flatly lit wooden box with a light gray background. How do you think the audience would react? On seeing the shot, most of us would assume that the image is important or is supposed to have some sort of meaning or purpose. After all, it is appearing on video. So we start by wondering what it is all about. What are we supposed to be looking at? Does the box have some significance that we've missed? Is someone coming on in a minute to explain?

Now the director has the audience's attention for a moment or two while they are trying to understand what is going on. If a word is stenciled on the box, the viewers will probably read the word and then try to puzzle out what it means. They will look and listen, and finally get bored. But all that has probably only taken a few seconds. Directors cannot rely on the subject alone to hold the audience's interest. How the subject is presented is very important.

Let us imagine ourselves again in darkness, but now on the screen appears a box, half-lit from behind with only part of the box visible as the rest falls away into a silhouette. A low rhythmical beat steadily fills our ears. The camera dollies slowly along the floor, creeps forward very slowly, pauses, then moves onward, stopping abruptly before moving on again. Slow chords from an instrument grow louder and louder.

How is your audience going to react? If it has been done well, they are now on the edges of their seats, anxious to find out what is in the box. It is the same box that appeared in the first illustration, only you have now held your audience's attention for much longer than a few seconds.

All right, we know that these dramatic techniques cannot be used in all productions. However, it does show how persuasive the video can be. It shows us how even a simple subject, like an empty box, can be influenced by production techniques. But it is also a reminder that the production treatment needs to be *appropriate*. It needs to create an ambience, an atmosphere that is suitable for the occasion. Whether your program is to have Hollywood glitter, the neutrality of a newscaster's report, the enthusiastic participation of a kids' show, or the reverential air of a remembrance ceremony, the style of your presentation should suit the occasion.

INTERCOM INSTRUCTIONS

In a multicamera production, the director gives instructions to the crew members (cameras, sound, etc.) through their headsets. Microphones, performers, or the viewing audience cannot overhear this intercom. It is only meant for the production crew (Figure 4.11).

FIGURE 4.11
Directors use intercoms to give instructions to the crew.

Ready to fade to 1	Production is beginning in video black. Director is warning the technical director and the camera 1 operator that he or she is going next to camera 1.
Fade to 1	Gradual transition from video black to camera 1.
Ready to take 2	Stand-by cue for camera 2.
Cam 2, give me a two-shot of Joe (host) and guest	Camera 2 operator should frame both people in the shot.
Zoom in	Use the zoom control on the lens to magnify the subject.
Tighten your shot	Slightly zoom in.
Go wider	Slight zoom out.
Dolly in/back (track)	Move the whole camera and mount slowly toward/away from the subject.
Pan left/right	Pivot the camera to the left/right.
Kill the flowers	Remove the flowers from the set (unwanted, obtrusive).
Lose focus on Joe	Let Joe become defocused (generally to be used as a transition or as a background for graphics).
Stand by for a rise (or sit)	Talent is about to stand (sit).
Let talent go	Allow talent to move out of shot.
Lose Joe	Recompose or tighten shot to exclude Joe.
Clear on Cam 2	Camera 2 can move to next position.
Stand by	Alert talent, ready for a cue.
Cue action/cue Joe	Give hand signal to Joe to begin action.
Back to the top/take it from the top	Begin again at start of scene; repeat the rehearsal.
Pick it up from 20	Recommence rehearsal (or shooting) from shot 20 (as listed on script or show format).
Would they just walk it?	Ask actors to move through their action, without dialog or performance.
Clear 2's shot	Something/someone is obscuring camera 2's shot.
Tighten them up	Move the people closer together.
Give Joe a mark	Make a floor mark (tape) to show Joe a location point.
Tell talent to look at 2	Talent should face camera 2.
Stretch	Tell talent to go more slowly (there is time to spare).
Tell talent to pad/keep talking	Tell talent to improvise until next item is ready.
Give host a minute	Host has a minute left (hand signal).
Clear talent	We have left talent. He or she is free to move away.

4.5 THE CAMERA'S ROLE

The camera is an "eye." But whose eye? It can be that of an onlooker, watching the action from the best possible position at each moment. This is its *objective* role. Or the camera can be used in a *subjective* way. Moving around within the scene, the camera represents the talent's point of view, allowing the audience to see through the talent's eyes as the camera moves through a crowd or pushes aside undergrowth. The effect can be dramatic, especially if people within the scene seem to speak to the viewer directly, through the camera's lens.

4.6 THE CAMERA AS AN OBSERVER

This is the way the camera is used in many types of productions. The program shows us the scene from *various viewpoints*, and we begin to feel a sense of space as we build up a mental image of a situation—although the camera is only showing us a small section of the scene in each shot. The camera becomes an observer, moving close to see detail and standing far back to take in the wider view.

We might, for example, watch two people sitting and talking. As one speaks, we see a close-up shot of the speaker. A moment later, the camera switches to show us the other person listening. From time to time, we see them together (Figure 4.12).

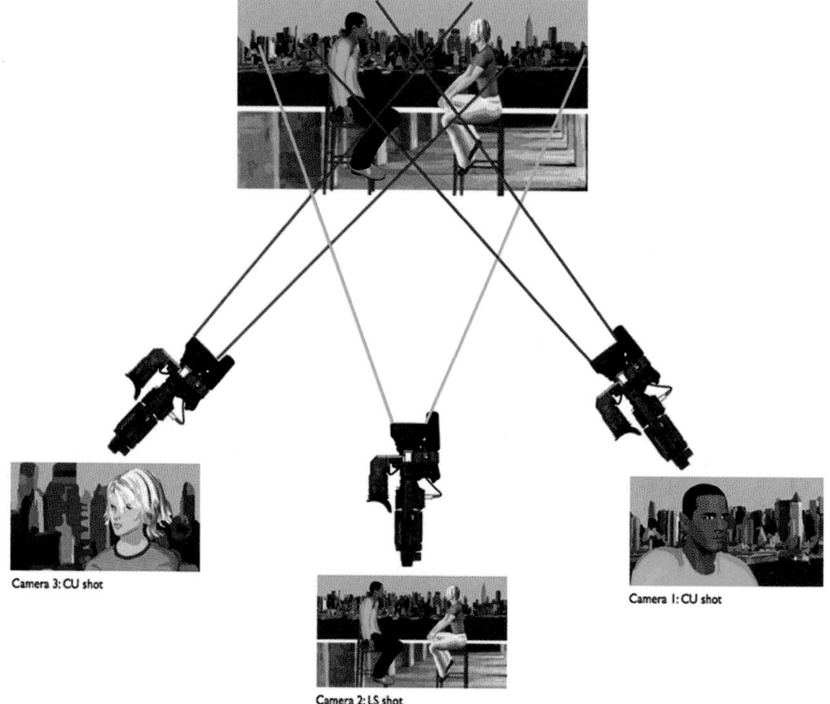

FIGURE 4.12
A basic three-camera shoot uses a mix of different shot angles to maximize communication.

There is nothing *imaginative* about this treatment; but then, it is not intended to work on the audience's emotions. It is intended to show us clearly what is going on, who is there, where they are, and what they are doing. It intermixes close-up shots to show the details we want to see at a specific moment (people's expressions) with long shots that help us establish the scene and give a more general view of the situation. In fact, treating a conversation in front of the camera in another way, by overdramatizing its presentation, would normally be inappropriate.

4.7 THE PERSUASIVE CAMERA

If, on the other hand, you are shooting a music video, shots may be as bizarre and varied as you can make them. Your aim is to excite and to shock, to create great visual variety. There is no room for subtlety. Picture impact, strange effects, and rapid changes in viewpoint thrust the music at your audience.

There is a world of difference between this brash display and the subtle play on the emotions that we discussed earlier. Yet they all demonstrate how directors can influence the audience through the way they choose and compose their shots, move the camera, and then cut those shots together.

A high-angle shot looking down on the subject can suggest an air of detachment. A low-angle shot can exaggerate the subject's importance. Tension increases as the camera dollies. These are typical ways in which the camera can affect the viewers' responses to what they are seeing.

4.8 BEGINNING AND ENDING

Part of a production's impact lies in the way it is packaged, how it is introduced, and how it is brought to an end. At its start, the main goal is to grab the audience's attention, to arouse their interest and to hold it. This can be done in a variety of ways: by shocking them, by intriguing them, by making them feel welcome, by impressing them.

One of the least interesting ways to introduce any program is to provide a series of titles in dead silence, giving the name of the program, followed by lists of those appearing in it and those responsible for the production. Music and graphics can set the scene—upbeat music and quirky titles for a comedy and regal music and formal titling for a solemn occasion.

At the end of a program, directors usually want their audience to be left with a feeling of completeness—that the program is now concluded, not that the show has just died off. This can be achieved a number of ways, including inflexions in the talent's voice during concluding words or by the way a musical background winds up. Generally speaking, it is considered poor practice to fade out in the middle of a song. It is best to edit the song to the appropriate length.

4.9 PRODUCTION METHODS

Most types of programs follow paths that have been trodden in the past. For instance, there is no sparkling new way of interviewing someone; pretty much all feasible methods have been tried at some time or other. But that does not have to make an interview any less interesting. It does mean, though, that directors can benefit from what others have discovered.

There are no infallible all-purpose formulas. But there certainly are approaches that experience has shown to work for specific subjects. In the following sections, you will find hints and reminders that could help when you are shooting various regular forms of productions.

4.10 HOW DO YOU VISUALIZE SOMETHING THAT DOES NOT EXIST?

We become so accustomed to seeing pictures to accompany seemingly every subject under the sun that sometimes we overlook one fundamental paradox: For many situations there is, strictly speaking, no subject to shoot. There are no images.

Directors have to deal with this problem on various occasions:

- Abstract subjects that have no direct visuals (philosophical, social, spiritual concepts) (Figure 4.13)
- General nonspecific subjects (transport, weather, humanity)
- Imaginary events (fantasy, literature, mythology)
- Historical events where no authentic illustrations exist (Figure 4.14)
- Upcoming events where the event has not yet happened

FIGURE 4.13
Abstract concepts can be very difficult to visualize. Cloud shots like this could be used to visualize spiritual concepts such as "heaven."

FIGURE 4.14
Historical or imaginary events are often visualized by using artists' drawings.

- Events where shooting is not possible, is prohibited, or the subject is inaccessible
- Events where shooting is impracticable, is dangerous, or you cannot get the optimum shots
- Events, now over, that were not photographed at the time
- Events where the appropriate visuals would prove too costly, would involve travel, or have copyright problems

Historical or imaginary events are often visualized by using artists' drawings.

So how do directors cope with these situations? The least interesting method is to have the talent stand outside of the building—where the camera was *not* allowed in to watch a meeting—and tell the audience what they would have seen if they had been there. Newscasts frequently use this approach when the event has already come to an end. The bank robbery, the explosion, or the fire is now over, and we can only look at the results.

Another method is to show still images or artwork of the people or places involved, utilizing explanatory commentary. This could be a good solution if the director is discussing history, such as the discovery of America or the burning of Rome. Some museum relics might even be available to show, to enliven interest, but items such as these are usually only peripheral to the main subject.

Sometimes the director can show substitutes—not a picture of the actual bear that escaped from the zoo but one like it. Although you cannot show photos of next week's parade, shots of last year's parade may illustrate the excitement of the upcoming event.

At times, directors may not be able to illustrate the subject directly. Instead, they have to use visuals that are closely associated with it. For instance, if the director does not have photographs or drawings of a composer, he or she might be able to show shots of the composer's native country or hometown.

Another possibility is to use shots that illustrate the composer's music, such as images of sunlight rippling on water, wind in trees, waves breaking on the shore, reflections, children at play, or any other associated image that would serve as a visual accompaniment. "Visual padding" of this kind is widely used in broadcast programs, in the form of general views of a town or countryside or shots of traffic or people moving around. These shots can be used as cutaways or wherever suitable visual material does not exist for one reason or another.

Interview with a Pro

Scott Rogers, Sports Producer

Scott Rogers, Sports Producer

What do you like about being a producer?
First and foremost I like being able to tell the "story" of a game my way. My guiding principle when I'm producing a game is "What do I want to know about?" Also, I like being the place where the buck stops. As the producer, the format is organized your way—how you think—so you can provide complete answers quickly. And, last but not least, the challenge of getting 25 people working toward the same goal without a script (most of the time).

How do you prepare for a specific assignment as a producer?
First you have to assess what is already in place so you can decide what needs more attention (i.e., crew—are they good at what you need, do you need to get all your own crew or truck, what is on the truck and what extra do you need to get?). Next I make a format with the open, breaks, and end and then build around that. At the same time I am reading everything I can get my hands on regarding the teams/players to select interesting stories that can be supported by tape and/or graphic elements. I also make sure I develop strong relationships with the people I will have to interact with, mostly because they control the timing of the event. Ideally, you need to get who is controlling the timing (which also includes refs/officials) to give you a little leeway about when to restart the event after commercial breaks. But, it is important you do not ask for extra time in every break. After you get your ideal scenario set up, you then have to make a mental "Plan B" if you have technical issues and know what elements are "must haves." The fact is, there is no substitute for experience when it comes to planning, but there are some things you have to (and will!!) learn the hard way.

What challenges do you have to deal with as a producer?
You have to be able to go "off plan" at any moment. You create a lot of plans/timelines of how you're going to accomplish things, and then something technical, etc. delays you, so you have to reaccess what needs to get done now and what can wait until later or not at all. Also, you need to know what areas you need help in and delegate someone to help you with that area.

Scott has been involved in productions for the NBA and multiple Olympics, as well as local television.

CHAPTER 5
Writing for Video

Action is character.

—F. Scott Fitzgerald

Key Terms

- ***Camera script*:** Adds full details of the production treatment to the left side of the "rehearsal script" and usually also includes the shot numbers, cameras used, positions of camera, basic shot details, camera moves, and switcher instructions (if used).
- ***Cue card*:** The talent may read questions or specific points from a cue card that is positioned near the camera. Generally it is held next to the camera lens.
- ***Format (running order)*:** The show format lists the items or program segments in a show in the order they are to be shot. The format generally shows the duration of each segment and possibly the camera assignments.
- ***Full script*:** A fully scripted program includes detailed information on all aspects of the production. This includes the precise words that the talent/actors are to use in the production.
- ***Outline script*:** Usually provides the prepared dialog for the opening and closing and then lists the order of topics that should be covered. The talent will use the list as they improvise throughout the production.
- ***Rehearsal script*:** Usually includes the cast/character list, production team details, rehearsal arrangements, and so forth. There is generally a synopsis of the plot or story line, location, time of day, stage/location instructions, action, dialog, effects cues, and audio instructions.
- ***Scene*:** Each scene covers a complete continuous action sequence.

5.1 THE SCRIPT'S PURPOSE

If you are working entirely by yourself on a simple production, you might get away with a few notes on the back of an envelope. But planning is an essential part of a serious production, and the script forms the basis for that plan.

Scripts do the following:

- Help the director to clarify ideas and to develop a project that works
- Help to coordinate the production team (Figure 5.1)
- Help the director to assess the resources needed for the production

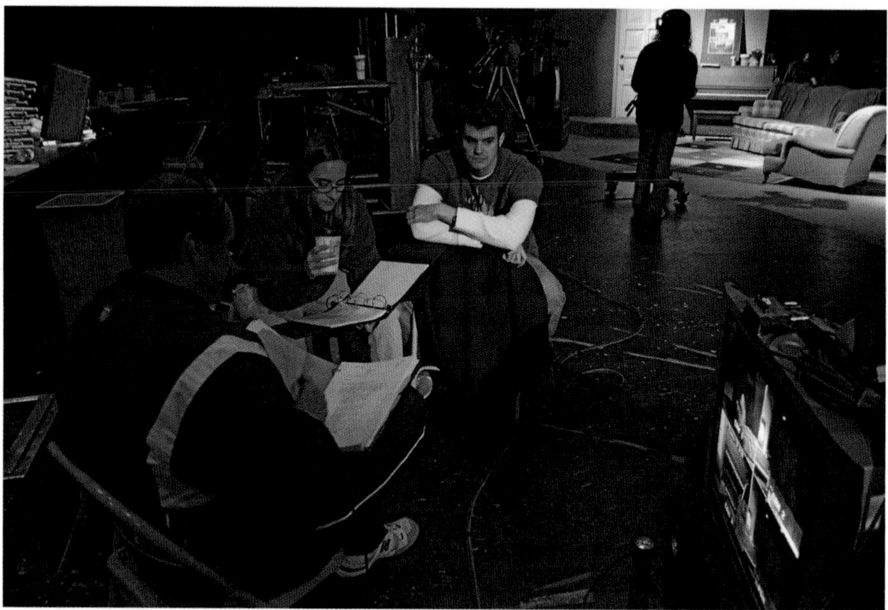

FIGURE 5.1
Director, on the set of a sitcom, discussing the script with the writers. Scripts help coordinate the production team.

Although some professional crews on location (at a news event, for instance) may appear to be shooting entirely spontaneously, they are invariably working through a process or pattern that has proved successful in the past.

For certain types of productions, such as a drama, the script generally begins the production process. The director reads the draft script, which usually contains general information on characters, locations, stage directions, and dialog. He or she then envisions the scenes and assesses possible treatment. The director must also anticipate the script's possibilities and potential problems. At this stage, changes may be made to improve the script or make it more practical. Next, the director prepares a camera treatment.

Another method of scripting begins with an *outline*. Here you decide on the various topics you want to cover and the amount of time you can allot to each topic. A script is then developed based on this outline, and a decision is made concerning the camera treatment for each segment.

When preparing a documentary, an extended outline becomes a *shooting script*, possibly showing the types of shots that will be required. It may also include rough questions for on-location interviews. All other commentary is usually written later, together with effects and music, to fit the edited program.

5.2 IS A SCRIPT NEEDED?

The type of script used will largely depend on the kind of program you are making. In some production situations, particularly where talent improvise as they speak or perform, the "script" simply lists details of the production group, facilities needed, and scheduling requirements, and it shows basic camera positions, among other fine points.

An *outline script* usually includes any prepared dialog such as the show opening and closing. If people are going to improvise, the script may simply list the order of topics to be covered. During the show, the list may be included on a card that the talent holds, on a cue card positioned near the camera, or on a teleprompter as a reminder for the host. If the show is complicated with multiple guests or events occurring, a show format is usually created (Figure 5.2) that lists the program segments (scenes) and shows the following:

- The topic (such as a guitar solo)
- The amount of time allocated for this specific segment
- The names of all talent involved (hosts and guests)
- Facilities (cameras, audio, and any other equipment and space needed)
- External content sources that will be required (tape, digital, satellite, etc.)

Example	
CARING FOR THE ELDERLY	Total duration 15 min
1. OPENING TITLES AND MUSIC	00:10
2. PROGRAM INTRO.	00:30
3. PROBLEMS OF MOBILITY	02:20
4. INJURIES	02:15
5. DIET	02:45
6. DAILY ACTIVITIES	03:40
7. EXERCISES	01:20
8. AIDS THAT CAN HELP	01:15
9. CLOSING	00:25
10. END TITLES	00:10
	15:00

FIGURE 5.2
Sample show format.

When segments (or edited packages) have been previously recorded to be inserted into the program, the script may show the opening and closing words of each segment and the package's duration, which enables accurate cueing.

5.3 BASIC SCRIPT FORMATS

There are many different script formats. However, basically, script layouts take one of two forms:

- A single-column format
- A two-column format

Single-Column Format

Although there are variations of the single-column format (Figure 5.3), all video and audio information is usually contained in a single main column. Before each scene, an explanatory introduction describes the location and the action.

```
FADE IN:
1. EXT: FRONT OF FARMHOUSE—DAY
   Front door opens. FARMER comes out, walks up to gate.
   Looks left and right along road.
2. EXT: LONG SHOT OF ROAD OUTSIDE FARM (Looking east)—DAY
   POV shot of FARMER looking along road, waiting for car.
3. EXT: FARM GATE—DAY
   Medium shot of farmer leaning over gate, looking
   anxiously. He turns to house, calling.
     FARMER:
     I can't see him. If he doesn't come soon, I'll be late.
4. INT: FARMHOUSE KITCHEN—DAY
   Wife is collecting breakfast things. Sound of radio
     WIFE:
     You're too impatient. There's plenty of time.
5. EXT: FARM GATE—DAY
   Medium shot of FARMER, same position. He looks in other
   direction. Sound of distant car approaching.
   Sudden bang, then silence.
```

FIGURE 5.3
Single-column format/single-camera shooting script.

Reminder notes can be made in a wide left-hand margin. They include transition symbols (for example, X = Cut; FU = fade-up), indicate cues and camera instructions, and incorporate thumbnail sketches of shots or action.

This type of script is widely used for narrative film-style production and single-camera video, where the director works alongside the camera operator. It is perhaps less useful in a multicamera setup, where the production team is more dispersed but everyone needs to know the director's production intentions.

Two-Column Format

Like the one-column format, there are many variations of the two-column format (Figure 5.4). This traditional television format is extremely flexible and informative. It gives all members of the production crew shot-by-shot details of what is going on. Crew members can also add their own specific information (e.g., details of lighting changes) as needed.

Two versions of the script are sometimes prepared. In the first (*rehearsal script*) the right column only is printed. Subsequently, after detailed planning and preproduction rehearsals, the production details are added to the left column to form the *camera script*.

5.4 THE FULL SCRIPT

When a program is fully scripted, it includes detailed information on all aspects of the production.

- *Scenes*. Most productions are divided into a series of scenes. Each scene covers a complete continuous action sequence and is identified with a number and location (Scene 3: Office set). A scene can involve anything from an interview to a dance routine, a song, or a demonstration sequence.
- *Shots*. When the director has decided how he or she is going to interpret the script, each scene is subdivided into a series of shots, each shot showing the action from a specific viewpoint. The shots are then numbered consecutively for easy reference on the script, in the order in which they will be screened. In a live production, the program is shot in the scripted order (running order). When taping a production, the director can shoot in whatever order is most convenient (shooting order) for the crew, actors, or director. The director may decide to omit shots ("drop shot 25") or to add extra shots ("add shots 24A and 24B"). He or she may decide to record shot 50 before shot 1 and then edit them into the correct running order at a later time.
- *Dialog*. The entire prepared dialog, spoken to camera or between people. (The talent may memorize the script or read it off teleprompters or cue cards.)
- *Equipment*. The script usually indicates which camera/microphone is being used for each shot (e.g., Cam. 2. Fishpole).

- *Basic camera instructions.* Details of each shot and camera moves (e.g., Cam. 1. CU on Joe's hand; dolly out to long shot).
- *Switcher (vision mixer) instructions.* For example: cut, fade.
- *Contributory sources.* Details of where videotape, graphics, remote feeds, and so forth appear in the program.

SHOT	CAM (Position)	SCENE/ACTION/AUDIO
CAMS:	1B, 2D, 3A	SOUND: BOOM POLE
		Scene 4. INT. BARN—NIGHT
15.	FU 2D LS DOORWAY Zoom in to MS as farmer enters	(FARMER ENTERS, HANGS LAMP ON WALL-HOOK BESIDE DOOR) TAPE 7: WIND DISC 5: RAIN FARMER: It's getting late. How is the poor beast doing?/
16.	1B O/S SHOT SON'S POV	SON: I don't think she'll last the night. She has a high fever./
17.	3A LS FARMER He comes in WS	(FARMER WALKS FORWARD TO THE STALL) FARMER: I called Willie. He's on his way. (FARMER KNEELS BESIDE COW)/
18.	2D CU SON	SON: D'you think he'll be able to get here?
19.	1C CU FARMER	FARMER: If the bridge holds. But the river is still rising./

Abbreviations used:
CU: Close-up
MS: Medium shot
LS: Long shot
FU: Fade up
O/S: Over the shoulder
POV: Point of view
___/: Indicates point to "cut to next shot"

FIGURE 5.4
Two-column format/multicamera shooting script.

TIPS

Tips for writing better dialog: keeping it brief

Writing better dialog frequently means removing existing dialog and replacing it with action, or substituting action before putting any dialog down. All writers have to seriously acquaint themselves with the great films of the silent era and how the Sennett two-reelers and the Chaplin shorts moved forward and kept the audience rapt. There is a set of ground rules. The great writers of today are not really doing anything different than the silent era gag writers. The secret? Brevity.

The stage loves words; television and the cinema love movement. Say what you want to say in the briefest possible way. If that means taking out an entire speech and replacing it with an arched eyebrow, do so. If you have to choose between the two, an arched eyebrow packs a greater punch.

Gangster plots and love stories: Why is the gangster genre so enduring? One of the reasons is because the gangster has to think half a second faster than his adversary; often his life depends on it. A nod speaks volumes; a facial tick can bring down an empire. This approach can guide writers to write more effective dialog in all other genres (love stories included). In the gangster picture, the dialog is qualitative, not quantitative.

As an exercise, try writing a classic vignette (8 to 10 minutes long), a la Mack Sennett or Buster Keaton. Note that silent movies have little to no dialog (except for, perhaps, a few title cards) and are composed of almost pure action. As with all visual writing, your character has to get from A to B using the shortest route possible; the obstacles create the tension and drama. The writer can create a tension-filled scenario where the protagonist has to get from A to B using no dialog. These circumstances could include a prison break, a prom date, or anything with obstacles to overcome. This is a great exercise for keeping the creative muscles in shape.

—Sabastian Corbascio, Writer and Director

5.5 THE DRAMA SCRIPT

The dramatic full script may be prepared in two stages: the *rehearsal script* and the *camera script*.

The rehearsal script usually begins with general information sheets, including a cast/character list, production team details, and rehearsal arrangements. There may be a synopsis of the plot or story line, particularly when scenes are to be shot/recorded out of order. The rehearsal script includes full details of the following elements:

- *Location*. The setting where the scene will be shot.
- *Time of day* and *weather conditions*.
- *Stage* or *location instructions*. For example, "The room is candlelit, and the log fire burns brightly."
- *Action*. Basic information on what is going to happen in the scene (i.e., actors' moves: Joe lights a cigar).

- *Dialog*. Speaker's name (character) followed by the person's dialog. This includes all delivered speech, voiceovers, voice inserts (e.g., phone conversations), commentary, announcements, and so on (perhaps with directional comments such as "sadly" or "sarcastically").
- *Effects cues*. Indicates the moment for a change to take place (lightning flash, explosion, Joe switches light out).
- *Audio instructions*. Music and sound effects.

The camera script adds full details of the production treatment to the left side of the rehearsal script and usually includes the following:

- The shot number
- The camera used for the shot and possibly the position of the camera
- Basic shot details and camera moves (CU on Joe; dolly back to a long shot LS as he rises)
- Switcher instructions (cut, dissolve, etc.)

5.6 SUGGESTIONS ON SCRIPTWRITING

There are no shortcuts to good scriptwriting, any more than there are to writing short stories, composing music, or painting a picture. Scriptwriters learn their techniques through observation, experience, and reading. But there are general guides that are worth keeping in mind as you prepare your script.

5.7 BE VISUAL

Although audio and video images are both important in a production, viewers perceive television as primarily a visual medium. Material should be presented in visual terms as much as possible. If planned and shot well, the images can powerfully move the audience, sometimes with very few words. At other times, programs rely almost entirely on the audio, using the video images to strengthen, support, and emphasize what the audience hears. Visual storytelling is difficult but powerful when done well.

When directors want their audience to concentrate on what they are hearing, they try to make the picture less demanding. If, for instance, the audience is listening to a detailed argument and trying to read a screen full of statistics at the same time, they may do neither successfully.

5.8 ASSIMILATION

Production scripts should be developed as a smooth-flowing sequence that makes one point at a time. Avoid the tempting diversions that distract the audience from the main theme. As much as possible, try not to move back and forth between one subject and another. Directors need to avoid the three-ring circus effect, which can occur when they are trying to cover several different activities simultaneously. Ideally, one sequence should seem to lead naturally on to the next.

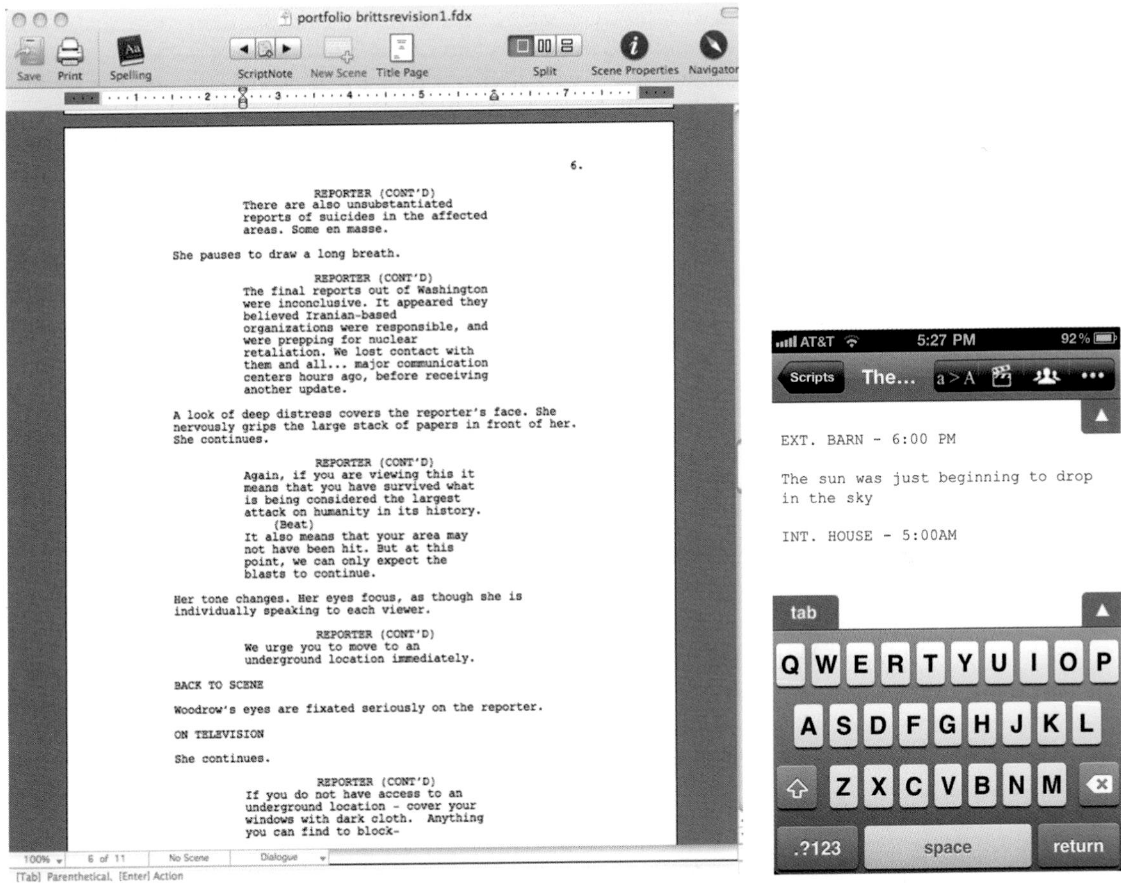

FIGURE 5.5
There are many different computer-based scriptwriting programs. The first photo shows a screen shot of Final Draft software and a script. The second photo shows a smart phone script writing app.

The previous paragraph presented a number of important points, but if a director presented ideas at that rate in a video program, there is a good chance that the audience would forget most of the information. Unlike them, you can read this book at your own pace, stop, and reread whatever you like. The audience viewing a video usually cannot. An essential point to remember when scripting is the difference between the rates at which we can take in information. A lot depends, of course, on how familiar the audience already is with the subject and the terms used. When details are new and the information is complicated, the director must take more time to communicate the information in a meaningful way. Ironically, something that can seem difficult and involved at the first viewing can appear slow and obvious a few viewings later. That is why it is so hard for directors to estimate the effect of material on those who are going to be seeing it for the first time. Directors become so familiar with the subject matter that they know it by heart and lose their objectivity.

Directors must simplify. The more complex the subject, the easier each stage should be. If the density of information or the rate at which it is delivered is too high, it will confuse, bewilder, or encourage the audience to switch it off—mentally if not physically.

5.9 RELATIVE PACE

As sequences are edited together, editors find that video images and the soundtrack have their own natural pace. That pace may be slow and leisurely, medium, fast, or brief. If editors are fortunate, the pace of the picture and the sound will be roughly the same. However, there will be occasions when editors find that they do not have enough images to fit the sound sequence or do not have enough soundtrack to put behind the amount of action in the picture.

Often when the talent has explained a point (perhaps taking 5 seconds), the picture is still showing the action (perhaps 20 seconds). The picture or action needs to finish before the commentary can move on to the next point. In the script, a little dialog may go a long way, as a series of interjections rather than a continual flow of verbiage.

The reverse can happen too, where the action in the picture is brief. For example, a locomotive passes through the shot in a few seconds, quicker than it takes the talent to talk about it. So more pictures of the subject are needed, from another viewpoint perhaps, to support the dialog.

Even when picture and sound are more or less keeping the same pace, do not habitually cut to a new shot as soon as the action in the picture is finished. Sometimes it is better to continue the picture briefly, to allow time for the audience to process the information that they have just seen and heard, rather than to move on with fast cutting and a rapid commentary.

It is all too easy to overload the soundtrack. Without pauses, a commentary can become an endless barrage of information. Moreover, if the editor has a detailed script that fits in with every moment of the image and the talent happens to slow down at all, the words can get out of step with the key shots they relate to. Then the editor has to either cut parts of the commentary or build out the picture (with appropriate shots) to bring the picture and sound back into sync.

5.10 STYLE

The worst type of script for video is the type that has been written in a formal literary style, as if for a newspaper article or an essay, where the words, phrases, and sentence construction are those of the printed page. When read aloud, this type of script tends to sound like an official statement or a pronouncement rather than the fluent everyday speech that usually communicates best with a television audience. This is not to say, of course, that we want a script that is so colloquial that it includes all the hesitations and slangy half-thoughts one tends to use, but we certainly prefer one that avoids complex sentence construction.

It takes some experience to be able to read any script fluently with the natural expression that brings it alive. But if the script itself is written in a stilted style, it is unlikely to improve with hearing. The material should be presented as if the talent is talking to an individual in the audience, rather than proclaiming on a stage or addressing a public meeting.

The way the information is delivered can influence how interesting the subject seems to be. The mind boggles at "The retainer lever actuates the integrated contour follower." But we immediately understand "Here you can see, as we pull this lever, the lock opens."

If the audience has to pause to figure out what the speaker means, they will not be listening closely to what the person is saying. Directors can often assist the audience by anticipating the problems and then inserting a passing explanation, a subtitle (especially useful for names), or a simple diagram.

5.11 TIPS ON DEVELOPING THE SCRIPT

How scripts are developed varies with the type of program and the way individual directors work. The techniques and processes of good script writing are a study in themselves, but we can take a look at some of the guiding principles and typical points that need to be considered.

The Nature of the Script

- The script may form the basis of the entire production treatment.

Here the production is staged, performed, and shot as indicated in the script. As far as possible, dialog and action follow the scripted version.

- The scriptwriter may prepare a draft script (i.e., a suggested treatment).

The director studies and develops this draft to form a shooting script.

- The script may be written after material has been shot.

Certain programs, such as documentaries, may be shot to a preconceived outline plan, but the final material will largely depend on the opportunities of the moment. The script is written to blend this material together in a coherent story line, adding explanatory commentary/dialog. Subsequent editing and postproduction work based on this scripted version.

- The script may be written after material has been edited.

Here the videotape editor assembles the shot material, creating continuity and a basis for a story line. The script is then developed to suit the edited program.

Occasionally, a new script may replace the program's original script with new or different text. For example, when the original program was made in a language that differs from that of the intended audience, it may be marketed as an M&E version, in which the soundtrack includes only "music and effects." All dialog or voiceover commentary is added (dubbed in) later by the recipient in another language.

Scriptwriting Basics

A successful script has to satisfy two important requirements:

- *It must fulfill the program's main purpose.* For example, it must be able to amuse, inform, intrigue, or persuade (i.e., the artistic, aesthetic, dramatic element of the script).
- *It must be practical.* The script must be a workable vehicle for the production crew.

Fundamentally, we need to ensure that the following occurs:

- *The script meets its deadline.* When is the script required? Is it for a specific occasion?
- *The treatment is feasible for the budget, facilities, and time available.* An overambitious script will necessarily have to be rearranged, edited, and scenes rewritten to provide a workable basis for the production.
- *The treatment fits the anticipated program length.* Otherwise it will become necessary to cut sequences or pad the production with added scenes afterward to fit the show to the allotted time slot.
- *The style and the form of presentation are appropriate for the subject.* An unsuitable style, such as a lighthearted approach to a serious topic, may trivialize the subject.
- *The subject treatment is suitable for the intended audience.* The style, complexity, concentration of information, and so on must be relative to their probable interest and attention span.

Ask Yourself These Questions

Who is the program for?

- What is our target age group? (e.g., children, college classes, mature students)
- Are the audience members specialists? (e.g., sales staff, teachers, hobbyists)
- Where is it to be shown? (e.g., classroom, home, theater, public place)
- What display device will be used? (e.g., television, I-mag screens, online, mobile telephone)

What is the purpose of this program?

- Is it for entertainment, information, or instruction?

- Is it intended to persuade? (as in advertising, program trailers, propaganda)
- Is there a follow-up to the program? (publicity offers, tests)

Is the program one of a series?

- Does it relate to or follow other programs?
- Do viewers need to be reminded of past information?
- Does the script style need to be similar to previous programs?
- Were there any omissions, weaknesses, or errors in previous programs we can correct in this program?

What does the audience already know?

- Is the audience familiar with the subject?
- Does the audience understand the terms used?
- Is the information complicated?
- Does previous information need to be recapped?
- Would a brief outline or introduction help (or remind) the audience?
- Is the audience likely to be prejudiced for or against the subject or the product? (e.g., necessitating diplomacy or careful unambiguous treatment)

What is the length of the program?

- Is it brief? (having to make an immediate impact)
- Is it long enough to develop arguments or explanations for a range of topics?

How much detail is required in the script?

- Is the script to be complete, with dialog and action? (actual visual treatment depends on the director)
- Is the script a basis for improvisation? (e.g., by a guide or lecturer)
- Is it an ideas sheet, giving an outline for treatment?

Are you writing dialog?

- Is it for actors or inexperienced performers to read? (for the latter, keep it brief, in short "bites" to be read from a prompter or spoken in the performer's own words)
- Is the dialog to be naturalistic or "character dialog"?

Is the subject a visual one?

- If the subjects are abstract or no longer exist, how will you illustrate them?

Have you considered the script's requirements?

- It only takes a few words on the page to suggest a situation, but reproducing it in pictures and sound may require considerable time, expense, and effort (e.g., a battle scene); you may have to rely on available stock library video.
- Does the script pose obvious problems for the director? (e.g., a script involving special effects, stunts, etc.)
- Does the script involve costly concepts that can be simplified? (e.g., an intercontinental conversation could be covered by an expensive two-way

video satellite transmission, or it can be accomplished by utilizing a telephone call accompanied by previously acquired footage or still images)

Does the subject involve research?

- Does the script depend on what researchers discover while investigating the subject?
- Do you already have information that can aid the director? (have contacts, know of suitable locations, availability of insert material, etc.)

Where will the images come from?

- Will the subjects be brought to the studio (which allows maximum control over the program treatment and presentation) or will cameras be going on location to the subjects? (this may include shooting in museums, etc.); script opportunities may depend on what is available when the production is being shot.

Remember

Start scripting with a simple outline.

- Before embarking on the main script treatment, it can be particularly helpful to rough out a skeleton version. This would usually include a general outline treatment that covers the various points that need to be included, in the order in which the director proposes to deal with them.

Be visual.

- Sometimes pictures alone can convey the information more powerfully than the spoken word.
- The way a commentary is written (and spoken) can influence how the audience interprets a picture (and vice versa).
- Pictures can distract. People may concentrate more on looking than on listening!
- Avoid "talking heads" wherever possible. Show the subject being talked about rather than the person who is speaking.
- The script can only indicate visual treatment. It will seldom be specific about shot details unless that is essential to the plot or situation. Directors have their own ideas!

Avoid overloading.

- Keep it simple. Don't be long-winded or use complicated sentences. Keep to the point. When a subject is difficult, an accompanying diagram, chart, or graph may make the information easier to understand.
- Do not give too much information at a time. Do not attempt to pack too much information into the program. It is better to do justice to a few topics than to cover many inadequately.

Develop a flow of ideas.

- Deal with one subject at a time. Generally avoid cutting between different topics, flashbacks, and flash forwards.

- If the screen has text to be read, either have an unseen voice read the same information or give the viewer enough time to read it.
- Do not have different information on the screen and in the commentary. This can be distracting and confusing to the viewer.
- Aim to have one subject or sequence lead naturally into the next.
- Where there are a number of topics, think through how they are related and the transitions necessary to keep the audience's interest.

Develop a pace.

- Vary the pace of the program. Avoid a fast pace when imparting facts. It conveys an overall impression, but facts do not sink in. A slow pace can be boring or restful, depending on the content.
- Remember that the audience cannot refer back to the program (unless it is interactive). If they miss a point, they may fail to understand the next point and will probably lose interest.

Develop a style.

- Use an appropriate writing style for the intended viewer. Generally aim at an informal, relaxed style.
- There is a world of difference between the style of the printed page and the way people normally speak. When you read from a prompter, it produces an unnatural, stilted effect.
- Be careful about introducing humor into the script.

Interview with a Pro

Robyn Sjogren, Writer

Robyn Sjogren, Writer

What do you like about being a writer?

- I like the creativity that's involved with writing. There's always an empty slate to work with, and, within reason, you can craft the script however you want. It really can be fun!
- I like the aspect of informing the public about current events. It's a public service. My writing has the potential to help someone else change the world, find a missing child, or compel them to write to their government leaders to address an important issue that needs changing.

How do you write visually for TV?

- You have to really think about the video the viewer will see when you write your copy.
- Write to the video. When appropriate, go ahead and describe what the viewer is seeing.

What suggestions do you have for new writers?

- Be conversational. Write like you're writing to a friend as much as possible.
- Read the wirecopy first, and then try to write without it. You can always go back to check for facts, but this way you're not leaning on the wirecopy as a crutch. Chances are, your writing will be more conversational in the end.
- Read what you've written out loud. If it sounds "newsy," it's not conversational enough.
- Put the best details first. Sometimes the new stuff isn't the best stuff. Sell the viewer on the story. Practice! The more you write, the better you will get. You will get faster and more comfortable with it as well.
- Short sentences are key so the anchor has a chance to breathe. It also makes it more conversational.

What are some challenges that you face as a writer?

- One of the biggest challenges is writing for "Day 2" or 3, or 4, and so on. The challenge is to keep the story current, but not boring and avoiding words like "another," "still," "continues," etc.
- Sometimes the story isn't something you'd tell to a friend, but you still have to make it conversational. That's a big challenge.

Robyn Sjogren is a writer for CNN and TruTV.

CHAPTER 6
The Camera

Perhaps it sounds ridiculous, but the best thing that young filmmakers should do is to get hold of a camera and shoot and make a movie of any kind at all.

—Stanley Kubrick, Director

Camera operators need to know their camera so well that they don't need to "think" about it technically. That knowledge allows them to spend their time shooting creatively in a way that effectively communicates.

Key Terms

- ***Aperture:*** The opening of the iris (see *iris*).
- ***CCD:*** This charged-coupled device is an image sensor used in most video cameras.
- ***CMOS:*** This complementary metal-oxide semiconductor image sensor has less power consumption, saving energy for longer shooting times.
- ***Depth of field:*** The distance between the nearest and farthest objects in focus.
- ***Digital zoom:*** Zooming is achieved by progressively reading out a smaller and smaller area of the same digitally constructed image. The image progressively deteriorates as the digital zoom is zoomed in.
- ***Dolly:*** This platform with wheels is used to smoothly move a camera during a shot toward or away from the talent. Dolly also refers to a movement of the camera closer to, or further away from, the subject.
- ***DSLR:*** Digital Single Lens Reflex still camera with video capabilities.
- ***f-stop:*** The measurement of the size of the aperture.
- ***Focal length:*** An optical measurement; the distance between the optical center of the lens and the image sensor, when you are focused at a great distance such as infinity; it is measured in millimeters (mm) or inches.
- ***Handheld camera:*** A camera that is held by a person and not supported by any type of camera mount.
- ***Iris:*** The diaphragm of the lens that is adjustable. This diaphragm is adjusted open or closed based on the amount of light needed to capture a quality image.

- ***Jib:*** A counterbalanced arm that fits onto a tripod that allows the camera to move up, down, and around.
- ***Normal lens:*** The type of lens that portrays the scene approximately the same way a human eye might see it.
- ***Optical zoom:*** The optical zoom uses a lens to maintain a high-quality image throughout its zoom range.
- ***Prime lens:*** A lens that has a fixed focal length.
- ***Telephoto lens:*** Gives a magnified view of the scene, making it appear closer.
- ***Tripod:*** A camera mount that is a three-legged stand with independently extendable legs.
- ***Tripod arms (pan bars):*** Handles that attach to the pan head on a tripod or other camera mount to accurately pan, tilt, and control the camera.
- ***Truck:*** The truck, trucking, or tracking shot is when the camera and mount move sideways with the subject.
- ***Viewfinder:*** Monitors the camera's picture. This allows the camera operator to focus, zoom, and frame the image.
- ***Wide-angle lens:*** Shows a greater area of the scene.
- ***Zoom lens:*** A lens that has a variable focal length.

6.1 A RANGE OF MODELS

Video cameras today come in a wide variety of shapes and sizes that suit all kinds of different situations. They range from units that fit in a pocket to cameras that are so heavy that they can take a couple of people to lift them (Figure 6.1). Historically there were consumer, industrial, and professional cameras. Many of those monikers have merged, with small, previously thought of as "consumer" cameras now being used in the professional workplace (Figure 6.2). Traditionally, for a multicamera production, high-cost cameras were used that required camera control units. Today's multicamera systems allow many types of cameras to be used in professional situations, including low-cost cameras. The right camera depends on how the end production is going to be used. What was considered a professional quality camera 10 years ago has been dwarfed by the quality of small, low-cost high-definition pocket-sized cameras available today. Television and film competitions are being won by directors who are using cameras that cost less than $1,000. That was unheard of in the 1990s. So now, no one can blame the lack of quality on his or her camera gear because almost anyone can afford the equipment. For all of the cool technological advancements, keep in mind that the important thing is to know how to visually communicate.

Most productions are created with a camera that is a stand-alone unit; they are known as single-camera productions. Single-camera productions are generally edited together during postproduction. The second major type of production is a multicamera production, where two or more cameras are used with a switcher selecting the image to be shown to the viewer, otherwise known as "live editing." We will be covering both of these types of production in more detail in a later chapter.

FIGURE 6.1
Video cameras come in all different shapes and sizes.
(Photos courtesy of Grass Valley/Thomson, Sony, JVC, and Panasonic.)

FIGURE 6.2
Traditionally thought of as consumer cameras, small HD cameras, such as the GoPro shown, are now being used by television networks for specialty shots. These HD cameras have gained popularity as a camera that can be connected to anything. For a relatively low cost, this high-quality little camera, with a 170 wide-angle lens and waterproof case, records to an SD card. The photo on the right was shot with this camera.

Single cameras generally have a built-in recorder. Cameras are increasingly moving away from videotape. Most cameras today use a flash card and/or a hard drive. Cameras may also be combined (by wire or wirelessly) with other recorders, such as a tape deck or a portable hard drive. Some of the studio cameras or remote production (outside broadcast) cameras are available without recorders because they are designed specifically for multicamera use (Figures 6.2, 6.3, and 6.4).

FIGURE 6.3
With their high-resolution sensors and HD capabilities, cell phones are becoming increasingly popular as video cameras. The iPhone 4 shown here is attached to an OWLE grip that includes tripod/light mounts, a professional mic, and an add-on wide-angle lens. One of the main advantages of these phones is that the video can easily be immediately edited on the phone and then transmitted back to a news station, client, or directly onto a website … right from the phone.

6.2 CAMERACRAFT

Most video cameras are easy to operate at the basic level. Designers have gone to a lot of trouble to make controls simple to use. The consumer-oriented cameras have been so automated that all one needs to do to get a decent image is to point them at the subject and press the record button. When shooting for fun, that's fine. So why make camerawork any more complicated?

It really depends on whether the director plans to use the camera as a *creative tool*. The weakness of automatic controls is that the camera is only designed to make *technical* judgments. Many times these technical decisions are something of a compromise. The camera cannot make *artistic* choices of any kind. Auto-circuitry can help the camera operator avoid poor-quality video images, but it cannot be relied on to produce attractive and meaningful pictures. Communicating visually will always depend on how *you* use the camera and the choices *you* make.

Obviously, good production is much more than just getting the shot. It begins with the way the camera is handled and controlled. It is not just a matter of getting a sharp image but of selecting which parts of the scene are to be sharp and which are to be presented in soft focus. It involves carefully selecting the best angle and arranging the framing and composition for maximum impact, as well as deciding what is to be included in the shot and what is to be left out. It is the art of adjusting the image tones by careful exposure. Automatic camera circuitry can help, particularly when shooting under difficult conditions, and can save the camera operator from having to worry about technicalities. However, automatic circuitry cannot create meaningful images. Let's take a look at the parts of a camera.

(A)

(B)

FIGURE 6.4
A number of different 3D cameras have been introduced, including a low-cost professional model (A) and a very low-cost consumer model (B).
(Photos courtesy of Panasonic.)

ENG/EFP Camera Components

- This type of *viewfinder* is generally called an electronic news gathering (ENG) or electronic field production (EFP) viewfinder. It is a small monitor designed to be placed next to the camera operator's eye.
- The *power switch* turns the camera on/off.
- The *manual zoom control* lens ring allows the camera operator to zoom in and out manually.
- The *power zoom rocker switch,* located on the side of the lens, allows the camera operator to electronically zoom the lens. The speed of the zoom may vary, depending on the switch pressure.
- The *focus control* ring on a lens allows the camera operator to turn the ring manually to obtain the optimal focus.
- The *lens aperture control* ring allows the camera operator to adjust the lens iris manually to control exposure.
- The *white and black balance* controls the circuitry in the camera that uses white or black to balance the color settings of the camera.
- The *filter wheel* includes a number of filters that can be used to correct the color in daylight, tungsten, and fluorescent lighting situations.
- Clip-on *camera batteries* allow the camera operator to carry multiple batteries.
- Although at this point it is not common, some cameras are equipped with a built-in *wireless microphone and antennas.*
- On-camera *shotgun microphones* are useful for picking up natural sound but often pick up camera and operator noises.
- *Lens shades* protect the lens elements from picking up light distortions from the sun or a bright light.

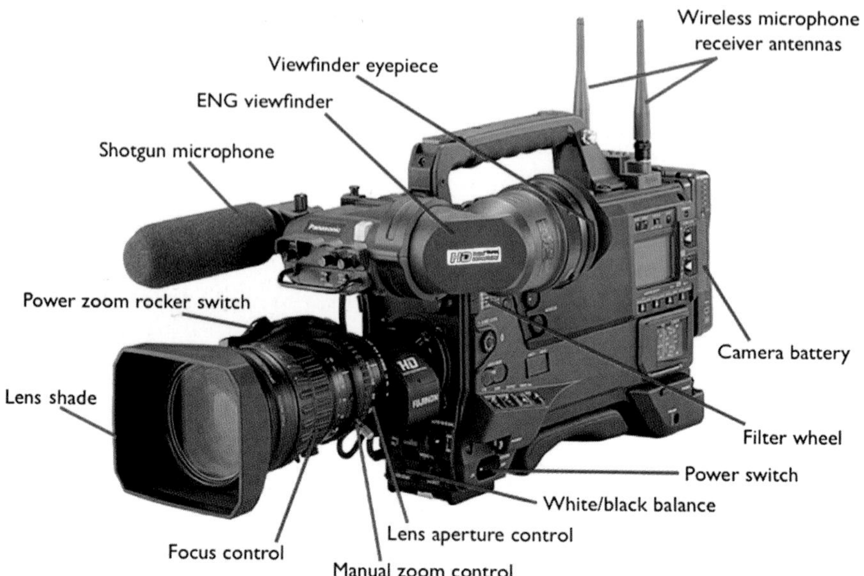

FIGURE 6.5
Video camera designs vary, but these are some of the common parts found in a professional ENG camera.
(Photo courtesy of Panasonic.)

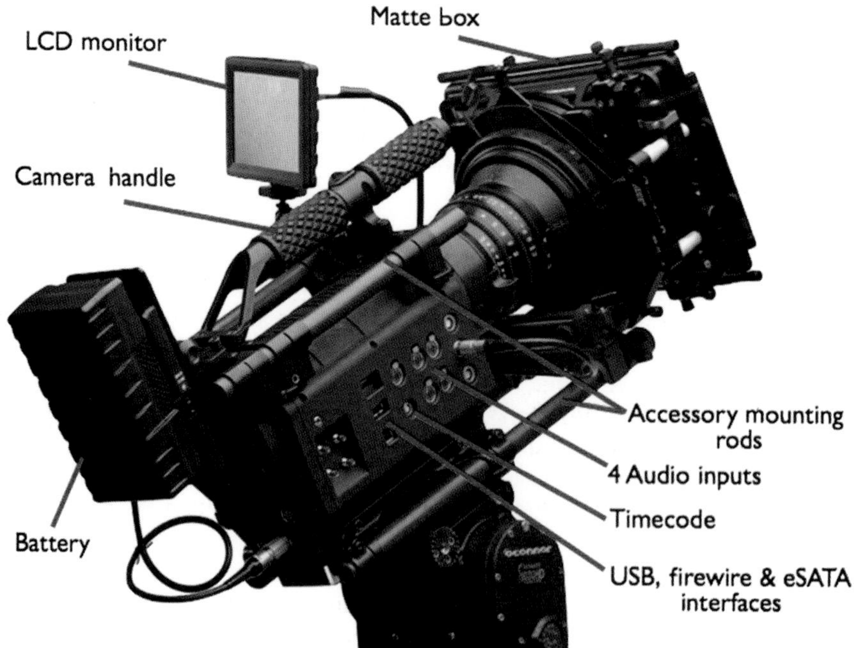

FIGURE 6.6
Parts of a high-quality (4K) camera.
(Photo courtesy of Rd.)

Stationary/Hard/Studio Camera Components

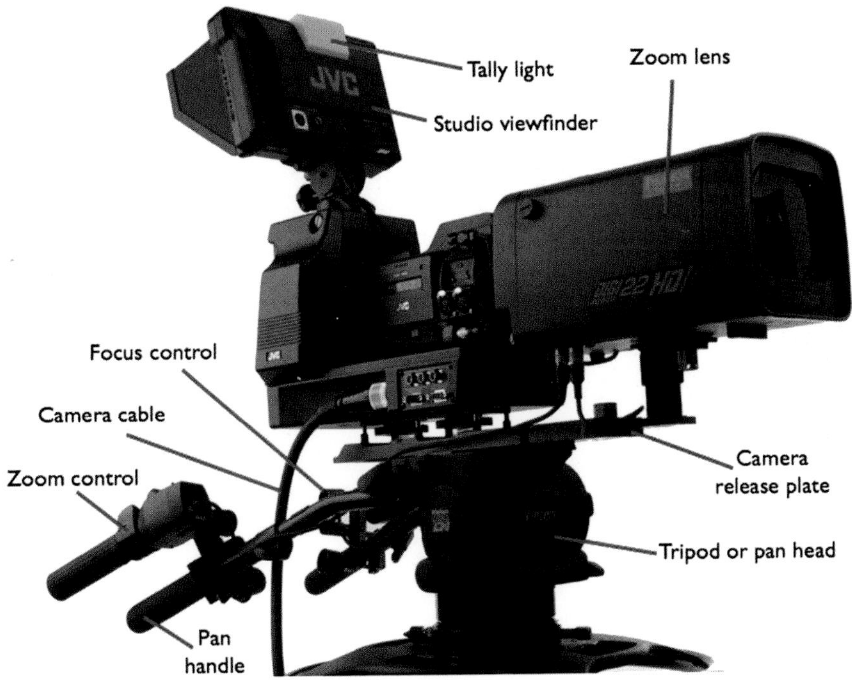

FIGURE 6.7
The "studio" or "hard" camera body is attached to a pan head. The zoom lens is then attached to the camera body and the pan head. This type of system is generally used in studio or remote production settings where the camera is stationary.

- The *camera cable* is a two-way cable that carries the video to a distant camera control unit (CCU) and allows the video operator to adjust the camera from a remote site (such as studio control or a remote truck).
- The *viewfinder (VF)* monitors the camera's picture. This allows the camera operator to focus, zoom, and frame the image.
- The *quick-release mount* is attached to the camera and fits into a corresponding recessed plate attached to the tripod/pan head. This allows the camera operator to quickly remove or attach the camera to the camera mount.
- The *tripod head* (panning head) enables the camera to tilt and pan smoothly. Variable friction controls (drag) steady these movements. The head can also be locked off in a fixed position. Tilt balance adjustments position the camera horizontally to assist in balancing the camera on the mount.
- One or two *tripod arms* (or panning bars/handles) attached to the pan head allow the operator to accurately pan, tilt, and control the camera.
- The *tripod*, or *camera mount* can take various forms such as a tripod, pedestal, or jib.

- The *zoom control* (Servo zoom), *focus control*, and remote controls allow the camera operator to zoom and focus the lens from behind the camera.

CAMERA FEATURES

6.3 MAIN FEATURES

Let's take a look at the main sections of a camera (see Figure 6.8):

- The *lens system* focuses a small image of the scene onto a light-sensitive sensor.
- This *light-sensitive chip*, or *sensor*, converts the image from the lens into a corresponding pattern of electrical charges, which are read out to provide the video signal.
- The camera's *viewfinder* displays the video image, enabling the camera operator to set up the shot, adjust focus, exposure, and so on.
- The camera's *recorder* captures the video images and stores them on tape, flash memory, or hard drive.
- The camera's *power supply* is usually either an external AC power supply that plugs into the wall or batteries that fit onto the camera.
- The *microphone* is either fitted internally or attached onto the camera and is intended for general sound pickup.

The instruction manual issued with the camera gives details and specifications of the specific model you are using. Table 6.1 presents a list of typical features.

FIGURE 6.8
The DSLR has become a popular choice as a video camera.
(Photo courtesy of Canon.)

Table 6.1	Camera Features
Gain control	Circuitry that manually or automatically adjusts video amplification to keep it within preset limits. Reduced during bright shots and increased under dimmer conditions, it alters overall picture brightness and contrast.
Auto-black	After capping the lens to exclude all light, this switch automatically sets the camera's circuitry to produce a standard black reference level.
Auto-focus	A mechanism that automatically adjusts the lens focus for maximum sharpness on the nearest subject in a selected zone of the frame. Whether this is the one *you* want sharpest is another matter. When shooting through foreground objects, focusing selectively, or if anything is likely to move between the camera and your subject, the camera should be switched to manual focusing. This option is always available on consumer cameras and rarely part of a high-end professional camera. However, medium-level professional cameras seem to increasingly be adding this option.
Auto-iris	This device automatically adjusts the lens aperture (*f*-stop) to suit the prevailing light levels (light intensities). By doing so, it prevents the image from being very over- or underexposed (washed-out or murky). However, there are times when the auto-iris misunderstands and changes the lens aperture when it should remain constant, such as during zooming or when a lighter area comes into the shot. Then it is necessary to switch the lens aperture control to *manual aperture* and operate it by hand.
White balance or auto-white	This control automatically adjusts the camera circuits' *color-balance* to suit the color quality of the prevailing light and ensure that white surfaces are accurately reproduced as neutral. Otherwise, all colors would be slightly warmer (red-orange) or colder (bluish) than normal, depending on the light source. To white-balance a camera, the operator pushes the white balance button while aiming the camera at a white surface (see Figure 6.5).
Backlight control	This control opens the lens aperture an arbitrary stop or so above that selected by the auto-iris system to avoid underexposure resulting from ambiguous readings.
Black stretch or gamma adjustment	Some cameras include an operator-controlled circuit adjustment to make shadow detail clearer and improve tonal gradation in darker picture tones. This is the opposite of "contrast compression," which emphasizes the contrast in picture tones. With a higher gamma setting such as 1.0, picture tones are more contrasty, coarse, and dramatic. A lower gamma setting such as a 0.4 provides more subtle, flatter tonal quality. These areas should be adjusted by someone who knows what he or she is doing and is utilizing a waveform monitor.
Camera cable	This may be a short "umbilical" multiwire cable connecting the camera to a recorder or a more substantial cable routed to a camera control unit (CCU). This cable provides power, sync, intercom, and so on, to the camera, and takes video and audio from the camera to the main video/audio equipment.

(*Continued*)

Table 6.1 Camera Features (*Continued*)

Color correction filters or filter wheel	Because the brain compensates, we tend to assume that most everyday light sources such as sunlight, tungsten light, quartz lamps, and candlelight are all producing "white" light. But in reality, these various luminants often have quite different color qualities. They may be bluish or reddish yellow, depending on the light source and the conditions. Unless the camera's color system is matched to the prevailing light, its pictures will appear unnaturally warm (orange) or cool (bluish). How far auto-white adjustment is able to rebalance the camera's color response to compensate for variations in the color quality of the prevailing light depends on equipment design. For greater compensation, filters may be required to obtain the best color. These are often fitted inside the video camera, just behind the lens on a *filter wheel*. Alternatively, an appropriate filter may be fitted on the front of the lens. Typical correction filters include *daylight* (5600), *artificial/tungsten light* (3200), and *fluorescent light* (4700). The filter wheel may also include or combine neutral-density (ND) filters to improve exposure.
Exposure modes	A series of preset savable exposure settings such as indoor/outdoor.
Exposure override	Switches from auto-iris system to manual to allow precise exposure adjustments.
Macro	Most zoom lenses have a *macro* position. This allows the lens to focus on very close objects—much closer than the lens's normal minimum focused distance.
Photo mode	Some video cameras have the ability to capture still pictures (freeze frames) of a scene.
Image stabilizer	This system compensates for accidental irregular camera movements such as camera shake.
Preset situations	Some consumer cameras offer prearranged adjustments selected for typical occasions such as sport action or snowy conditions. These are general exposure selections and are not recommended for the serious camera operator.
Shutter speed	To avoid movement blur and improve detail in fast action, a much briefer exposure rate than the normal 1/60 sec (PAL 1/50) is needed. A variable high-speed electronic shutter (settings from, e.g., 1/125 to 1/400 sec) reduces blur considerably but needs higher light levels.
Standby switch	This setting is used to save battery power by switching off unused units when rehearsing or during standby. Some cameras have *auto switch-off*, which cuts the system's power when the camera has not been used for several minutes.
Timecode	This series of frame-accurate numbers is assigned to a specific video frame. The number includes hours, minutes, seconds, and elapsed frames.
Genlock input	When working as an ENG camera, the camera generates its own *internal* synchronizing pulses to stabilize the scanning circuits. Genlock allows external sync to be put into the camera. In multicamera production, a genlock cable may be plugged into the genlock input, using sync from a communal sync generator.

THE DSLR (PROS AND CONS)

Digital Single Lens Reflex cameras (DSLR) have become a formidable force in the video world today. While originally they were designed as a still camera that has some video capability, directors are using them to shoot corporate videos, commercials, television network shows, and even feature films. Some camera model's high megapixel sensors and 1080p quality, combined with their small size and low cost, make them a cost-effective option in video production. However, there are positives and negatives about the current class of DSLR cameras. While they are continually improving, the current models are good for some projects and not a good camera for other projects. Here are some of the pros and cons:

Advantages:

- Low cost: When compared to video cameras with similar image quality, the DSLR is very cost effective.
- Depth-of-field: The large sensor size can provide a very shallow depth-of-field.
- Weight: Its light weight makes it easier to move around.
- Low profile: When shooting documentaries, the camera is less obvious.
- Low light: DSLRs can shoot in very low light situations and still maintain their quality.

Disadvantages:

- Recording time: The current DSLR models have somewhere around a 12-minute maximum continuous recording time. While the camera can be immediately restarted, this does create some recording limitations.
- Audio: DSLRs usually have automatic gain control, unbalanced inputs, and no phantom power. All of these mean that you have to record your audio on a separate high-quality audio device and then sync it later. Another audio disadvantage is that most DSLRs do not include a headphone input to allow you to monitor the audio quality. In order to ensure quality audio, it must be recorded independently and then synced later in postproduction. There are a number of software options available that will assist you in syncing the audio.
- Stability: Due to their small size, DSLRs are handheld, not shoulder mounted. This is not a great design for stability while recording motion. Most camera operators use a shoulder-mounted support when handholding them.
- Timecode: The lack of timecode can create some problems when attempting to sync audio in the postproduction process.
- Quality: In order to obtain the 1080 image from their sensor, some models use a type of line skipping when capturing the image. While this type of down-resing reduces the amount of processing for the camera, it can cause some serious aliasing issues, which causes problems when shooting highly detailed patterns.

Other DSLR Issues:

- The terms used on a still camera are not the same as the terms on a video camera. For example, still cameras use "ISO" while video cameras use "gain."
- There are few video controls on a DSLR compared to a prosumer or professional video camera. This can limit the camera operator's ability to adjust blacks or other fine-tune adjustments.
- The DSLR does not always look professional if you are working for a client. Compared to a typical size professional camera, they may look amateurish.

6.4 THE LENS SYSTEM

Engraved on the front of almost every lens are two important numbers:

- The lens's *focal length*—or in the case of zoom lenses, its range of focal lengths. This gives you a clue to the variations in shot sizes the lens will provide.
- The lens's *largest aperture* or *f*-stop (e.g., *f*/2)—the smaller this *f*-stop number, the larger the lens's maximum aperture, so the better its performance under dim lighting (*low-light*) conditions.

There are two fundamental types of lenses on video cameras:

- Prime lens (primary lens), which has a specific (unchangeable) focal length. Prime lenses have become specialty items, primarily used by filmmakers, digital filmmakers, and in special use situations such as security or scientific research.
- Zoom lens, which has a variable focal length. Zoom lenses are by far the most popular lens on cameras because of their ability to move easily from wide-angle to telephoto focal lengths.

6.5 FOCAL LENGTH AND LENS ANGLE

The term *focal length* is simply an optical measurement—the distance between the optical center of the lens and the image sensor when you are focused at a great distance, such as infinity. It is generally measured in millimeters (mm).

FIGURE 6.9
Cameras can be white-balanced by filling the viewfinder with the white card held by an assistant. The white-balance button on the camera is pushed and held for a few seconds.

A lens designed to have a *long focal length* (long focus) behaves as a *narrow angle* or *telephoto* system. The subject appears much closer than normal, but you can only see a smaller part of the scene. Depth and distance can look unnaturally compressed in the shot.

When the lens has a *short focal length* (short focus), this *wide-angle* system takes in correspondingly more of the scene. But now subjects will look much farther away; depth and distance appear exaggerated. The exact coverage of any lens depends on its focal length relative to the size of the camera's sensor (Figures 6.9, 6.10, and 6.11).

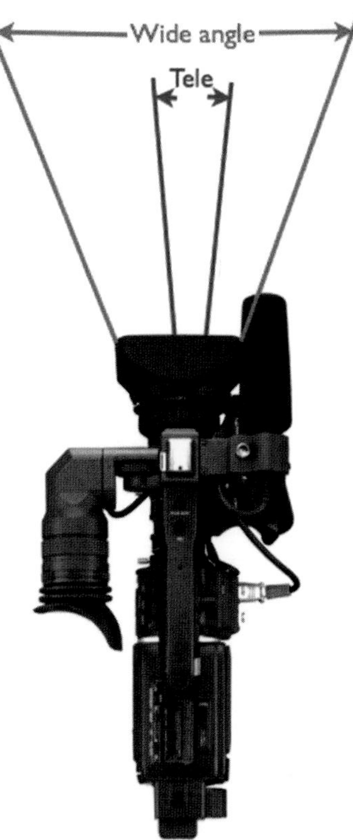

FIGURE 6.10
A lens designed to have a *long focal length* behaves as a *narrow-angle* or *telephoto* system. When the lens has a *short focal length*, this *wide-angle* system takes in correspondingly more of the scene.

6.6 THE PRIME LENS

The *prime lens,* which stands for primary lens, is a fixed-focal-length lens (Figures 6.13 and 6.14). Only the *iris* (diaphragm) within the lens barrel is adjustable. Changing its aperture (*f*-stop) varies the lens's image brightness, which controls the picture's exposure. The focus ring varies the entire lens system's distance from the receiving camera image sensor.

If a video camera with a single prime lens is being used and a closer or more distant shot of the subject is needed, the camera

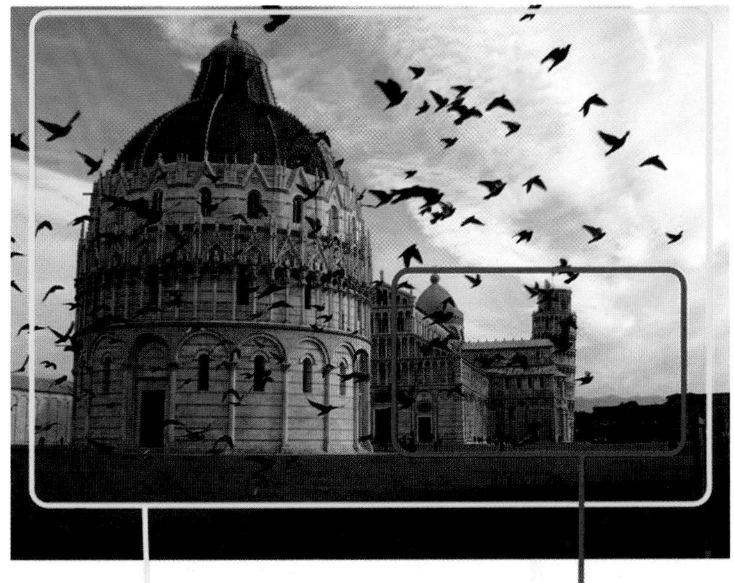

FIGURE 6.11
The various shots that can be obtained by different lenses. The wide-angle and telephoto shots can be taken while standing in one place and exchanging lenses.

FIGURE 6.12
This mobile phone app, Artemis, uses the internal video camera to show the various lenses that can be used to shoot a scene. The image can then be saved for future use.

FIGURE 6.13
A prime lens has few features, focus, and aperture.
(Photo courtesy of Zeiss and BandPro.)

operator has to move the camera nearer or farther from the subject. The alternative is to have a selection of prime lenses of various focal lengths to choose from.

6.7 THE ZOOM LENS

A *zoom lens* is a variable focal length lens. It allows the camera operator to zoom in and zoom out on a subject without moving the camera forward or backward. The zoom lens enables the camera operator to select any coverage within its range. Most video and television cameras come with optical zoom lenses. An optical zoom uses a lens to magnify the image and send it to the image sensor. The optical zoom retains the original quality of the camera's sensor (Figure 6.15).

An increasing number of consumer video cameras are fitted with a lens system that combines both an *optical zoom* and a *digital zoom*. A camera might, for instance, have a 20X optical zoom and 100X digital zoom. Depending on the quality of its design, the optical zoom system should give a consistently high-quality image throughout its zoom range; the focus and picture clarity should remain optimal at all settings. In a *digital system,* the impression of zooming in is achieved by progressively reading out a smaller and smaller area of the same digitally constructed picture. Consequently, viewers are likely to see the quality of the image progressively deteriorating as they zoom in because fewer of the original picture's pixels are being spread across the television screen.

FIGURE 6.14
A set of prime lenses. This set allows the camera operator to utilize a wide variety of focal lengths.
(Photo courtesy of Zeiss/BandPro.)

Lens design involves many technical compromises, particularly in small systems. The problems with providing high performance from a lightweight, robust unit at a reasonable cost have been challenging for manufacturers. So the optical quality of budget systems is generally below that of an equivalent prime lens.

When the camera operator wants to get a "closer" shot of the subject or is trying to avoid something at the edge of the picture coming into the shot, it is obviously a lot easier to zoom in than to move the camera, particularly when using a tripod. In fact, many people simply stand wherever it is convenient and zoom in or out to vary the

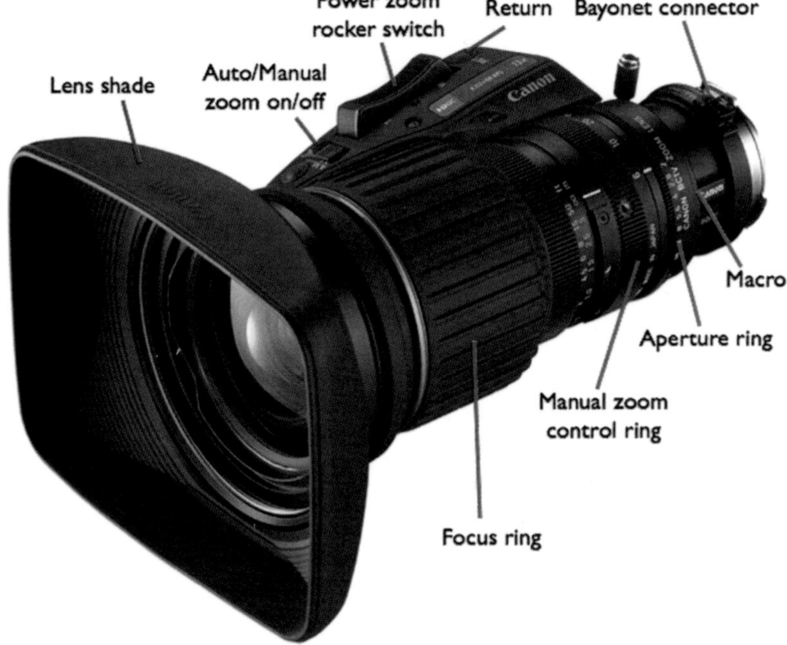

FIGURE 6.15
The zoom lens.
(Photo courtesy of Canon.)

size of the shot. However, the focal length of the lens does not just determine the image size. It also affects the following factors:

- *How much of the scene is sharp*. The longer the telephoto used, the less amount of depth of field (the distance between the nearest and farthest objects in focus).
- *How prominent the background is in closer shots*. The background is magnified at the same time as the foreground subject. Instead of zooming, if the camera were moved closer to the subject, the background size would be different from the zoom shot (see Figure 6.16).

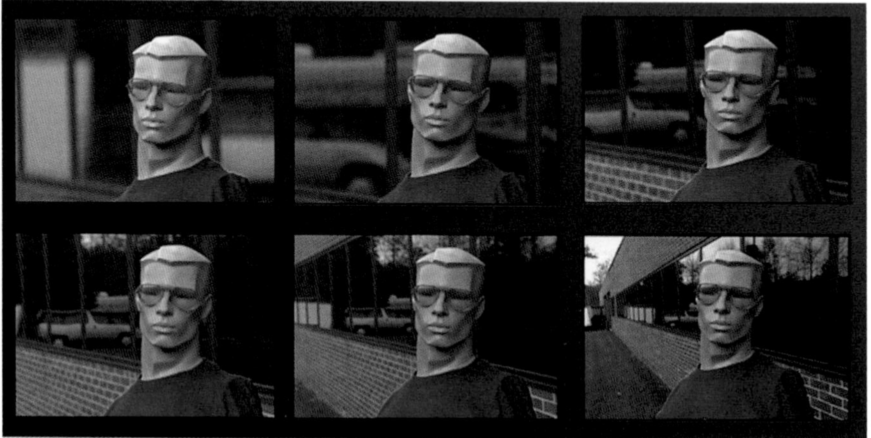

FIGURE 6.16
The background changes in size are due to the lens used. Note that the first photo was shot with a telephoto lens and the last shot was taken with a wide-angle lens. The camera had to be moved closer to the subject for each shot as a wider lens was attached so that the subject would stay the same approximate size.
(Photo by K. Brown.)

- *How hard it is to focus*. The longer the telephoto, the smaller the depth of field.
- *Camera shake*. The longer the telephoto, the more the operator's shake is magnified. The wider the shot, the less amount of shake.
- *The accuracy of shapes* (geometry). Lenses can easily distort shapes. For example, when a very wide-angle lens is tilted up at a tall building, the building will distort, looking as though it is going to fall.

As you can see, the zoom lens needs to be used with care, although amateurs do ignore such distortions and varying perspective. The zooming action, too, can be overused, producing distracting and amateurish effects.

6.8 ZOOM LENS REMOTE CONTROLS

Zoom lens remote controls are an important tool for camera operators. Standing close to the camera to manipulate the controls on the lens is uncomfortable if required for a long period of time. Remote controls allow the camera operator to adjust the focus and focal length of a zoom lens while standing at the back of the camera (Figure 6.17).

FIGURE 6.17
The remote focus and zoom controls allow the operator to manage the lens while working behind the camera. Note in photo (B) that the control cables fit directly into the lens. When the camera is fitted to a camera mount, it is not really convenient for the camera operator to reach around to the front of the camera to adjust the lens. The lens focus and zoom can be adjusted from remote controls attached to the pan bars located at the back of the camera.

6.9 THE APERTURE OF THE CAMERA

When the aperture (size of the opening) is fully opened (probably around *f*/1.4), it lets the most light into the camera. Its minimum opening, when "stopped down" (under very bright lighting), may be *f*/22. Remember, the smaller the opening, the bigger the number. Some irises can be stopped down until the picture fades out altogether.

When a camera operator alters the aperture of the lens, two things happen simultaneously:

- The aperture changes the brightness of the lens image falling onto the chip, altering the picture's *exposure* (Figure 6.18).
- The aperture modifies the *depth of field*, affecting the sharpness of anything nearer and farther than the actual focused distance (Figures 6.19 and 6.20).

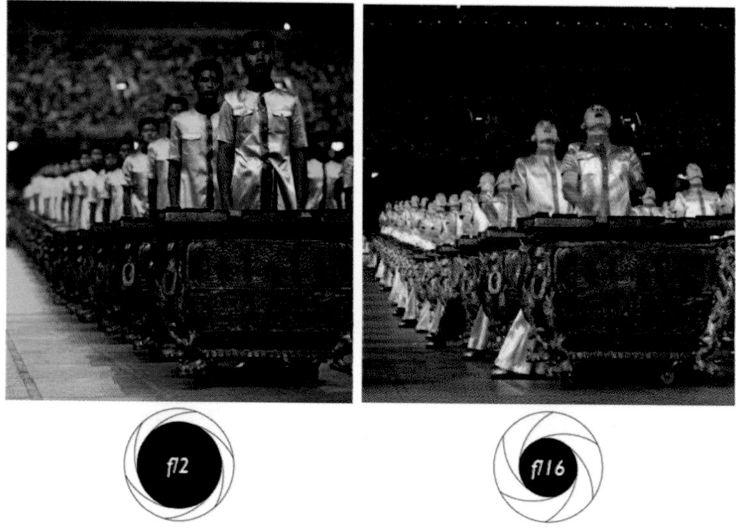

FIGURE 6.18
The lens aperture is adjustable in this illustration from a maximum of *f*/2 to a minimum of *f*/16. The larger the aperture (opening), the smaller the *f*-number (such as *f*/2) and the shallower the depth of field. Less light is needed in this situation. The smaller the lens aperture, the larger the *f*-number (such as *f*/16) and the larger the depth of field. More light is needed to shoot at higher-number *f*-stops.

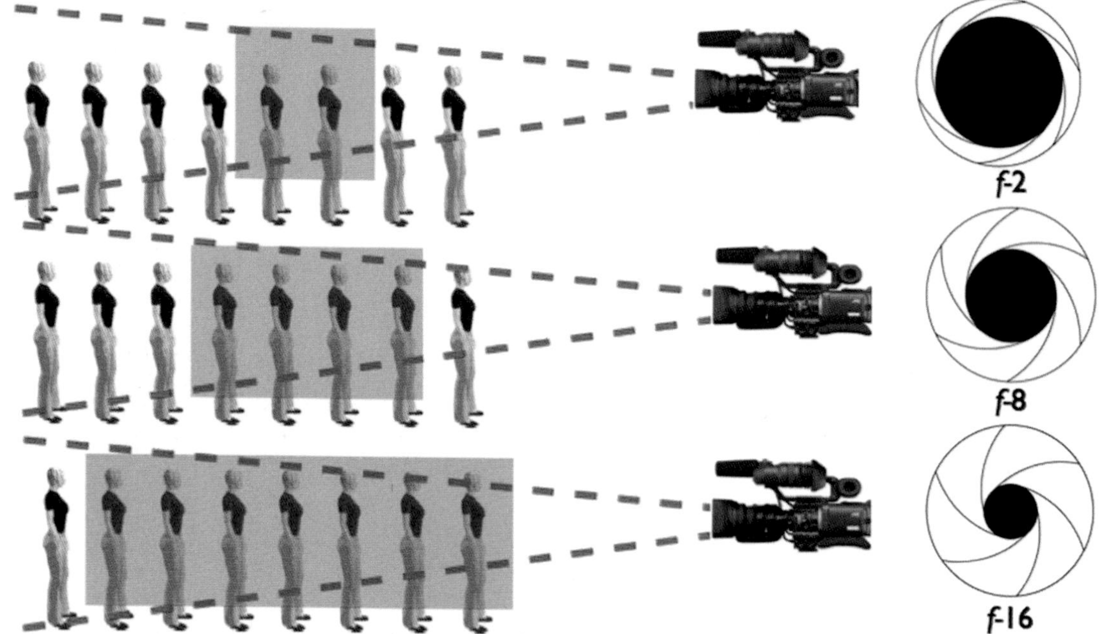

FIGURE 6.19
By adjusting the aperture (*f*-stop), the camera operator can increase or decrease the depth of field. The larger the *f*-stop number, the larger the depth of field.

You have three options when selecting the lens aperture:

- *Choose an f-stop to suit the exposure.* Adjust the lens aperture to give a properly exposed picture so that you can see tonal gradation and details clearly in the subject. If there is insufficient light, you may need to add additional lighting. If there is too much light, so that the shot is overexposed, the lighting on the subject may need to be reduced, reduce the lens aperture (stop down) or add a neutral-density filter.
- *Choose an f-stop that gives a specific depth of field.* People usually concentrate on getting the exposure right and accept whatever depth of field results. However, there will be times, especially in close-up shots, when it is not possible to get the entire subject in sharp focus; in other words, there is insufficient depth of field. Then it is necessary to reduce the aperture and increase the amount of light going into the camera until the exposure is right. The camera operator may want a shallow depth of field so that only the subject itself is sharply defined. Or deep focus can be used, in which everything in shot appears clear-cut.
- *Settle on an f-stop that averages the lighting situation.* There may be times when the camera operator has little or no control over the amount of light on the scene or when the camera needs to move around under varying light conditions. In these situations, there may be little choice but to adjust the lens aperture manually for the best average exposure or to switch on the camera's automatic iris control and accept whatever depth of field results.

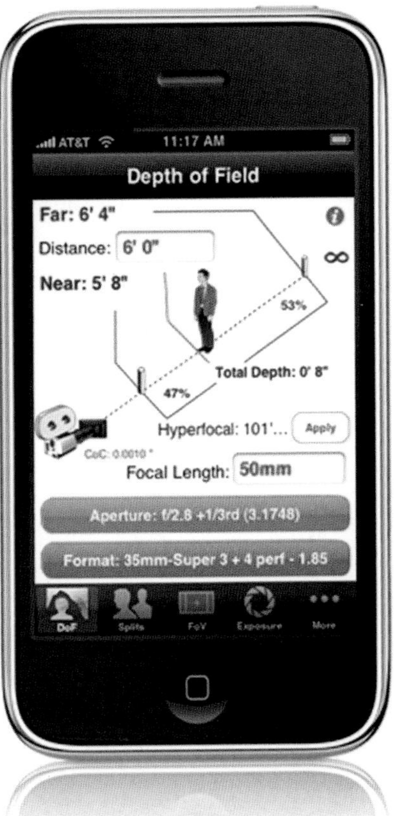

FIGURE 6.20
This screenshot is from an app called pCAM. The software helps the director or cameraperson calculate the correct lens, depth of field, and settings.
(Photo by David Eubank.)

6.10 LENS ACCESSORIES

There are three sometimes neglected accessories that fit onto the lens: the lens cap, the UV filter, and the lens hood:

- *Lens cap.* When the camera is not actually being used, get into the habit of attaching the lens cap. This protective plastic cover clips onto the front of the lens and keeps grime from accumulating on the front surface of the protection filter (UV) or the lens surface. The lens surface has a special bluish coating, which improves picture contrast and tonal gradation by reducing the internal reflections that cause "lens flares" or overall graying. Careless cleaning or scratching (from blown sand, grit, etc.) can easily damage this thin film. The lens cap not only prevents anything from scratching or rubbing against the lens surface, but it helps to keep out grit or moisture.
- *The clear or UV filter.* A clear filter is usually kept on the front of the lens to protect the front lens element from damage. See the preceding lens

cap section for a description of some of the issues that can arise with lens coatings.

- The *lens hood* (sun shade). This is a cylindrical or conical shield fitted around the end of the lens. When there is a strong light source just out of shot ahead of the camera, it shields off stray light rays that could otherwise interreflect within internal lens elements. Although special lens coatings considerably reduce these lens flares, the lens hood helps to avoid the spurious effects of light, mottling, or overall veiling that could otherwise develop.

6.11 THE IMAGE SENSOR

The type of image sensor in a camera greatly affects the quality of the image in its resolution (definition), picture defects, and limitations.

There are several types and sizes of image sensors. These chips typically include hundreds of thousands of tiny independent cells (called pixels or elements). Each cell develops an electrical charge according to the strength of the light that falls on it. The result is an overall pattern of electrical charges that corresponds to the light and shade in the lens image.

There are significant advantages and disadvantages to these different sensors. The quarter-inch sensors are inexpensive but generally are in focus from close-up to infinity. That means the camera operator has limited creative ability because everything is in focus. The larger the chips, the more ability the camera operator has to selectively focus on the subjects, isolating some with a shallow depth of field while using wide focus in other situations. Of course, the largest sensors are also more expensive and are found in the most expensive cameras.

6.12 SENSITIVITY

All camera systems must have a certain amount of light to produce good, clear pictures. How much will depend on camera design and adjustment and on how light or dark the surroundings are. However, what if the surroundings are not bright enough for you to get good images? You have two options. You must either adjust the camera or improve the lighting.

The simplest solution is to open up the lens aperture to let more of the available light through to the image sensor, up to the maximum lens-stop available (e.g., *f*/1.4). But then the depth of the field becomes shallower, which may make focusing difficult for close-up shots.

Another possible solution where there is insufficient light is to increase the video gain (video amplification) in the camera. Although the image sensor itself still lacks light, this electronic boost will strengthen the picture signal. Most cameras include two or three manual positions, and some have an automatic gain. A 6-dB increase will double the gain, and a 12-dB increase will quadruple it. A 6-dB boost would give you acceptable quality images in low light levels. A high gain of 12 dB would allow you to obtain a recognizable image, but the quality of the image may be poor. It is best to keep gain to a minimum wherever possible because it increases picture noise (grain) and the picture sharpness deteriorates. However, there will be times when high image technical quality is less important than getting the right shot (Figure 6.21).

(A) (B)

FIGURE 6.21
Camera operators often need to shoot in low light (A). One way to increase the detail is to increase the video gain. However, the more the gain is adjusted, the more the image deteriorates in quality (B).

6.13 THE VIEWFINDER

There are basically three types of viewfinders for cameras: an *ENG/EFP* viewfinder, a *studio* viewfinder, and a *swing-out LCD screen*.

Camcorders generally use the ENG/EFP viewfinder. This viewfinder contains a small television (typically 1.5 inches in diameter) with a magnifying lens that enlarges the image to be viewed by the camera operator. With its flexible cup eyepiece held up against one eye, all ambient light is shielded from its picture so that the camera operator cannot only compose the shot but also gets a good idea of exposure and relative tonal values. Some camera designs will allow the camera operator to reposition the eyepiece onto whichever side of the camera is more convenient. It may also angle up and down (or swivel) so that the camera operator can still see the image when using the camera above or below eye level (Figure 6.22).

When the camera is working from a fixed viewpoint or mounted on a dolly, it is possible to use a larger viewfinder. This larger monitor is easier to watch for sustained periods, compared with an eyepiece continually held up to the eye.

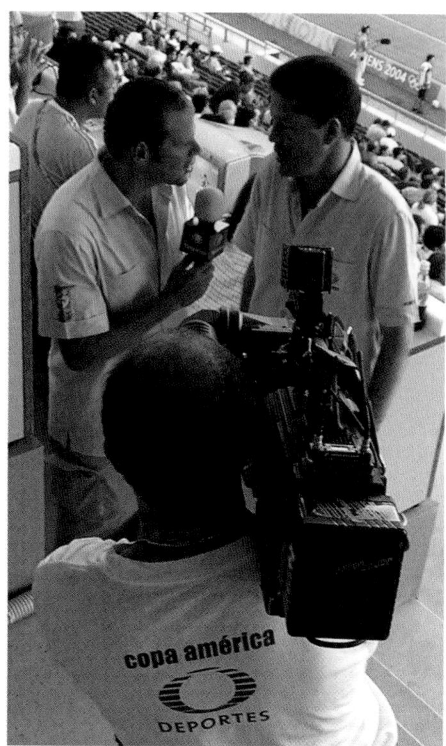

FIGURE 6.22
This camera operator is using the ENG viewfinder to view the image.

FIGURE 6.23
The camera operator is using a studio viewfinder on his remote camera. Note that he has taped cardboard onto the visor to reduce the amount of sunlight falling on the monitor.
(Photo by Shannon Mizell.)

Focusing can also be more precise than when watching a small image. A *hooded visor* is usually fitted around the monitor screen to shield stray light from falling on its picture. This type of viewfinder may be either black and white (monochromatic) or color (Figure 6.23).

- *LCD swing-out viewfinder*. An increasing number of video cameras are fitted with a foldout rectangular *LCD screen* (liquid crystal display), which is typically 2.5 to 3.5 inches wide and shows the shot in color. It is lightweight and conveniently folds flat against the camera body when out of use. However, stray light falling onto the screen can degrade its image, making it more difficult for the camera operator to focus and to judge picture quality (Figure 6.24).

Like all television monitors, viewfinders have brightness, contrast, and focus (sharpness) adjustments. Some of the newer viewfinders have a setting that assists the camera operator in focusing (called focus assist). Remember, viewfinder adjustments do not affect the camera's video image in any way.

The viewfinder on a camcorder not only shows the video image being shot, but it can also be switched so that the camera operator sees a replay of the newly shot images. Camera operators can check for any faults in camerawork, performance, or continuity and can then reshoot the sequence if necessary.

6.14 INDICATORS

Even if the camera is set in a completely automatic mode (*full auto*), the camera operator will still need information from time to time about basics such as how much of the recording media is left and the charge level of the batteries. Video cameras carry a range of indicators that give a variety of information and warnings: small meters, liquid crystal panels, indicator lights, and switch markings. Most of the indicators are on the body of the camera, but because the camera operator's attention is concentrated on the viewfinder much of the time while shooting, several indicators are arranged within the viewfinder. Table 6.2 presents a selection of typical indicators. Keep in mind that no camera has them all.

FIGURE 6.24
This professional camera includes a flip-out LCD screen as well as an ENG/EFP viewfinder.
(Photo courtesy of JVC.)

Table 6.2 Common Camera Indicators

Indicators of various kinds, including the following, are fitted to video cameras.	
Auto-focusing zone selected	Shows whether auto-focus is controlled by a small central area of the shot or the nearest subject in the scene
Back light exposure correction	System that opens the lens an arbitrary stop or so to improve exposure against bright backgrounds
Gain	Amount of video amplification (gain) being used
End of tape warning	Shows the number of minutes remaining on the tape
Full auto-indicator	Shows that camera is in fully automatic mode (auto-iris, auto-focus, etc.)
Low light level warning	Insufficient light falling onto image sensor, causing underexposure
Manual aperture setting	Shows lens iris is in the manual mode
Shutter speed	Indicates which shutter speed has been chosen
Tally light (cue light)	A red light showing that the camera is recording or, when used in a multicamera setup, shows that the camera is "on-air"
Time indicator	Shows running time (elapsed time/tape time used) or the amount of time remaining on the record device
Video/audio recording	Indicates that the recorder is recording (audio and video)

6.15 AUDIO

Most portable video cameras include a microphone intended for environmental (natural) sound pickup (Figure 6.25). It may be built in or removable. A foam sponge cover over the mic reduces low-pitched wind rumble.

FIGURE 6.25
Microphones attached to the camera are generally used to pick up environmental sounds.

To position the microphone more effectively, it is sometimes attached to a short telescopic "boom," which can be extended to reach out in front of the camera. The use of this type of microphone generally requires the use of a *boom operator* (Figure 6.26).

An *audio monitor* earphone/headphone jack enables the camera operator or audio person to monitor the microphone sound pickup during the recording. Audio needs to be assessed continually for quality, balance, background, and other factors. Often background noises that seemed low to the ear during the recording prove obtrusive on the soundtrack. You also can use the earpiece to listen to a replay of the video soundtrack.

An *external mic* socket on the camera is generally included to plug in a separate microphone for better sound quality and more accurate mic positioning.

An *audio input* socket may be included to allow a second sound source (such as music or effects) to be recorded on a separate track during the video recording.

During a multicamera production, cameras are connected by an intercom, which allows the camera operator to speak with the director and anyone utilizing the camera operator's channel. The intercom is usually connected using the camera control unit (CCU).

FIGURE 6.26
A microphone on a "boom" pole is often used to get the mic physically closer to the talent (presenter).

6.16 POWER

Video cameras normally require a low-voltage direct current DC power supply. This power generally comes from an on-camera battery (which is DC) or an alternating current (AC) adapter that converts AC to DC. Camera operators generally carry multiple camera batteries. There are other power options, including battery belts and special power supplies.

When using batteries, there are a number of precautions you should take to avoid being left without power at a critical moment. The most obvious is to either switch the equipment off when it is not actually being used or switch the camera to a standby (warmup) mode so that it is only using minimum power.

Remember, the camera system (including its viewfinder), the video recorder, any picture monitor you may be using, an audio recorder, and lights attached to the camera are all drawing current. When setting up shots, organizing action, shooting, doing retakes, reviewing the recording, and writing notes, it is easy to squander valuable battery power. Fully charged standby batteries are a must (Figure 6.27).

CONTROLLING THE CAMERA

6.17 HANDLING THE CAMERA

Pictures that are shaky, bounce around, or lean to one side are a pain to watch. So it is worth that extra care to make sure that camera shots are steady and carefully controlled. There may be times when the audience's attention is so riveted to exciting action on the screen that they are unconcerned if the picture does weave from side to side or move about. But don't rely on it! Particularly when there is little movement in the shot, an unsteady picture can be distracting and

FIGURE 6.27
The large battery pack attached to the back of this camera will provide hours of power.
(Photo courtesy of JVC.)

irritating to watch. As a general rule, the camera should be held perfectly still, mounted to a camera support, unless the camera operator is deliberately *panning* it (turning it to one side) or *tilting* it (pointing it up or down) for a good reason.

So what stops us from holding the camera steady? There are a number of difficulties. Even "lightweight" cameras grow heavier with time. Muscles tire. Body movements (breathing, heartbeat) can cause camera movement. Wind can buffet the camera. The camera operator may be shooting from an unsteady

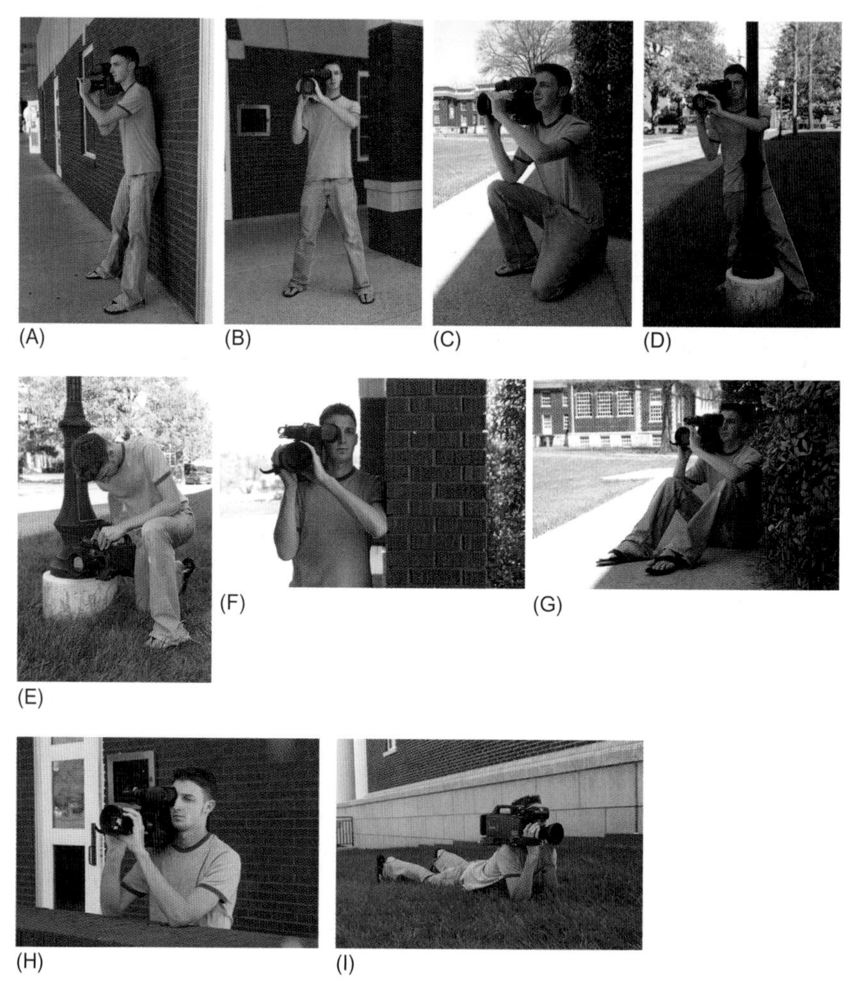

FIGURE 6.28

Keeping the handheld camera steady takes practice. Here are some techniques to handhold a camera: (A) Rest your back against a wall. (B) Bracing the legs apart provides a better foundation for the camera. (C) Kneel, with an elbow resting on one leg. (D) Rest your body against a post. (E) Lean the camera against something solid. (F) Lean your side against a wall. (G) Sit down, with your elbows on your knees. (H) Rest your elbows on a low wall, fence, railings, car, or some other stationary object. (I) Rest your elbows on the ground.

(Photos by Josh Taber.)

position, such as a moving car or a rocking boat. On top of all that, if a telephoto lens is being used, any sort of camera shake will be considerably exaggerated. To overcome or reduce this problem and provide a stable base for the camera, several methods of camera support have been developed (Figure 6.28).

FIGURE 6.29
A body brace helps to firmly support the camera.
(Photo courtesy of Videosmith.)

6.18 SUPPORTING THE CAMERA

There are three basic ways to support a camera:

- *Use the camera operator's body*. With practice, cameras can be *handheld* successfully. Depending on the camera's design, a handheld camera may be steadied against the camera operator's head or shoulder while he or she looks through the viewfinder eyepiece.
- *Use some type of body support*. A number of body supports are available for cameras of different sizes. They add a mechanical support of some type to give the camera added stability (see Figure 6.29).
- *Attach it to a camera mount*. The camera can be attached to a camera mount of some type (monopod, tripod) with a screw socket in its base. A quick-release plate may be fastened to the bottom of the camera, allowing it to be removed in a moment.

6.19 HANDHELD CAMERAS

When the decision is made to have the operator hold the camera by hand, it is usually because the camera has to be mobile, able to change positions quickly. This method is most commonly used by news crews, for documentaries, at sports events, or for shooting music videos. In all of these situations, the camera generally needs to move around to follow the action (Figure 6.30).

Some of the more lightweight consumer and lower-end professional cameras can be held in one hand. They are not large enough to be shoulder mounted. A camera operator can maintain steadiness fairly easily for short periods of time. However, over longer periods, even lightweight cameras can become difficult to hold steady.

Larger cameras are designed to be shoulder mounted. The body of the camera rests on the camera operator's right shoulder. The operator places his or her right hand through a support loop on the side of the lens. This way, the operator's fingers are free to control the zoom rocker (servo zoom) switch while the thumb presses the record/pause switch. The camera operator's left hand adjusts the manual zoom ring, the focusing ring, and the lens aperture (Figure 6.31).

FIGURE 6.30
Handholding a camera for a long period of time will generally produce unsteady shots.
(Photo by Paul Dupree.)

The secret to good camera control with a handheld camera is to adopt a comfortable, well-balanced position, with legs apart and slightly bent and elbows tucked in on the sides. Grip the camera firmly but not too tightly, or your muscles will tire and cause camera shake. Enhance steadiness by resting your elbows against your body or something really secure. This may be a wall, a fence, or perhaps a nearby car (see Figure 6.28).

The comfort and success of handholding a camera depends largely on the camera operator's stamina and how long he or she will be using the camera. Standing with upraised arms supporting a shoulder-mounted camera can be very tiring, so several body braces and shoulder harnesses are available that help the camera operator to keep the camera steady when shooting for long periods (Figure 6.29).

(A)

(B)

FIGURE 6.31
(A) The shoulder-mounted handheld camera is steadied by the right hand, positioned through the strap on the zoom lens.
(B) That same right hand also operates the record button and the zoom rocker (servo zoom) switch.
(Photos by Josh Taber and Sony.)

6.20 THE MONOPOD

The monopod is an easily carried, lightweight mounting. It consists of a collapsible metal tube of adjustable length that screws to the camera base. This extendable tube can be set to any convenient length. Braced against a knee, foot, or leg, the monopod can provide a firm support for the camera, yet allow the operator to move it around rapidly for a new viewpoint. Its main disadvantage is that it is easy to accidentally lean the camera sideways and get sloping horizons. And, of course, the monopod is not self-supporting (Figure 6.32).

FIGURE 6.32
The monopod.
(Photo courtesy of Manfrotto.)

6.21 THE PAN HEAD (PANNING HEAD OR TRIPOD HEAD)

If the camera were mounted straight onto any mount, it would be rigid, unable to move around to follow the action. Instead, it is better to use a tripod head. Not only does this enable the camera operator to swivel the camera from side to side (*pan*) and tilt it up and down, but the freedom of movement (friction, drag) can be adjusted as well. The tripod head can also lock in either or both directions (Figure 6.33).

FIGURE 6.33
The gray tripod head (pan head) allows the camera to pan and tilt.
(Photo by Taylor Vinson.)

Although a camera can be controlled by holding it, it is usually much easier to control the pans, tilts, zooms, and focus by using the tripod arms (also known as a pan bar or panning handles) attached to the head.

Whenever the camera is tilted or panned, the camera operator needs to feel a certain amount of resistance to control it properly. If there is too little resistance, the camera operator is likely to overshoot the camera move at the end of a pan or tilt. It will also be difficult to follow the action accurately. On the

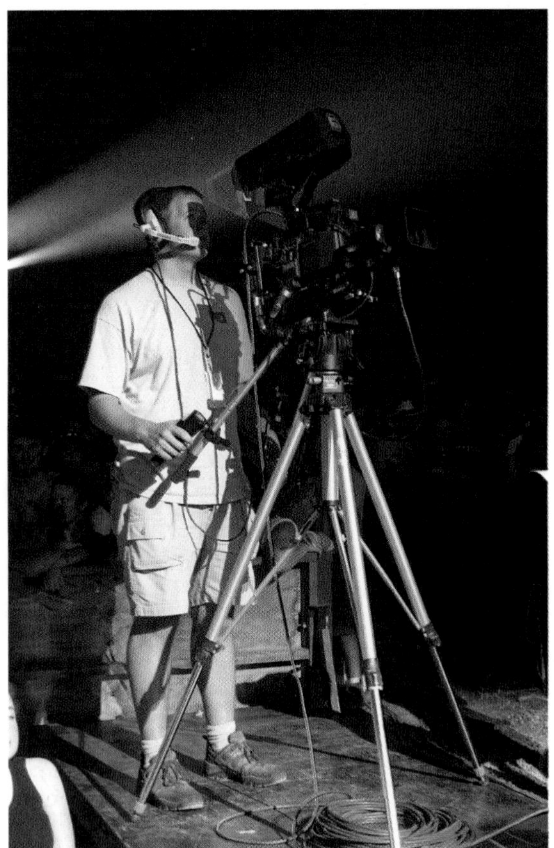

FIGURE 6.34
A tripod is a simple three-legged stand with independently extendable legs that can be set up on rough, uneven ground.
(Photo by Paul Dupree.)

other hand, if the camera operator needs to exert too much effort, panning will be bumpy and erratic. So the friction (drag) for both pan and tilt is generally adjustable.

Tripod heads for video cameras usually use either friction or fluid to dampen movements. The cheaper, simpler friction head has disadvantages: As pressure is gradually exerted to start a pan, the head may suddenly move with a jerk. And at the end of a slow pan, it can stick unexpectedly. With a fluid head, though, all movements should be steady and controlled.

Locking controls are part of the tripod head. These controls prevent the head from panning or tilting. Whenever the camera is left unattended, it should be locked off. Otherwise, the camera may suddenly tilt and not only jolt its delicate mechanism but even tip the tripod over. Locking controls are useful when the camera needs to be very steady (such as when shooting with a long telephoto lens).

6.22 USING A TRIPOD

A tripod offers a compact, convenient method of holding a camera steady, provided it is used properly. It has three legs of independently adjustable length that are spread apart to provide a stable base for the camera (Figure 6.34). However, tripods are certainly not foolproof. In fact, precautions need to be taken in order to avoid possible disaster, so here are some useful tips:

- Ideally, the tripod should be set up before the camera is attached to make sure that it is stable.
- Don't leave the camera on its tripod unattended, particularly if people or animals are likely to knock against or trip over it. Take special care whenever the ground is slippery, sloping, or soft.
- To prevent the feet from slipping, tripods normally have either rubber pads for smooth ground or spikes (screw-out or retractable) for rough surfaces. (Be sure, though, not to use spikes when they are likely to damage the floor surface.)
- If the ground is uneven, such as on rocks or a staircase, the tripod legs can be adjusted to different lengths so that the camera itself remains level when panned around. Otherwise horizontals will tilt as the camera pans. Many tripods are fitted with bubble levels to help level the camera.

- Tripods fitted with a camera tend to be top-heavy, so always make sure that the tripod's legs are fully spread and that it is resting on a firm surface.
- There are several techniques for improving a tripod's stability. The simplest is to add a central weight, such as a sandbag, hung by rope or chain beneath the tripod's center. The legs can be tied to spikes in the ground. Or use a folding device known as a "spreader" to provide a portable base (Figure 6.35).

FIGURE 6.35
The tripod uses a "spreader" to give more stabilization. Note that the camera operator also moved the camera low when not in use. This gives the camera a lower center of gravity, making it more difficult to knock it over.

6.23 THE ROLLING TRIPOD/ TRIPOD DOLLY

One practical disadvantage of the tripod is that the camera operator cannot move it around while shooting. However, tripods can use a tripod dolly, a set of wheels that fit directly on the tripod, or a wheeled base (called a camera dolly) to become a rolling tripod.

Although it sounds obvious, before moving a rolling dolly, remember to check that there is no cable or obstruction in the camera's path. It sometimes helps to give a slight push to align the casters in the appropriate direction before the dolly begins. Otherwise the video image may bump a little as the tripod starts to move.

Although widely used in smaller studios, the rolling tripod dolly does not lend itself to subtle camerawork. Camera moves tend to be approximate. Camera height is adjusted by resetting the heights of the tripod legs. So height changes while shooting are not practical unless a jib is attached to the dolly (Figure 6.36).

6.24 THE PEDESTAL

For many years, the *pedestal* (or *ped*, as it is widely known) has been the all-purpose camera mounting used in TV studios throughout the world. It can support even the heaviest studio cameras, yet it still allows a range of maneuvers on smooth, level surfaces.

Basically, the pedestal consists of a three-wheeled base supporting a central column of adjustable height. A concentric steering wheel is used to push and steer the mounting around and to alter the camera's height. Thanks to a compensatory pneumatic, spring, or counterbalance mechanism within the column, its

FIGURE 6.36
A tripod on a dolly. A dolly can operate on a smooth floor or on a dolly track.
(Photo by Will Adams.)

FIGURE 6.37
While primarily used in studios, camera pedestals can also be used outside. Pedestals come in all different sizes, from lightweight to extremely heavy, like the one shown.

height can be adjusted easily and smoothly, even while on shot. There may be occasions when a second operator's assistance is needed to help push the pedestal and to look after the camera cable (Figure 6.37).

6.25 GORILLAPOD

The Gorillapod's flexible, jointed arms allow you to wrap it around a railing, twist it around a tree branch, or loop it onto a shopping cart. This type of camera support is extremely light and easy to travel with, as well as providing great camera support (Figure 6.38).

6.26 BEANBAG

Beanbag camera supports allow the camera to be positioned in all types of angles while holding the camera steady. This type of support is very light and flexible. There are many different brands available (Figures 6.39).

FIGURE 6.38
A Gorillapod's legs can be twisted around to hold a camera securely in place.
(Photo courtesy of Joby.)

6.27 JIB ARMS

In the golden days of filmed musicals, large *camera cranes* came into their own: bird's-eye shots of the action, swooping down to a group, sweeping along at floor level, shots of dancing feet climbing to follow the action as dancers ascended staircases—in the right hands, such camerawork is very impressive (Figure 6.40).

Some television production companies still use small camera cranes (jibs), but they need skilled handling and occupy a lot of floor space compared with a pedestal. If you want a wide variation in camera heights, a much less costly and more convenient mounting is the *jib* (or jib arm) (Figure 6.41).

(A)

(B)

FIGURE 6.39
Beanbags can securely hold a camera in place without the need for a tripod.
(Photos courtesy of The Pod and Cinesaddle.)

The long jib arm (*boom*) is counterbalanced on a central column. This column is generally supported on a tripod or camera pedestal. The video camera is fixed into a cradle at the far end of the jib, remotely controlled by the camera operator who stands beside the mounting, watching an attached picture monitor. There is a wide range of jib designs, from the lightweight mountings used with smaller cameras with a maximum camera height of 6 feet to heavy-duty jibs that will reach up to 40 feet.

The jib has a variety of operational advantages. It can reach over obstructions that would bring a rolling tripod or pedestal to a halt. It can take level shots of action that occur high above the floor while other mounts working on the floor level can only shoot the subject from a low angle. However, as the jib is swung, the camera always moves in an arc, whether it is being raised, lowered, or turned sideways. It cannot travel parallel with subjects moving across the action area. Whether an operator can turn and raise/lower the jib while on shot and keep the moving subjects in focus and in a well-composed picture will depend on the operator's skills—and a bit of luck.

FIGURE 6.40
This small, relatively inexpensive jib arm fits onto a standard video tripod. It also folds up into a travel case.

(A)

(B)

FIGURE 6.41
(A) Large jibs require skilled talent. (B) The operator remotely controls the head from the red control box while viewing the image on the attached monitor.

6.28 SPECIALTY CAMERA MOUNTS

Several devices are available that can help camera operators cope with those awkward occasions when the camera needs to be secured in unusual places. Typical equipment that can prove handy for smaller production units include the following:

- *Camera clamps*. Metal brackets or clamps of various designs, which allow the camera to be fastened to a wall, fence, rail, door, or other structure (Figure 6.42).
- *Car rig* (or *car mount*). A car mount that attaches to the car, inside or outside of the car, in order to capture images that would otherwise be difficult to obtain. Some mounts use suction cups to fit onto the car, others fit over the side door, and some sit in a beanbag-type mount as shown in Figure 6.43.

FIGURE 6.42
A variety of camera clamps have been designed to mount the camera to almost anything.
(Photo courtesy of Manfrotto.)

The *Steadicam*, *Glidecam*, and *Fig Rig* are just some of the special camera stabilizers that take the shake and shudder out of wide camera movements. These systems allow the camera operator to take smooth traveling shots while panning, tilting, walking, running, climbing, and so forth. An LCD color screen

(A)

(B)

FIGURE 6.43
Car mounts can be anything from a "saddlebag" (large beanbag) (A) to a rigid metal brace with suction cups (B). The goal is to make sure the camera is safe while shooting.
((A) by Taylor Vincent and (B) courtesy of VFGadgets.)

FIGURE 6.44
Smaller cameras can be supported by a handheld steady device like this Steadicam. However, larger cameras must be steadied by a device that includes a body brace.
(Photo courtesy of Steadicam/Tiffen.)

(treated to reduce reflections) allows the operator to monitor the shots (Figures 6.44 and 6.45).

The main theme you will find running through this book is that *it's the result that matters, not how you get it.* The camera needs to be firmly supported. The audience does not know or care whether the camera operator is using a tripod or resting the camera against a handy post. A moving shot can be taken from a car, the back of a motorcycle, a hospital trolley, a wheelchair, or even roller skates or skis. It is the result that counts, although some methods are a lot safer and more convenient than others.

FIGURE 6.45
This "Fig Rig" was designed to hold a camera steadily during extreme movement. It includes mounts for microphones and other accessories.
(Photo courtesy of Manfrotto.)

6.29 HANDLING CARE

It's easy to endanger video equipment, especially when shooting on location. Although some units are rugged and almost foolproof, others are easily damaged. A moment's oversight can put the equipment out of action altogether—a camera momentarily rested on the ground, a spilled drink, the jolts, and vibration of a traveling vehicle. It takes just a moment to protect the camera with a waterproof cover (rain hood) against wind-blown dust and grit, sea-spray, or rain (Figure 6.46). Extreme cold, heat, or moisture can create problems too. A car's trunk can become an oven in the hot sun. High humidity can wreak havoc with videotape recorders.

Moving from a cold exterior to warm surroundings is liable to result in condensation (dew) in VCRs and can cause tape or machine damage. Condensation can also cause major problems with lens element misting, and care must be taken to protect internal elements if the lens is not sealed. The newer memory card cameras are not as susceptible to tape types of problems. Wrapping the equipment (even in a plastic bag) may help fight the condensation.

FIGURE 6.46
Weather gear protects the camera from the elements.
(Photo by Josh Taber.)

Interview with a Pro

Keith Brown, Videographer

Keith Brown, Videographer

What do you like about shooting?
The camera is a tool that allows me to be a storyteller. Whether a concept has been storyboarded or is just simple notes on a napkin, it's the art of turning that concept into something that conveys a visual message. It comes through previsualization, collaboration with other crew members, and deciding how to manipulate the camera to tell that story. What focal length will best illustrate this point, how does depth of field contribute or distract, what do I include or exclude from the frame?

It's the art of allowing viewers to experience the feelings I had at that particular moment, showing them more than just what the experience was factually. It's the challenge of eliciting the same emotional response to an event or story that I had as the camera operator.

There's also the joy of the unexpected moment when light, subject, and movement combined with framing, lens selection, creative use of white balance, and being in the right place at the right time all come together to create something magical.

What are the features that you believe are essential for professional production?
Quality—quality camera work, lighting, audio, scripting when applicable.

A complete understanding of the production:

1. What's the age group? This helps determine the style and approach of your presentation.
2. How familiar are they with the topic? This might determine how much background information you have to give.
3. Why are they watching or listening to your program? This determines what information you need to provide.
4. Do they all speak the same language—both literally and figuratively?
5. Will they answer a call to action, or is the presentation purely informative?
6. How long can you hold their attention?
7. What's the walk away? What's the main thing you want the audience to remember?
8. What's the best way to deliver the message—live, on a DVD, over the web, or some other method?

What kind of support do you use for your camera (mainly tripod?), or do you primarily handhold it? Why?
The style of the show obviously dictates whether it's shot handheld or on a tripod. Shooting pace, setting (is there even room for a tripod or is one allowed?), and the feeling one's trying to convey all come into play.

There are dozens of reasons or situations that help determine the choice; these are a few.

A tripod is employed if:

1. It's a slower-paced show
2. Shots are held longer
3. Scenics
4. Long focal lengths are used
5. Traditional interview situation

Handheld is employed for:

1. A faster pace
2. Mobility
3. Movement
4. Frenetic
5. Walking and talking (without a Steadicam, unfortunately)
6. Intensity
7. Run and gun filming

What advice would you give someone about caring for a camera?

1. Always have a filter on the lens. Start with a UV or Skylight, screwed on or in a mattebox.
2. Learn how to properly clean filters.
3. Keep it in the case when not shooting, especially when travelling.
4. Develop a strategy for keeping track of batteries and recording media, and stick to it so you're never caught guessing. That includes offloading and backing up footage.
5. Learn everything you can about the camera to get the most out of it.

What are the challenges you deal with when shooting?

1. Humidity – Plan on extra time if you're going from a cold to warm environment. Putting the camera in a plastic bag helps because condensation will transfer to the bag instead of the camera.
2. Air travel – Depending on the size of the aircraft, if your camera travels in a soft case, you might have to hand-carry the camera on board. Checking baggage is becoming more expensive, which sometimes determines the amount of gear taken.
3. Audio – Shooting interviews requires good location planning. When will grass be cut, is there any construction in the area, is there any possible interference with wireless signals, what do surrounding offices sound like, are we close to an airport, how loud are the crickets, is the road noise a problem?
4. Lighting – Do I have enough in my lighting package to do the job, or do I need to rent equipment? What time of day does the shoot occur and how long will it take? What are the power considerations?
5. What size crew can I expect to work with?

Keith Brown is a videographer who travels around the world shooting short documentaries that highlight world issues for a nonprofit organization.

CHAPTER 7
Using the Camera

In the hands of even a moderately skilled photographer who knows the capabilities of the camera, even a cell phone can produce reasonable pictures. Unfortunately, owning a camera and knowing which button to push doesn't make you a photographer, any more than owning an automobile makes you a Formula One racecar driver.

—Andy Ciddor, *TV Technology*

Today's cameras can create high-quality images. With the right techniques, you can produce interesting and persuasive images. A working knowledge of the camera, lenses, depth of field, shutters, and *f*-stops is essential to obtain images with the maximum impact.

Key Terms

- ***Action line:*** Also known as an *eye line*, the *180 line*, or the *proscenium line*, this is the line along the direction of the action in a scene. It is the line that separates the "stage" from the audience. Cameras should only shoot from one side of this line.
- ***Auto-focus:*** Some lenses are designed to automatically focus on the subject.
- ***Backlight control:*** When there is more light in the background than on the subject, some cameras use a backlight control button, which opens up the iris an arbitrary stop or so above the auto-iris setting to improve the subject's exposure.
- ***Black-stretch control:*** Some cameras include a black-stretch control menu or button that can be adjusted to make shadow detail clearer and improve tonal gradation in darker tones.
- ***Close-up shot:*** Encourages the audience to concentrate on a specific feature. Shows emotion on people and draws the viewer's attention to a detail/aspect/portion of an object.
- ***Follow focus:*** This technique requires the camera operator to continually change the focus as the camera follows the action.
- ***Long shot or wide-angle shot:*** Helps establish the scene for the viewer.

- ***Macro:*** Some lenses include a macro setting, which is designed to provide a sharp image almost up to the actual lens surface.
- ***Medium shot:*** The medium shot tells the story; it is close enough to show the emotion of the scene but far enough away to show some of the relevant context of the event. Generally shot from the waist up on a person.
- ***Pan shot:*** When the camera pivots to the left or right with the camera pivoting on a camera mount.
- ***Telephoto lens:*** A narrow-angle lens that gives a magnified view of the scene, making it appear closer.
- ***Tilt shot:*** When the camera pivots up or down on a camera mount.
- ***Waveform monitor:*** An oscilloscope that displays a fluctuating line that traces the variations of the video signal, the sync pulses, and so forth. Individual picture lines can be selected and examined. Its several uses include checking for exposure errors, ensuring that the video does not exceed the system's limits, and checking the accuracy of sync pulses.
- ***Wide-angle lens:*** Shows us a greater area of the scene than is normal. The subject looks unusually distant.
- ***Zone focus:*** Camera operators are focused on a portion of the scene. Any time the subject comes into that area, the camera has been prefocused to make sure the action is sharp.

7.1 JUST POINT AND SHOOT

Many people just point and shoot. They assume that the camera should be set on automatic, and therefore they don't worry about it. There are times when the automatic setting is the way to go. However, most of the time the results will be disappointing. The exposure may be incorrect, the auto-iris may fluctuate, and the subject may be blurry. Many times the shots are just plain boring. The audience's attention will wander and the picture quality varies. That's unfortunate, considering that by mastering a few basic principles, effective images can be created that look professional.

7.2 WHAT GETS ON THE SCREEN?

Occasionally, the camera is described as the "eye of the audience." However, that can be a misleading oversimplification. The camera can be used to *deliberately* create that impression, but the camera doesn't automatically convey a true picture of any situation to the audience. If individuals are at a location, their eyes flick around, refocusing, taking in what is happening. They know where they are and can decide for themselves what they look at. Everyone makes his or her own selection from a scene. Television viewers can only see what the director chooses to show them. Only that part of the scene selected by the lens is visible on the rectangular screen in front of them. The audience can only guess at what lies outside the lens's *angle of view*. Other things quite near the camera would fill the screen if the lens turned just a little, but these things remain unseen, "out of shot," because framing is highly selective (Figure 7.1).

FIGURE 7.1
The camera isolates. The camera only shows what is going on in its frame of the scene. The audience does not really know what is outside the field of view.
(Photo by Josh Taber.)

A hallmark of good directors is their ability to select from moment to moment exactly the right features within the scene that suit their dramatic purpose, yet at the same time convince their audience that this is exactly what *they* want to see at that instant.

7.3 HOW CLOSE SHOULD YOU GET?

- A *close-up shot* (CU) is great for revealing detail, intimacy, emotion, and drama. Sometimes it can even reveal too much: It encourages the audience to concentrate on a specific feature.
- Keep in mind that restricting how much the viewers can see might frustrate them, particularly if they feel that they are missing something going on elsewhere.

Be careful not to throw details at the audience too blatantly as if to say, "Pay attention! Look at these details!" Good production techniques are based on *persuasion*. There are many subtle ways of influencing exactly where your audience looks, without throwing out intense close-ups all the time. You can persuade with images by controlling the way the composition is arranged, such as by moving people around or positioning the lighting.

A *long shot,* or *wide shot,* shows the audience a wide view of the scene:

- It establishes the scene by showing the audience where the action is located.
- It lets viewers see how one thing relates to another (such as the various relationships between team members on a basketball team).
- It can give them a good idea of space, unless the director deliberately misleads them by using a much wider lens angle than normal to exaggerate perspective.

An overall view of this type does have its disadvantages. Although HD helps this situation, the audience may not be able to see subject details clearly in a wide shot. The viewer can see the speed with which the player runs after the ball, but not the expression when he or she drops it (Figure 7.2).

CAMERA SHOTS

- Extreme close-up (ECU or XCU) or big close-up (BCU) is a detail shot.
- Close-up (CU) is generally framed just above the head to the upper chest. This shot is sometimes called a "head and shoulders" shot.
- Medium shot or midshot (MS) cuts the body just below or above the waist.
- Long shot (LS) or wide shot (WS) generally features the entire person in the frame, just above and below the body. The European term for a long shot of a person is a full shot (FS).
- Extreme (or extra) long shot (ELS or XLS) or very long shot (VLS) shows significant space above and/or below the subject.

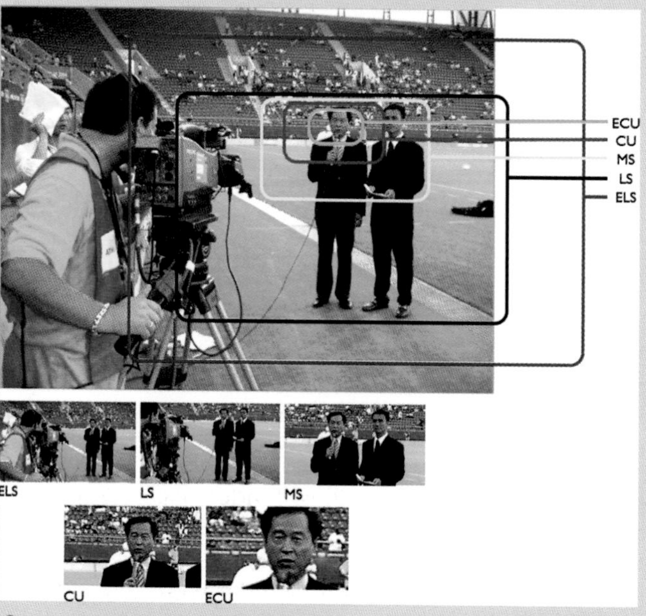

FIGURE 7.2
When shooting people, shots are classified by the amount of a person taken in.

Long shots have the advantage of allowing the viewers to select, to choose whatever attracts their attention in the wide view. But it also gives them the opportunity to look around and start thinking about whatever catches their interest rather than concentrating on the specific point that the program is trying to make at that moment.

Any well-edited program needs a series of closer and wide shots, each carefully chosen for its purpose. These shots assist the audience to establish the scene, observe what is going on, interpret action, and see details.

SHOOTING FOR THE INTERNET

Compressing video to be used on the Internet deteriorates the overall quality of the video. Any time footage is compressed, a bit of the quality has to be sacrificed. Here are a few points to keep in mind when shooting something that will be streamed on the Internet:

- Do not use more camera motion than you need. Whenever there is camera motion, the result is more compression.
- Use a tripod to give the most stable shot possible (you usually should use a tripod anyway).
- Limit camera pans and tilts; when you do use them, make sure the motions are slow and smooth.
- Light the subject well.
- Keep the background simple. The more detailed it is, the more the video will need to compress.

7.4 HOW MUCH CAN WE SEE?

How much of the scene the camera shows will depend on several factors:

- The camera's viewpoint (angle)
- How far the camera is from the subject
- The angle its lens covers

As we noted earlier, the lens's coverage (*lens angle, angle of view*) varies with its focal length. The *zoom lens* can be adjusted to any focal length within its range. If it is a 6:1 (six to one) system, then its widest angle will be six times the narrowest.

Some zoom lenses are fitted with a 2X extender (Figure 7.3). You can flip in this extender when you need a longer lens. The extender will double the focal length of the lens. However, there will be a noticeable light loss. Another way of altering the maximum or minimum angle of your lens system is to clip or screw on a *supplementary lens* (*diopter lens*). There are both telephoto and wide-angle conversion lenses available for this purpose. However, there can be some light loss, depending on the diopter (Figure 7.4).

FIGURE 7.3
The 2X extender is located on the side of the lens.
(Photo courtesy of Canon.)

FIGURE 7.4
Wide-angle lens adapter.
(Photo courtesy of VF Gadgets.)

7.5 LENS ANGLES

Lens angles significantly impact the video images that the camera will capture, as well as the audience's interpretation of those images.

If the angle from the viewer's eyes to the sides of the TV screen is reasonably similar to that of the camera's horizontal lens angle, the viewer will get a realistic impression of space, distance, and proportions. This is referred to as a *"normal" lens angle.* With today's variety of screen sizes and shapes, this angle is by no means precise, but for all practical purposes we can assume that it is around 20 to 28 degrees.

What are the disadvantages if the camera operator shoots with a lens angle that is appreciably different from "normal"? Well, some interesting things can happen to the image. With some subjects, the audience may not even notice anything. However, wherever the audience can judge proportions and perspectives, such as looking up at a tall building or a close-up of a person, differences between images shot with different lens angles will be obvious.

A *telephoto* or *narrow-angle* lens (long focal length) will give a magnified view of the scene, making it appear closer. The telephoto lens is advantageous when the camera operator cannot move the camera closer to the subject or does not want to. But there are also disadvantages. The telephoto lens often has the effect of flattening subjects because it compresses depth. This compression can also make subjects look unnaturally close (Figure 7.5). Movements are affected as well. Even fast-moving subjects seem strangely slowed by a telephoto lens as they move toward or away from the camera. The telephoto/narrow-angle lens is also difficult to hold steady; even the slightest vibration is magnified and causes image shake. The camera needs to be mounted or rested on something firm in order to obtain a steady image.

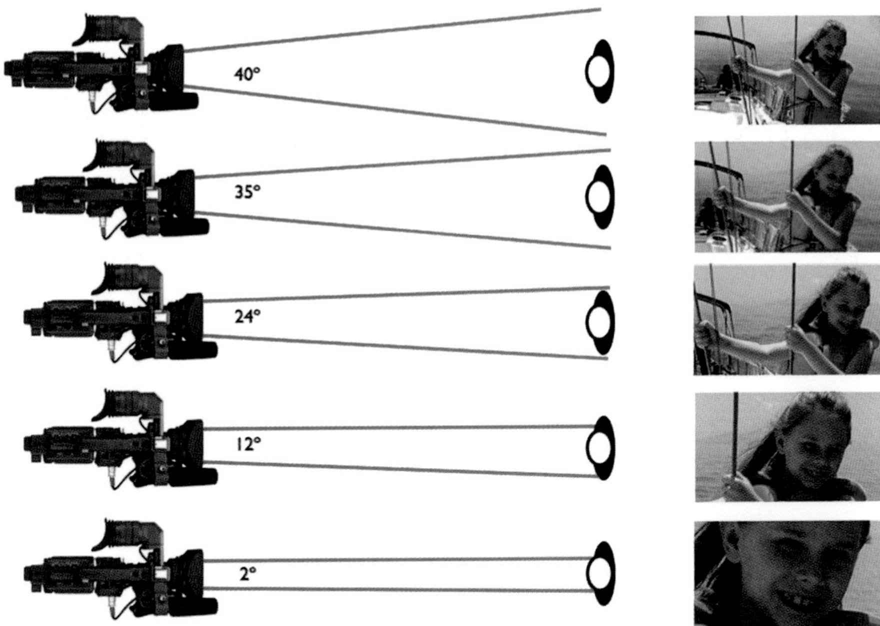

FIGURE 7.5
Changing the lens's focal length alters its coverage proportion. In this situation, the camera stayed the exact same distance from the subject but the lens was changed.
(Camera photo courtesy of JVC.)

A *wide-angle* lens, on the other hand, shows us a much greater area of the scene. Everything in the image looks unusually distant. The lens seems to emphasize space and depth. Movements toward and away from the camera seem faster than they really are.

The wider the lens angle (i.e., the shorter the focal length), the easier it is to hold the camera steady and to move around smoothly while shooting. Although the wide-angle lens has many advantages, it cannot be used all of the time because there will be too many long shots. If the camera is moved in close to the subject in order to get a close-up shot, subjects will look distorted with a wide-angle lens.

7.6 SO WHY MOVE AROUND?

If the subject can appear closer and farther away by simply varying the lens angle, why bother to move the camera? Why not just zoom the lens? It is far less trouble.

Although, at first glance, changing the focal length *seems* to give more or less similar results to those obtained when repositioning the camera, when you look at the image critically, it becomes obvious that there are distinct differences in the results (Figure 7.6). You'll find these differences summarized in Tables 7.1 and 7.2.

FIGURE 7.6
Changing the focal length (lens angle) of the lens significantly alters the proportions of the image. Subjects will be compressed or appear farther away. Note the impact that the telephoto and wide-angle lenses have on how the image looks.
(Photos by Josh Taber.)

Table 7.1 Selecting the Right Lens

How much of the scene is sharp?	▪ When using a wide lens angle (short focal length), most of the scene will usually appear sharply focused because there is a large depth of field.
	▪ With a narrow lens angle (long focal length), the depth of field is considerably less, and only subjects located within this restricted zone will be sharply focused.
	▪ The depth of field varies with the following factors:
	  ▪ The actual lens angle (the focal length of the lens). The zone's depth increases as you increase the lens angle.
	  ▪ The lens aperture (the *f*-stop you are using). The zone's depth increases as you decrease the lens aperture.
	  ▪ The distance at which the lens is focused. Depth increases as you focus farther away (which increases the camera's focused distance).
	  ▪ Camera sensor size. Depth of field is also determined by the image size. For example, quarter-inch camera sensors provide an extremely large depth of field.

(*Continued*)

Table 7.1 Selecting the Right Lens (*Continued*)

How prominent is the background in closer shots?	■ With the lens aperture stopped down (large *f*-stop number), the depth of field will be greater. ■ With the lens aperture opened up (small *f*-stop number), the depth of field will be reduced. ■ Backgrounds are likely to be defocused if the lens is working wide open (small *f*-stop number).
How hard is it to focus?	■ The longer the focal length, the more difficult it is to focus accurately because the depth of field becomes shallower and reveals focusing errors. In close shots of a nearby object, using a long focal length (telephoto) may make it hard to get the entire objects sharply focused. ■ Working with a wide-angle lens, the depth of field is much greater and focusing is correspondingly easier. But there are still drawbacks. It can be difficult to judge exactly where the lens is focused if there is a large depth of field. When set to a wide angle, the camera must be closer to the subject in order to get an appropriate image size on the screen. There can also be problems with distortions.
Camera shake	■ The longer the focal length, the more sensitive the camera becomes to shake, particularly when the camera operator is standing still to shoot a stationary distant subject.
The impression of distance and depth in the picture	Because distant planes appear closer when shot with a narrow-angle lens, a distant back wall will look nearer and the room will appear smaller. Planes in the picture that are at an oblique angle to the camera (a side wall) will be shortened. Three-dimensional subjects will look squashed because their depth or thickness along the z-axis (near-to-far direction) is compressed. Conversely, a wide-angle lens will cause these same dimensions to appear stretched or deeper than usual. All planes will look abnormally far away. Impressions of size and space are exaggerated.
The accuracy of the shapes (geometry)	The wider the lens angle, the greater the distortion in closer shots of three-dimensional subjects.

The lens's focal length affects a number of areas simultaneously. How noticeable these effects are in the image depends on the subject and the scene.

It's a good general working principle to use a *normal lens angle* as much as possible and to move the camera viewpoint rather than just zooming in and out with a stationary camera. Actual camera movement gives life to an image. Whenever a camera moves, we see significant changes in the image. Various surfaces become progressively hidden as the camera moves past; others are gradually revealed. Although this effect becomes most obvious when travelling

Table 7.2	Why Change the Lens Angle?
To adjust framing	**A slight change in lens angle:** When excluding or including certain objects and repositioning the camera or subject would ruin the proportions.
For otherwise unobtainable shots	**Using a narrow-angle lens:** To capture subjects that are situated a long distance from the camera and are inaccessible or where the camera cannot be moved (located on a camera platform). **Using a wide-angle lens:** Where the normal lens does not provide a wide enough shot because of space restrictions.
To adjust effective perspective	Altering the lens angle and changing the distance between the camera and subject alters the subject/background proportions. **Using a wider lens angle** enhances spatial impression and increases the depth of field. **Using a narrower lens angle** reduces spatial impression and compresses the depth.
To provide simpler or more reliable changing operations	**Zooming in/out instead of dollying** may produce smoother, easier changes in shot size (but the perspective changes because of the focal lengths of the lens) (Figure 7.7). Zooming provides **rapid changes in image size** more safely than fast dollying (for dramatic effect or to suddenly reveal detail). **Zooming in/out on a flat subject** is indistinguishable from dollying, but it avoids focus-following problems. Lens angle changes can avoid close-up cameras coming into picture.

past foreground images, such as a series of columns or through a group of trees, it is one of those natural everyday phenomena that help us to interpret our three-dimensional world. It is even more pronounced when the camera *trucks* (or *crabs*) sideways.

Whenever a lens is zoomed, it simply magnifies and reduces the exact same shot. The natural effects that make shots from a moving camera so persuasive are simply not there.

There will certainly be times when the camera operator will deliberately widen or narrow the lens angle for practical or artistic reasons (Table 7.1). Don't hesitate to vary the lens angle as needed to overcome a problem or to get an effect. Don't just alter it casually. For example, if a camera operator is shooting a parade from a balcony and getting useful group shots with a normal lens angle, the operator may also use a wide-angle lens to take in the lengthy procession or a narrow-angle lens to show details. Using one lens angle would significantly limit the shot opportunities. The camera operator certainly couldn't rely on running up and down to new viewpoints to provide the variety of shots needed.

If the director wants to show details on a distant statue located at the top of a building, he or she will certainly need to use a really *narrow lens angle* (*long focal length*). There will be some compromises to make. However, it's unavoidable. Space will be squashed, and the form of the building itself may appear distorted. If you are using a narrow-angle lens when alternative camera positions are available, such distortions are unjustified.

On the positive side, the way in which a *wide-angle lens* exaggerates space offers invaluable opportunities in a crowded location or where the budget is limited. A wide-angle lens can make the smallest setting appear spacious. Even a couple of scenic flats linked together can create the illusion of an entire room if shot strategically with a wide-angle lens. Table 7.2 summarizes the practical advantages of the wide-angle lens.

7.7 THE ZOOMING PROCESS

There are several methods of controlling the lens's zooming action. A camera operator working on a dramatic production may prefer a *manual zoom system,* which allows the shot's coverage to be subtly readjusted as picture composition varies. But for the split-second decisions and fast zooms involved when shooting a sports event, *motorized systems* may prove more convenient.

Controlling the Zoom

There are three primary ways to control a zoom lens:

- *Manual zoom control ring (or barrel ring).* Turning a ring on the lens barrel varies the zoom lens's focal length. This is a precise method, giving total control over the zoom action throughout the shot.
- *Power zoom.* Many zoom lens systems can be controlled by a two-way *rocker switch* (see Figure 7.7), which activates a small motor. This will drive the zoom toward either the wide-angle or the telephoto end of its range, stopping where needed. The zoom speed may be adjustable or vary with finger pressure on the switch. The power zoom is widely used and particularly adaptable to all types of production in the studio and in the field. Zoom lenses on professional cameras generally have the switchable option of selecting between remote/manual/auto methods of iris control using the same hand.
- *Remote control.* Remote control units are available for most cameras. They allow the camera operator to zoom the camera's lens from behind the camera. This unit is generally mounted on a tripod arm (pan bar).

The zoom lens can be a creative tool when used with discretion. When shooting a ballgame, zoom in to a closer shot as the action grows tenser. Zooming

Zoom Lens Shot | **Dolly Shot**

1a

2a

1b

2b

1c

2c

1d

2d

FIGURE 7.7
Zooming simply magnifies and reduces the picture. It does not produce the changes in the scene that arise as the dolly is moved through a scene. Increasing the focal length narrows the lens angle, filling the screen with a smaller and smaller section of the shot. These photographs illustrate the difference between the zoom and the dolly. Notice that there is not much of a difference between images 1b and 2b. However, as the dolly continues in 2c, it begins to show a different perspective, showing that there is a table between the two chairs on the left. Photo 1d zooms past the table, whereas the dolly perspective in 2d takes viewers up to the table and allows them to see the top of it.

in rapidly so that the camera seems to swoop into a scene, particularly if it is on a jib arm arcing over the action, can produce dynamic results. But if you use a similar zooming action at the wrong time, your audience will probably get frustrated.

To test this effect, try dollying in toward a person while zooming out at a corresponding speed and keeping the person the same size in the frame throughout. The result is bizarre, but it demonstrates the extent to which the lens angle and camera distance can affect a shot.

7.8 FOCUSING

Focus is an incredibly effective tool for directing the audience's attention. The eye is always attracted to the part of the image that is in focus. This means that a knowledge of focus, depth of field, and lenses is essential if the camera operator and director want to use the camera creatively as a tool for storytelling.

There are a number of techniques that camera operators use to capture the action in focus.

- The most popular method is called *follow focus.* This technique requires the camera operator to continually change the focus as he or she follows the action, constantly turning the focus ring to keep the subject sharp whenever it begins to soften. However, focusing is not always as easy as that. With practice it can become a reflexive action. That does not mean it becomes easy.
- *Zone focusing* refers to when camera operators are assigned a "zone" on the field of play or at a news event. They calculate the aperture so that basically everything will be in focus when the player or other subject moves into their zone. They generally do not try to shoot the subject when they are outside of their zone.
- *Prefocusing* is when the camera operator focuses the camera on the subject before beginning to record. An example would be when a talk show host wants to show the audience a still photograph. Usually the host will place the photo on a stand located on his or her desk. Because one of the cameras has usually prefocused on the stand, the photo is instantly framed and in focus. Prefocusing is also required whenever a zoom lens is used. We will continue our discussion of prefocusing later in this chapter.

Many lenses also include *macro* systems, which are designed to provide a sharp image almost up to the actual lens surface. However, it is difficult to avoid a camera shadow when lighting such close subjects.

As the subject gets closer to the camera, the depth of field becomes shallower, so focusing is more critical. How noticeable a fall-off in sharpness is will depend on the amount of fine detail and tonal contrast in the subject.

7.9 AUTO-FOCUS

Many video cameras are fitted with an *automatic focusing* feature. This is a useful device for the occasions when the camera operator is preoccupied with following the action, is not sure where the subject is going to move to next, and might get the focusing wrong in the heat of the moment. But why not switch to auto-focus all the time so that we can forget about focusing altogether?

If the camera operator relies entirely on the automatic focus features in the camera, the resulting images will vary greatly. The auto-focus system simply sharpens the focus in a selected zone of the shot, irrespective of what is appearing there. So it needs to be used with care.

While auto-focusing can be very accurate, here are some situations that can be problematic:

- When the subject is not in the center of the picture. If two people are placed on either side of the frame, auto-focus may sharpen on an unimportant distant object in the center of the screen and leave the subjects soft-focused.
- The camera operator may want to focus on someone near the camera and a distant person at the same time, but auto-focus may sharpen on one or the other—or neither.
- If shooting a subject through a foreground framework, such as a fence or branches, the system will focus on this foreground rather than the more distant subject (Figure 7.8).
- If following someone who is moving around within a crowd, the auto-focus system is likely to readjust itself continually, focusing on nearby people instead of the intended subject.
- When the camera operator zooms to change the size of the shot, the auto-focus system may refocus as the shot is recomposed.
- If the camera operator is shooting a distant view and anyone (or anything) moves into the shot, closer to camera, the system may refocus on the secondary subject instead and defocus on the real subject. If, for example, the camera operator is panning around a scene and moves past a foreground tree, the system may readjust to focus on the tree.

When dealing with any of these situations, the best solution is to switch to *manual* focus to avoid the problems. Nevertheless, when used wisely, auto-focus can be a useful tool.

7.10 DEPTH OF FIELD

Depth of field, or the *focused zone*, is usually defined as the distance between the nearest and farthest objects in focus. When shooting something in a distance, everything seems clearly focused. But refocus the lens onto something a few feet away, and only a limited amount of the shot will really appear sharply

FIGURE 7.8
Auto-focus systems cannot accurately focus on subjects behind broken-up foregrounds such as fences, branches, or the cage in the photo shown here.
(Photo by Lynn Owens.)

focused. Now focus on something very close to the camera, and sharpness becomes restricted to an even shallower zone.

How obvious this effect is varies with the amount of detail in the scene.

The depth of field varies with the following factors:

- The *distance* at which the lens is focused
- The size of the *image sensors*
- The *focal length* of the lens
- The lens *f*-stop (*aperture*)

Alter any of these elements, and the depth of field changes.

Depth is *greatest* when any of the following is true:

- The lens is focused at a distance
- A wide-angle lens is being used
- The lens aperture is stopped down (*f*/16) (Figure 7.9)

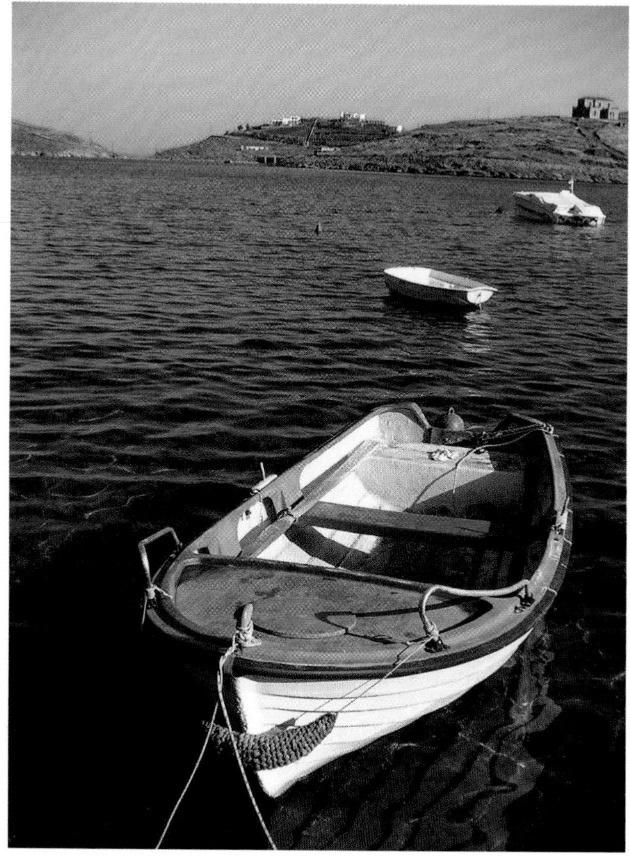

FIGURE 7.9
You can achieve a large depth of field by using a wide-angle lens and a large-numbered *f*-stop such as *f*/22. The bright sunlight in this photo allowed the large-numbered aperture.

Depth of field is *shallow* in the following situations:

- When you are focusing on subjects close to the camera
- When you are using a telephoto (narrow angle) lens
- When you open up the lens aperture (*f*/2) (Figure 7.10)

Don't be misled into thinking that you can use a wide-angle lens to improve depth of field in a shot every time. In some situations, the wide-angle lens works well at increasing the depth of field. However, when you switch to a wide-angle lens, the subject will look smaller, and by the time the camera gets close enough to compensate, the focused depth may become the same as before—only now there may be distortion and exaggerated depth too. It all comes down to the type of shot the director is trying to capture.

FIGURE 7.10
The shallow depth of field shown here was achieved with the use of a telephoto (narrow-angle) lens along with a fairly small-numbered *f*-stop such as *f*/4.
(Photo by Chad Crouch.)

7.11 MAXIMUM SHARPNESS?

Of course, it is not necessary to always get everything in the picture as sharp as possible. There are certainly situations when the director will want to see everything in the shot clearly—for example, when showing widespread action such as in a ballgame or when presenting an interesting building. Another example is when the director wants to create depth in the picture by having the shot include a person near the camera and another some distance away, both sharply focused. Then the camera operator could use a wide-angle lens, stopped down as far as the light levels permit.

There will be other times, though, when the director wants the audience to concentrate on a specific subject and disregard the surroundings. This can be achieved by deliberately restricting the depth of field or by using a larger lens aperture or a narrower lens angle. Now, because of the limited depth of field, the subject will appear sharp against a defocused background, where anything likely to confuse or distract merges into an indistinct blur.

7.12 DIFFICULT TO FOCUS?

Sometimes there is insufficient depth of field to focus clearly on the whole subject. That is a specific problem in close-up shots. Stopping the lens down would help, of course, but there may not be enough light to do so without underexposing the image. If it is impossible to increase the light level, what can one do? Several compromise solutions are available. However, please note the word "compromise"—the results may not always be optimum (Figure 7.11).

- The best method may be to sharpen focus on the *most important part* of the subject and leave the rest defocused. Although this situation is not ideal, it is a way to show the viewers exactly what you want them to see.

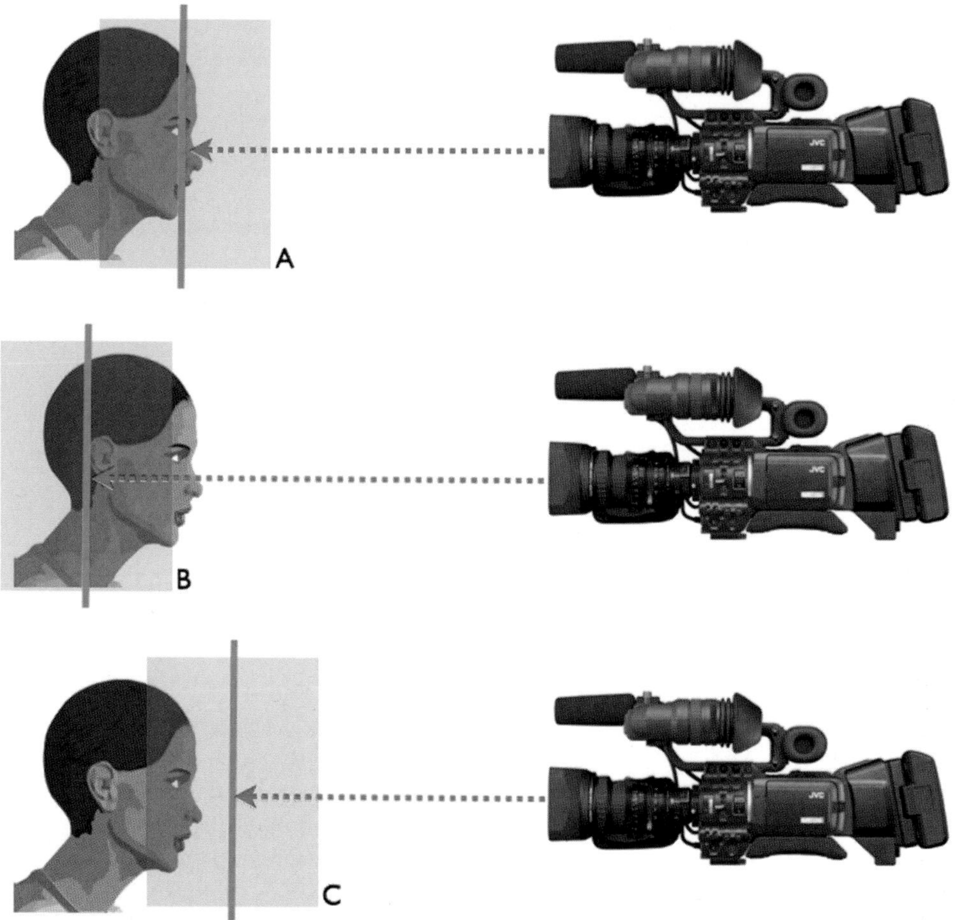

FIGURE 7.11
When accurately focused, (A), the most important part of the subject should be the sharpest. The specific focus point (as represented by the darker blue line in the illustrations) should have a large enough depth of field (represented by the light blue field) to keep the subject in focus as she moves a little forward or backward. Note that the incorrect focus point, as demonstrated in B and C, would make it easier for the subject to move out of focus.
(Camera photo courtesy of JVC.)

- It is possible to *split focus* and choose a compromise focusing distance that keeps all subjects clearly enough in focus.
- Sometimes a *pull focus* or *throw focus* is appropriate. For example, suppose that two people are being shot at different distances from the camera and it is not possible to get them both in sharp focus. The camera operator might start by focusing on the first person, and then, at the appropriate moment, change the focus to sharpen on the second person. The method successfully directs the audience's attention, and the effect can be dramatic. So it is a technique that needs to be reserved for the right occasion.
- Ideally the situation can be improved by moving the subjects or altering the camera position so that they are both about the same distance from the camera and within the available depth of field.

Limited Depth of Field

If the depth of field is too limited for your purposes, you can do the following (Figures 7.12 and 7.13):

- *Stop down*. Increasing the depth of field will require a high light level.
- *Focus on one subject*. Let others soften.
- *Split focus*. Spread the available depth between both subjects (now none is really sharp).
- *Move subjects closer together*. This way, they will be roughly the same distance from the camera.
- *Use a wide-angle lens*. The depth of field will increase, but the subject will now appear smaller.

FIGURE 7.12
***Pulling focus* can be used to guide the viewer through a scene. Notice the change of focus in the two photos shown here.**
(Photos by Josh Taber.)

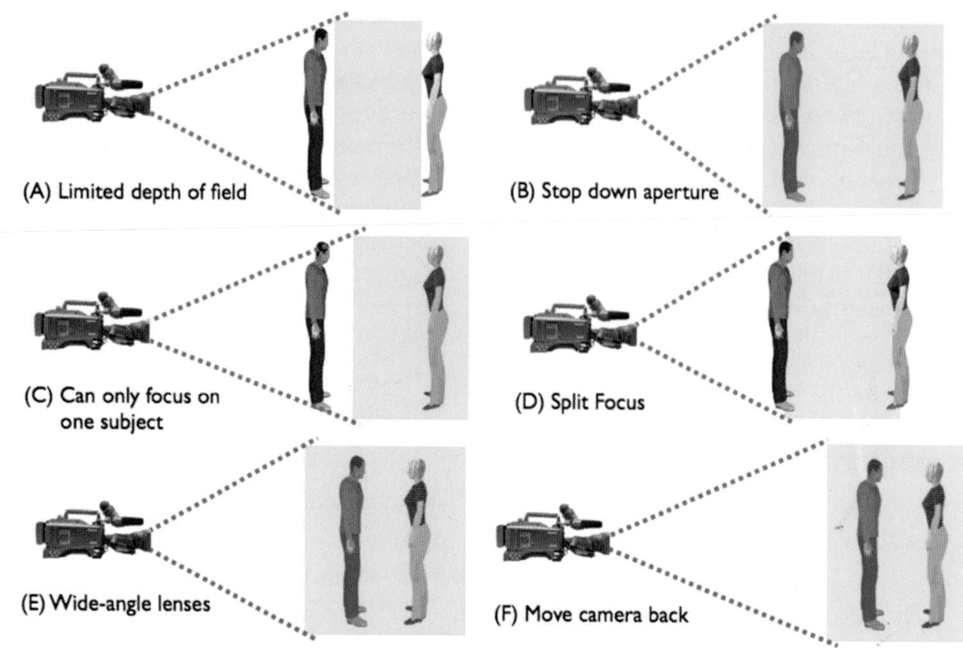

FIGURE 7.13
Dealing with a limited depth of field. When a limited depth of field creates problems (A), here are a few solutions:

- *If the aperture is stopped down (a higher f-stop number), the depth of field will increase (B).*
- *If there is not enough depth to cover two people (C), it may be possible to split focus (D).*
- *Wide-angle lenses have a much wider depth of field than a telephoto lens (E).*
- *The closer the camera is to the subject, the shallower the depth of field. By moving the camera farther back, a wider depth of field will be created. However, the subject will be smaller.*
  (Camera photo courtesy of Panasonic.)

7.13 PREFOCUSING THE ZOOM LENS

The zoom lens is a fine tool for the creative camera operator, but it also has some nasty pitfalls for the unwary. When following fast-moving action, the camera operator may run into difficulties.

Depth of field will significantly change as a zoom lens moves through its focal length range. When zoomed out (wide-angle view), there is normally considerable depth of field available, and focusing is easy. Usually, so much looks sharp in the picture that the camera operator cannot judge exactly where the best focus is. But zoom in to a close-up shot (telephoto or narrow-angle view), and the depth of field becomes relatively shallow. In fact, there is always the danger that instead of being focused exactly on the subject, the lens was really focused some distance nearer or farther away. Consequently, when zooming in from a good, sharp long shot to a close-up, the image may be completely defocused, and then the camera operator has to hurry to correct the focus. This is especially tense for live, on-air productions (Figure 7.14).

FIGURE 7.14
When focusing is extremely critical, especially in dramatic productions, a *focus puller* is often used to adjust the focus of the camera. This allows the camera operator to concentrate on framing.

The only solution to this dilemma is to remember to *prefocus the zoom* before taking the shot. The camera operator takes a trial close-up shot of the subject immediately beforehand so that the focus can be crisply adjusted; then he or she zooms back to the wide shot (without changing distance), ready to start shooting the action.

PREFOCUSING THE ZOOM

If zoom lenses have not been prefocused on the subject by zooming in for the close-up, the picture may become defocused during the zoom move from long shot to close-up.

- The long shot may look perfectly in focus. However, this is because of the depth of field created by the wide-angle lens.
- As the lens zooms in to a telephoto (narrower angle), the depth of field becomes much more restricted, and it is possible that the shot will be totally out of focus.
- The best method of keeping zoom shots in focus is to zoom in close to the subject, focus, and then zoom out. This should allow the camera operator to zoom in and out, keeping everything in focus.

EXPOSURE

7.14 What Is "Exposure"?

Every video camera requires a certain amount of light to function effectively and produce quality images. However, the camera's sensors can only handle a limited range of tones. When shots contain a wide range of tones (brightness values), directors cannot hope to reproduce them all absolutely accurately in the final image.

- If the amount of light from a surface exceeds the chip's upper limit, it will reproduce as white in the video picture. It will *burn out* or *clip* to a blank white.
- Conversely, where a surface reflects too little light, it will fall beyond the system's lower limit and crush to an overall black tone.

The average brightness of the lens image falling onto the sensor is primarily determined by the *lens aperture* (*f*-stop). The goal is to adjust the aperture so that the most important tones, usually people's faces, are clearly visible. This process is called "adjusting the exposure." "Correct exposure" is a subjective choice.

The video camera operator can always see the image in the viewfinder or on the screen. The operator can assess the picture continually, and if it is over- or underexposed, he or she can immediately compensate. In video/television production, the camera itself is the light meter.

Let's take a practical example. The camera operator shoots someone who is standing out in the sunlight. He or she adjusts the exposure by altering the lens aperture until the person looks good in the viewfinder or, better still, on a high-grade picture monitor. The subject's face tones, in particular, appear quite natural—neither too light nor too dark. However, the subject's white shirt looks washed out and has no detail, or maybe the subject's pants look black, with no signs of modeling in the material at all. The director might be willing to accept these results, unless this is a fashion shoot, meant to show off the quality and attractiveness of the clothing.

Don't expect to always show good tonal gradation in *everything* in the scene. There will usually be something in the shot that crushes out to white or black. How successfully the shot is exposed will depend not only on the range of the tones appearing in it but also on the effect the director wants to capture. The director may want to deliberately underexpose an image to make it look more shadowy and mysterious. Or he or she might overexpose a shot of the seashore to create a high-key effect (Figure 7.15).

It is easier to control the tones in a studio by altering the lighting or by adjusting the aperture. But elsewhere, particularly on location, the camera operator may have to make the most of what is available, and at times the selected lens aperture may have to be something of a compromise.

If parts of the location scene appear as large blank white or black areas in the image, there may not be much you can do about it. The obvious remedy is to reframe the shot or change the camera position to keep the harsh white or black areas out of the picture altogether. If lighting equipment is available, it may be possible to lighten darker tones or shadowy areas (Figures 7.16 and 7.17). Occasionally, troublesome surfaces can be masked off (have someone

FIGURE 7.15
Directors cannot expect that every image will be captured with good tonal qualities. In this image, the director could choose to get good exposure of either the field of play or the audience.
(Photo by Shannon Mizell.)

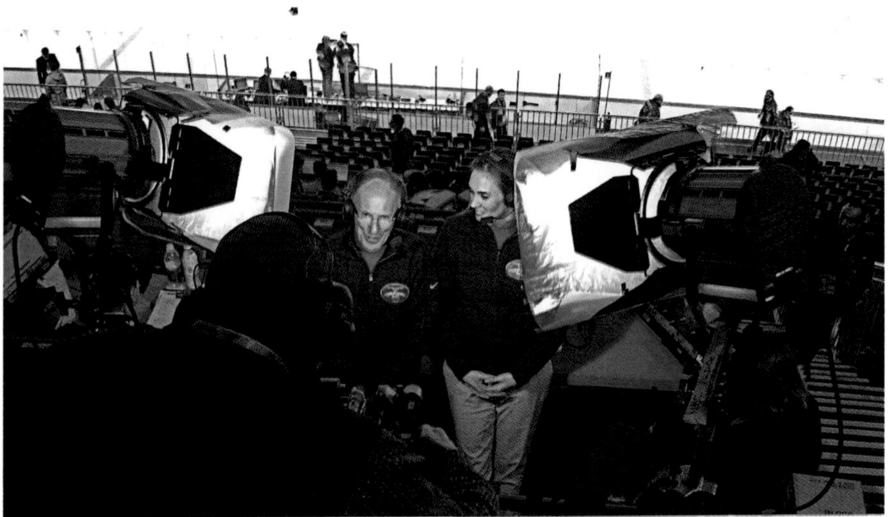

FIGURE 7.16
Lights were used to try to match the exposure of the presenter to the details on the ice of the hockey rink behind the talent. Otherwise, the ice would be entirely white or the talent would be entirely black.

standing in the foreground to obscure a large blank white wall). If the object that catches the eye is small, such as the sun reflected in a table mirror, it may be possible to reangle it or remove the mirror altogether. Again, choosing the optimum exposure may involve a certain amount of compromise.

FIGURE 7.17
Additional lighting or some type of reflector can be used to lighten darker areas when working outdoors.

7.15 UNDEREXPOSURE AND OVEREXPOSURE

When a picture is *underexposed*, all of its tones will appear much darker. Results are usually dull and lifeless. Detail and modeling may be clear in light tones (even clearer than usual), but middle to dark areas look muddy and merge to black (Figure 7.18).

Underexposed

Correctly Exposed

Overerexposed

FIGURE 7.18
Taking the time to expose an image properly is essential for quality pictures.

It is worth remembering too that when the camera receives insufficient light from the scene, other image defects can also develop, such as *lag* (image smearing on movement) and picture noise.

To fix underexposure, open the lens aperture to provide the camera's chips with a brighter lens image. (Of course, this will reduce the depth of field to some extent and could make focusing harder, particularly when using a narrow-angle lens.)

Increasing the *video gain* on a camera does not really compensate when the camera sensor is not getting enough light for maximum performance; it simply boosts the video signal. However, it will certainly enhance the picture, perhaps even making it look bright and well contrasted. The downside to video gain is that the quality of the image deteriorates the higher the gain is set.

When a picture is *overexposed*, all of its tones will appear unusually light. Even fairly light tones in the scene will block off, whereas darker areas of the scene will often be easier to discern than normal. Stopping down a little improves reproduction in light tones but reduces the visibility of shadows. However, it is impossible to electronically compensate for grossly over- or underexposed areas. They will have little detail. Again, lowering the video gain setting is not a good solution. It will simply reduce the overall brightness of the image (Figure 7.18).

7.16 AUTOMATIC EXPOSURE

If judging exposure is a matter of artistic choice, how is it that so many video cameras utilize an automatic iris most of the time? Leaving aside those people who would otherwise be careless about exposure, the auto-iris is a useful tool when you are in a difficult spot. It continually adjusts the lens aperture to maintain an average video signal.

Under typical location conditions, whether outside or inside, light levels can change considerably as the camera's viewpoint changes. If you were to walk around a location with a light meter, you would probably see its needle bouncing up and down each time you repositioned. The camera may need to be stopped down to *f*/16 in a sunlit courtyard but opened up to *f*/2 inside a house.

Strictly speaking, if the camera needs to follow along with action that moves from the exterior to the interior, then the camera operator needs to keep an eye on the viewfinder and adjust the exposure to match the different light levels.

Some may wonder, if camera operators already have to follow focus as they move and keep the shot properly framed, how can they adjust the exposure at the same time? That is why even experienced camera operators under these conditions may leave exposure to the auto-iris and concentrate on focusing and composing the picture.

Ideally, the lens aperture is set for the correct exposure of the main subject. If the same subject appears in a succession of shots in the same scene, the exposure needs to be constant, not change about as incidental background tones vary. Yet changes of this kind are unavoidable when using an auto-iris.

It is easy to fool an auto-iris. If a lighter tone is brought into the shot (e.g., the subject opens a newspaper or takes off a jacket to reveal a white shirt), the iris will close down a little and darken all the other tones in the picture, including the subject's face. Take the light area out of the shot or pan away from it, and the auto-iris will open up. Image tones will lighten. Take a long shot, and face tones may look dark, but zoom in to a close shot, and because other picture tones are now excluded, the face reproduces much lighter.

Under certain conditions, the auto-iris can also cause bad underexposure. Normally, if you are shooting inside a room, the system will open up and produce well-exposed images. However, suppose the person being filmed moves over to a window. The auto-iris will see the intense daylight and stop the lens

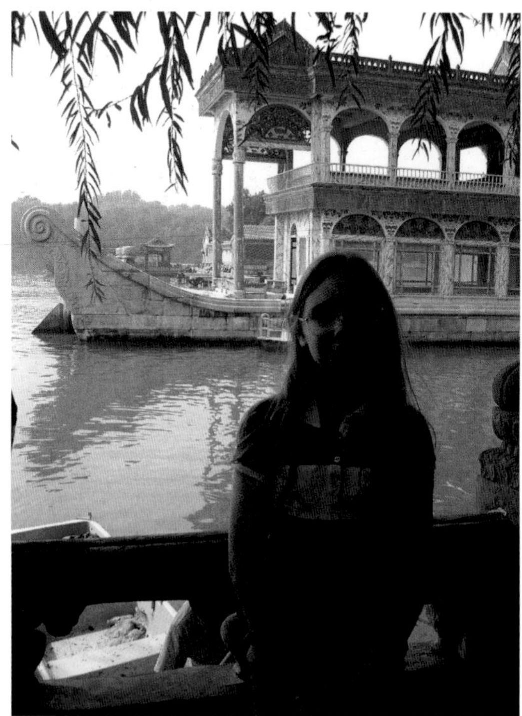

FIGURE 7.19
Brightly lit backgrounds will cause the auto-iris to underexpose the main subject.

down. As a result, the person could now appear as a silhouette, while the sky may be well exposed (Figure 7.19).

Some cameras have a *backlight* control that can be switched on when the background is bright in the image. This opens up the iris an arbitrary stop or so above the auto-iris setting to improve the subject's exposure. This may overexpose the lightest areas, but the subject would now be better exposed.

Although the auto-iris system has its own problems, these variations are often preferable to badly overexposed or underexposed images. And in practice, they may be too slight to worry about or may even pass unnoticed by the viewer. However, they are still there. Your decision about how to respond to these challenges all depends on how critical the final result is.

7.17 CAMERA ADJUSTMENTS

Manufacturers create a default that will give the camera operator the best average setting. Generally these settings produce a good image. However, there are times when a few adjustments can lead to great images. Our impressions of picture quality are very subjective. It is surprising how often we prefer a picture that looks just a little warmer or has slightly exaggerated contrast when compared with the original scene.

The most common camera adjustments relate to the lens, focus, lens aperture, shutter, video gain, and white balance. These changes can usually be completed on the camera or with a camera control unit (Figure 7.20). Within certain limitations, almost all of these areas also can be adjusted with editing

FIGURE 7.20
Instead of using a white card to white-balance the camera, one can use light blue cards for the color balance process, resulting in a warmer image.
(Photos courtesy of Vortex.)

software. Image quality can be altered in a number of ways, for a specific shot or perhaps for an entire scene:

- *Sharpness.* Sharpness can be adjusted (or manipulated) by the use of special-effect filters (mist, soft focus, ripple, etc.) and by defocusing the lens.
- *Brightness.* Brightness can be adjusted with the lens aperture or *video gain.*
- *Tonal range and contrast.* Tone and contrast can be modified by adjusting the *gamma* (higher gamma settings produce a coarser, exaggerated contrast; lower settings result in thin and reduced tonal contrasts). Lowering the picture's *black level* moves all picture tones toward black and crushes the lowest tones. Raising the *black level* lightens all picture tones but does not reveal detail in blackest tones.
- *Color intensity.* Increased *saturation* emphasizes the strength of color. Reduced saturation (diluting with white) gives a more pastel effect.
- *Color fidelity.* To simulate firelight or moonlight or make a picture warmer or cooler, shooting with "wrong" *color temperature* filters or gels may suffice. Otherwise, color balance can be changed by adjusting the video gain, white balance, black level, or gamma of the separate red, green, or blue color channels (Figure 7.21).

FIGURE 7.21
Camera remote control unit (CCU). The CCU can be used from a remote location to control the main electronic adjustments in the camera that affect picture quality (exposure, black level, gain, etc.).
(Photo courtesy of JVC.)

Changing Camera Settings

Changes in black level or gamma should only be made if a waveform monitor is available. I would never suggest altering individual RGB settings in camera. These changes should be left until post. Furthermore, whatever settings you choose to alter, I would recommend that you always carefully mark the original settings of the controls so that they can be returned to their original positions/settings, thus restoring the camera to its former status (Figure 7.22).

—Tony Grant, Producer/Director

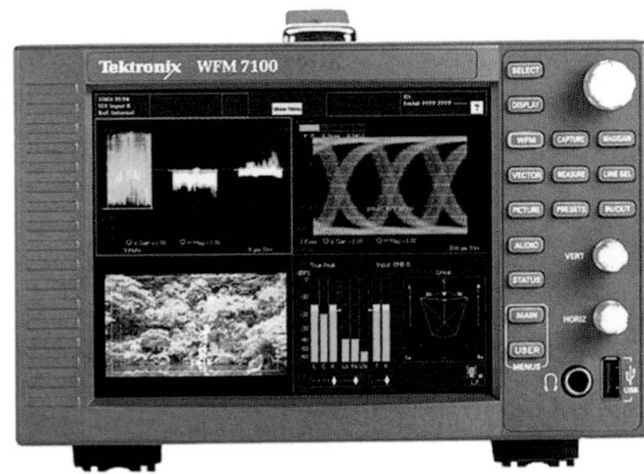

FIGURE 7.22
Waveform monitors are used when adjusting camera settings.
(Photo courtesy of Tektronix.)

7.18 PRACTICAL SOLUTIONS

When shooting a scene that contains a variety of tones, it may not be possible to accommodate the entire range. There are times when the director may have to accept that the lightest or the darkest areas will be lost in detail-less highlights or shadows. However, a few other options can be utilized to enhance the image in some limited situations.

Graduated Filters

When shooting in the field, there are times when you will find that the main subject is properly exposed, but distant skies are far too bright and distracting. This can be a particular problem when the foreground subjects are dark toned.

A graduated filter can often help you to overcome this dilemma. Its upper section has a neutral gray tint, which reduces the brightness of the image in that part of the picture. So it will "hold back" the overbright skies while leaving anything in the clear lower section unaffected.

Graduated filters have a gradual tonal transition, giving a soft blend between the treated and untreated areas. There are also graduated filters that can be used to create a deliberate effect (Figure 7.23). One-half of the filter may be orange and the other half clear or blue tinted. Some color filters have a central horizontal orange or yellow band, which, with care, may simulate the effect of a sunset.

(A)

(B)

(C)

FIGURE 7.23
(A) A graduated filter. (B) A scene shown without the use of a filter. (C) Here the camera operator used a graduated filter to enhance the sky.
(Photos courtesy of Tiffen.)

The main disadvantages of this otherwise useful device are the following:

- The filter will not work for every shot; it only works in specific situations.
- You cannot pan or tilt the camera when using this filter, or the effect will be obvious to the viewer.

Tonal Adjustments

How successfully can a camera reproduce the scene that is being shot? The tones that are seen on the screen are usually expected to correspond exactly to those in the scene. However, in practice, video has a tendency to exaggerate or to reduce apparent tonal contrasts in the reproduced picture. At the lightest and darkest extremes, video cannot distinguish between subtle differences in brightness, so those tones appear merged into dense shadow or blank highlights.

As we saw earlier, if there is a difficulty in seeing detail or tonal differences in shadows, trying to improve things by opening up the lens aperture will probably overexpose the lightest tones. Extra video amplification won't help either. Some cameras include a *black stretch* control, which will make shadow detail clearer and improve tonal gradation in darker tones. There may even be corresponding camera circuitry to improve reproduction of the lightest tones.

TEN COMMANDMENTS OF SHOOTING VIDEO

1. *White balance must be done.* Don't forget to white balance your camera in every lighting situation.
2. *Take plenty of recording material.* Take two to three times as much recording medium (flash memory, hard drives, or tape) than you think you will need. It is better to have too much than not enough.
3. *Take more batteries than you think you can possibly use.* Also, take your power adapter and charger with you even if you think you won't be near power ... you never know.
4. *Use manual focus.* Since auto-focus always searches around as you move your camera or your subject moves, you have more control when you manually focus the camera. Plus, it also saves your battery for other things.
5. *Don't zoom when shooting.* (Okay, you can do it sometimes.). However, zooming during the shooting of a production is often the sign of an amateur. Don't overuse it.
6. *Get a mic.* Use an external microphone to capture your audio. The in-camera microphone picks up distracting camera sounds. Also, always monitor your audio with a headphone. Not listening to your sound is like not looking at your viewfinder.
7. *Use a tripod.* There is nothing like a steady shot. Most professionals use tripods 90% of the time.
8. *Don't use a tripod.* Okay, I know that this sounds like I just contradicted #7... oh well. Video is made to capture motion—either your subject's motion or your camera's motion. There is nothing like a dynamic shot, such as following someone through a crowd. This movement may require more takes and is difficult to master. When successful, it really adds energy to a production.

9. *Make sure that you shoot plenty of footage.* You don't want to have to go back to shoot additional cover footage. Shoot plenty of cutaways and extra material. Today's recording medium is cheap.
10. *Take care of your gear.* You need it to work. Keep it in protective cases, keep it from dust, and keep the lenses clean.

HANDLING THE CAMERA

7.19 Panning and Tilting

If it is not possible to get a sufficiently wide shot of the subject to show it completely, or if the distant view does not have enough detail, there are two general solutions.

The first possibility is that a series of separate shots can be taken, which are then edited to build an overall image in the minds of your audience. However, when developing this sequence, avoid amassing a disjointed, random collection of images.

Alternatively, the camera can be panned or tilted carefully and systematically over the scene to relate various parts (Figures 7.24 and 7.25). Take care, though, to avoid a series of brief, erratic pans or long, "empty" pans that wander over unimportant things. Each pan needs to have a clear purpose and finish by settling on an interesting feature of the scene. Above all, avoid panning from side to side over the scene. Although this can be a great temptation, you are not likely to use these sequences when you see the results.

FIGURE 7.24
A pan shot is when the camera pivots left or right on a camera mount, such as a tripod, or as a handheld camera. In a pan shot, the camera mount or handheld operator pivots the camera.
(Photo courtesy of Vortex Media.)

FIGURE 7.25
A tilt shot pivots the camera up or down on a camera mount. The correct command is "tilt up" or "tilt down."

Like all camerawork, panning and tilting should be smooth and controlled. Above all, avoid overshooting, such as going beyond the final point and then having to correct the shot by reversing the pan a little. It draws attention to the error. Ideally, each movement should be brought to a smooth finish. If the pan has a jerky start or finish, is hesitant, its speed is uneven, or it wavers up and down, the result will look crude in the finished production.

Don't be tempted to pan or tilt too quickly because the image may become an indecipherable blur. Most of us fall into that trap when first shooting a landscape. We pan briskly, trying to show everything, only to find that the result on the screen is extremely disappointing as details break up ("strobe") during the movement.

FIGURE 7.26 When following the subject in a wide arc, the camera operator's feet should face the midpoint of the arc. This will allow the camera operator to pan smoothly with the action.

Try panning or tilting across a scene so that it takes an object roughly 5 seconds to travel from one edge of the screen to the other. That is about the fastest rate that can be used to avoid movement breakup. There are situations in which a rapid *whip pan* or *zip pan* can be used deliberately for a startling dramatic effect, but the technique is seldom used.

If a handheld camera is required to follow the action over a wide arc, camera operators should not try to turn their bodies on their heels. Instead, the body should be facing midway through the action, ready to make a smooth, balanced movement, and the camera operator will twist his or her body to follow the action. The result will be much more controlled. Keeping the knees slightly bent can also help (Figure 7.26). When using a tripod, remember to check that it is level before panning, or the framing may move upward or downward during the pan.

7.20 FOLLOWING MOVING SUBJECTS

There is a lot more to taking shots of a moving subject than simply keeping up with it. Dealing effectively with a moving camera is the difference between a good camera operator and a great camera operator.

When one is handholding a camera still, anything moving around in the shot can quickly reach the edge of the frame and move out of sight, particularly if it is moving quickly in a "tight" shot that is filling most of the screen. There are several ways to deal with this situation:

- The moving subject can be allowed to *move out of the frame altogether* ("exit"). This is a good idea if the director wants the audience's attention to move on to a new subject.

- The camera operator can widen the shot by zooming out or moving back to include the movement. This is often the best solution if someone is pacing back and forth or waving his or her arms around (Figure 7.27).
- The operator can pan or tilt the camera to keep the subject in the shot (for example, to follow somebody as the person moves around a room). However, don't use too close a shot here. Not only will the subject itself look cramped in the frame, but it will also be difficult to follow the action smoothly.
- The camera position can be moved, such as an arc, so that the subject remains in shot.
- The camera can move along with the subject, such as a tracking shot, keeping the subject in the frame throughout the action.
- Instead of following the movement, you can let it leave the frame and then pick up the action from a new viewpoint.

FIGURE 7.27
It can be difficult to shoot close-ups during fast-moving action. Generally the camera operator needs to zoom out a little to effectively cover the action.

If a single camera is being used to cover the action, the camera operator would need to stop recording, move to the next position, set up the new shot, and begin recording again. In the meantime, some of the action has been missed—unless, of course, the action can be repeated. In that situation, the action begins again from just before the camera was moved to the second position. If two or more cameras are being used, none of the action has to be missed; just cut to the second camera at the right moment.

All of these methods work. The camera operator or director must consider which one is most appropriate, both artistically and practically.

7.21 FRAMING MOVEMENT

At first sight, it seems logical to keep a moving subject exactly in the middle of the picture. However, the image will look unbalanced and boring. Instead, when panning with a moving subject that is running toward something, position the subject a little behind the center of the frame. If the subject is running away from something (such as a thief in a police chase scene), keep the subject just over the center frame (Figure 7.28). The image will look more dynamic; the faster the movement, the greater the offset. Most important, don't let the subject "move around the frame" through uneven planning.

FIGURE 7.28
When shooting a fast-moving subject, keep the subject behind the center of the frame. The image will be more dynamic.
(Photo by Mark Stokl.)

7.22 WALKING

Handheld shooting is difficult. Unless the director is looking for a bouncy camera style, handholding a camera takes a lot of practice. It is not as easy as it seems to keep the camera level steady and well-composed shots in sharp focus.

When the subject moves away, the obvious response is to have the camera operator walk with the person. However, this can be a significant problem. The route has to be checked in advance to ensure that there are no carpets, steps, cables, people, or posts in the pathway. The camera operator could easily meet unseen hazards as he or she concentrates on the viewfinder image. That is why experienced camera operators develop habits of glancing around (to check out their surroundings and nearby action) and keeping both eyes open when using an eyepiece viewfinder. The safest and best strategy is to use a camera assistant who can get people out of the camera operator's way or guide the operator around problematic obstacles (Figure 7.29).

FIGURE 7.29
Camera assistants are invaluable to a handheld or Steadicam operator. The assistants can guide the operator around obstacles.

There is always a certain amount of bounce in the camera's shot as the camera operator walks, especially if he or she is moving quickly. This unevenness may be unimportant or even dramatic if the camera is following someone's moves over uneven ground, through a crowd, or through a forest. But it can be distracting when the operator is walking within a building.

If moving shots, particularly over rough terrain, are required, the most practical way to avoid camera bounce is to attach the camera to a stabilizer unit such as the Steadicam. This camera mount compensates for irregular movements. There are also several forms of optical or electronic *image stabilization,* which diminish vibrations and smooth out variations.

7.23 SHOOTING FROM VEHICLES

Whenever shooting from any vehicle, there are a number of points worth bearing in mind:

- Resist the temptation to rest the lens or the camera on the glass or the vehicle's body, since vibration can damage the equipment and blur the images.
- Smeary, rain-speckled, dusty, or tinted windows can significantly degrade picture quality, especially if sunlight is falling on them. The images will show a flattened contrast, defocused blurs, and changing color values that become particularly obvious when edited with other shots.

The position of the camera in the vehicle will influence the audience impact of the images. Facing forward, subjects appear to move toward the camera, getting closer and increasingly clearer. This is a powerful viewpoint that provides continual interest. A rear view, however, shows everything moving away from the camera, and the audience's interest tends to fall. No sooner does something come into shot than it quickly becomes too small to see properly. Side windows are useful for shooting distant subjects, but anything close rapidly moves across the screen out of focus.

Shooting someone inside a moving car requires a certain amount of agility. A wide-angle (short-focus) lens is essential because it enables the camera operator to get sufficiently wide shots of the driver. Typical camera positions include the following: seated beside the driver, crouched in the passenger's foot space, or leaning over from a rear seat. Cameras can also be mounted outside the car, using beanbags, bolt-on brackets, or suction-held pads (Figure 7.30).

FIGURE 7.30
Many devices can be used to secure a camera to a moving car. This photo illustrates how a Cine Saddle (a sophisticated beanbag) can be tied onto a car for forward (toward the road) or backward (toward the driver) shots (also see Figure 8.15).

THE BASICS OF SHOOTING

7.24 Practical Conditions

There are no absolute "rules" for shooting effective images. In fact, if the images are arranged too systematically, the results can look boring and artificial. But there are a number of situations that need to be avoided.

During a busy shooting schedule, there generally is not time to experiment with the composition of each shot. Many times, quick decisions have to be made because a live event is unfolding, there may be production or broadcast deadlines, the crew is standing by, and, from a practical standpoint, time is money. So the pressure is generally on to make quick decisions. However, if the camera operator and director understand composition basics, they will know what to look out for and realize how to adjust the shot for the most appropriate effect. Once camera operators recognize the characteristics that make images unsuccessful, and many are a matter of common sense, they will avoid them instinctively.

Unlike a painter, who can arrange objects on the canvas to suit his or her ideas, a video camera operator usually has to make the most of what is already there. But that does not mean that what the viewer sees cannot be controlled. The director and camera operator can do a great deal to change an image's appeal. They can select the viewpoint carefully, choose the appropriate lens angle, or control the way the shot is framed. Sometimes they can reposition the subject or some of the objects to further improve the image.

SHOOTING IN 3D

Audiences tend to want to explore a 3D frame longer than they would a 2D frame. Since there is more information to be imparted, most shots tend to stay on the screen a bit longer.

—Steve Schklaire, CEO, 3ality Digital Systems

When shooting in 3D everything is multidimensional. That means all the objects seen on the screen are typically in constant focus as they are with human vision. This is one of the reasons a rack focus effect in 3D looks uncomfortable to the eye and should be avoided.

—David Kenneth, President, I.E. Effects

7.25 SELECTING THE RIGHT SHOTS

Whether you are shooting a single-camera or a multicamera production, you must create a smooth-flowing sequence that makes sense to the audience. This will not happen automatically.

The worst thing you can do is to take a series of random "good shots" of the subject without any thought about how they are going to be interrelated on the screen. Planning is essential before the shoot begins. Thinking through the required shots and how they can be composed in advance will save time for everyone once the production begins. It also allows more production time because less time is spent experimenting and trying to make a decision.

7.26 PERSUASIVE SHOTS

Picture making is not just about creating beautiful pictures; it is about providing appropriate pictures. There may even be moments when an ugly shot is deliberately introduced in order to shock the audience with harsh reality. The camera too easily glamorizes. A scene of squalid decay can become a vision of interesting textures and hues in the evening sunlight.

A well-chosen sequence of shots should do more than just illustrate the subject for the audience. The chosen and arranged images express a point of view; they show how the director has interpreted the situation, what he or she wants to say about it. That is what creating programs is all about. It is almost as if the director were there beside the viewers, guiding their choices and interpretations of the events.

When showing the audience images of a bustling marketplace, the director is offering an unspoken invitation: "Look around at anything that happens to interest you." More often, though, the director wants to draw the audience's attention to certain aspects of a scene. The director is selecting shots that will invite the audience to concentrate on an interesting feature: "See how this object differs from that one. Notice the intricate details there." Or on another occasion the director might be saying, "See how she is reacting to what he said. See what she is doing. Watch how she is doing it."

7.27 GUIDING THE VIEWER THROUGH THE SCENE

As each shot appears on the screen, the audience is seeing and hearing it for the first time. In an instant, the audience has to interpret what the director has selected to put there. It is not surprising that viewers can occasionally become confused.

Unless the director is careful, the audience may "look at the wrong thing"—that is, the viewer's attention might alight on something else in the picture that is more prominent, more colorful, or more interesting.

The duration of a shot is important too. If the director hangs on to any shot for too long, the audience will begin to lose interest. If the shots are too brief, they may flick past the viewer's eyes without entering the brain.

The director's goal is to help the viewers understand, to guide their thoughts, whether the scene is describing a technical process or telling a joke. The director does not want to confuse or distract them by irrelevancies. It is important to present a logical sequence of ideas that the audience can easily follow. The audience cannot stop to ask what the director meant or to reread what was said. Viewers have to get the point the first time around.

If the director does not take the trouble to choose shots carefully, people have to look around each picture, trying to decide what it is all about, correctly or incorrectly. If they do not have any idea of what they are supposed to be looking at (or don't find it interesting), they will look at whatever draws their attention. Random pictures produce random thoughts.

Occasionally, the director may actually *want* to puzzle or intrigue the audience in order to create a dramatic or comic buildup of tension. The camera enters a quiet room. The viewers are left wondering; they see a threatening shadow of someone standing there, but a moment later they realize that it is only coming from garments on a coatrack. They have been fooled.

But, in most situations, if the audience is left puzzled, wondering where the shadow is, or what it is supposed to be, or why they have been switched away from something they found interesting to this new unexplained scene, then something is very wrong. Some directors do this all too often when they try to introduce some variety or do something different. The shot cuts to a building reflected in a puddle, or some wayside flowers, or a dog sleeping beside the road, or to some other image that seems to have nothing to do with the story. Even shooting the subject through a decorative foreground screen can be puzzling at times.

If a shot is appropriate and moves the story forward, it can be as unusual as the director likes. But if the audience is distracted by it or begins to think about how interesting the shot is rather than focusing on the subject, then the experiment has failed.

7.28 CLUTTER

If the audience's attention is not guided to specific features of the scene, viewers are just as likely to look at the wrong thing or become bored.

When an image is absolutely full of things (a crowd of people, shelves of articles, or a wall of paintings), it is hard for the viewer to concentrate on any one of them properly, or even see them clearly. The director may be trying to say, "Aren't there a lot of different versions?" or "See how big the collection is!" However, the viewers could end up feeling as though they missed out, especially when they can't see any of the items clearly.

It is often far better to *isolate* the item the audience needs to see:

- Get closer (tighter framing).
- Change the camera's viewpoint.
- Use a shallow depth of field so that only the main subject is in focus (Figure 7.31).
- Move it apart from the rest.
- Use contrasting tones.
- Use strong compositional lines.
- Position the subject higher in the frame.
- Use lighting to isolate the item (light pool, shadows).

7.29 I CAN'T SEE IT PROPERLY

There will be times when the director will deliberately set out to intrigue, to mystify, and to keep the audience guessing. Diffusion or dramatic lighting may

FIGURE 7.31
Depth of field can be used to isolate a subject by emphasizing where the audience should look.

be used to make the subject look strange, mysterious, or just different. But these are the exceptions. Most times the director will want the audience to see the subject clearly.

Look out for those moments when the viewer cannot see important aspects of the show because the shot is too distant, or something is shadowing the subject, or even someone's thumb is over the label that the viewers are supposed to be reading.

Close-up shots are great for showing detail. But sometimes a close shot can prevent the audience from seeing enough of the subject. It may show a few cogs, when the audience really needs to see much more of a piece of machinery to understand how it works.

Although all of these situations are obvious, problems of this sort happen regularly.

COMPOSING PICTURES

7.30 Composition Rules and Guidelines

The goal of composition is to create an image that is attractive or that at least captures and keeps the audience's attention and effectively communicates the production's message. Throughout the years, a series of composition "rules" have been established. However, the word "rules" is not really appropriate for composition; they should be treated as guidelines. They are designed to be adapted, or even broken. Television would be boring if everyone composed every shot the same way. Your goal should be to look for imaginative ways to adapt or take advantage of these rules or guidelines. Don't let them imprison your creativity; instead, let them motivate and inspire you.

COMPOSING THE SHOT

Good composition does not have to be difficult. However, it does take careful planning if you are to get the best image. Here are some key factors to consider that will ensure that your images effectively communicate the message of the production:

- *Symbolism*. Does the image have meaning to the viewer? When viewers see the image, what do they immediately think of? Is that what you are trying to communicate?
- *Meaningful context*. The content of the image should allow the viewer to understand the subject better. Compose the shot in such a way that it includes a background, or foreground, that adds additional information or context to the image (Figure 7.32).
- *Motion and emotion*. The video images should give the audience the same emotional response that you had while shooting. Does the image portray emotion or motion in some way?

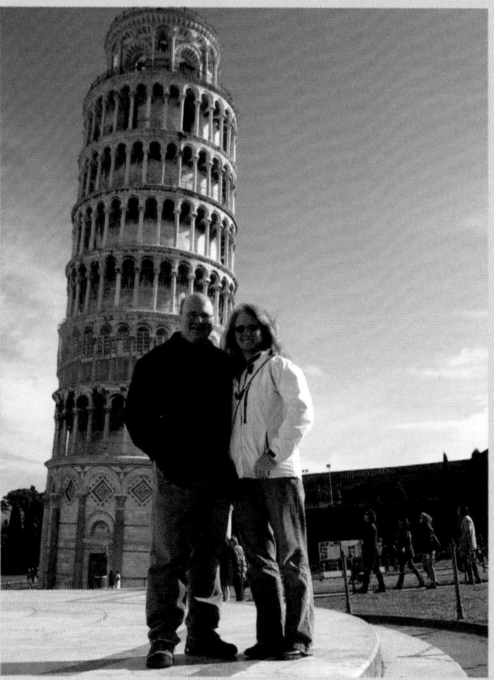

FIGURE 7.32
Because the image was shot with meaningful context, the viewer knows it was shot in Italy. *(Photo by Sarah Owens.)*

7.31 THE BRIEF SHOT

When we look at a still picture, whether it is on the printed page or hung in an art gallery, there is an opportunity to linger. We can scrutinize it for as long as we want.

On a television screen, shots do not encourage browsing. Each is there for only a brief time, from a fraction of a second to perhaps half a minute at most. Then another replaces it. Each shot has to make its point quickly. Each creates its own impact.

7.32 "BORING" IS IN THE MIND

What makes a shot boring? A lot depends on the audience's attitude toward what they are seeing. Any shot can be boring when someone personally finds little worth in looking at it or if the audience does not care to know who the people are, where they are, or what they are doing. That's why other people's vacation videos may lack some of the appeal for you that they have for those who took them.

A shot may seem to show just a boring stretch of ocean. But if the commentary tells us, "At this dangerous spot, after years of painstaking exploration, divers found the Spanish treasure ship," we look at the picture with new eyes, although in reality there isn't anything special to see! Without the influence of the commentary, such shots could be an instant yawn. But because our interest is aroused, and the images are there for only a short time, they attract and hold our attention.

So the appeal of any picture depends partly on what it *shows*, partly on what it is *about*, and partly on how *interested* the audience has been persuaded to be in it.

A shot of open desert may quickly pall, but when the audience sees a tiny moving shape in the distance, its curiosity is aroused. What happens if the director continues to hold that shot? Usually, people lose interest. But in different circumstances, while viewing exactly the same shot, they may be on the edge of their seats, waiting perhaps to discover which of the travelers has managed to survive.

If there is *too much* to see in the picture, the eye flits around hopefully but probably finishes up concentrating on nothing. If there is *too little* in the shot, attention soon falls.

When there are no visual accents to grab the attention, the eye wanders. But if things can be arranged so that the main subject stands out from its surroundings, then the audience will concentrate on it and is less likely to look at other things in the picture.

7.33 SHOTS THAT ARE DIFFERENT

It is tempting to devise shots that are *different*, shots that make the eye stop and wonder. Wildly distorted perspectives from a close wide-angle lens, very low-angle shots, or pictures using weird reflections are fine when you need them for a dramatic or comic effect. But extremely unusual viewpoints don't just make a picture look different; they also draw attention to themselves. They may distract the audience from the real subject.

7.34 FITTING THE FRAME

The TV screen has a horizontal rectangular shape (unless you are putting cell phone video on a website), and many subjects fit comfortably into this format (Figure 7.33). So we can get quite a close-up shot of them, filling the entire screen, without losing parts outside the frame area.

Others are too tall for the screen. So they can be shown completely only through a long shot, or they can be shot in sections, either by panning over them or by cutting between a series of close-up shots. Sometimes when the subject does not fit the screen, an oblique viewpoint must be selected in order to get it all into the picture.

As the camera gets closer, parts of the subject are bound to be lost outside the frame of the picture. Most television receivers are adjusted to get the maximum picture size possible, so they cut off the edges of the shot. To make sure that the audience does not miss anything important, such as titling, it is important to compose the shot to keep these details within the "safe area" of the screen (Figure 7.34).

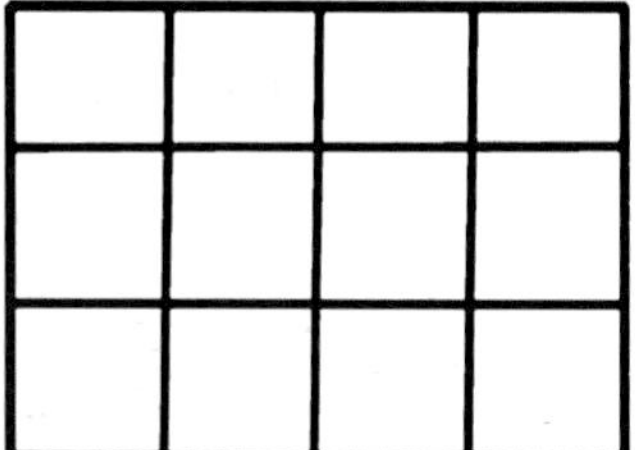

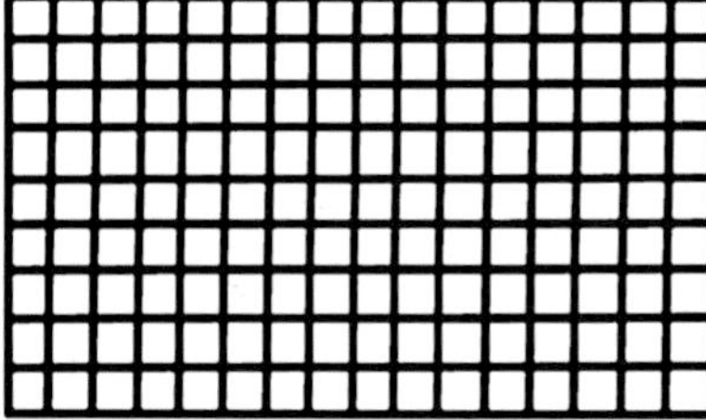

FIGURE 7.33
Television screen ratios: The proportions of a standard television picture are four units horizontally and three units vertically. If a picture is 18 inches wide, it is 13.5 inches high. In the HDTV 16 × 9 format, if the image is 16 inches across, it is 9 inches high.

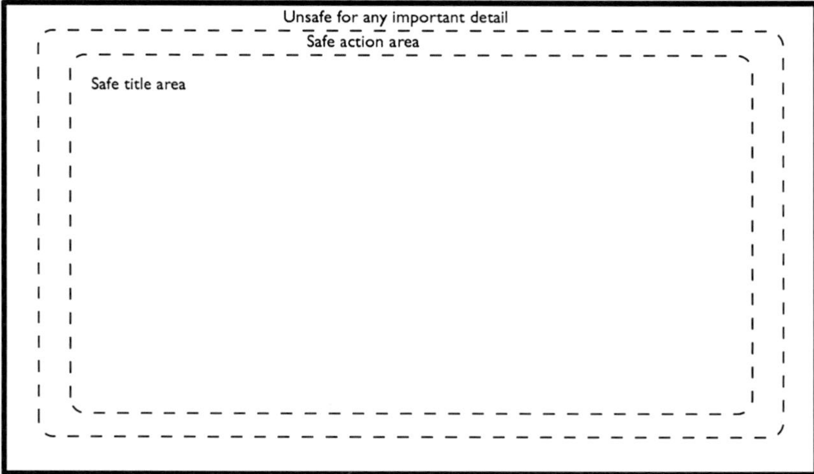

FIGURE 7.34
The picture edges are usually lost on the screen (as a result of overscanning the picture tube). To ensure that no important action or titling is lost, keep it within the borders shown.

If a person is shot so that the frame chops off their head, hands, or feet, the result looks odd. But if you alter the shot slightly so that the frame cuts part-way along the individual's limbs, the effect may seem much more natural.

FRAMING PEOPLE

- Don't let the frame cut people at natural joints; it is more attractive to cut at intermediate points.
- Avoid having people seem to lean or sit on the edge of the picture.
- If the shot is framed too close to contain the subject's motion, the subject will keep moving in and out of the picture. The result is disconcerting and distracting (Figure 7.35).

FIGURE 7.35
If shooting too close, the camera operator may not be able to keep up with the movement of the subject.
(Photo by Josh Taber.)

It is interesting to see how the frame of the screen affects how comfortable we feel with the picture. If a shot is taken in which the subject just fills the screen, it will look cramped and hemmed in by the frame. Get a little closer, so that parts of the subject are cut off, and all at once the shot looks great. Take a shot in which the subject only fills a small part of the screen, and we may get the impression that there is too much air around the subject.

7.35 WATCH THE BACKGROUND

Directors and camera operators need to be detail oriented. New directors often concentrate so much on the main subject that they miss things in the background that pop out to the audience. Items in the background of a shot can cause the audience to easily become distracted, moving them away from the program's content. Repositioning the camera may be all it takes to create a great shot (Figure 7.36).

FIGURE 7.36
While the tree is beautiful, the portable restrooms in the background distract the audience. By simply moving the camera to another angle, the attention is drawn back to the tree.

In order to draw the audience's attention to your primary subject, it is important to simplify the background of the images so that the audience knows where to look. Otherwise, they are left searching through the image, trying to figure out what they are seeing (Figure 7.37).

FIGURE 7.37
Simplify the background. The first photo shows an airplane in front of a ship—the airplane is difficult to see. By shooting the plane with a simple background, the audience is drawn to the airplane.
(Photos by Sarah Owens.)

7.36 DIVIDING THE IMAGE INTO THIRDS

If the screen is divided into even proportions (halves, quarters), either vertically or horizontally, the result is generally boring. For example, a horizon located exactly halfway up the frame should be avoided.

The *rule of thirds* is a useful aid to composing the picture. Divide the screen into thirds both horizontally and vertically (Figure 7.38). The main subject should be on one of those lines or, ideally, on the intersection of two of the lines. The thirds rule suggests that the main subject should not be in the middle of the image (Figure 7.39). Instead, it should be placed before or after the center of the image, depending on the effect the director would like. Keep in mind that the "thirds" is merely a guideline; sometimes it may be closer to a fifth or somewhere in between. Remember also that, ultimately, the subjects' positions depend on their size, shape, tone, the background, and their relative importance. Good camera operators instinctively compose shots with these features in the back of their minds.

FIGURE 7.38
The thirds rule suggests that the main subject should not be in the exact center of the image.
(Photo by Sarah Owens.)

FIGURE 7.39
While placing the main subject in the exact center of the image allows formal balance, it can be boring. By placing the subject slightly to the left or right of the frame's centerline, the image becomes more dynamic.
(Photo by Chad Crouch.)

7.37 SHOOTING FROM DIFFERENT ANGLES

The majority of the images seen on television have been shot at the eye level of the camera operator. Shoot from high angles looking down on the subject. Look at the scene from low angles. Try to find angles that communicate the subject to the audience and hold their attention.

When shooting people, low-angle shots make them look important (Figure 7.40). A high-angle shot, which looks down on the subject, can make the person look small and insignificant.

FIGURE 7.40
Low-angle shots portray strength while high-angle shots can make people look inferior.

7.38 SHOWING SCALE

The audience does not always understand the size of the subject being shot. When shooting a subject that is very large or very small, it is important to compose the image in a way that puts the subject in context so that the audience can understand the size without being told (Figure 7.41).

FIGURE 7.41
If shooting something unusually large or small, show it next to something that the audience is familiar with so that the audience can understand its size.

7.39 FRAMING THE SUBJECT

Framing the subject can add depth to the scene. The frame could be a tree, a fence, or, better yet, something that adds meaningful context to the subject. It is important that the frame not detract from the subject or message (Figure 7.42).

FIGURE 7.42
Flowers frame the subject.
(Photo by Josh Taber.)

7.40 LEADING LINES

Leading lines composition is when the lines within the image lead the viewers' eyes to what the director wants them to look at. These lines can create specific feelings:

- Horizontal lines can portray calm and tranquility.
- Vertical lines can show strength and dignity.
- Diagonal lines can show movement and speed.
- Curved lines can portray serenity.
- Converging lines can show depth (Figure 7.43).

7.41 HEADROOM

If there is not enough space between the top of a person's head and the top of the picture (too little "headroom"), the frame will seem to crush down on the

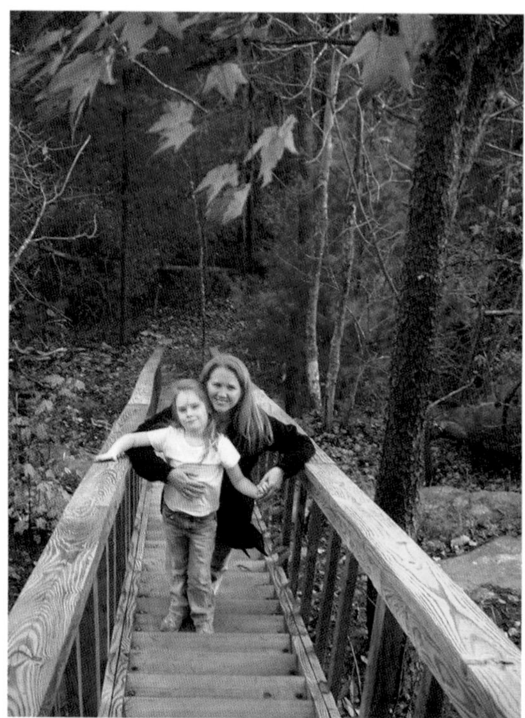

FIGURE 7.43
Converging leading lines portray depth in the image. Also, note that the leaves do provide some framing.

subject, and parts of the head may be cut off by the television overscan. If there is too much space, then the image becomes unbalanced and the audience's attention goes up to the space to see what is there (Figure 7.44). The subject's height in the frame alters the feeling of the picture's vertical balance, so when taking shots of people, always look out for the headroom. It will be considerable in a long shot and will reduce correspondingly as the shot gets closer. As a very rough guide, keep the eyes at about a third of the screen height from the top of the picture. However, headroom is influenced by whatever else is visible in the top of the picture.

FIGURE 7.44
The first image has too little headroom, the second image has too much headroom, and the last one is correct.
(Photo by Josh Taber.)

7.42 GOOD BALANCE

Looking at a well-balanced image, we see that it has a settled, stable look. An unbalanced shot, on the other hand, has an insecure, uncertain feel to it.

Sometimes that might be just what the director wants. An unstable, incomplete look increases tension and creates dramatic impact. An easy way to achieve this is to make the picture topheavy or lopsided. Usually shots are arranged so that they look balanced and complete.

Other subjects within the frame can significantly impact the balance. The impact of other subjects depends on their relative sizes and tones. Obviously, a large subject a long distance away may appear smaller than a tiny object close to the camera. It is the effect that counts. A large subject on one side of the frame can actually be balanced with several smaller ones on the other side. It is all a matter of their relative sizes, tones, and distance from the center of the frame (Figure 7.45).

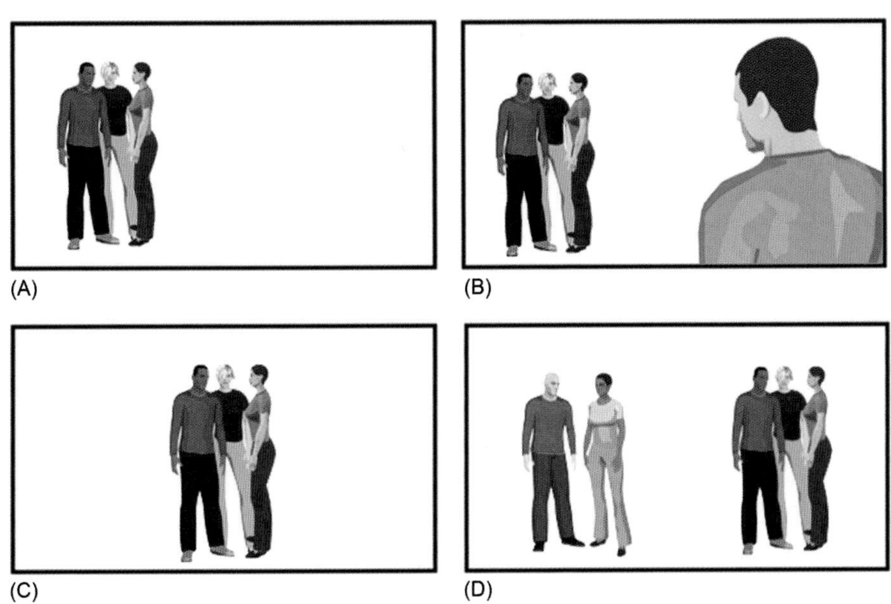

FIGURE 7.45
A group that would look lopsided and unbalance the picture (A) can be counterbalanced by another mass in another part of the screen (B). If centered (C), the picture is balanced, even without other subjects, but continual centering gets monotonous. Different-sized masses can balance each other, but take care not to split the audience's attention (D).

The key to interesting, well-balanced images is not shots that are continually, monotonously centered every time, but shots that are balanced across the frame, depending on the tones and proportions of the subjects we see there.

7.43 CHANGING THE PERSPECTIVE

You can vary the perspective and position of things in a picture simply by doing the following:

- *Adjusting the camera's distance.* The closer things are to the camera, the larger they appear in the frame. Even a slight change in the camera's distance can affect the apparent size of foreground items considerably, while anything in the background can remain about the same size in the picture.
- *Changing the camera height.* Lower the camera's viewpoint, and things in the foreground may become more prominent until they dominate the entire image. However, raise the camera a little, and it may be possible to shoot past them altogether. The viewer may not even realize that they are there.
- *Adjusting the lens angle.* Use a wide-angle lens and everything looks much smaller and farther away than usual. Size diminishes rapidly with distance from the camera. Even items relatively close to the lens appear farther away than normal. The wide-angle shot generally emphasizes distance and depth, noticeably distorting subjects in the foreground.
- Conversely, when a telephoto or narrow-angle lens is used, the reverse happens. Everything looks much closer than usual. Relative sizes do not seem to change much with distance. Even things that are far off still look pretty close. Depth appears reduced.

So by selecting an appropriate lens and adjusting the camera's distance, you can significantly control the perspective of the shot.

7.44 GROUPING (UNITY)

When showing a number of items in an image, avoid having them scattered around the frame. It is better to centralize the viewers' attention by grouping subjects in some way; otherwise the audience is more likely to look around the image at random. Grouping creates a sense of unity in a picture by pulling its subjects together.

Sometimes groupings can be created by deliberately positioning the subjects to suit the composition. Other times the camera's viewpoint is deliberately selected to frame the subjects in a way that creates unity.

7.45 CAMERA VIEWPOINT

The location of the camera, in relation to the subject, will have a strong influence on what the subject looks like to the viewers and how they feel about it. The smaller a subject appears in the frame, the less important it seems to become, and less detail is visible. Its surroundings become more prominent and can take attention from the subject.

Although closer shots emphasize the subject, care needs to be taken that they do not become so enlarged on the screen that the effect is overpowering. Really close-up shots often lose scale and make the audience forget the true size and proportions of the subject.

Looking down at any subject tends to make it look less impressive than looking up at it. Although steeply angled viewpoints are usually too dramatic for most purposes, even a slight variation from an eye-level position can affect the impact of a subject.

7.46 DISTORTIONS

Controlled distortion can be an effective camera/lens technique in appropriate situations. For example, use a close wide-angle lens to distort a Halloween mask and create a frightening effect. Or use this technique to make a small group of trees look like a threatening forest.

However, take care so that shapes do not become badly distorted by accident. Let's use an example of shooting an oil painting situated high on the wall of a historic house. Either to avoid light reflections or to get an unobstructed view, the camera operator may decide to take close shots of it from a side position using a telephoto lens. While he or she may get the shot, the result may be a squashed version of the painting that does little justice to the original.

When shooting in a small room, you may need to use a wide-angle lens to prevent everything from looking too close. However, there is a good chance that now the room will look much larger than it really is, and if people appear in the shot, they may appear warped because of wide-angle distortions. Most people really don't want to look as though they have gained weight (Figure 7.46)!

FIGURE 7.46
When using a wide-angle lens, close to the subject, the subject will distort.

ANTICIPATING EDITING

An editing session will go much more smoothly if the camera operator keeps the final postproduction editing phase in mind when shooting.

—Kathy Bruner, Producer

7.47 CONTINUITY

Every time the camera is set up to take the next action shot, think about *editing;* otherwise you may end up with a series of shots that do not fit together smoothly. This especially happens when repositioning the camera to shoot a repeated scene from a different location.

The most frequent problems are as follows:

- Part of the action is *missing.*
- The action shot from another angle does not *match* that from a previous shot of the subject.
- The *direction* of the action has changed between successive shots.
- The *shot sizes* are too similar or too extreme.
- Action leaves the frame and reenters it on the same side.
- Successive shots show continuity differences; for example, the talent is and then is not wearing eyeglasses, shows different attitudes/expressions, or is dressed differently.

7.48 IMPROVING EDITING FLEXIBILITY

When shooting, editing flexibility can help in various ways.

Avoid Brief Shots

- Always tape the *run-in* and *run-out* to an action to allow editing flexibility. Do not wait to record until the instant the action starts. Extra footage on each side of the action, or *head* or *tails,* will give the editor the opportunity to utilize dissolves and fades and will allow him or her to trim the footage in an optimal way.
- Where possible, start and finish a long panning shot with a still shot.

Extra Editing Material

- Always shoot some *cutaways* showing the surroundings, general scene, bystanders' reactions, and so on.
- Determine whether specific reaction shots/nod shots are needed.
- It is sometimes helpful to shoot the same scene at a leisurely pace and at a faster pace (slow pan and faster pan) to allow editing flexibility.

Faulty Takes

- Do not record over an unsuccessful shot. Parts of it may be usable during the editing process.
- If an action sequence goes wrong, it is sometimes better to retake it entirely. At other times, just change the camera angle (or shot size), and retake the action from just before the error was made (a "pickup" shot).

Establishing Shots

- Always begin shooting with a wide shot of the scene (*establishing shot*), even if it is not used ultimately. This shot allows the editor to understand the placement of the other shots.
- Consider taking a long shot (*cover shot* or *master shot*) of all of the action in a scene, and then repeat the action while taking closer shots.

COMMON FAULTS WHILE SHOOTING

- Make sure that the camera was white balanced properly and the appropriate color correction filter was used.
- The camera operator must take the time to make sure that the lens is properly focused.
- The camera should be mounted on a tripod or some other type of mount as much as possible. Most people cannot handhold a camera very steadily, especially for an extended period of time.
- Taking the time to level the camera may be time-consuming but is essential—the horizons need to be straight.
- Each time the camera is repositioned, the headroom must be reviewed.
- Make sure that the subject is properly framed. Do not cut on a natural bend of a body.
- Advanced planning, possibly even including storyboarding, will help make sure that your shots are not too similar, the camera is at the right height, the focusing is on the right subject, and the necessary type of shot (CU, MS, or LS) is used.
- All subjects should not be center-frame: Keep the rule of thirds in mind when shooting.
- Think "transitions" as you select your shots.
- Carefully review the foregrounds and backgrounds of a scene for distraction objects.
- It is better to have a clip that is too long than too short. Make sure that you begin shooting before the action begins and continue shooting briefly after the action is complete.
- Zoom shots must be motivated; they need to be there for a reason.
- If panning is not smooth, the tripod may need to be adjusted.
- When the talent has to handle an object, it is important to practice with the talent so that they understand what you need them to do.

MORE SHOOTING TIPS

7.49 What Does a Filter Do?

Lens filters can be used in several ways:

- To reduce the image brightness in strong sunlight or to allow a wider lens aperture
- To give the picture an overall tint in order to:
  - correct the color temperature of the prevailing light
  - simulate lighting conditions, such as candlelight, a sunset, or firelight
- To reduce the overall image contrast
- To cut through haze on location (improve image contrast)
- To create an atmospheric effect, such as fog, mist, or haze
- To create a decorative effect, such as rays around highlights (starburst)
- To distort the image in various ways, such as creating a ripple effect
- To soften the image (such as localized or overall diffusion)
- To reduce a bright sky or to enhance clouds
- To suppress light reflections or glare

Filters also come in a number of different forms (Table 7.3). Some camera filters are made of plastic or glass and can be square or rectangular. These filters are slipped into a matt box, which is supported in front of the lens (Figure 7.47). Other glass filters are circular and screw into threads on the front of the lens. The third type of glass filter is a small piece of glass that is housed inside the camera, called a filter wheel, for quick selection. Most professional cameras include two or three filters in their filter wheel, with room for a couple of others. There are also digital filters that can be integrated into editing systems and allow the editor to experiment with a variety of filters.

7.50 CROSSING THE LINE

Camera viewpoints can easily confuse the audience's sense of direction and their impression of spatial relationships if care is not taken when selecting camera positions. For example, during a basketball game, if cameras are placed on both sides of the court, it is confusing to see a player running toward the left side of the screen and then, when the director cuts to the camera on the other side of the court, to see the player running toward the right side of the court.

To avoid this confusion, keep in mind that there is an axis of action (also called the action line, proscenium line, or eye line) that runs along the direction of the action. The camera must be kept on one side of this "line." It is generally not crossed when covering an action. It is possible to dolly across the line, or shoot along it, or change its direction by regrouping people, but cutting between cameras on both sides of this imaginary line produces a *reverse cut* or *jump cut* (Figures 7.48 and 7.49).

Table 7.3	The Most Common Types of Filters
Neutral density filter	Obtainable in a series of densities from 80.0% to 0.01% transmission. These transparent gray-tinted filters reduce the amount of light but do not affect the color quality. These filters can also be purchased as gels and placed over windows or other light sources to reduce the light intensity.
Color correction filter	Compensates for the color quality of the prevailing light. A “daylight filter” (light blue) adjusts the orange-yellow color quality of tungsten lighting to match the bluish quality of daylight.
Color conversion filter	Colored filter giving the entire picture a specific color. For example, a light blue filter simulating moonlight.
Ultraviolet (UV) filter	A coated filter that blocks the ultraviolet light that creates glare and reduces picture contrast when shooting in the open air.
Fog filter	A filter that diffuses the image and simulates a foggy or misty effect. There are a number of different types of these filters available, some with an etched or finely ground surface, to open-weave net material stretched across the lens.
Diffusion filter	Provides overall softening of the image, from slight “defocusing” to strong diffusion. Created by ribbing, embossing, or scribing the filter’s surface.
Star filter	A clear disc with a closely scribed or grooved grid, which produces multiray starburst patterns (e.g., 4, 6, 8 ray) around highlights and point light-sources. On turning the filter, the ray pattern rotates.
Graduated ND filter	A graduated neutral density filter that reduces the brightness of the upper part of the image (possibly the sky), while remaining clear below (see Section 7.17).
Polarizing filter	A filter material that is selective to light direction. Rotated to the appropriate angle, found by trial and error, this filter can selectively reduce light reflections from shiny surfaces (such as glass, water, metal, road surfaces), and darken blue skies, while making clouds more prominent.

FIGURE 7.47
Square or rectangular filters can be slid into a matt box like the one pictured here.
(Photo courtesy of JVC.)

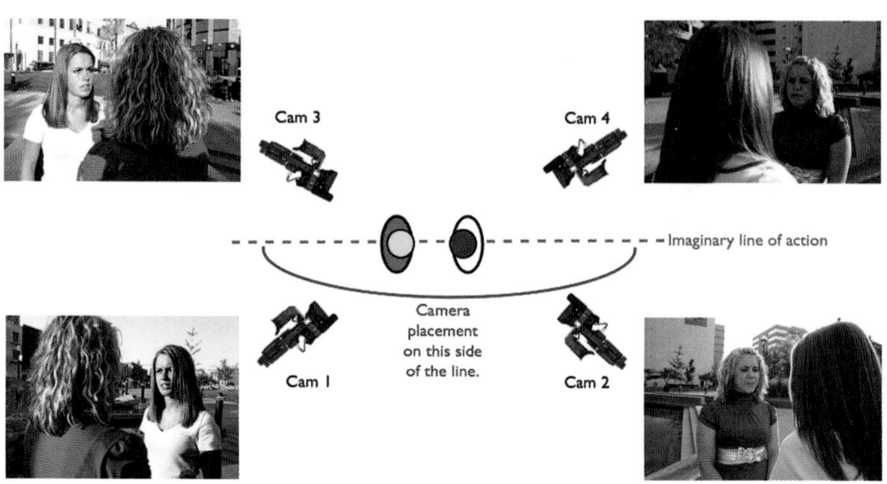

FIGURE 7.48
The line of action. Shots can be cut between cameras located on the same side of the imaginary line of action: between 1 and 2, or 3 and 4. Cutting between cameras on opposite sides of this line could cause a jump cut (1 and 3, 1 and 4, 2 and 3, and 2 and 4).
(Photos by Josh Taber.)

FIGURE 7.49
Crossing the line. Because the camera has been moved across the line of action, the walk appears to have changed direction, confusing the audience.
(Photos by Josh Taber.)

Interview with a Pro

Nathan White, Videographer

Nathan White, Videographer

What do you like about being a videographer?
Few positions within television production can put a person in the middle of the action quite like being a videographer. Whatever is unfolding in the production is literally taking place directly in front of the videographer.

An example is that of the fall of the Berlin Wall. When looking back in history, the image that demonstrates what happened is not an anchor speaking; few remember what they said. It is the video of liberated West Germans tearing down the wall and standing above the crowd with arms raised in triumph. A videographer's work lives forever in archives and the minds of viewers. There is nothing like having people all over the world coming to a stop to look at my video. It is an experience that few others will ever have.

How do you decide what shot to use?
Shot selection for a videographer is an art. If the right angles are not shot, then the whole piece may not edit together very well at all. When I was first starting out, editors complained that my video was a series of shots that were well composed, but did not fit together in a sequence.

Every shot conveys something different to the audience. When a videographer understands what each shot can do, they can better know what shot to get. Long shots establish context, close-ups convey intimacy and emotion, and medium shots propel the piece along.

Long shots should only be used long enough to lead the viewer into a scene or away from it. If they are used too often, the audience will become bored. Dramatic vistas look better as a painting than as video.

Close-ups bring viewers in very close to the action. A CU of a pair of hands putting something together, or of gears in a machine, can show how something is done, and they are easy to use as cutaway shots. CUs of a person's face are an excellent way to show emotion. These make excellent cutaways. Shoot as many close-ups as possible, because they are easily edited and add intimacy.

Medium shots are the most-used shot in videography. They are easily edited, close enough to show action and intimacy, and wide enough for the viewer to still see some context. If there is a single event that can only be captured once, the MS is the best shot to use.

Do you ever use auto settings on your camera?
It is best to learn how to use a camera without using any of the auto settings. It is rare that auto settings can completely ruin a shot, but manual settings put the control in the hands of the videographer. Auto settings can be very useful in situations where there is little time to make adjustments (on breaking news, for example). Or they can be used as a reference point when setting up the shot.

Nathan White is a videographer for a local television station.

CHAPTER 8

Shooting People and Objects

Images should not tell you what you already know. It takes no great powers or magic to reproduce somebody's face in a photograph. The magic is in seeing people in new ways.

—Duane Michals, Photographer

While shooting can be a simple process, camera operators and directors must be very intentional in order to shoot the subject in a way that attracts the audience's attention, holds their attention, *and* communicates the message effectively (Figures 8.1 and 8.2).

FIGURE 8.1
When the talent is speaking directly to the camera, directors generally want a close-up. This shot gives viewers the feeling that the talent is speaking to them; it is inclusive.

FIGURE 8.2
When shooting talent who is sitting down, be prepared to either follow him with the camera or have a second camera ready, which is already zoomed out, when he stands. Otherwise, his head will be cut off. Similarly, be ready for him to sit if he is standing. Both situations remind us that camera operators cannot lock off the tripod head during action.

SHOOTING PEOPLE

8.1 THE SINGLE PERSON

Let's examine the basics of shooting a single person.

It is important to make your talent feel comfortable with you whenever possible. As they relax, you will get a better performance.

Framing People

Framing is an issue that significantly impacts your final image. The talent needs to understand how tight the shots will be if he or she is making a presentation. That way they know how much room is available to move around in. If a person moves around a lot in a chair (leans, settles back, or waves arms), then a wider shot will be needed. While an extreme close-up shot does intensify emotion, the audience is also more likely to start inspecting more than listening if the shot is held too long. They begin to look at the trim of a mustache, a facial detail, or teeth. A screen-filled full face shot is out of place most of the time, although it can be dramatically powered when used at the right moment. (Figures 8.3 and 8.4).

FIGURE 8.3
Incorrect framing: When panning with a moving subject, try to keep it steady in the frame, just behind image center. Correct framing: The amount of offset increases with the subject's speed.

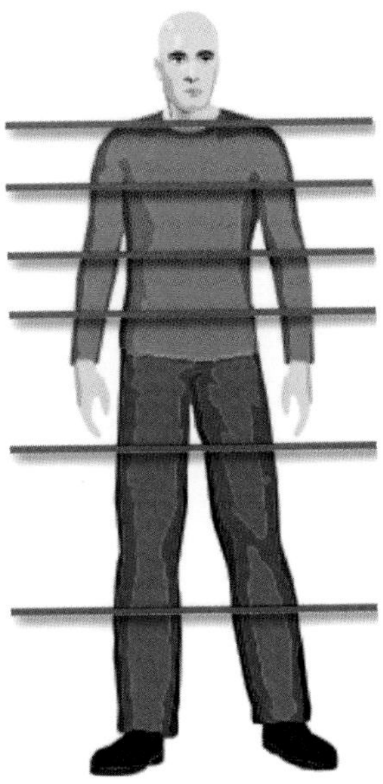

FIGURE 8.4
When framing shots of a person, do not cut off a shot at a natural bend of the body. Go slightly above or below the bend.

Contextual Shots

Including context to your shot gives your audience additional information about your subject. While a long shot generally gives you plenty of context, it does not show the facial expression well. So, a medium shot is generally used to show context and expression. (Figure 8.5).

Camera Movement

A sustained shot of someone speaking directly to the camera soon becomes boring to the viewer. Sometimes the shot can be improved by gradually tightening the shot to increase interest or slowly widening it to relax the audience's concentration. However, don't overdo the camera movement or it will become tiresome and distracting.

In order to create some visual variety when using multiple cameras, cut to different-sized shots. Cuts made at the end of a sentence or thought sequence will not usually disrupt the visual flow.

FIGURE 8.5
The buildings in the background give context to the image. They provide additional information to help the audience understand more about the individual.
(Photo by Lynn Owens.)

Subject Movement

Directors can help to "motivate a cut" by having the talent turn at an agreed moment to be shot from another direction, although this can look staged if it is not done well. This type of cut can be useful when the talent has made a mistake and has to restart from before the mistake. In these circumstances, the cut will hide the intermittent shooting and result in a smoothly flowing narrative. When someone is walking, a medium shot is generally the closest shot that can be used comfortably.

Show the Talent or Subject?

Instead of continually showing shots of the talent talking, try wherever possible to show what the talent is talking about. This not only makes the production more interesting to watch, but it becomes more informative because it gives the viewer time to examine the subject itself, rather than just hear about it.

If the program is intended to concentrate on the *personality* of the speaker, then use plenty of shots of the talent. However, if it is really intended to show the viewer how to do something or how something works, that should decide the sort of shots that you use—that is, do not show us repeated shots of the cook; instead show us shots of the cooking process.

8.2 ARRANGING PEOPLE SHOTS

Shots showing people talking generally fall into formal, informal, or grouped arrangements:

Formal situations are the normal format seen in studio interviews, newscasts, public affairs programs, games shows, and similar situations where people are intentionally positioned (sitting or standing) in a specific way.

The *informal* style includes people sitting in their own homes, standing in the street, walking, driving, or speaking while working. Informal approaches may also include *wildtrack interviews*, in which we see images of someone busily occupied (sawing wood, for instance) and yet hear the person in a non-synchronous audio wildtrack of an interview made separately. The audience accepts this convention without wondering how the talent can speak without moving his or her lips.

Arranged groups are mostly found in dramatic productions, where people are deliberately positioned to form compositional patterns that direct the eye and influence our response to the action.

8.3 EFFECTIVE SHOTS

When shooting groups of people (two or more), the shots should always answer the basic questions: Who are they? Where are they? What do they have to say?

We want to see their reactions and hear their replies. Shots of people just sitting and listening quietly without expression have limited visual value. So effective shooting is a matter of the appropriate selection of the right person and the right shot at the right time. A common production approach is to begin with a group shot that shows everyone present (this establishes where everyone is located and sets the scene), cut to the host of the show, then cut to close-ups of individuals as they speak (cutting in reaction shots). Shots of part of the group are often included, such as a shot of a person with his or her partner. But if a shot includes more than three people, details of their expressions will probably be lost.

FIGURE 8.6
The full frontal shot or the three-quarter frontal shots are considered the most effective close-up shots when the talent is speaking.

For most purposes, frontal shots (with the person facing the camera) or three-quarter frontal shots (looking 45 degrees to either side) are the most effective. In a profile shot (side view), which is the least familiar view of most people, the camera seems to be scrutinizing the guest, and the effect is not particularly attractive, although admittedly it can be dramatic in a strong, aggressive interview (Figure 8.6).

DIRECTION AND SPEED

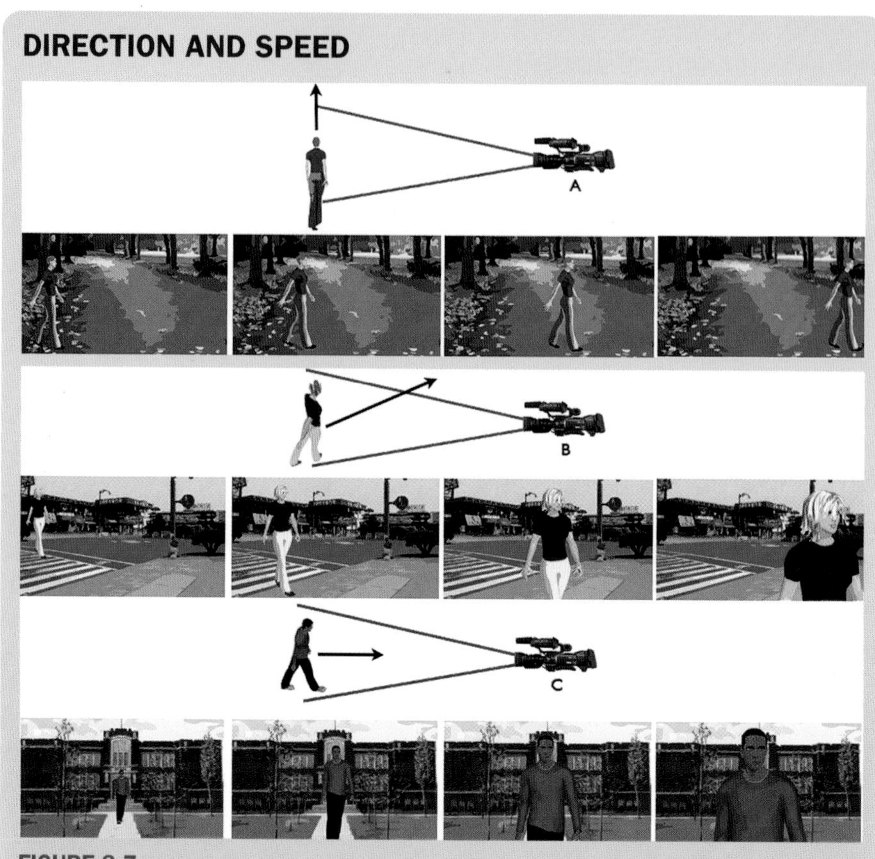

FIGURE 8.7
Direction and effective speed. (A) Talent moving across the screen quickly passes out of shot. Direction and effective speed. (B) Diagonal moves are more interesting (and take longer). (C) Moves toward (or away from) the camera are sustained the longest. However, they may take too long.

WIDELY SPACED MOVES

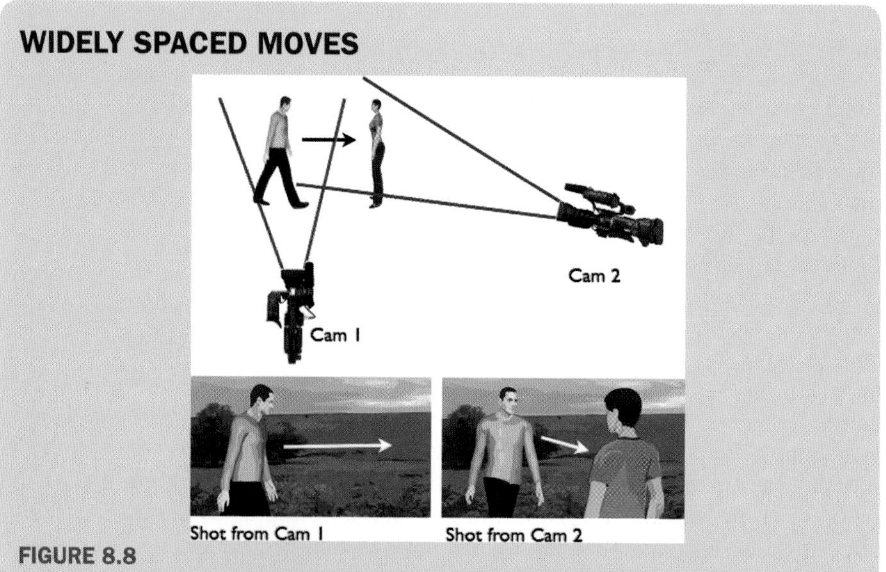

FIGURE 8.8
Widely spaced moves. If two people are quite a distance apart, you can cut between them, pan between them, or just shoot the action from a different angle.

8.4 SELECTING THE RIGHT SHOT

When watching someone at work—painting, cooking, quilting, or whatever else—it is natural for the camera to concentrate on what they are *doing* and *how they are doing it* instead of dwelling on their expressions. When directors cut away from the center of interest for too long to shots of an interviewer, the audience can become impatient, feeling as though they are missing the real action. However, these talent cutaway shots are effective editing techniques that can be used to reduce overlengthy shots of the action. Instead of going on and on watching the bread dough being kneaded, show part of the action with an establishing shot, then go to a cutaway shot (ideally to something that is *relevant*) to cover the fact that the action has been interrupted and removed during postproduction.

When showing a situation where there is a continual feeling of apprehension as to whether the action will succeed (such as during a cliff climb), regular cutting between the action itself and the person's expressions of concentration will heighten the impact on the audience. We have all seen situations where the director includes shots of drumming fingers, hands fiddling with jewelry, straightening a tie, and so on. Although such shots may reveal the guest's unconscious reactions, at times they distract the audience from what is being said.

If someone is being cross-examined during an interview, directors sometimes use a tighter shot than normal. If the situation becomes especially heated, the camera operator can move even closer to the "guest" during questioning. But these are not techniques to be used lightly during a normal, cool, polite interview. There is always the risk that once the closest shot has been reached, anything after it is anticlimactic.

8.5 SINGLE-CAMERA INTERVIEWS

When shooting two people in a continuous interview or discussion with a single camera, treatment is inevitably restricted to some extent. But with a little preplanning, the audience will not even realize that there were any coverage problems.

There are two ways of shooting an interview:

- In the first, the camera moves around, changing its viewpoint.
- In the second, the camera remains with the guest throughout.

Interviews are best shot in one continuous take. When restricted to just one camera, the camera operator might, for example, open with an establishing long shot that shows the participants and where they are. Slowly the camera moves in to a medium shot of the interviewer who is introducing the guest. As he or she turns to face the guest, the camera pans slightly and the shot is widened to include them both again. The shot can then be tightened to a single close-up of the guest (Figures 8.9 and 8.10).

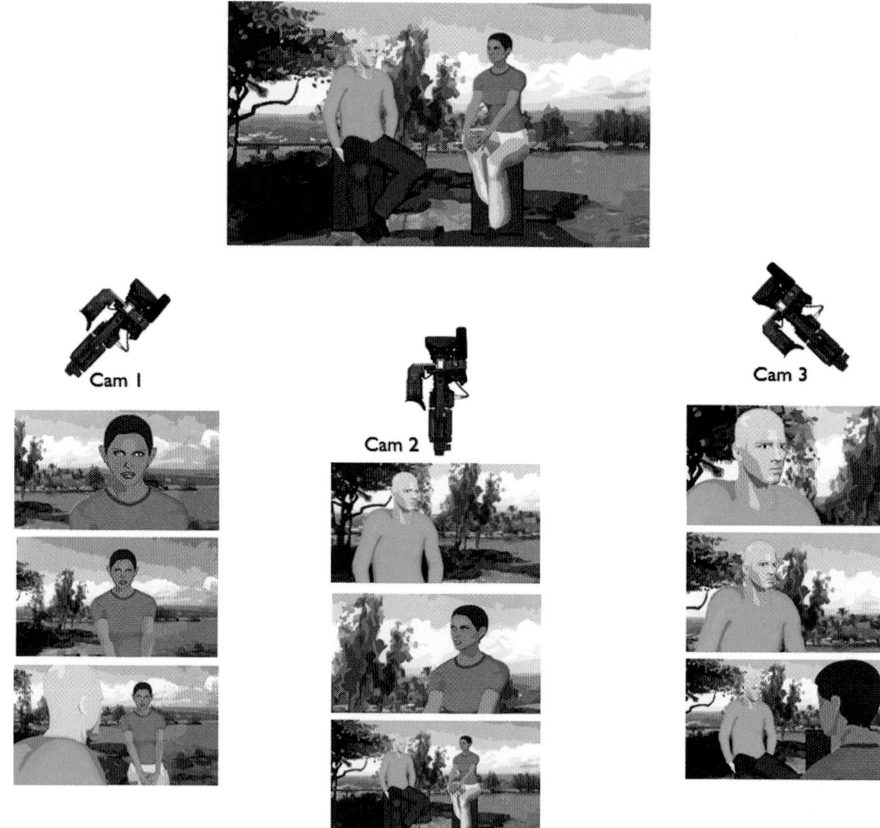

FIGURE 8.9
In a formal interview, there are relatively few effective shots.

Using a different approach, the camera operator could begin with a medium shot of the interviewer, slowly pull out (zoom or dolly) to include the guest in a two-shot, then gradually pan over and move in at the same time to concentrate on the guest and exclude the interviewer. As the interview ends, the camera operator can simultaneously pull out and pan over to a two-shot, finally tightening on the interviewer for his or her closing words. If the interview is long, the camera operator can vary the guest's shot from time to time by gradually zooming in and out. However, much depends on how interesting and animated the guest proves to be.

Location interviews are often "one-take" opportunities, in which the camera concentrates on the guest (slowly zooming to vary the shot size). The interviewer, who is unseen, stands near the camera to ask the questions (out of shot, off-camera).

Once a one-camera interview has concluded, it is common practice for the interviewer to record a series of brief on-camera segments. This practice avoids

Camera I Position
This camera position is used to capture the guest 's responses to the host's questions.

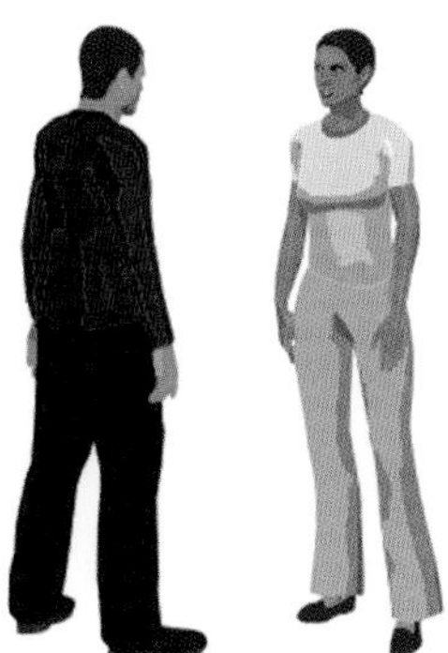

Camera 2 Position
This camera position is used to capture interview questions and reaction shots after the interview.

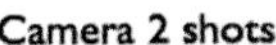

FIGURE 8.10
Single-camera interviews generally require moving the camera into two different positions.

disrupting the actual interview or continually panning between the two people as they talk. Speaking directly to the camera afterward, the interviewer may introduce the guest(s) to the audience. If useful, this segment could be cut in during editing, or it can be used as a voiceover introduction accompanied by informational shots about the subject discussed. The interviewer may also choose to ask the guest some of the original questions, usually looking past the camera as though it was part of the actual interview. Later, these questions can be edited into the interview tape at the appropriate points. When the questions are scripted, this usually means referring to notes or a script. When they are spontaneous, it may involve checking the interview tape itself to get the wording correct. In either case, it is imperative that these are the *actual questions,* asked with similar *intonation* to those asked the guest.

Many interviews and discussions simply involve straightforward recording. However, results can be disappointing. When the images do not work, do it again and select the best version or use parts of each take. Another approach to interviewing is to tape a much longer session than you really need and then extract the highlights to suit the required program length (Figure 8.11).

FIGURE 8.11
It can be difficult shooting a single-camera interview. The camera operator must zoom from close-ups to two shots, sometimes repeatedly.
(Photo by Kara Laufenberger.)

8.6 EDITING CONTINUOUS INTERVIEWS

A regular method of handling interviews with a single camera is to concentrate the camera on the guest throughout. The interviewer remains out of shot. This treatment is simple and least likely to distract the guest. But it does leave the director with one very long take. The result is usually a sequence that is far too long to hold the audience's attention. It needs "tightening." Use the most important and interesting segments, and discard any unwanted or irrelevant portions.

FIGURE 8.12
Cutting between two images of the same subject using the same shot, such as these two close-up shots, will result in a jump cut.

If the editor simply cuts out the segments needed for the interview and then joins them together in the editing process, there will be a distracting *jump cut* at the start of each new section, with sudden changes in positions, expressions, and shot sizes (Figure 8.12). Directors often try to cover these cuts with quick dissolves or wipes, but the result is seldom satisfactory. The answer to this dilemma is to take a series of *reaction shots* at the end of the interview and then edit them into the main sequence.

The *reaction shot* is a familiar feature in all interviews. It is simply a silent reaction shot of the interviewer looking with interest or reacting with occasional head nods, smiles, or concern. The director may even ask the guest to oblige with similar reaction shots to give some variety to the editing. During postproduction, directors use the original interview shot with its soundtrack and then cut in the reaction shots wherever necessary, without interrupting the sound. To be convincing, it is important that the person in the reaction shot doesn't speak. If you are using an over-the-shoulder shot, make sure that the mouth of the person with their back to the camera cannot be seen moving. Too often an interviewer will chat to the guest while the reaction shot is being taken; the result is that after editing, the speaker's mouth movements do not match the sound.

8.7 SHOOTING GROUPS

Shooting a group effectively with a single camera is a challenge, but it can be done well. You use the movement techniques we have just discussed for the interview.

If possible, avoid continually panning across the group from one person to another. It looks clumsy, particularly if people are sitting some distance apart and the camera is panning over meaningless background. When shooting with one camera, it is usually better to zoom out, to include the new speaker in a wide shot, then perhaps zoom in on him or her (Figure 8.13).

The exception is when something really dramatic happens (such as when someone suddenly stands and shouts in opposition). Then the camera can pan over rapidly to show the interrupter. However, the disadvantage of a *whip pan* (zip pan, blur pan) of this kind is that, although it makes a strong visual impact, you are likely to end up with a defocused or badly framed picture that has to be corrected. While this can be edited in postproduction, it is a bigger problem if the image is being broadcast live.

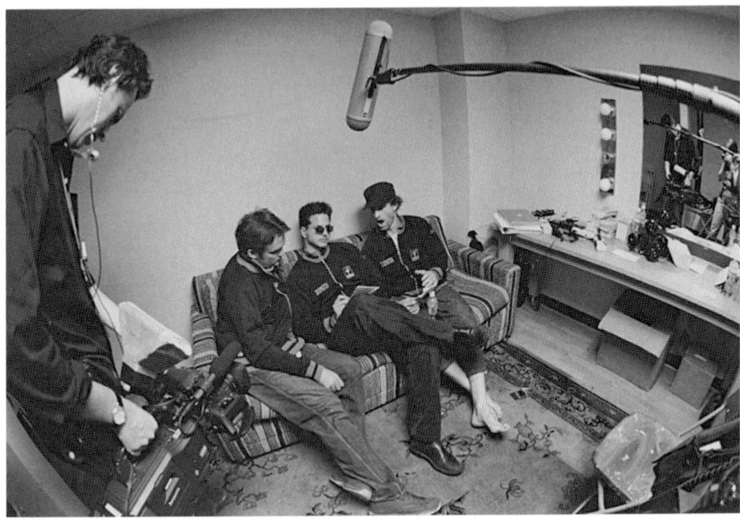

FIGURE 8.13
When shooting with one camera, it is better to zoom out, include the new speaker in the wide shot, and then sometimes zoom back in on the speaker.
(Photo courtesy of Sodium Entertainment.)

However, if instead of a whip pan, the camera operator had quickly zoomed out from a close-up to a group shot, then immediately zoomed in to a close shot of the interrupter, the out-in movement would have looked extremely awkward to the viewer. When shooting a group in which people speak at random, avoid the temptation to continually arc around and move to new positions, particularly when someone out of the shot suddenly begins talking. It is usually less obtrusive to zoom out and include them in a wide shot.

The trick is to make every camera move appear as natural as possible. Think about covering a street interview. The camera operator might begin with a medium shot of the interviewer speaking to the camera, introducing someone. Then, as the talent turns toward them saying, "Tell me, Mr. Able, what were the first signs…?" the camera arcs around on the talent's turn to shoot Mr. Able for the rest of the segment.

As a general principle, use movement to "motivate a pan" (such as following something or someone moving past). The result will look much more natural and unobtrusive than simply panning over the empty air.

If two or more cameras are being used to shoot a group, various shots can be prearranged between them. For example, camera 1 can take a long shot (wide shot, master shot, or cover shot) of the entire action and shots of the interviewer or host. Camera 2 can capture the shots of the guest.

If there are more guests, the director can introduce various shots of singles, pairs, subgroups, and group shots. Always be ready to come back to a long shot if somebody, speaks unexpectedly when you are in a close-up on the other camera (see Figure 8.14).

FIGURE 8.14
Shooting groups. Static groups can be broken into a series of smaller individual shots. For single-camera shooting, this involves repositioning the camera (or repeated action). With multicamera shooting, the director can cut between the various viewpoints.

There is an important difference between shooting a group where members are going to speak in an agreed order and a group where members speak whenever they wish. In the first case, cameras and microphones can follow along systematically. When people speak at random, the camera operator, who has been concentrating on a shot, now has to look around, turn, reframe, and refocus on the new speaker before the shot can be used. Again, zooming out to a wide shot may save the situation. If you are shooting a group of people, it is often an advantage to put people in the front row who you know are going to speak.

During shooting, it is best to check that shots are reasonably compatible so that there are no wild jumps in size, variations in headroom (the space from the top of the head to the upper frame), or changes in camera height. Eye lines (where people appear to be looking) should be sufficiently related to suggest that people are talking to each other. If directors are not careful when cutting between various camera positions around a group, the talent can appear to be looking off-camera or at the wrong person.

8.8 CAR INTERVIEWS

Interviews in cars are common, but how successful they are will vary between individuals. Some drivers find the nearby camera distracting. Their replies are liable to be perfunctory because they are concentrating on driving conditions. The audience may even find the passing scene more interesting than the interview. Camera operators must be careful not to distract the talent to the point of an accident.

A steady camera is essential, whether the operator is located beside the driver (seated or crouched down) or shooting over the front seats. The camera can even be clamped to the outside of the car, looking in (Figure 8.15).

To give the shots variety or to provide cutaways, directors can cheat by reshooting the driver alone or with the interviewer (and no camera in the car) from another vehicle traveling alongside or slightly ahead. Some directors create cutaway shots by showing the passing scene through the car windows, shots reflected in the rearview mirror, shots showing a gear change, and so on. But unless these pictures are directly related to the interview (such as discussing road safety, the route, or driving techniques), they are simply a distraction.

FIGURE 8.15
Car mounts provide a convenient way to shoot a car interview.
(Photo courtesy of VFGadgets.)

8.9 WALKING INTERVIEWS

Walking interviews get away from the regular seated situation, but don't underestimate their problems. Generally a wireless mic is clipped to the interviewer and guest. However, audio interference from other transmissions can be a problem. That may not be the only problem. Inexperienced talent may not be able to walk and talk naturally. The interview may be stilted, especially if the interviewee has to walk up or down stairs. Arrange the walking interview so that you do not pick up a lot of extraneous noise, such as the crunch of gravel underfoot, wind, or traffic.

If serious sound pickup problems occur, one strategy is to shoot the action so that the interviewee's mouth movements are not obvious in the image; use long shots or rear views and then lay the speech that you have recorded separately over the pictures during the editing process. Occasionally, what looks like a "walking interview" is actually a studio interview, with pictures of the people walking, taken with a carefully angled camera and sweetened with audio effects.

During a walking interview, the camera operator has the option of doing the following:

- Walking backward (usually guided by an assistant's hand on a back or shoulder)
- Sitting on a dolly of some type (anything from a wheelchair to a professional dolly) being pulled in front of the action
- Locating the camera at an uninterrupted vantage point and panning with the action
- Walking behind the talent, taking a three-quarter back or a rear view

None of these methods lends itself to steady camerawork for any length of time, especially if the camera is hand or shoulder supported and the ground is uneven. The best solution is usually to break up the walk into a series of sections, perhaps letting the talent walk out of frame at the end of a section. Remember, though, if the person exits frame left, he or she must enter the next shot from frame right so that the person appears to be walking in the same direction. Alternatively, the director can cut to a head-on view of the person coming toward the camera. To avoid any walk becoming unduly long, the talent can pause at intervals and, still talking, lean on a fence, sit on a log, stand and look at the landscape, or engage in some other natural activity.

SHOOTING AN EFFECTIVE INTERVIEW

Interviews range from casual street encounters to friendly chats and probing interviews. Here are a variety of areas to consider and techniques that you can use to capture an effective interview:

- Why is this person being interviewed? Is he or she a well-known person? Has he or she done something unusual? Or seen something unusual? Is an expert explaining something or giving an opinion? Whatever the reason, this information will form the basis for the type of questions and influences how you approach the interview.
- Preliminary research on the person always pays off, whether this takes the form of reading the person's book, biography, newspaper profile, or just asking around.

- Try to get to know guests whenever possible before the recording begins. This will put them at ease. It is also a good time to explain what will be happening during shooting.
- Avoid going over the whole interview in advance. You don't want the recorded version to lose its freshness. In addition, the talent may leave out information during the second time, thinking that he or she has already covered those points. If that happens, the interviewer can always prompt the talent by saying, "Earlier, you were telling me…"
- Does the guest have any personal items, such as mementos or family album photos, that would be interesting to show during the recording? These may be shot later as cutaway or insert shots. It would also be good to let the guest know, before the interview begins, when the personal items will be discussed during the recording.
- If there is a video monitor nearby, angle it so that the guest cannot see it. Monitors can make a guest either nervous or vain.
- Before beginning the interview, test the audio level of the microphones. Both the interviewer and guest should speak at a normal volume so that the audio channel gain can be properly adjusted for optimum sound.
- Develop a fact sheet or background card, noting the points that need to be discussed. Create these points based on research and conversation. Don't prepare detailed, written-out questions, which can seem forced and artificial. The interviewer can introduce the guest or refer to any statistics or data by reading from a prompter.
- It is best if questions *appear* to develop from the guest's answers, moving back to prepared topics when possible. Do not simply work through a list of questions. It is better for a host to glance at notes briefly than it is for the host to ignore replies while reading the notes in detail.

There are regular dos and don'ts for interviewers:

- Be punctual for the interview and the preliminary checks (i.e., fitting intercom earpiece, checking voice levels, checking the prompter, shot checks of hair, tie, clothing, etc.).
- Try to maintain eye contact with your guest as much as possible. It helps him or her to feel "involved" rather than being interrogated.
- Ask specific questions, not general ones, and keep to the point of the interview. If, for example, you are talking to a witness of a fire, his or her opinions about the neighborhood may be relevant or a distraction.
- These questions will help focus the interview: Where? When? Why? How? Who? Which? What? (Figure 8.16).
- Use invitations such as "Tell me about…"; "Let's talk about…"; "Do you remember, you were telling me about …?" to prompt the guest to talk (Figure 8.17).
- Ask one question at a time and wait for replies. Some interviewers get their best responses by simply waiting. The talent feels uneasy at the silence and says something (often revealing) to break it, giving the interviewer the opportunity for further questions.
- Never interrupt interesting replies for the sake of asking prepared questions, and never ignore the guest's answers. Even if the reply is "I see" or a nod, this avoids a feeling of interrogation.

FIGURE 8.16
Who, what, when, where, and why questions will focus the interview.

- Do not say too much. (Some interviewers do most of the speaking.)
- Use a polite, friendly style, not a solemn or overreacting one. Smiles help as long as they appear genuine.
- Persuade guests not to wear dark glasses. They can prevent the host and audience from seeing expressions.

FIGURE 8.17
Avoid questions that can be answered yes or no. The goal is to elicit more information from the guest.

SHOOTING INSTRUCTIONAL PRODUCTIONS

8.10 TYPICAL INSTRUCTIONAL PRODUCTIONS

A wide range of video programs can be described as "instruction." Besides the programming found on the networks, niche cable channels are filled with shows about cooking, hunting, home improvement, medicine (surgery), and many other topics. Most of these programs are instructional and are designed for specific markets, such as educational, professional, specialist trades, and so on.

8.11 APPROACHES TO INSTRUCTION

There are some subjects that cannot really be demonstrated effectively in a video program. Instead, directors have to rely on *verbal descriptions* of processes. Other subjects may be only partly successful because of the *limitations* of the system, such as a demonstration of sound quality.

One of the weakest instructional methods in a video program is an illustrated talk that shows still photographs, diagrams, maps, and so on. To enhance the project, pan or tilt the camera across the still photo or slowly zoom in and out of the still.

FIGURE 8.18
Since cooking shows are full of visual movement and a process that develops as the audience watches, they are popular on television. This photo is from a cooking segment on NBC's *Today* show.

A cooking demonstration, on the other hand, can be extremely effective; it is full of visual movement and change, a process that develops as we watch—even though the audience cannot smell or taste whether it is as successful as it looks (Figure 8.18).

One of the most powerful forms of instruction is when the talent speaks to us directly through the camera, pointing out each feature of the subject (Figure 8.19).

The "documentary format," in which the host may be heard as a *voiceover* making observations on the images, is much less personal. However, it can be more authoritative, especially if the speaker's visual presence is not particularly impressive on camera for any reason. But the documentary approach is extremely greedy for imagery. Compared to the "direct approach," where directors can always take shots of the talent speaking to the camera, the "documentary" method requires that the camera is continually looking at the subject and

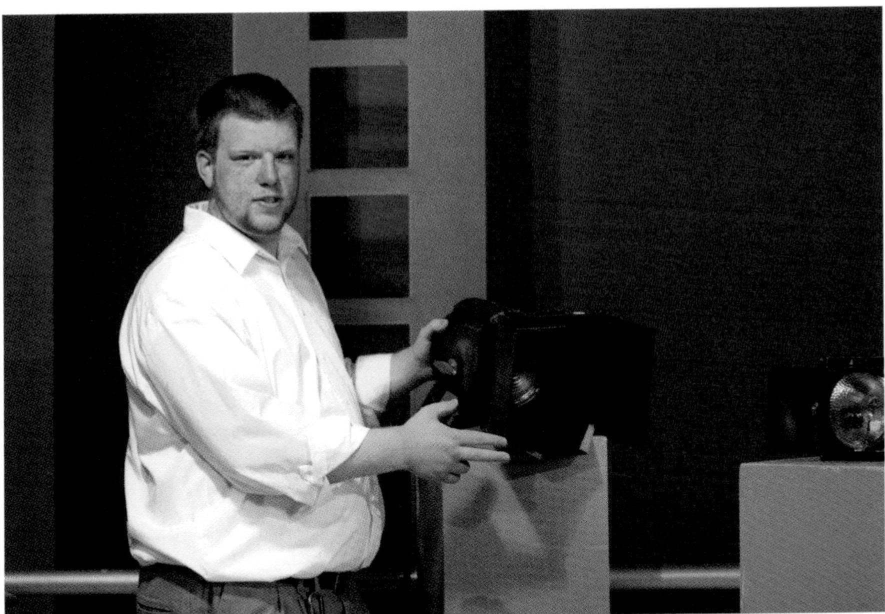

FIGURE 8.19
The most common and usually the most effective form of presentation is when someone speaks to us *directly* through the camera, pointing out each feature of the subject.
(Photo by Josh Taber.)

its surroundings—which may not have enough interest to sustain the viewer's attention.

8.12 ADVANCE PLANNING

On the face of it, one might assume that instructional productions merely involve presenting the item before the camera and pointing out its features. Some very boring programs are made this way. The secrets of really successful demonstrations are *planning, preparation,* and *rehearsal,* even for the most familiar subjects. In fact, the more familiar it is, the more difficult it can be to make the program interesting and hold the audience's attention. Too easily, the director can assume that the viewers "know all about that."

A good instructional program is designed to fit its audience. If it is produced at too high a level, the uninitiated become bewildered and embarrassed at not being able to grasp the facts. They become confused. They lose their self-confidence. While sorting out what has been said, they get lost.

A successful program encourages curiosity and intrigues, leaving the audience with a sense of satisfaction and fulfillment. "What do you think will happen now?" is much more involving than "When we do this, that happens."

8.13 CREATING THE INSTRUCTIONAL PROGRAM

Instructional programs can take anything from a few minutes to years to complete. Directors often need to stretch or condense time in various ways to suit the occasion:

- Shoot everything from start to finish. This ensures that the audience misses none of the action and gets an accurate idea of how long everything takes. Clearly this is a good approach for relatively brief productions, but it is unsuitable when producing a program such as "How to Build a House."
- The video can be recorded continuously, then edit out the time-consuming, repetitious, or boring parts. This can produce a shorter, better-paced program and ensures that the audience concentrates on the important stages.
- Portions of a show can be arranged in prepared sections. For instance, when showing how to bake a cake, the director may first display the ingredients, begin the method of mixing, and then place the prepared mixture in an oven (or not, if one is not available). The talent can then remove the cooked cake and begin to decorate it, and we end with a shot of the fully decorated cake. Not only does this method save a great deal of time, but it ensures that the results turn out right at each stage. However, directors have to guard against leaving out important information when shortcutting time in this way. For instance, the audience may inadvertently be left wondering how to tell when the food is fully cooked. Preferably the host would both tell and show the audience how to test for doneness.
- For demonstrations that take a long time to develop, such as a plant growing, the simplest plan is to shoot short sequences at strategic moments (hours, days, or weeks apart) and show them one after the other. The alternative is to use some type of an automatic timer that takes a brief video shot at regular intervals.
- Sometimes a demonstration program has to be made to a prescribed length in order to fit a scheduled time slot. You can achieve this goal by deliberately including material that is interesting but can be trimmed or omitted as necessary.
- If the video program is to be used as part of a live presentation, such as a classroom lecture where a teacher will also be speaking and answering questions, the production can be designed to be extremely flexible. The program can be arranged as a series of pretimed, self-contained sections so that the teacher can use as much as is needed for a specific lesson without the students feeling that they are being prevented from seeing the entire program.

8.14 SHOOTING OBJECTS

Here are a few reminders of how you can attain quality shots of objects. Even though they are obvious, it is amazing how often these errors occur in programs (Figure 8.20).

- Black backgrounds need to be used with care. Although they can create great contrast with a much lighter subject, they may emphasize color, and dark areas around the edges of the subject may vanish into the surroundings. If the backlight is increased to prevent this from happening, it can produce an inappropriate glittering halo of light around the subject.
- Strong background colors such as red, yellow, or bright green may not only be distracting, but they will modify the apparent colors of the subject.
- If the subject is *flat* such as framed artwork, shoot it from a straight-on viewpoint and tilt the frame down a slight bit to avoid light reflections, camera reflections, or shadows.
- If a demonstrator has to put the item in position for the camera, it is often a good idea to have an unobtrusive mark on the table to guide where the object should be placed. This way, the camera can also prefocus on the spot.
- Solid objects are best lit with "three-point lighting" (key, fill, backlight) or a side light to left and right with some frontal fill light.
- Close-up shots with a wide-angle lens will create considerable distortion.
- If the depth of field is too limited in an extreme close-up or "detail" shot, use a smaller *f*-stop; but this requires higher light levels. Instead of trying to increase the overall light level, take a separate close-up shot of the item afterward under stronger localized lighting, and insert this image.
- Instead of moving the camera in an arc around a smaller object (a difficult move to carry out smoothly), it is better to place the object on a turntable (manual or motor driven) that can be slowly turned, allowing the audience to see the object from all directions.

SHOOTING OBJECTS

FIGURE 8.20A
The goal is to simplify the shot so that the viewer does not get distracted.

FIGURE 8.20B
Avoid confusing or distracting backgrounds.

FIGURE 8.20C
Do not show an extreme close-up of the object unless you are showing detail that has already been shown in an establishing shot.

FIGURE 8.20D
Do not unintentionally crop parts of the object. See that handling does not obscure important detail.

Interview with a Pro

Sarah Leckie, Director/Videographer

Sarah Leckie, Director/Videographer

When shooting people, what do you think about? What do you look for?
Most of the action I film is people sitting and talking, which can get really boring. Because the action is extremely boring, I have to liven up the shot with something interesting. So I have to look for interesting angles. I usually try to look for something I can juxtapose the action with—for example, a guitar in the foreground or something. You can't just think about the action. You have to think about what surrounds the action and whether or not it's relevant to the shot or will make it more appealing or more understandable.

If I am filming someone playing soccer, I have to think about how relevant the context of the action is to the image. For instance, if I am filming a soccer game at a stadium, people know what stadiums look like and don't need a lot of stadium shots. I can focus on close-ups of the action. However, if I am filming a soccer game inside a prison, I'll probably want to widen up my shots to shoot the context of the prison. It will make the shots more dramatic.

What are challenges of shooting people?
Usually the challenge is to get people to not look at the camera, to get them to act like I am not there. Communicating exactly what I have pictured in my head, and getting them to see that image can be extremely difficult. Also, getting the camera actions perfectly lined up with the people's actions is a challenge. For instance, if I am rack focusing or zooming or tracking while they look away and then at the camera, the timing has to be perfect! This is difficult.

How do you get people to do what you need them to do in your productions?
I usually have to do a lot of coaching. I have to be able to not only tell them what to do in an interview, but often I have to take the time to show them exactly what I want them to do. It takes a lot of patience.

Sarah Leckie is a corporate television producer/director who creates international documentaries.

CHAPTER 9
Working with the Talent

Actors are the life's blood of any show. The best screenplay is only as good as the players performing the text.

—David K. Irving, Director

Always get more sleep than your actors.

—Orson Welles, Director

People have an incredible impact on a production. The face and the body language of a person communicate faster to an audience than any other method. Showing a close-up shot of the face quickly communicates the story as the actor expresses disgust, joy, sorrow, and seriousness. Many video productions totally rely on how well people perform in front of the camera. It is up to the director to get the best performance from the talent. The director must be able to communicate his or her vision for the program and keep the talent motivated and informed. Coaxing the best performance can be tough, but it is well worth it in the end.

> With the competing television channels, newspapers, magazines, and Internet, television commentators have the difficult task of being innovative every time they are on the air. Research is the commentator's weapon in being able to comment on the really important issues and describe the images provided to the audience.
>
> **—Kostas Kapatais, Producer**

9.1 TALENT

Although the broad term "talent" is widely used to refer to those appearing in front of the camera, we must always remember how varied this talent really is. "Talent" covers a remarkable spread of experience and temperaments, from the professional actor working to a script and playing a part, to the impromptu, unrehearsed interview with a passerby on the street (Figure 9.1).

FIGURE 9.1
"Talent" generally refers to anyone who appears in front of the camera. That can include a wide variety of people, from anchors to actors to athletes to the man on the street doing an interview.

When the director invites someone to appear in front of the camera, that is only the beginning of the story. The person's performance can have an incredible influence on the program's success. It is important that the director helps in any way needed to make the talent's contribution as effective as possible. The talent's specific role may be major or it may be slight, but the impression he or she makes on the audience can decide whether that part of the program is a success or failure. The television camera can be an unwavering critic. Under its scrutiny, the audience weighs arrogance, attitude, and credibility, while sending sympathy to those who are shy and ill at ease.

For practical purposes, we can divide talent into the *professional performers*, who are used to appearing in front of the camera, and the *inexperienced*, for whom the program is likely to be a new, strange, and exciting, yet worrying event.

HIGH-DEFINITION MAKEUP

HD is forcing the industry to produce better artists. HD makeup artists have to watch what they do more, watch how much paint they use, and be more artistic.

—Matthew Mungle, Oscar Winner

Makeup is changing with the onset of high-definition television (HD). It intimidates some actors because they know that the clarity of the HD signal can show every flaw. HD can show a single strand of out-of-place hair:

- It is important that the talent feels comfortable with his or her new makeup on HD.
- Usually artists select makeup that is much less colored than traditional set makeup.
- More attention is usually spent on application.
- More and more artists are using an airbrush for makeup application.

Professional performers usually like to work through a prepared format. Some, like an actor in a play, will learn their lines, their moves, and the mechanics of the production. Others work from an abbreviated cue sheet near the camera or read running text from the screen of a teleprompter. Some will extemporize from guide notes, while others will read from a printed script (Figures 9.2 and 9.3).

FIGURE 9.2

Teleprompters are generally attached in front of the lens of the video camera. Video or text can be placed on the prompter, allowing the talent to see the program or read the script while looking into the camera lens. Portable teleprompters, such as the software/app used on an iPhone in the second photo, are increasingly being used in the field.

(App photo courtesy of Bodelin Technologies.)

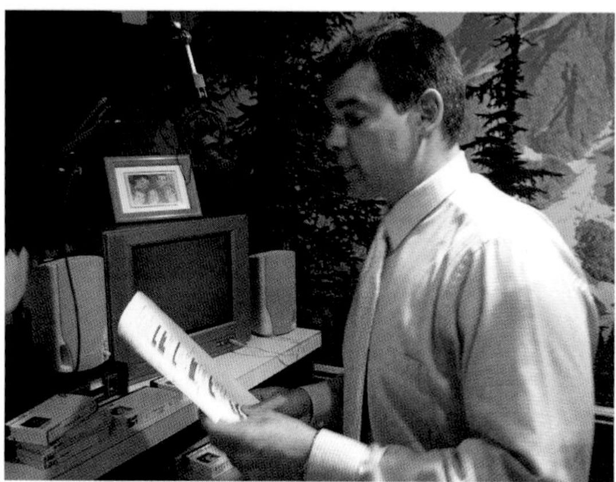

FIGURE 9.3
News talent records voiceovers for story packages.
(Photo by Jon Greenhoe.)

FIGURE 9.4
Talent must be able to concentrate on the work, even with a lot of distractions going on involving cameras, audio personnel, lighting, and other crew members.

The best professionals can be relied on to repeat, during the actual taping, the dialog, the moves, the pace, and the timing that they gave in rehearsal. The talent needs to know what he or she is going to say and that he or she can modify the delivery of the piece to fit the situation, showing enthusiasm, vigor, calm detachment, patience, or reverence. Talent can take guidance and instructions and follow this through without being confused. Good talent can improvise when things go wrong and remain calm if the unexpected happens (Figures 9.4, 9.5, and 9.6).

FIGURE 9.5
Note that while these two sports commentators rehearse, audio and production personnel are working around them, testing their mics and adjusting the talent's headset on his neck.
(Photo by Josh Taber.)

FIGURE 9.6
A "standup" is when talent are placed in front of something that provides context for the story being covered.

9.2 TALENT AND PRODUCTION STYLES

The talent needs to understand the various types of programs in order to know how to act:

- *Recorded (or taped) program.* Because this type of program is being recorded and then edited in postproduction, the recording can be stopped and started again. This takes pressure off of the talent, knowing that everything can be edited after the show has been recorded.
- *Live program.* During a program that is live, the show is being broadcast and cannot be stopped and restarted. This puts the ultimate amount of tension on the talent because, no matter what happens, the show must go on. This means that the talent must be able to work without a script at times, ad-libbing as needed.
- *Live-to-tape program.* This type of program is treated like a "live" program, without stopping the action. However, errors can be corrected in postproduction before it is broadcast or distributed.

Any director using talent who is not used to working to a camera has to make certain allowances and take precautions that are not necessary when professional performers are involved. How well inexperienced people fit into their roles in the program will depend to an extent on the director. Do not expect new talent to have the self-discipline and efficiency of a professional. There is, after all, a scary novelty about finding yourself faced with an impersonal camera, a microphone pointing to pick up your slightest remark, unfamiliar people grouped around, lighting, and all kinds of disruptions. The occasion can become unreal to inexperienced talent.

> The difference between being a director and being an actor is the difference between being the carpenter banging the nails into the wood and being the piece of wood the nails are being banged into.
>
> **—Sean Penn, Actor**

WHAT DO I WEAR?

Talent often ask the question: "What do I wear to this shoot?" Good question. Here are some basic guidelines:

- *Appropriateness is key.* The clothing needs to fit the situation. If it is a studio interview, you want the talent to wear nice clothes and polished shoes. If they are on location at a car race, you won't want them in a suit. If they are on a dramatic set, they need to dress to fit the character, which may mean dirty shoes, T-shirt, and jeans. The clothing needs to fit the situation.
- *Wear low-contrast clothes.* Contrasting colors are a major problem. Video cameras see differently than the human eye. Cameras cannot handle the contrast between light and dark objects. When the camera shows detail in the light object, the dark

becomes indistinguishable. The reverse is also true: when detail is shown in the dark, the light colors become washed out, losing all of their detail. Contrast is also a problem for clothing and skin tone. Very light-skinned people should stay away from black or dark clothing when on television, and dark-skinned people should avoid wearing white or very light colors such as white, pink, and yellow. White clothing, including shirts or blouses, is discouraged for television.

- *Blue is universal on television.* The clothing color that seems to work best on television is a medium blue.
- *Watch the details.* Socks or stockings should be high enough so that they cover the leg when crossed. Collars should be positioned correctly. Hair should be in place.
- *Minimal jewelry is used on television.* Generally talent wears small jewelry, since large, shiny objects cause glares from the lighting. Small chains or pearls are usually non reflective. There are times that even watches can cause problems.
- *Street makeup is usually appropriate.* HD cameras are so sensitive that they no longer require the heavy makeup used in early television. Of course, special makeup may be required in order to fit a certain look or character.

9.3 THE INTERVIEW: GO BEYOND THE OBVIOUS

Asking the right questions when doing an interview is the key to capturing the audience's attention. However, many times it is tough to know how far to push to get the needed information. Here are a few suggestions about interviewing:

- Try to bring a fresh perspective. This requires the talent to think about the various story angles. It also may include trying to find new sources for information.
- Talk about the time leading up to the event being discussed. This will provide background information that may shed light on what happened.
- Knowing the terminology will keep the talent from getting lost in the middle of the interview. That means it may be important to explain that terminology to the viewers to increase their understanding.
- Do some research. Make phone calls and ask questions, look for information online, visit the site where the event took place, find photos or video of the event. Be knowledgeable about the subject.
- Talent should get multiple sources about the subject so that they can see the various perspectives.

9.4 SELECTING TALENT

New directors often have to deal with limited budgets, and one of the areas they often are tempted to cut is the budget line for professional talent. There are basically three types of talent for productions:

- *Professional talent.* Professionals cost more money up front. However, their quality usually facilitates a better final project, and they usually can complete the project much faster than the two types of talent discussed next.

- *University/college theater performance students.* Directors can usually "hire" students for very little money or even for free. The advantage is that these students have usually received training in acting and are often willing to work hard just for an experience they can put on their resume. So these students cost less than professionals but may take a bit more time to create the final project, including more retakes.
- *Amateur talent.* It is always tempting to grab a relative or friend to be the talent on a project. The problem is that amateurs do not have the experience needed to complete the project in a timely fashion or to master the pronunciation.

In summary, although they may be free, amateur talent may actually cost more money than professional talent if equipment or studio space is being rented for the production. The cost you save on talent may be spent on rental costs, because the amateur can take much more time to complete a script. Not only can you save money by using professional talent, but the overall quality will be better.

WORKING WITH NEW TALENT

FIGURE 9.7
The experienced interviewer can help inexperienced guests in many ways:

- Put them at ease. Explain what will be happening.
- Give them clear instructions, such as where to look and the direction you want the interview to go.
- Keep the area clear of distractions.
- Place items on a prearranged mark.
- Be aware of the time limits.

9.5 INEXPERIENCED TALENT

Many people who appear to be "natural performers" in the final program are really the product of an understanding, yet wily, director. Typical ways of handling inexperienced talent include the following:

- You can put your performers at ease by making them feel welcome, letting them know what they need to do, making them feel that their contribution is an important and interesting part of the program, and assuring them that if anything goes wrong, there is nothing to worry about because the scene can be recorded again (unless it is a live program).
- Let them do it their way, and then edit the result.
- Let them reminisce, for example, and then select the most interesting or the most relevant parts.
- Interview them in a situation that is natural for them (such as their workshop) rather than in a formal studio setting.
- Whenever possible, avoid showing the talent just standing, waiting for their part. They will feel more at ease (particularly in their own surroundings) if they have something to do. For example, a cook might be cutting up some vegetables before speaking.
- Give them a few instructions, such as telling them when, where, or how to hold the items in front of the camera.
- Use plenty of cutaway shots so that the program does not concentrate on the talent all of the time. As much as possible, look at what they are talking about. During the editing phase, the cutaways can be cut into the program.
- Some directors keep the tension down by shooting when the talent does not know they are being recorded.

In a scripted program, it may be wise to record the dress rehearsal and, if possible, to run through the material several times, recording everything, so that the director can select and combine the best parts of each version.

If sections do not edit well, the interviewer can record a question or a statement later that will bridge what would otherwise be disjointed material. With care, this can be done quite well, even though it was not part of the original interview.

THE ACTOR'S CRAFT

The best advice I've ever received about directing came from a veteran motion picture cameraman who had successfully switched to feature film directing in mid career. The advice was this: "No matter which medium, video, film, theater, etc., and no matter what kind of production—sales training tapes to news segments to documentaries to feature films—as long as people are involved, a good director must have a knowledge of the craft of acting."

A knowledge of the actor's craft will fundamentally change your approach to directing any kind of program in which people appear on camera. I took his advice and can now declare: "He was right!"

—Frank Beacham, Director

9.6 THE HOST

Many of the problems of handling inexperienced talent can be reduced if someone who is familiar with the production routine offers support. The person who serves as the host will probably meet the guest beforehand, help the person to feel at ease, and explain what will be happening during the program (Figure 9.8). The host can also gently guide the guest through the interview by posing the questions within the right context: "Earlier, you were telling me about ..." or "I wonder if we could look at ..." or "Isn't the construction of this piece interesting?" The host can move the program smoothly from one topic to the next. Especially when shooting intermittently or out of order—both very confusing to the novice talent—the host can be very effective at guiding the guest through the production.

FIGURE 9.8
One of the hosts from NBC's *Today* show, sitting in the light shirt, is prepping his guest for the next segment of the program.

THE ACTOR

A jolt of panic rises in even the most experienced actor when he starts to perform in front of other people, even if it is just a rehearsal. He is putting all his talent and self-image on the line and is probably terrified that his audience may not buy into what he is doing. What if the crew hates it? It would be a personal rejection of the actor. The more he uses his own psyche to build the character, the more vulnerable he becomes. There is one key principle about working with actors: Actors must feel they are in a place where they are totally safe.

—John Badham, Director

In situations where the talent will be discussing an object that must appear on camera, the host can help the guest know how to handle the object. Instead of the nervous guest holding the prop in a way that does not work for television (partly hiding it, reflecting the lights, or moving it around in a close-up shot), the host can tactfully take it from the guest to look at it and then hold it in a way that facilitates a good camera shot. At times, the host can also look in a nearby monitor to check the shot.

9.7 THE OFF-CAMERA HOST

Talent does not always appear on camera. Some hosts are required to sit in a booth and commentate while watching the event on monitors. As pay-per-view Internet extended versions of broadcast programs continue to grow in popularity, this practice will increase. The problem with off-camera broadcasting is that the talent needs to keep the excitement in their voice and act as though they are there. This can be difficult at times when the talent may not even be in the area of the event (Figure 9.9).

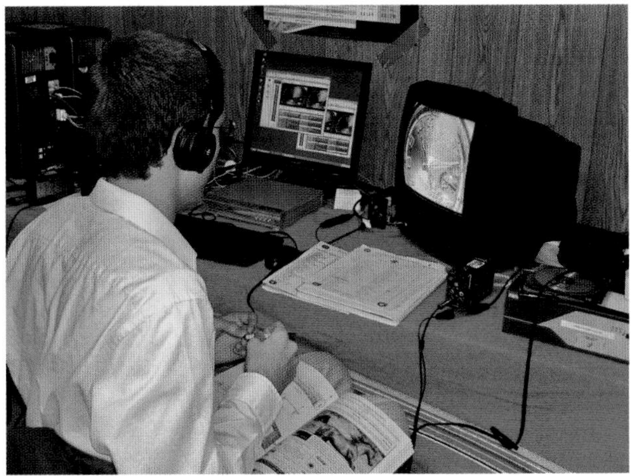

FIGURE 9.9
This reporter is commenting on a sporting event broadcast worldwide on NBC.com. Keeping your energy going as a commentator, when you are not actually at the event, can be difficult.

When There Are Problems

There are times when the invited guests simply do not live up to expectations. Perhaps he is too stiff. Or maybe she is so hesitant and nervous that she does herself little justice. Then there are the guests who overcompensate and become loud and obnoxious. In a live show, there may be little opportunity to actually replace someone. If there is a rehearsal and it is obvious that the guest is not going to work, it is possible to cut that individual from the show. However, doing so can create a difficult situation. It may be possible to tape the segment instead of going live, in the hope you will be able to use at least some of the person's contribution. If a shaky performance becomes a serious issue, it can be cut in postproduction.

Other ways to deal with a problematic guest are to simplify or to shorten the person's segment. You can use multiple cutaways, such as close-ups of details, to cover the edits during postproduction. If necessary, these cutaways can be shot after the main show is recorded.

Another approach is to have the host present the items in the program while continually referring to the guest. For example, the host could pick up an item, hold it to camera, and remind the guest of the information they discussed before or during rehearsal. At worst, the guest has to do little more than say yes and no.

As a last resort, you can use a voiceover track for the guest's segment and use video images of the subject matter.

9.8 PRESENTING THE INFORMATION

Just because the talent may be an expert about a specific subject does not mean that he or she can present it convincingly to the camera. Ironically, there are times when a talent working from a teleprompter script may appear more authentic, even though the words may have been written by someone else.

How the action is shot is influenced not only by the nature of the subject but by the talent involved. The camera can behave like a bystander who moves around to get a good view of whatever is going on. This happens in street interviews. At best, one hopes that whoever is being interviewed will be preoccupied with the questioner and barely notice the camera and microphone. However, it can sometimes be difficult to relax when one is being besieged by the curiosity of bystanders.

9.9 IMPORTANCE OF PEOPLE IN THE SCENE

Suppose you are shooting a production about a town. You are describing its character and its special features and showing details of its buildings. Shooting early in the morning, before people are moving around, provides a great opportunity to get clear, uncluttered views. However, do the shots really convey the town's typical atmosphere?

On the other hand, if you begin shooting once the town has come to life so that you can capture the hustle and bustle of passing traffic, it may be difficult to get the required shots, although the place now has exactly the right feel to it. This is a reminder that there may be advantages to shooting various aspects of

FIGURE 9.10
People bring life to scenes, making the image more interesting to the audience. This image captured the atmosphere of the red carpet at the British Academy Awards.

the subject at different times, according to the light, the weather, and the passing crowd (Figure 9.10).

Finally, do not overlook how important people are in giving life to a scene. Rather than pan along an empty sidewalk, it is more interesting to follow someone who is passing (although there is the possibility that the audience may now wonder who this newcomer is, speculating on the person instead of on the real subject).

A shot looking along an empty bridge is likely to bore your audience within a few seconds. But have someone walk across that same bridge, and the scene immediately becomes more interesting. Now you can hold the shot much longer while a voiceover tells us about the bridge's history.

Selecting the right talent to fit the script and then helping the talent understand what you need from him or her to make a successful production are two of the director's greatest challenges. However, when the talent gets it right, with the right script and with the right director, the results can be incredible.

9.10 SAFETY

The crew always needs to look out for the talent's safety. The talent is often looking at the camera or concentrating on the script and may not see someone or something approaching from the side. They have to be protected against tripping on cables, walking off curbs, or getting too close to hot lights. When working in heat, you also have to make sure that they are hydrated.

Interview with a Pro

Kristin Ross Lauterbach, Director

Kristin Ross Lauterbach, Director

Why do you like to direct?

I have always been a visual storyteller. I love the collaborative nature of the process, as well as the interaction with all the arts. As a director, I have the opportunity to experience the whole journey of the film from words on a page to moving, talking images on a screen. As a lover of books, art, and music, directing utilizes all these crafts without the need to be an expert in any of them. Sometimes the process is daunting, as you are the driving force behind the project, but it's such a wonderful feeling when you sit back at the end and all of the senses are stimulated by the story you have worked so hard to tell.

What are the challenges to working with actors/talent?

I think any time that you work in a celebrative profession, which filmmaking is, you will have challenges and struggles because everyone has their own vision. As a director, you are steering the ship, but you have to give everyone enough freedom to express their own talents. You cast your actor because you believe in their ability to make the script come to life, so give them enough room to let it. One of the best compliments I received from an actor was that I gave him a box to play in and he had total freedom to experiment inside it, but I let him know if he went outside that box. As a director, you are looking at the bigger picture, and you have to help everyone see their part of that vision with confidence and compassion.

What suggestions do you have for the beginning director for working with talent?

Take the time to rehearse and talk scenes out with your talent before you ever get to the set. Your entire cast and crew is looking to you for vision and guidance, so make the time to help your talent develop their characters so you are not holding up the entire crew on shoot day. With that said, be willing to take a break on set if your actor is struggling with a scene. It might feel like you don't have time to do it, but you will thank yourself when you get back to the cutting room.

How do you select an actor for a production? Are there things that you specifically look for?

Go with your gut. Listen to that little voice that says, "This is right," and definitely listen to it when it says "This is NOT right," especially if it looks right on paper. It's not. We read all type of subconscious body language without even realizing it.

I like to have a conversation with talent before I ever have them read a word of the script. I think performing the scene is more a formality, and it's not the best representation of the actor; get to know them. I know what I am looking for, and when I see it, I know. In the past, when I didn't listen to my gut, it always came back to bite me, and it made for very long, painful productions.

Kristin Lauterbach has worked in television and film.

CHAPTER 10
Audio for Video

The true mark of an audio track's success—to sound so natural under a given scene that it draws no attention to itself.
—Walter Schoenknecht, Midnight Media Group

Historically, audio has been slighted in the world of television. Most manufacturers and producers have cared more about the image, relegating audio to an inexpensive, poor-sounding little speaker on television sets. However, if you really want to find out how important audio is to a video production, just turn off the audio and try to follow the story. You will soon get lost. Look away from the screen, with the audio up, and you can still follow the story. Audio is as important to television as the video image. Audio gives images a convincing realism. It helps the audience feel involved. As Dennis Baxter, sound designer for the Olympics, has written, "Audio, in partnership with video, delivers a holistic experience with all of the intense emotion and interesting nuances to the viewer."

Key Audio Terms and Equipment

- ***Audio filters:*** Used to reduce background noises (traffic, air conditioners, wind) or compensate for boomy surroundings.
- ***Audio mixer:*** Used to select, control, and intermix audio sources. It may include filter circuits, reverberation control, and other features. It is usually operated by the audio mixer (a job title as well as the name of the board) or A-1 (sound supervisor).
- ***Bidirectional microphone:*** This microphone can hear equally well both in front and in back but is deaf on either side of it. This is sometimes called a "figure of eight" pattern.
- ***Compressor/expander:*** Deliberately used to reduce or emphasize the audio dynamic range (i.e., the difference between the quietest and loudest sounds).
- ***Condenser microphone:*** A high-quality microphone that can be very small and is generally powered by an onboard battery, phantom power, or a power supply.
- ***Directional microphone:*** This type of microphone can hear sounds directly in front of it.

- ***Dynamic microphone:*** A rugged, low-maintenance, not easily distorted microphone.
- ***Graphic equalizer (shaping filter):*** This unit is equipped with a series of slider controls, which allows selected parts of the audio spectrum to be boosted or reduced.
- ***Handheld microphone:*** Widely used by news reporters and musicians.
- ***Lavalier microphone (mini-mic, clip-on, lapel mic):*** These small "Lav" microphones clip onto the talent's clothing and provide fairly consistent, hands-free, audio pickup of the talent's voice.
- ***Limiter:*** A device for preventing loud audio from exceeding the system's upper limit (causing overload distortion) by progressively reducing circuit amplification for louder sounds.
- ***Monaural (mono):*** One audio track.
- ***Natural sound:*** The recording of ambient or environmental sounds on location.
- ***Omnidirectional microphone:*** This type of microphone can pick up audio equally well in all directions.
- ***Patch panel/jackfield:*** Rows of sockets to which the inputs and outputs of a variety of audio units are permanently wired. Units may be interconnected with a series of plugged cables (patch cords).
- ***Preamplifier:*** An amplifier used to adjust the strength of audio from one or more audio sources to a standard level (intensity). It may include source switching and basic filtering.
- ***Reverberation:*** Device for increasing or adjusting the amount of echo accompanying a sound.
- ***Shotgun microphone:*** A highly directional microphone used to pick up sound from a distance.
- ***Stereo:*** Stereo sound uses two audio tracks to create an illusion of space and dimension.
- ***Surround sound:*** 5.1 surround uses six audio tracks to create a sense of envelopment.

10.1 THE ESSENTIAL COMPONENT

The valuable contribution that sound makes to television cannot be underestimated. In a good production, sound is never a casual afterthought. It is an essential part of the production's appeal.

People often think of television as pictures accompanied by sound. Yet when the best television productions are analyzed, people are usually surprised that most of the time it is the *sound* that conveys the information and stimulates the audience's imagination, while the image itself can be a visual accompaniment. Audio has the power to help the audience conjure up mental images that enhance what is being seen.

Sounds are evocative. For example, consider an image of a couple of people leaning against a wall with the open sky as a background. If we hear noises of waves breaking and the shrill cry of birds, we quickly assume that the couple is near the seashore. Add the sound of children at play, and now we are sure that our subjects are near the beach. Replace all those sounds with the noise of a battle, explosions, and passing tanks, and they are immediately transported to a war zone. They might even appear particularly brave and unfazed, as they remain so calm in the middle of this tumult.

In fact, all we really have here is a shot of two people leaning on a wall. The wall itself might have been anywhere—up a mountain, in a desert, or near a replica in a studio. The location and the mood of the occasion have been conjured up by the sound and our imagination.

Successful audio is a blend of two things:

- Appropriate *techniques*. The way the equipment is used to capture the audio.
- Appropriate *artistic choices*. How the sounds are selected and mixed.
- Both are largely a matter of technical knowledge combined with experience.

10.2 THE NATURE OF SOUND

The world about us is filled with such an endless variety of sounds that it is difficult to believe each can be resolved into a single complex vibration pattern. When several sources sound together, their separate patterns combine into an even more complicated form. Yet our eardrums, the microphone diaphragm, and the loudspeaker all follow this combined vibration, and, more miraculous still, our brain interprets the result.

The simplest possible sound vibrations make a regular *sinusoidal* movement, and we hear the pure tones from a tuning fork, a flute, or an audio oscillator. The faster this oscillation, the higher the pitch. Very slow vibrations (subsonic, below about 15 times a second) and extremely fast vibrations (ultrasonic, above about 20,000 times a second) fall outside our audible range. The frequency or rate of these vibrations is measured in *hertz*.

The stronger the sound's vibrations (the greater their *amplitude*), the louder it seems. Slight vibrations are inaudible, whereas extremely loud sounds can become painful to listen to, as they exceed our threshold of feeling.

Few sources emit "pure" sounds. Most are a complex combination of the main note (the *fundamental*) and multiples of that note (*harmonics* or *overtones*). The apparent quality of a sound will depend on the proportions or relative strengths of these harmonics.

Broadly speaking, a note played by a double bass, an oboe, or a bassoon can be judged by its overall quality. If the response of the audio system is not even over the whole audible range (because of filtering or limitations in the equipment), the proportions of the harmonics can change. Then the quality of the reproduced sound may no longer be recognizable as the original instrument.

10.3 ACOUSTICS

You have only to compare sound in an empty room with the difference that occurs when that same room is furnished or filled with people to realize how acoustics alter sound quality. If we understand the basics of acoustics, we can avoid many of the audio problems that might arise during the production (Table 10.1).

Table 10.1 Coping with Acoustics

When Surroundings Are Too "Live," Reduce Acoustic Reflections
▪ Move the microphone closer to the sound source. ▪ Pull curtains if available. ▪ Add thick rugs. ▪ Add cushions. ▪ Use upholstered furniture. ▪ Drape blankets on frames or over chairs. ▪ Add acoustic panels (Figure 10.2).
When Surroundings Are Too "Dead," Increase Acoustic Reflections
▪ Move the microphone farther away. ▪ Open curtains to increase hard surface space. ▪ Remove rugs. ▪ Remove cushions. ▪ Remove upholstered furniture. ▪ Add board or plastic surfaced panels. ▪ Add floor panels (wood, fiberboard). ▪ Add artificial reverberation.

When a sound wave hits a *hard surface* (plastic, glass, tile, stone walls, metal), little is absorbed, so the reflected sound is almost as loud as the original. This is referred to as a live surrounding. Where there are a lot of hard surfaces around (as in a bathroom, a large hall, or a church), a place can become extremely reverberant or live. Sound waves rebound from one surface to another so easily that the original and the reflected versions, completely intermixed, are heard. This can cause considerable changes in the overall sound quality and significantly degrade its clarity. When surroundings are reverberant, reflections are often heard seconds after the sound itself has stopped; in extreme cases, these sounds reflect as a repeated echo. Whether reverberations add richness to the original sound or simply confuse it will vary with the design of the space, the position of the sound source, the pitch and quality of the sound, and the position of the microphone (or mic).

When a sound wave hits a *soft surface* (curtains, couches, rugs), some of its energy is absorbed within the material. Soft surfaces create a *dead* surrounding.

Higher notes are the most absorbed, so the sound reflected from this sort of surface is not only quieter than the original sound wave, but it lacks the higher frequencies. Its quality is more mellow, less resonant, even dull and muted. Certain soft materials absorb the sound so well that virtually none is reflected (Figures 10.1 and 10.2). If, on the other hand, the sound is made in a place with many soft surfaces, both the original sound and any reflections can be significantly muffled. When outside, in an open area, sound can be very dead. This is due to the air quickly absorbing the sound because there are few reflecting surfaces. Microphones used outside often have to get closer to a subject than normal to pick up sufficient sound, especially if a person is speaking quietly (Figure 10.3).

FIGURE 10.1
The variety of angles of the set walls, the curtains, carpet, furniture, and people help dampen the live sound—but not too much.

10.4 MONO SOUND

In everyday life, each member of the audience is used to listening with the aid of two ears. As listeners compare these two separate sound images of the external world, they build up a three-dimensional impression from which the direction and distance of sound is estimated.

FIGURE 10.2
Acoustic panels were placed on the walls of this audio room to reduce the "liveness" of the room.

FIGURE 10.3
During the shooting of a dramatic program, the boom operator got the microphone as close as possible, while still being off camera, because open-air sound does not usually travel far.

Nonstereo television sound is not as sophisticated as this. It presents a "single-eared" monaural ("mono") representation of sound in space. The only clue to distance is loudness, and direction cannot be conveyed at all. When listening to mono reproduction, we are not able to distinguish between direct and reflected sounds, as we can when listening in stereo. Instead, these sounds become intermixed so that the combined sound is often muddy and less distinct. In mono sound, we become much more aware of the effects of reverberation.

Because the audience cannot easily distinguish direction and distance, the mono microphone needs to be carefully positioned. Audio personnel need to be careful to consider the following:

- Too many sound reflections are not picked up.
- Louder sounds do not mask a quieter sound (particularly in an orchestra).
- Extraneous sounds do not interfere with the ones we want to hear.

10.5 STEREO SOUND

Stereo sound creates an illusion of space and dimension. It enhances clarity. Stereo gives the viewer the ability to localize the direction of the sound. This localization gives the audience a sense of depth, a spatial awareness of the visual image and the sound. However, because the speakers in television receivers are close together, the effect can be somewhat limited. Sound quality and realism are enhanced, but our impressions of direction and depth are less obvious.

FIRST SURROUND SOUND

Disney introduced surround sound to the cinemas with the movie *Fantasia*, released in 1940. Three channels were used behind the theater screen, with three additional speakers used on either side and at the rear. However, implementing this system was extremely expensive, and the system was used in only two theaters.

10.6 SURROUND SOUND

Surround sound can provide a sense of envelopment when mixed correctly. Instead of the one channel for mono or two channels for stereo, 5.1 surround has six discrete (distinct, individual) channels: left front, right front (sometimes called stereo left and right), center, a subwoofer for low-frequency effects (LFE), left rear, and right rear speakers (sometimes called surround left and right). To present the feeling of depth, direction, and realism, audio personnel pan between the five main channels and route effects to the LFE channel (Figure 10.4).

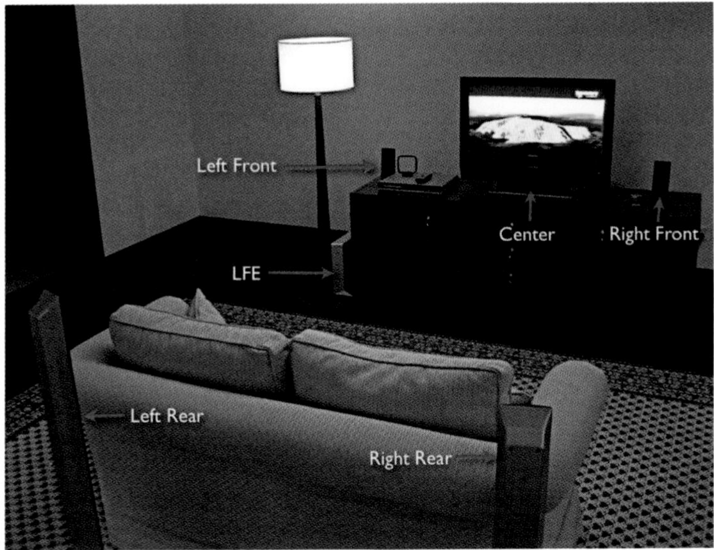

FIGURE 10.4
A home surround system utilizes six speakers.

10.7 MICROPHONE CARE

Although most people regard the video camera with a certain apprehension, there are those who tend to dismiss the microphone (or mic) all too casually. They clip it onto the guest's jacket with an air of "that's all we have to do for audio" instead of treating the mic as a delicate tool. The microphone (and how it is used) is really at the heart of television program sound. If the microphone is inferior, if it is damaged, or if it is poorly positioned, the program sound will suffer. No amount of postproduction work with the audio can compensate for doing it right from the beginning. *Program sound all begins with the microphone.*

It is not important to know how various types of microphones work to use them properly. They all convert sound waves in the air into a fluctuating electrical voltage (the audio signal). It does help, though, to be aware of their different characteristics.

Although most microphones are reasonably robust, they do need careful handling if they are to remain reliable and perform up to specification. If you drop them, knock them, or get liquid on them, you are asking for trouble.

10.8 DIRECTIONAL FEATURES

Microphones do not all behave in the same way. Some are designed to be *nondirectional* (*omnidirectional*), meaning they can pick up equally well sounds coming from all directions. Others are *directional*, meaning they can pick up sounds directly in front of them clearly but are comparatively deaf to sounds in all other directions. A further design has a bidirectional or "figure-of-eight" pattern, meaning it can pick up equally well both forward and backward, but it is deaf on either side.

The advantage of an *omnidirectional* mic (Figure 10.5) is that it can pick up sound equally well over a wide area. It is great for covering a group of people or someone who is moving around. The disadvantage is that it cannot discriminate between the sound you want to hear and unwanted sounds such as reflections from walls, noises from nearby people or equipment, ventilation noise, footsteps, and so on. The more reverberant the surroundings, the worse the problem. The mic must be positioned so that it is closer to the wanted sounds than to the extraneous noises. This mic is great for picking up ambient or natural (NAT) sounds.

When a directional mic (Figure 10.6) is pointed at the desired sound, it will tend to ignore sounds from other directions, providing a much cleaner result. On the other hand, the directional mic needs to be aimed very carefully. It is also important to make sure that the audio source does not move out of the main pickup zone; if it does, the source will be "off mic." The off-mic sound becomes weaker, and the audience may hear what the mic is pointed at instead of the desired source.

FIGURE 10.5
The omnidirectional pickup pattern is equally sensitive in all directions, generally rugged, and not too susceptible to impact shock. This mic cannot distinguish between direct and reflected sounds, so it must be placed close to the sound source.
(Drawing courtesy of Audio-Technica.)

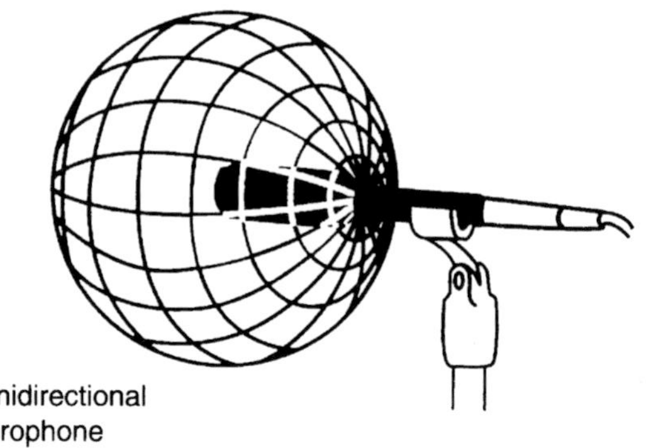

There are several forms of unidirectional pickup patterns. The *cardioid* (Figure 10.6) or heart-shaped pattern is broad enough for general use

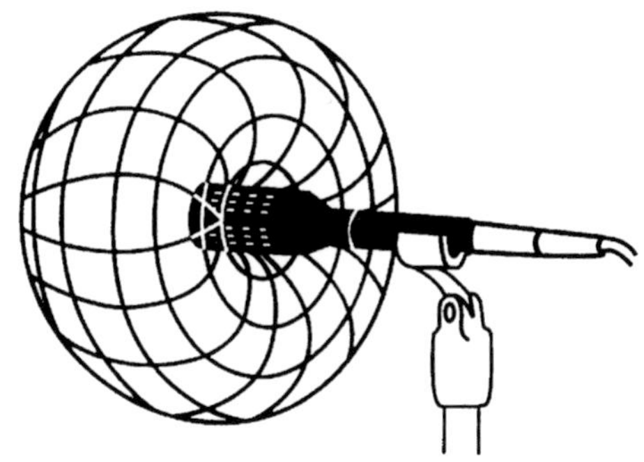

FIGURE 10.6
The directional (or cardioid) mic pickup pattern. This broad, heart-shaped pickup pattern (roughly 160) is insensitive on its rear side.
(Drawing courtesy of Audio-Technica.)

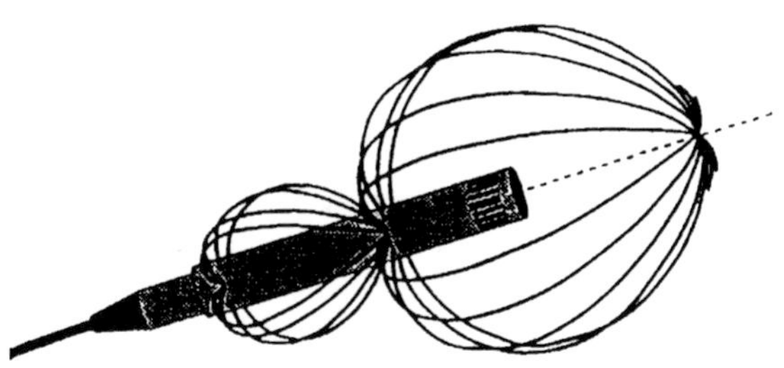

FIGURE 10.7
Use a supercardioid (or highly directional) pickup pattern wherever you want extremely selective pickup, to avoid environmental noises, or for distance sources.
(Drawing courtesy of Audio-Technica.)

but not overselective, whereas the *super-* or *hypercardioid* (Figure 10.7) response has also a limited pickup area at its rear to receive reflected sounds.

10.9 POPULAR TYPES OF MICROPHONES

There are two predominant methods for converting sound energy to an electrical equivalent signal: electrodynamic and electrostatic, better known as *dynamic* and *condenser*.

Dynamic microphones are the most rugged, provide good quality sound, and are not easily distorted by loud sounds such as nearby drums. These mics need little or no regular maintenance. They can be handheld without causing unwanted "handling noise" and used in all types of microphone mountings. However, they are just as high quality as the condenser microphone.

The condenser microphone produces very high audio quality and is ideal for picking up music. A significant advantage to the condenser is that it can be very small, making it the logical choice for a shotgun, lavalier mic, and other miniature microphones. The condenser mic is generally powered by an inboard battery, phantom-powered audio board, or a special power supply. The electret condenser microphone has a permanent charge applied when it is manufactured, which remains for the life of the microphone and does not need to be externally powered.

> Just as you should preplan camera angles for a shoot, you should preplan mic types and positioning. Carefully plan cable runs and connections, and scout every location to determine if it will cause undesirable noise from air conditioners, trains, traffic, or other uncontrollable sounds that will end up being recorded.
>
> **—Douglas Spotted Eagle, Grammy Award-Winning Producer**

SUPPORTING THE MICROPHONE

10.10 CAMERA MICROPHONES

If the camera is fitted with a microphone, the theory is that when it is aimed at the subject to capture the video, the mic will also pick up quality audio. However, a lot depends on the situation and the type of sound involved. Nothing beats a separate, high-quality microphone placed in exactly the right place. However, single-camera operators, working by themselves and moving around to various shooting positions, may have to use the camera microphone.

The simplest form of camera microphone is a small built-in mic at the front of the camera. These mics are known to pick up sound from all around the camera, including noise from the camera zoom lens and camera operator sounds. With care, though, this basic microphone is useful for general atmospheric background sounds (traffic, crowds) and is almost adequate for close-up voice. However, it should only be used for voice when better options are not available. With most camera mics, trying to pick up a voice more than four to six feet away results in unacceptably high levels of background noise or acoustical reflections.

The most popular type of camera microphone is the shotgun mic, attached to the top of the camera (Figure 10.8). Plugged into the camera's external mic socket, this mic will give the best quality long-distance pickup from the subject. As always with directional mics, the *shotgun mic* must be aimed accurately.

At first thought, a camera microphone provides the simplest method of picking up program sound:

- The microphone is positioned on the camera, so you do not need a second person to look after the audio.
- Wherever the camera points, the microphone will follow.
- There are no problems with microphone boom shadows.

FIGURE 10.8
Shotgun mics are the most popular type of camera microphones.

However, the camera microphone has a number of drawbacks too:

- The microphone is often too far away from the subject for the best sound. Its position is determined by the camera's shot, not by the optimum place for the microphone.
- Unless the microphone zooms with the zoom lens, and some do, the microphone's distance is the same for all shots. The camera may zoom in to a close-up shot or take a wide-angle shot, but the sound level remains the same.

- The camera microphone cannot follow somebody if they turn away from a frontal position, such as to point to a nearby wall map. The sound's volume and quality will fall off as the subject moves off mic.

10.11 THE HANDHELD MICROPHONE

The handheld mic (stick mic) is a familiar sight on television, as it is used by interviewers, singers, and commentators (Figure 10.9). It is a simple, convenient method of sound pickup, provided it is used properly. The handheld mic is best held just below shoulder height, pointed slightly toward the person speaking. It should be as unobtrusive as possible.

FIGURE 10.9
The handheld microphone is widely used for interviews, commentaries, and stage work. If the mic has a cardioid directional response, extraneous noise pickup is lower. If the mic is omnidirectional, it may need to be held closer to the subject to reduce atmosphere sounds. The mic is normally held just below shoulder height.

To reduce the low rumbling noises of wind on the microphone and explosive breath-pops when it is held too close to the mouth, attach a foam windshield on the microphone. Note the yellow foam windshield in the interview photo in Figure 10.9. Whenever possible, talk across the microphone rather than directly into it. This will provide the optimal audio quality.

Handheld microphones with cardioid patterns help reduce the amount of extraneous sound overheard, so this type of mic can be used about 1 to 1.5 feet from the person speaking. An omnidirectional handheld mic will normally have to be held much closer, about 9 inches away.

When the talent is walking around with a handheld mic, make sure he or she has plenty of mic cable, or use a wireless handheld. The talent should be able to move around easily without the cable limiting movement. It is important to run the cable out of sight of the camera. Gaffer tape can be used to tape the cable to the floor.

10.12 THE SHOTGUN MICROPHONE

The shotgun microphone (hypercardioid) consists of a slotted tube containing an electret microphone at one end. This microphone is designed to pick up sound within a narrow angle while remaining less sensitive to sounds from other directions. It is great for isolating a subject within a crowd or for excluding nearby noises (Figure 10.10).

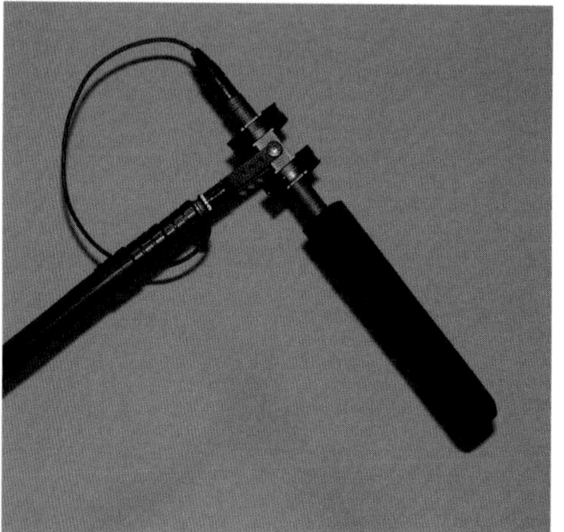

FIGURE 10.10
The shotgun microphone is one of the most used mics in television. These microphones are very susceptible to handling noise and must be held or connected to a pole or stand with a shock mount.

When shooting in very "live" (reverberant) surroundings, a shotgun microphone has advantages because it will pick up the subject's sound successfully while reducing unwanted reflections, although how effectively it does this will depend on the pitch or coloration of the reflected sounds.

The shotgun microphone is adaptable and is regularly used as follows:

- A handheld microphone supported by some type of shock mount (see Figure 10.10)
- Connected to the end of a boom pole or fishpole (see Figure 10.12)
- In the swiveled cradle support of a regular sound boom or perambulator boom (see Figure 10.1)
- As a camera microphone, fitted to the top of the camera head (see Figure 10.8)

Most people working in the field fit a shotgun microphone with some type of a windshield (windjammer or wind muffler; see Figure 10.11). The most effective types for suppressing obtrusive wind noises are a furry overcoat with "hairs" or a plastic/fabric tube. An alternative design of wind filter is a tubular plastic

FIGURE 10.11
Different types of windshields are used to protect a shotgun mic from wind noise.

sponge (see Figure 10.10). Although much lighter, this may prove inadequate except in the lightest breeze.

10.13 USING THE SHOTGUN MICROPHONE

Selecting the best position for a shotgun microphone takes some preplanning. Audio personnel need a clear idea of how the action is going to develop. They may get this from a briefing beforehand or find out from a camera rehearsal:

- Will the shotgun be used for long takes or for brief shots? It is one thing to stand in a fixed position as someone talks directly to the camera and another to have to follow action around as people and cameras move through a sequence.
- Will audio personnel have an uninterrupted view of the action?
- Is anyone or anything going to get in their way, or are they going to get in anyone else's way?

Audio personnel should try to position themselves so that the action moves toward them instead of away from them. Whenever the mic boom holder or the talent moves around, it is easy for the talent to pass in and out of the microphone's main pickup area. If the talent turns away from the microphone, there is usually no way the mic boom holder can compensate or move onto the sound axis.

10.14 THE SHOTGUN AND THE BOOM POLE (FISHPOLE)

The boom pole has become the most popular choice for sound pickup on location and in many smaller studios. This adjustable lightweight aluminum pole is usually about six to nine feet long and carries a microphone at its far end. The sound cable is either designed inside the pole or is taped securely along the pole.

There are many ways to hold a boom pole:

- Above the head, with arms fully extended along the pole to balance it (see Figure 10.12).
- Set across the shoulders for added stability.
- With the end of the pole tucked under one shoulder. The goal is to get the microphone close enough without showing up at the bottom of the camera's shot (also see Figure 10.3).

FIGURE 10.12
A *mic boom* (or fishpole) is a regular method of mounting the shotgun microphone, particularly in the field. It allows the operator to stand several feet away from the subject, reaching over any foreground obstacles to place the microphone at an optimum angle. This position can be tiring if it has to be maintained for a long period of time. However, it may be the only solution when people are standing or walking about.
(Photo courtesy of Dennis Baxter.)

10.15 LAVALIER (LAPEL OR CLIP-ON MIC) MICROPHONES

The lavalier microphone, also known as a "lav," lapel, or clip-on mic, has become a favorite mic in productions where it is unimportant whether the viewer sees a mic attached to someone's clothing (Figures 10.13 and 10.14). These microphones are compact, unobtrusive, and provide high sound quality. But they must be used judiciously for optimum results. Clip the microphone

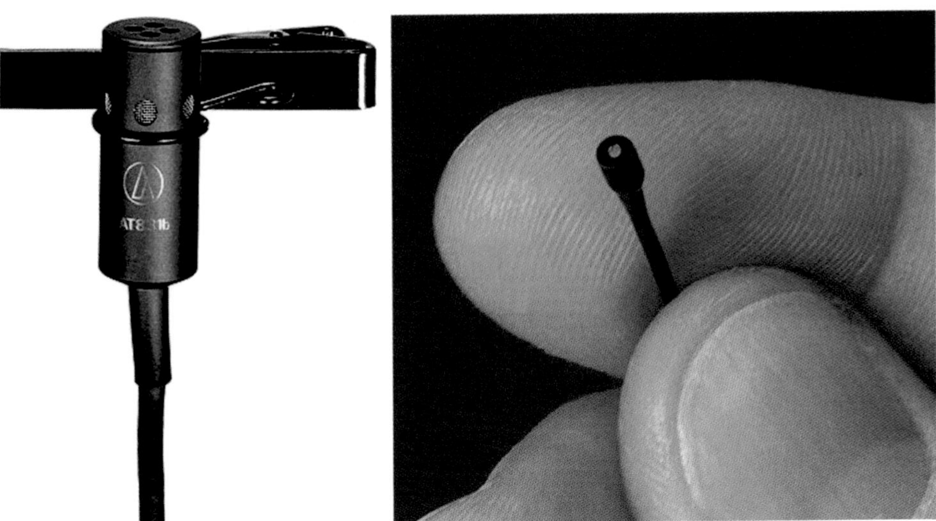

FIGURE 10.13
Lavalier microphones come in different sizes and shapes. Generally, a lavalier mic is clipped to a necktie, lapel, or shirt. Sometimes a "dual redundancy" pair is used whenever a standby mic is desired.
(Photo courtesy of Audio-Technica and Countryman Associates.)

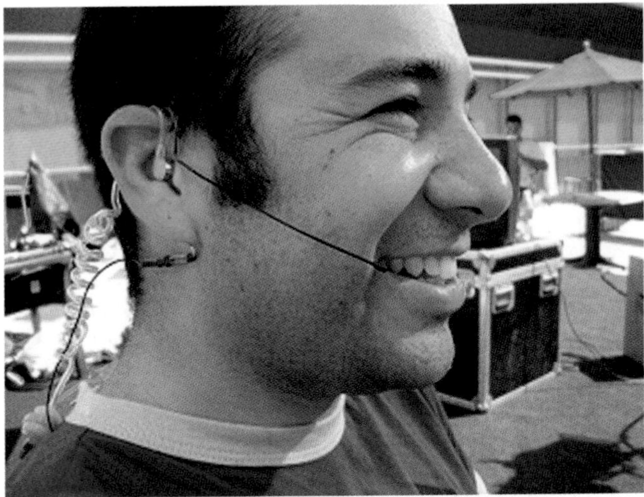

FIGURE 10.14
The talent is using an "earset" microphone that utilizes the lavalier microphone. It is mounted on a tiny mic "boom" and attached to the ear. It is also available in a flesh color and is almost invisible to the viewing audience. In this situation, it was used on ESPN's X-Games.
(Photo by Dennis Baxter.)

to outside clothing (such as the tie, lapel, shirt, or blouse), and noises from clothing rubbing will be kept to a minimum. One of the challenges when using a lavalier mic is that the volume and clarity of the sound can change as a wearer turns his or her head left and right, or toward and away from the microphone.

A lavalier mic can only be relied on to effectively pick up the sound of the person wearing it. When two or three people are speaking, each will need to wear his or her own microphone. This does not mean that the mics won't pick up the sound from others; it just won't be the same quality and will not be the same level. When working in noisy surroundings, a small foam windshield over the end of the microphone will reduce the rumble of wind noise. As always, it is important to conceal the lavalier mic's cable beneath a jacket or shirt.

Lavalier microphones can also be used to record subjects other than people. They are used effectively in sports productions (mounted in places like the nets at a soccer field), and they can be used to pick up the sound of some musical instruments. The clip-on mic in Figure 10.15 is actually a type of lavalier mic.

FIGURE 10.15
Lavalier microphones are often used to record musical instruments or any other subject that requires close miking.
(Photos courtesy of Audio-Technica.)

10.16 BOUNDARY OR PZM MICROPHONE

The *boundary microphone* and *pressure zone microphone* (PZM) are low-profile mics that can be used to capture audio from talent that is six or more feet away and do not produce the hollow sound of a hanging handheld mic (Figure 10.16). Although the pickup technology is very different, these two mics are used similarly. These microphones are especially good for dramatic productions where microphones should not be seen (they can be adhered to the back of set pieces). They are also good for stage performances of large groups. They can be hung from the ceiling, set on a floor, or adhered to furniture. The pickup distance can be increased by mounting these mics on a hard surface.

FIGURE 10.16
The boundary microphone is a low-profile mic that can pick up accurate sounds from six or more feet away.

10.17 HANGING MICROPHONE

Hanging microphones are especially designed for high-quality sound reinforcement of dramatic productions, orchestras, and choirs. These mics are suspended over the performance area. Their small size is ideal because they will probably be visible to the viewing audience (Figure 10.17).

FIGURE 10.17
Hanging microphone.
(Photo courtesy of Audio-Technica.)

10.18 SURROUND SOUND MICROPHONE

Surround sound microphones can capture 5.1 to 7.1 channels of discrete (separate) audio with the multidirectional pickup pattern. Using the small microphone shown in Figure 10.18, the audio can be recorded directly onto the camera's internal media along with the video image. The small microphone has five microphone elements—left front (L), right front (R), center (C), left rear or left surround (LS), right rear or right surround (RS)—and a dedicated low-frequency effects (LFE) (.1) microphone. Some high-end versions provide 7.1 surround sound. Smaller systems, designed specifically for a camcorder, utilize an internal Dolby Pro-Logic II Encoded line-level stereo output for connection directly to the camera on a single 3.5-mm stereo female miniplug jack (Figure 10.18).

Some of the nonlinear editing systems, like Final Cut Pro, have a Dolby logic decoder built in, allowing the channels from the stereo input to be split into the five surround channels. This allows a user to record programs in surround sound without the need for a full surround mixing board.

Surround sound microphones must be positioned carefully (Figure 10.19). They should not just be mounted on top of a camera if the camera will be

FIGURE 10.18
This small surround sound microphone includes a Dolby Pro-Logic II encoder with a line-level stereo output designed for camcorders.
(Photo courtesy of Holophone.)

FIGURE 10.19
ABC Television's *Extreme Home Makeover* uses a professional surround sound microphone, separate from the camera, to capture the audio.
(Photo courtesy of Holophone.)

panning and tilting around. Moving the microphone around with the camera can spatially disorient the audience. Generally these microphones are mounted on a separate stand or clamped to something stationary in order to pick up a quality ambient sound.

Suggestions for using a surround sound microphone:

- Use the surround mic to provide the "base" ambient surround sound for the audio mix.
- For a concert situation with arena-style seating, place the sound mic a little higher than the orchestra, tilting the nose down toward the performers.
- In most situations, try to position the surround mic as close to "front row center" as possible rather than near the back of the room.
- When shooting sports events, it is best to place the surround mic either near the center of the field or near a main camera position. Always keep in mind the perspective of the television viewer. Mounting the surround mic on a side of a field or rink opposite to the main camera angle would seem backward and unnatural.
- For surround recording of acoustic instruments, including drum kits, pianos, and voice at close range, try placing the mic near or above the instrument that is being recorded. For vocal or choirs, position the singers around the mic and monitor in surround to hear the results.

10.19 MICROPHONE STANDS AND MOUNTS

Microphone stands and mics are useful in situations where the director does not mind the microphone possibly appearing in the shot (Figures 10.20 and 10.21). It is especially useful for stage announcements, singing groups, and for miking musical instruments. It does have some disadvantages. If people move around much, they can easily walk out of the mic's range. Directors have to rely on the talent to get to the right place and keep the right distance from the mic. It is a good idea to give talent taped marks on the floor to guide them. And, of course, there is always the danger that the talent will kick the stand or trip over the cable.

FIGURE 10.20
An audio person adjusts a microphone stand for an on-location interview project.

10.20 WIRELESS MICROPHONE

The most commonly used wireless microphones are the lavalier mic and the handheld mics (Figures 10.22 and 10.23). Both can be purchased with the wireless transmitter built into the mic (or belt pack) and include a matching receiver. The lavalier mic has been popular because it allows the talent to generally have

FIGURE 10.21
There are many types of microphone stands and mounts, from bottom-weighted telescopic stands to small versions with thin, flexible, or curved tubing intended for lavalier or miniature mics.
(Photos by Paul Dupree and Dennis Baxter.)

FIGURE 10.22
Pictured here is a wireless (radio) belt pack transmitter and receiver. A lavalier microphone can be plugged into the transmitter.
(Photo courtesy of Audio-Technica.)

FIGURE 10.23
Any type of microphone can become a wireless microphone if some type of *wireless plug-on transmitter* is used. This transmitter converts a dynamic or condenser microphone to wireless, transmitting the signal back to a receiver.
(Photo courtesy of Audio-Technica.)

unrestricted movement while on location. They are used in the studio with interview shows, on referees to pick up their calls, and hidden on actors to catch their words.

Wireless microphones generally work on radio frequencies (RF) and many are "frequency programmable," allowing the audio personnel to select the best frequency for a specific location.

There can be a number of challenges when working with wireless microphones:

- These mics work off of batteries. Each battery life is roughly four to six hours. In freezing temperatures, the battery life is usually cut in half. New batteries should be placed in the mic before each new session. Do not leave it to chance, assuming that there is enough capacity left from last time.
- If two or more wireless microphones are being used in an area, it is advisable to set them to different RF channels to avoid interference.
- When working near large metal structures, there can be difficulties with RF dead spots, fading, distortion, or interference. While diversity reception, using multiple antennas, has improved this situation, it is still cause for some concern.

10.21 HIDDEN MICS

When other methods of sound pickup are difficult, a hidden microphone may be the solution to the problem. Mics can be concealed among a bunch of flowers on a table, behind props, or in a piece of furniture, for example.

However, hidden mics do have their limitations. Although the mic can be hidden, the cable must not be visible or the transmitter must be out of site. Sound quality may also be affected by nearby reflecting or absorbing surfaces. Because the microphone covers a fixed localized area, the talent has to be relied on to play to the mic and not speak off mic.

CONTROLLING DYNAMICS

10.22 DYNAMIC RANGE

Everyday sounds can cover a considerable volume range. Fortunately for us, our ears are able to readjust to an astonishing extent to cope with these variations. But audio systems do not have this ability. If audio signals are larger than the system can accept, they will overload it and become badly distorted. If, on the other hand, sounds are too weak, they get lost in general background noise. To reproduce audio clearly, with fidelity, it has to be kept within the system's limits.

A lot of sounds pose no problems at all. They don't get particularly soft or loud—that is, they do not have a wide dynamic range. When recording sounds of this type, there is little need to alter the gain (amplification) of the system once it has been set to an appropriate average position.

It can be difficult to capture audio that ranges from a whisper to an ear-shattering blast. Because the blast will exceed the system's handling capacity, the audio person must compensate in some way. The most obvious thing to do is to turn down the system's audio gain so that the loud parts never reach its upper limit. But then the quiet passages may be so faint that they are inaudible. Somehow the audio levels need to be controlled.

10.23 AUTOMATIC GAIN CONTROL (AGC) FOR AUDIO

Cameras generally allow the operator to set the audio manually or automatically. To avoid loud sounds overloading the audio system and causing distortion, most audio and video recording equipment include automatic gain control. When the sound signal exceeds a certain level, the auto gain control automatically reduces the audio input.

In a completely automatic gain system, which amplifies all incoming sounds to a specific preset level, it "irons out" sound dynamics by preventing over- or underamplification. Quiet sounds are increased in volume, and loud sounds are held back. There are no adjustments to make, and the camera operator must accept the results.

The problem with completely automatic gain systems is that when there is a pause in the audio, the automatic gain system amplifies the room sound, which does not sound natural. Whenever possible, use the manual gain control.

Some auto gain systems do have manual adjustments. The idea is to ensure that the gain control is set high enough to amplify the quietest passages without overamplifying the loudest sounds. The auto gain control circuitry only limits sound peaks as an occasional safety measure, depending on the gain adjustment.

10.24 MANUAL CONTROL

The other method of controlling the audio level is to continuously monitor the program while watching an audio level meter. The audio person is responsible for readjusting the audio system's gain (amplification) whenever necessary to obtain a quality audio signal. That does not mean that the dynamics should be ironed out by making all the quiet sections loud and holding back all the loud passages. "Riding the gain" in this way can ruin the sound of the program. Instead, when sounds are going to be weak, anticipate by gradually increasing the gain and, conversely, slowly move the gain back before loud passages. Then the listeners are unaware that changes are being made to accommodate the audio system's limitations.

How quiet the softest sound is allowed to be will depend on the purpose of the program. If, for example, the recording will be used in noisy surroundings or shown in the open air, it may be best to keep the gain up to prevent the quietest sounds from falling below −15 or 120 dB. If a piano performance is being shot, to be heard indoors, take care not to overcontrol the music's dynamics, and use the system's full volume range.

Unlike automatic control circuits, audio personnel are able to anticipate and make artistic judgments, which can make the final audio far superior. The drawback to manual control is that the audio personnel need to be vigilant all the time, ready to make any necessary readjustments. If they are not careful, the resulting audio may be less satisfactory than the auto circuits would have produced.

FIGURE 10.24
VU meters and bar graphs are used to monitor the audio signal.

There are several types of volume indicators, but the most common on video equipment take the form of visual displays using bar graphs or some type of volume unit *VU meters*.

A bar graph (Figure 10.24) has a strip made up of tiny segments. This varies in length with the audio signal's strength. Calibrations vary, but it might have a decibel scale from 250 to 110 dB, with an upper working limit of about 12 dB. Simply adjust the audio gain control so that the sound peaks reach this upper mark. Twin bar graphs are used to monitor the left and right channels.

The VU (Figure 10.24) meter is a widely used volume indicator. It has two scales: a "volume unit" scale marked in decibels and another showing the "percentage modulation." Although accurate for steady tones, the VU meter can give deceptively low readings for brief loud sounds or transients such as percussion.

Maximum signal coincides with 100% modulation /0 dB. Above that, in the red sector, sounds will distort, although occasional peaks are acceptable. The normal range used is 220 to 0 dB, typically peaking between 22 and 0 dB.

In summary, if the camera operator needs the audio system to look after itself because he or she is preoccupied with shooting the scene or is coping with unpredictable sounds, then the automatic gain control has its merits; it will prevent loud sounds from overloading the system. However, if an assistant is available who can monitor the sound as it is being recorded and adjust the gain for optimum results, then this has significant artistic advantages.

10.25 MONITORING THE AUDIO

Monitoring sound for a video program involves the following:

- *Watching.* Check the volume indicator and watch a video monitor to make sure that the microphone does not pop into the shot inadvertently.
- *Listening.* On high-grade earphones or a loudspeaker, listen to check sound quality and balance and to detect any unwanted background noises.

Ideally the audio level can be adjusted during a rehearsal. However, if a performance is going to be recorded without a rehearsal, such as an interview, ask the talent to speak a few lines so that the audio level can be accurately adjusted. It is best if the talent can chat with the host in a normal voice for a few minutes, or he or she can read from a script or book long enough to adjust the level. Do not have the talent count or say "test." Both can give inaccurate readings because they do not necessarily reflect normal speaking levels.

It is important to monitor the sound to also get an impression of the dynamic range while watching the volume level. If the results are not satisfactory, you may need to ask the talent to speak louder, more quietly, or to reposition the mic.

10.26 THE AUDIO MIXER

An *audio mixer* is needed whenever there are a number of sound sources to select, blend together, and control (such as a couple of microphones, CD, audio output from a video recording, etc.). The output of this unit is fed to the recorder (Figure 10.25).

FIGURE 10.25
The portable audio mixer is used in the field to mix up to three mics; the overall output is controlled by a master fader. A VU meter provides the volume indicator. Some mixers include a limiter to prevent audio overload.
(Photo courtesy of Shure Incorporated.)

On the front panel of the audio mixer are a series of knobs or sliders. Each of these "pots" (potentiometers) or "faders" (Figure 10.26) can adjust its channel's volume from full audio to fade-out (silence). In some designs, the channel can be switched on or off on cue with a mute button.

On a large audio mixing panel, there may be *group faders* (group masters, submasters). Each of these group faders controls the *combined* outputs of several channels, and it may have its own group volume indicator. For instance, one group fader can be used for all the mics on the audience.

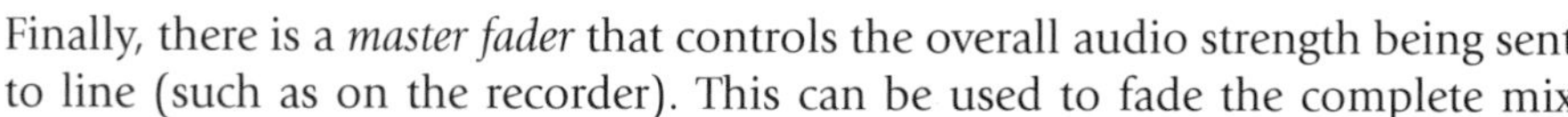

Finally, there is a *master fader* that controls the overall audio strength being sent to line (such as on the recorder). This can be used to fade the complete mix in or out. A master volume indicator shows the combined strength of the mixed audio.

FIGURE 10.26
Faders (potentiometers) on a large audio mixer.

Larger audio mixers include a *cue circuit* (audition, prehear, prefade), which enables audio personnel to listen privately on earphones or a loudspeaker to the output of any individual channel, even when its pot is faded out. That way, the source, such as a CD, can be set up at exactly the right spot, ready to be started on cue, without this being overheard on air. Mixers are slowly incorporating more and more surround sound capabilities (Figure 10.27).

FIGURE 10.27
A large surround sound audio mixer for television productions.

10.27 USING THE AUDIO MIXER

Is operating an audio mixer a matter of just fading up a microphone or two and controlling the sound levels, or is it a complex process involving edge-of-seat decisions? The answer depends on the type of production. Consider these examples:

- A "live" show, which is transmitted or recorded as it happens, involves rapid decisions. There is inevitably a feeling of urgency, tempered with caution. When working on a production that is being taped scene by scene, there is time to set up complicated audio treatments. Anything that goes wrong can usually be corrected and improved.
- When a number of sound sources need to be cued in at precisely the right moment, the situation poses different problems than those posed by a less complicated program such as an interview.
- Have the incoming sources already been prepared, such as when using pre-recorded material, or do the live incoming sources need to be controlled and continually monitored and adjusted?

These are just a few of the issues that decide how complex the audio mix needs to be. Let's look at typical operations in some detail:

- Sound sources should be faded in just before they begin (to the appropriate pot setting), and they should fade out when the audio source is finished.
- Source channels should not be left "open" (live) when not in use. Apart from accidentally recording overheard remarks ("Was that all right?") and other unwanted sounds, the channel may pick up someone who is on another mic.
- It is important that the right source is selected and faded up/down at the right moment. Individual or group faders can be used. Here is an example: Imagine a scene for a drama production is being shot. The audience sees the interior of a home, where the radio (actually from a CD player located near the mixer) plays quietly. An actor is talking (on live mic 1) to another person (on live mic 2) who is not shown in the shot. A nearby telephone rings (fade up using a special effects CD of a phone ringing). The actor turns down the radio (we fade down the CD) and picks up the phone (we stop the special effects CD). Continuous background noises of a storm (from another special effects CD) can be heard at a low level throughout the scene. All these fades must be completed on individual channel pots. The different tape and CD machines must be operated by the person at the mixer or by an assistant.
- When combining several sound sources, all of them should not be faded up to their full level. They should be blended for a specific overall effect. For example, if a single microphone was used to pick up the sound of a music group, chances are that the one microphone would pick up certain instruments much better than others. Loud ones would dominate and quiet ones would be lost. The overall balance would be poor. Instead, use several microphones, devoted to different parts of the group. Then the volume of

the weaker instruments, such as a flute, could be increased, and the volume of the louder ones, such as drums, can be decreased. With care, the result would sound perfectly natural and have a clearer overall balance.

- Sometimes the relative volume of a sound will need to be adjusted to create an illusion of *distance*. If the sound of a telephone ringing is loud, we assume it is nearby; if it is faint, it must be some distance away.
- Sounds may need to be deliberately emphasized. For example, you may choose to readjust the pot controlling the crowd noise to make it louder at an exciting moment and give it a more dramatic impact.
- The final audio mix needs to fit the mood of the overall production.

10.28 NATURAL SOUND

Most video productions are made up of a series of shots, taken in whatever order is most convenient, and edited together later to form the final program. This approach has both advantages and drawbacks. As far as the program sound is concerned, there are several complications.

First of all, although the various shots in a sequence have been taken at different times, it is important that their quality and volume match when they are edited together. Otherwise there will be sudden jumps whenever the shot changes. If, for instance, a shot is taken of a person walking down a hallway, using a close mic, and then a side view is shot of the same action, using a more distant mic, the difference in the sound, when cutting from one shot to the other, could be quite noticeable. The overall effect would draw attention to the editing.

When editing together a sequence of images shot at different times, the background sounds may not match. In the time between shooting one shot, repositioning the camera, adjusting the light, and then retaking the shot, the background noises often significantly change. Because the crew is busy, they may not notice that the background sounds are different. Sounds that we became accustomed to while shooting the scene—such as overhead aircraft, farm equipment, hammering, or typing—can have a nasty habit of instantly disappearing and reappearing when the shots are edited together.

When on location, it is a good habit to record a few minutes of ambient sound, background noise, on the recorder. It does not matter what the video is showing at this point; we are only really concerned with the audio. However, it is sometimes helpful to shoot the scene being recorded so that it gives the editor a visual reference as to where it was recorded. It is surprising how often this natural (NAT) sound or *wild track* comes in handy during audio editing for use as background sounds.

Even when shooting under what seems to be quiet conditions, there is a certain amount of background noise from air conditioners, equipment hum, and so on. A wild track of this natural sound can be used later to cover any periods where there is a break in the soundtrack during editing. Wild tracks also can help during those awkward moments when background sounds in successive shots do not match. They can serve as a bridge to disguise when silent and sound shots are edited together.

10.29 ANTICIPATION

Anticipation comes with experience. When something goes wrong, learn from it and prepare better next time. There are a number of ways to anticipate audio challenges:

Preparation

- Check through the script or preplanning paperwork, and then pull together the appropriate equipment so that every audio situation in the production can be covered.
- Check prerecorded audio inserts before the show. Make sure that each one is appropriate. Is the duration too long or too short? Is the quality satisfactory? Is the insert material arranged in the order in which it is to be used?
- Check all of the equipment to make sure that it is working correctly. Don't rely on the notion that it was okay yesterday. If additional plug-in equipment is being used, such as a portable audio mixer, have someone fade up each source (microphones or CD) to ensure that each one is working.
- Go to each microphone in turn, scratch its housing (which is an easy way to test the microphone), and state its location to make sure that the microphone is working and plugged into the correct input ("this is boom A").
- Have a backup microphone ready in case the main microphone fails. If it is a one-time-only occasion and you are using a lavalier mic, it may be advisable to add a second "dual redundancy" lavalier mic too (see Figure 10.28).
- Is the microphone cable long enough to allow the boom pole to move around freely?

Of course, these are all a matter of common sense, but it is surprising how often the obvious and the familiar are overlooked. These are just reminders of what should become a regular routine.

FIGURE 10.28
This lavalier clip is designed to hold two microphones, providing a backup microphone in case one fails.

10.30 ANTICIPATING SOUND EDITING

When shooting a scene, it is important to overcome the challenges of sound editing by anticipating the types of problems that will occur:

- *Continuity*. Try to ensure that the quality and level of successive shots in the same scene match as much as possible.
- *Natural/atmosphere sounds*. Record some general natural sounds (for atmosphere) and

typical background sounds (wild track) in case you need them during postproduction.

- *Questions.* When shooting an interview and concentrating on the guest, the questions of the interviewer may not be audible. Make sure the host has his or her own microphone, or go back and have them ask the same questions after the interview so that they are recorded.

10.31 FILTERED SOUND

Significant changes can be made to the quality of sound by introducing an audio filter into the system. It can be adjusted to increase or decrease the chosen part of the audio spectrum and to exaggerate or suppress the higher notes, bass, or middle register, depending on the type of filter system used and how it is adjusted.

The simplest "tone control" progressively reduces higher notes during reproduction. A more flexible type of audio filter is called an *equalizer*, which can boost or reduce any segment(s) of the audio spectrum by changing the slider pots.

Here are typical ways in which filtering can enhance the subjective effect of the sound:

- Cutting low bass can reduce rumble or hum, improve speech clarity, lessen the boomy or hollow sound of some small rooms, and weaken the background noise from ventilation, passing traffic, and so on. Overdone, the result sounds thin and lacks body.
- Cutting higher notes can make hiss, whistles, tape noise, sibilant speech, and other high-pitched sound less prominent. However, if you cut them too much, the sound will lack clarity and intelligibility.
- If the bass and top are cut, the sound will have a much more open-air quality—a useful cheat when shooting an "exterior" scene in a studio.
- By slightly increasing the bass, the impression of size and grandeur of a large interior can be increased.
- The clarity and presence of many sounds can be improved by making them appear closer; do this by boosting the middle part of the audio spectrum (such as 2 to 6 kHz).
- Filtering can make the quality of sound recorded in different places more similar (such as shots of someone inside and outside a building). It can help you to match the sound quality of different microphones.

10.32 REVERBERATION

As we saw earlier, most of the everyday sounds we hear are a mixture of direct sound from the source itself together with "colored" versions reflected from nearby surfaces. The quality of that reflected sound is affected by the nature of those surfaces. Some surfaces absorb the higher notes (curtains, cushions, carpeting). This reflected sound may even be muffled. Conversely, where surroundings reflect higher notes more readily, these hard reflections will add harshness (edginess) to the final sound.

This is a reminder that the room tone will depend on its size, shape, carpeting, drapes, easy chairs, and similar factors. Where there are *no* reflections, as in open spaces away from buildings or other hard surfaces, the resulting sound will seem *dead*. The only way we can simulate dead surroundings within a building is to use carefully positioned sound-absorbing materials. On the other hand, if there is too much reverberation, the result is a confused mixture of sound that reduces its clarity.

In practice, the appeal of many sounds can be enhanced by adding a certain amount of real or simulated reverberation to them. Today, the most commonly used method of adding some "liveness" is to use a reverberation unit that digitally stores the sound and is selectively reread over and over to give the impression of reflected sounds.

10.33 PROGRAM MUSIC

The role of music in television programs is so established that we don't need to dwell on it here. Musical themes often remain in the memory long after the program itself has faded from the mind.

Music can have various purposes:

- *Identifying*. Music associated with a specific show, person, or country.
- *Atmospheric*. Melodies that are intended to induce a certain mood, such as excitement.
- *Associative*. Music reminiscent of, for example, the American West or the Far East.
- *Imitative*. Music that directly imitates, such as a bird song, or music with a rhythm or melody that copies the subject's features, such as the jog-trot accompaniment to a horse and wagon.
- *Environmental*. Music heard at a specific place, such as a ballroom.

10.34 SOUND EFFECTS

Sound effects add depth and realism to a video production. They significantly impact the audience's experience. Interestingly, if a production is shot in a real location yet is missing the everyday sounds that occur there, the audience will perceive that it is a contrived location. However, if the same scene is shot in a well-designed television studio setting but is accompanied by the appropriate sound effects, the audience can easily be convinced that it was shot on location. The barely heard sounds of a clock ticking, wind whistling through trees, bird song, passing traffic, the barking of a distant dog, or whatever other noises are appropriate bring the scene to life.

Sound effects can come from a number of sources:

- *The original sounds recorded during a scene*. For example, a person's own footsteps accompanying the picture, which may be filtered, reverberation added, and so on.

- *Reused original sounds.* Examples would include the sounds of wind, traffic, or children at play that were recorded during a scene and are copied and mixed with that same scene's soundtrack to reinforce the overall effect.
- *Foley.* Creating sounds in a studio that can replace the original sounds. For example, introducing sounds of your own footsteps for the original ones; keeping in time with those in the picture.
- *Sound effects library.* Effects from a commercial audio effects library on CD or DVD.
- *Digital processing or sound sampling.* Computer software offers a plethora of options for creating and manipulating sounds. With the use of a keyboard, these effects can be repeated and changed in an endless variety of ways.

Interview with a Pro

Noel Dannemiller, Sound Mixer

Noel Dannemiller, Sound Mixer

What do you like about the field of audio?
I love working as a location sound mixer because I work in a different location with a different crew doing the same job everyday. The world is my office. I've recorded sound on the Great Wall of China, Red Square in Moscow, the beaches of Madagascar, and in my own living room. It beats working for a living.

What advice do you have for someone starting out in audio?
I would advise a new person in location sound to meet as many people in the biz as possible. Then call them all of the time to see what work is available. Once they start to hire you, back off on the calls, and hopefully your work speaks for itself and you become a regular on their crew. Also, move to an area where there are a lot of gigs.

How do you select the right microphone for a situation?
I choose the mic based on a couple of factors. These include the number of actors in the scene, location, camera angle, and wardrobe.

What are the challenges you have to deal with in audio?
Most of the challenges I deal with are the talent's wardrobe and environment we shoot in. Sometimes the wardrobe won't work with a hidden lavalier microphone. Then you have to use a boom pole to capture the talent or get creative. As far as locations are concerned, nobody ever scouts locations for sound. The picture is always the primary concern. If we have problems with the live audio, we either live with the ambience or do everything possible to deaden the sounds. Sometimes you can be saved by a music bed.

Noel Dannemiller has mixed sound for all types of productions.

CHAPTER 11
Lighting for Video

When it comes to image acquisition, lighting is still the art that separates the amateurs from the pros.

—Jay Holben, Producer

You light with the lights you have, not the lights you wish you had. The difference between a good gaffer and a great gaffer is knowing how to best use the lights you have.

—Jefrey M. Hamel, Lighting Director

Many times the difference between a good show and a great show is the lighting! Good lighting can transform a routine, uninteresting shot into an attractive, appealing image that draws the audience's attention.

Lighting allows the camera to record a quality image and is usually needed to increase or reduce depth of field. However, lighting is also a great manipulator of the audience. The eye is drawn to the brightest portion of an image. That means that the audience can be subtly directed where to look and what subject is the most important. Lighting is also used to add depth to a scene and allows the director to "color" a scene to create a mood and time period.

Key Terms

- ***Barn doors:*** These metal flaps are usually attached to the top, bottom, and sides of the light in order to shape the beam.
- ***Diffusion material:*** Can be attached to the front of a light in order to reduce the intensity of the light beam.
- ***Ellipsoidal:*** The ellipsoidal light is a sharply focused/defined spotlight.
- ***Floodlighting:*** This light scatters in all directions, providing a broad, nondirectional light.
- ***Fresnel:*** An unfocused spotlight. It is lightweight and less expensive than an ellipsoidal, and it has an adjustable beam.

- ***Gaffer:*** The head of the electrical department, many times in charge of lighting on a television set.
- ***Gel:*** Colored flexible plastic filters used to adjust the color of the lights.
- ***Grip clamps:*** Designed so that a light can easily be attached. The clamp is then used to attach the light to almost anything.
- ***LED light panel:*** A camera or studio light that is made from a series of small LED bulbs.
- ***Photographic lighting:*** See *Three-point lighting.*
- ***Scoop:*** A simple floodlight. It is inexpensive, usually not adjustable, lightweight, and does not have a sharp outline.
- ***Soft light:*** Provides a large level of diffused light.
- ***Spotlight:*** A highly directional light.
- ***Three-point lighting:*** A lighting technique that utilizes three lights (key, fill, and backlights) to illuminate the subject. Also known as photographic lighting.
- ***Triangle lighting:*** See *Three-point lighting.*

11.1 LIGHTING THE SCENE

Many people are apprehensive about lighting because they are afraid of doing the wrong thing and looking foolish. Others think of lighting as an unnecessary luxury when working with a small production crew. They assume it requires a lot of equipment and a lot of power. It can, if a large studio drama is being lit or if you are shooting the inside of a stadium. However, it is worth the time to make sure that the lighting treatment provides a quality image.

There are many situations where just one light, or a well-placed reflector, is all that you will need to make an image spring to life. Even in large-scale production, foresight and imagination can often make a little light go a long way. It is really a matter of knowing what the goal is, what to look out for, and what can be done about the problems that develop.

Why not simply shoot in whatever light is available? Of course, that is possible. On good days, the result will be clear, attractive, and interesting images, where realistic color makes the image jump at the audience. But there will certainly be days when the images will be lifeless, drab, or have a little too much contrast; when the subject is not clear; or when the subject's texture is lost.

So much depends on where and when the shooting takes place. Is the shoot occurring inside a building (interior) or out in the open (exterior)? Is it day or night? Are the surroundings well illuminated or in shadowy gloom? Are the shots very tight or spacious and long? Finally, a lot will depend on the sort of atmosphere the director is aiming to convey to the audience: a realistic everyday scene or a moody, dramatic situation.

Obviously, it is not smart to introduce any extra lighting into a scene unless it is really going to enhance the images. Often, the crew does not have the time or opportunity to set up lights anyway. For our purposes, we will assume that, for the most part, crews only carry around a few lights. There will be many situations, particularly when shooting outside, where even these lights will not be needed, provided the subject is correctly arranged in the existing light.

11.2 THE CAMERA DOES NOT COMPENSATE

One of the most important things to bear in mind when lighting is the essential difference between the way the human eye and brain registers a scene and the limited, literal way the camera reproduces it. The eyes and brain compensate (sometimes overcompensate) in many subtle ways as the lighting of the surroundings vary. Our eyes seem to be able to see details in shadows, and variations in color values pass unnoticed. We are able to see a remarkable amount, even when the lighting conditions are poor.

However, the camera cannot interpret. It responds to what is there, within its limitations. If a surface reflects too much light for the video system, whether it is a reflection from a shiny surface or a very light tone, it blocks off to a blank white in the picture. Darker-toned furniture, clothing, foliage, or shadows often crush out to black on camera. When we are at the same location, looking at the scene with our own eyes, we have none of these problems. That means that directors and camera operators need to watch how the camera is really reproducing what they are seeing.

Loss of detail and modeling in certain parts of the picture may not be important unless the audience specifically wants to see the features of a white wedding dress or a black velvet costume. Where those tones do matter, the camera operator may need to manipulate the scene a bit. For example, the dark background can be lit to bring it within the range of the camera, or you can change the camera's position in order to deliberately keep the background out of shot.

11.3 THE KEY FACTORS

Lighting involves a lot more than simply having enough illumination around to let the camera see what is going on. Light influences what the subject looks like, how the viewers feel about what they see, and what attracts their attention. That means that we not only need to think about where to place the lights but also the type of illumination that we are getting from these lights and how all this affects the quality of our images.

To use illumination, or lighting, successfully, we need to take a look at some of its interesting characteristics:

- The light's *intensity* (brightness) affects exposure.
- A light's *quality* refers to whether it is concentrated "hard" shadow-forming light or diffused "soft" shadowless illumination.
- Lighting impacts *contrast*, which is the relative brightness of the lightest and darkest areas in the shot.

- The *direction* of the light has an effect on the appearance of the subject.
- The light's *color temperature* refers to its overall color quality.

When using *colored light* for effect, directors need to be concerned with:

- Its *hue* (the predominant color; for example, blue, green, and yellow)
- Its *saturation* (chroma, purity, intensity) referring to its richness or paleness
- Its *luminance* (brightness, value), or how light or dark it appears

Understanding how to control or compensate for these various features will make the difference in whether you create consistent high-quality images. If you ignore them, the results may be fine, but then again, they will probably be unpredictable.

11.4 THE LIGHT'S INTENSITY

The camera requires a certain amount of light to produce a quality image. If there is too little light, then the shot will be underexposed (all tones reproduce too dark). If there is too much light, then everything will be overexposed (all tones reproduce too light). You can evaluate the intensity of the lighting by using an external light meter, the camera's internal exposure indicator, or by reviewing the image in the viewfinder or on a monitor.

The camera will not receive sufficient light in the following conditions:

- The light falling on the subject is too dim (low light levels).
- The lens aperture (*f*-stop) is too small.
- You are using a filter that is too dense relative to the tones in the scene or its overall brightness.

Clearly, less light is required to achieve good images in a white-walled room than is needed in a dark-paneled one. Remember that extra video gain can only partly compensate for underexposure, because although it boosts the picture strength, the camera's sensor itself is still getting too little light from the scene, which causes the image to deteriorate.

> High-definition television (HDTV) does not require a fewer number of lights. While HD is more sensitive to lighting, the number of lights is still required to create the tone and mood of the scene.
>
> **—Geoff Dunlap, Director of Photography**

11.5 IF THERE IS NOT ENOUGH LIGHT

When shooting inside buildings or outdoors at night, there generally is not really enough light to obtain the best-quality images. There are several solutions:

- Move the subject to where there is more light.
- Open up the lens aperture. However, this reduces the depth of field.
- Increase the camera's sensitivity by boosting the video gain. The problem is that this will increase picture noise.

- Increase the available lighting (switch on more room lights or open a curtain).
- Add additional lighting instruments.

11.6 IF THERE IS TOO MUCH LIGHT

If the lighting is too intense (high light levels), lighting personnel may compensate by doing the following:

- Move the subject to where there is less light.
- Stop down the lens (selecting a smaller aperture).
- Use a neutral density filter to reduce the light.
- Switch off some of the existing lighting.
- Pull the shades or blinds.

If video lights are being used and the lighting is too intense, the following actions will reduce the intensity:

- Switch off some of your light sources.
- Use lower-power sources.
- Use a dimmer.
- Place diffuser material over a light (Figure 11.2).

FIGURE 11.1
Barn doors are used to control and to limit the spread of the light.

- Move the light farther away from the subject.
- Flood (spread) or limit the lamp's beam (Figures 11.1 and 11.3).
- Use "bounce light" instead of direct lighting.

FIGURE 11.2
Diffusion material can be attached to the front of a light to reduce the intensity of the light beam.

FIGURE 11.3
Blackwrap or Cinefoil is used to cut the light beam completely out. It can easily be molded into custom shapes compared to a standard set of barn doors.

11.7 HARD LIGHT QUALITY (SPOTLIGHT)

Because the sun is so distant, it works like a localized point source of light. Its rays are directional and travel to us in straight lines. They cast distinct, sharp shadows, which emphasize the texture and contours of any subject, especially when the light falls at an oblique angle. Because it is directional, the light can be blocked off to prevent it from falling onto any surface.

Many manmade light sources, such as a match, a candle, or a bare lightbulb, also behave in this way. Because they are limited in size, they act as point sources and produce hard light, irrespective of how powerful or weak they are.

Rather than allowing the light to spread around in all directions (as with a bare bulb hanging from the ceiling), many lighting instruments include a specially shaped *parabolic* reflector that directs light rays forward in a narrow beam. They may also be fitted with a *Fresnel* ("stepped") lens to concentrate the beam further. This light gathering improves the lamp's efficiency and helps restrict the light to selected parts of the scene.

By adjusting the position of the reflector or the lens in relation to the bulb, the beam can be spread, and, to a certain extent, the intensity can be adjusted.

FIGURE 11.4
The ellipsoidal light is a sharply focused spotlight. The focusing ability allows it to project patterns on the set. It is heavier, includes internal shutters, is more expensive than other spots, and has an adjustable beam.
(Photo courtesy of Mole-Richardson.)

Barn doors, flaps attached to the sides of the light, can be used to cut off parts of the light beam (Figure 11.4).

Here are the good things about a spotlight:

- It is directional, so it can easily be restricted to illuminate just the desired areas.
- It casts sharp shadows and amplifies texture.
- It can produce vigorous, bold, well-defined effects.
- The intensity of a hard light source does not fall off appreciably with distance. So subjects can be effectively illuminated from some distance away.

Here are the bad things about spotlights:

- Distracting or ugly shadows can be difficult to avoid (such as shadows projected onto the set behind the talent).
- Results may look harsh and have a very high contrast.
- Texture may be too emphasized, such as revealing the irregularities in someone's skin.
- Spotlight sources have restricted coverage, so several lights may be required to cover a wide area.
- When more than one hard light source is used, the multishadows can be distracting.

11.8 SOFT LIGHT QUALITY (FLOODLIGHT)

Soft light or diffused light, usually known as a *floodlight*, scatters in all directions.

FIGURE 11.5
Weighing three pounds, the LED light panel projects a bright soft light. It is extremely lightweight and offers low power consumption and accurate color reproduction. It is heat free and can be dimmed. LED light panels are available as floodlights, spotlights, or a combination.
(Photo courtesy of Litepanels.)

FIGURE 11.6
The LitePad is nicknamed the "Everywhere Light." At a third of an inch thick, it can be placed anywhere to add a little soft light.
(Photo courtesy of Rosco.)

It occurs naturally, when the sun is obscured by clouds and whenever sunlight is reflected from rough light-toned surfaces. When subjects are illuminated by this *soft light*, there are no distinct shadows, only slight variations in surface brightness. So texture and surface contours are not pronounced in the picture. In fact, they may not be visible at all (Figure 11.7).

Several techniques can be used to provide soft light. Some rely on diffusion material such as a spun-glass sheet, frosted plastic, or wire mesh to scatter the light. (A diffuser can be placed over a hard light source to reduce its intensity

FIGURE 11.7
This outdoor spotlight has been transformed into a floodlight by shooting its light beam through diffusion material. This light was used to lighten the shadows on the talent's face.

and soften its quality to some extent.) In others, the light from the lamp hits a reflector and then scatters.

Another form of soft light uses a group or bank of open lamps. Their overlapping beams combine to give shadowless illumination. A compact "soft light" can be created by placing two or three layers of diffusion material, such as spun glass, over a hard light source such as a spot.

Here are the good things about soft light:

- It can produce subtle, delicate shading.
- It does not generally create unwanted shadows.
- It avoids emphasizing modeling and texture.
- It can lighten the shadows cast by hard light sources so that details are visible.
- It can cover a wide area of the scene.

Here are the bad things about soft light:

- It can flatten out all signs of surface shape and texture in the picture, because it does not emphasize texture.
- It spreads around, flooding all surfaces with light. It can be difficult to restrict the light from selected areas.
- It quickly falls off in intensity as the lamp's distance from the subject increases. So something fairly near the source may be overlit, while another subject a little distance away is insufficiently lit.

11.9 LIGHTING CONTRAST

The "contrast" in a scene is simply the difference between the brightness of its lightest and darkest tones. If the range is too great for the camera to handle, as is the case when strong sunlight casts deep shadows, the extreme tones are lost in the image. The tonal contrasts that the camera sees will depend partly on the tones of the subjects, partly on variations in the light's intensity, and partly on the shadows the light casts.

Excessive lighting contrast produces burned-out highlights and detail-less lower tones. Whether the result looks highly dramatic or difficult to interpret depends on the situation.

When the lighting is high contrast (lots of hard light from one direction and no fill light), picture quality can alter considerably as the camera's position varies. If you shoot with the light behind the camera, subjects may look bright, flat, and unmodeled. If you shoot toward the light, only the edges of subjects will be illuminated, while the rest remains unlit.

The other extreme is the effect obtained when the scene is lit with soft, shadowless lighting. Now everything is subtly modeled. Even if the camera is moved around over a wide angle, the tonal quality of the picture remains reasonably constant under soft lighting.

In practice, you usually want to avoid the harshness that comes from a high lighting contrast and the flatness that you get with a low lighting contrast. The best solution is to use a careful balance of hard lights (which creates a three-dimensional illusion) and some soft light to illuminate any shadows (i.e., "fill" them) without casting extra ones.

LIGHT DIRECTION EXERCISE

The direction of the light has a tremendous influence on what any subject looks like. The best way to demonstrate this for yourself is to grab a flashlight and sit in front of a mirror in a dark room. You will see how the light affects the image as it moves around.

First hold the flashlight beside your head, pointing it straight into the mirror. This is the equivalent of a light just beside the camera. Notice how this direct frontal light seems to flatten out the texture and shape of the front of your face. If there is a smooth or shiny surface behind you, the light bounces straight back into your eyes (back into the camera lens) and appears as a hot spot on the background. Even a rough surface, such as stone or concrete, may look smooth under direct frontal lighting. It reminds you too of how unpleasantly dazzling it can be for people if you light them this way.

Move your flashlight to above your head, shining it straight downward. See how the light emphasizes every wrinkle! The top of your head and your nose are now bright ("hot"), and your eyes are hidden in dark sockets. You have instantly aged a number of years! (Always try to avoid top, overhead, downward lighting, particularly when shooting people.)

Hold the flashlight down low, shining upward, and the effect is spooky, because we are not used to seeing people lit in this way—except in horror movies. Now the eyes and the neck are strongly lit. Again, surface details are emphasized with upward shadows.

Take the light around to one side. You will see how only half of your head is lit, and the surface texture and contours of your face are unattractively exaggerated.

If someone takes the flashlight and holds it behind you, shining onto the back of your head, you will see that only the edges of your head will be lit (hair, ears, and shoulders if the lamp is high). This sort of *backlight* is successful when you are lighting solid subjects, because it helps to make them stand out from the background and creates a three-dimensional illusion. If the subject is made of transparent or translucent material, the backlight will reveal this.

11.10 THREE-POINT LIGHTING

For most situations, the best lighting results come from using some variation of the three basic light directions (Figure 11.8).

The main light, or *key light*, is positioned slightly above and to one side of the camera. This is normally a spotlight (hard light), and it reveals the shape and surface features of the subject. The key light produces distinct, harsh shadows.

The *fill light* is a floodlight (soft light) that is placed on the opposite side of the camera from the key light. It reduces the shadows (made by the key light) but should not eliminate the shadows. The fill light also reduces the lighting contrast. The more the key light is offset, the more important this soft *fill light* (filler or fill-in) becomes. If the key is nearly frontal, you may not need fill light at all. Note that in the subject's image in Figure 11.8, the shadows on her face have not been eliminated. This helps give the face texture and shape.

Finally, a *backlight* is angled down onto the subject from behind to separate the subject and the background. The backlight emphasizes the shape of the subject.

The key light and backlight are generally the same intensity. However, the backlight may need to be reduced, depending on the subject's hair color. The fill light is usually one-half or three-quarters the intensity of the key and backlight.

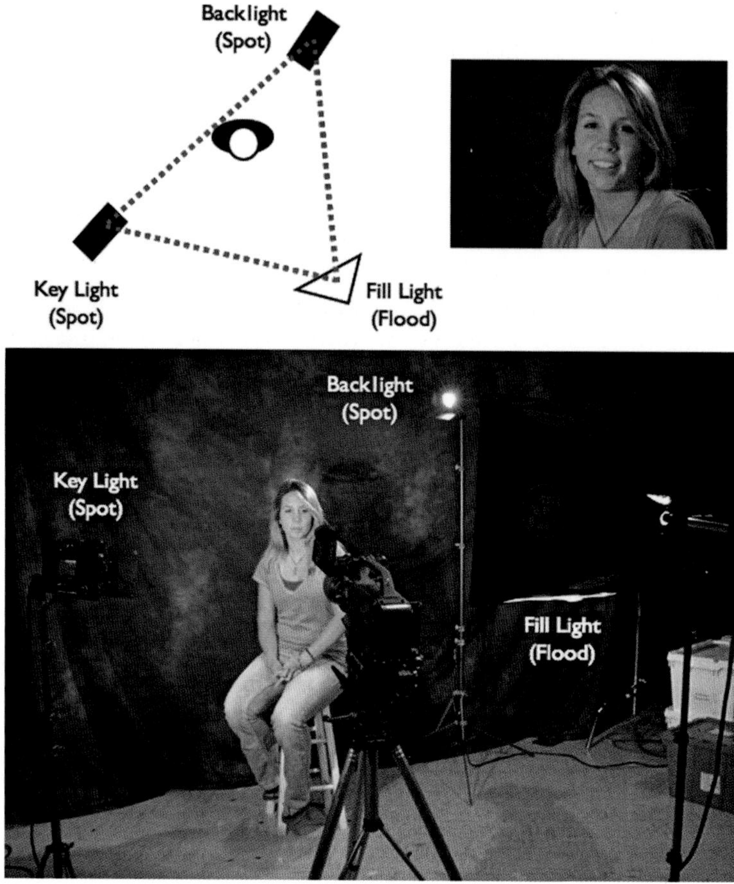

FIGURE 11.8
Three-point lighting is also known as "triangle lighting" or "photographic lighting." Three lights are used to create the lighting treatment: the key, fill, and backlights.
(Photo by Josh Taber.)

Wherever possible, additional lights can be used to illuminate the background behind the subject. But where space or facilities are limited, spill illumination from the key and fill lights may be used to cover the background areas.

11.11 COLOR TEMPERATURE COMPENSATION

The color quality of light can vary considerably, from the orange-yellow of candlelight or small tungsten lamps to the bluish illumination of daylight, from the warm hues of a sunset to the greenish quality of many fluorescent lights. For good color quality, the camera system's color response and the color quality of the prevailing light need to match reasonably well. If they do not, the pictures will have a pronounced bluish or orange-yellow color cast. The camera can be matched to the lighting by rotating in the appropriate color-correction filter on the camera or readjusting the camera's white balance.

Sometimes there will be a mixture of lighting—for example, daylight coming through the windows and a tungsten light inside a room. When that occurs, you have a number of options:

- Block the window so that the daylight will be obscured. The camera can then balance with the remaining tungsten lighting.
- Place light blue correction filters over the tungsten light to raise its color temperature to match the daylight.
- Attach large sheets of orange-yellow color filter material (gels) over the windows so that the incoming daylight will match the tungsten light.
- Shoot the scene with its mixture of daylight and tungsten and accept the results.

With the camera balanced to "daylight," the daylight will look right and the tungsten will look overwarm (yellow-orange). When the camera is balanced to "tungsten," the daylight will look very blue, and the tungsten light will look natural. The color-quality of light (its *color temperature*) is measured in kelvins (K). For most purposes, it is sufficient to switch the camera to its nearest color-correction filter position (e.g., "daylight," "artificial," "fluorescent," or the color temperature filters, 5,600 K (daylight), 3,200 K (tungsten)) and white-balance to these conditions.

11.12 USING COLORED LIGHT

Because video is usually in color, it seems reasonable to assume that a lot of colored light is used. However, colored lighting is really only needed when creating decorative effects such as for a display, a dance or musical routine, firelight or moonlight, or to change the appearance of backgrounds (such as to introduce some color on a plain neutral wall).

When colored lighting is needed, a sheet of colored plastic, called gelatin or a "gel," is clipped onto the front of a lighting instrument, making sure that the gel does not restrict the ventilation of the lamp (which will overheat and fail) (see Figure 11.9). It is also important not to put gel so close to the lamp that the intense heat destroys the color sheet.

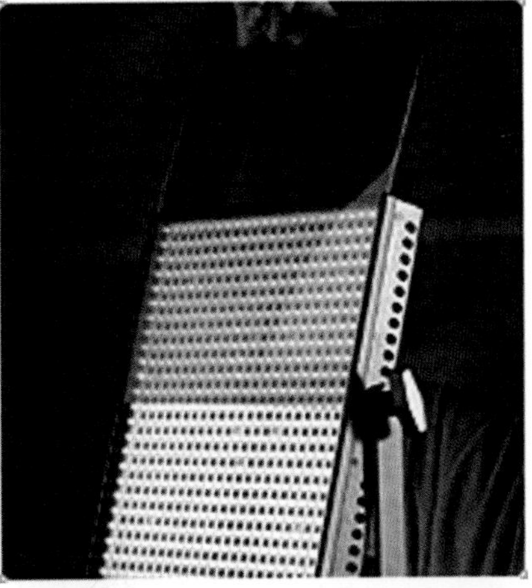

FIGURE 11.9
Colored "gels" are used to adjust the color of the lights.
(Top photo courtesy of Litepanels.)

Colored gelatin is inexpensive, but it burns up, quickly becomes brittle and torn, and pales out in use. Special plastic sheeting (of acetate, polyester, Mylar, or acrylic) is more expensive but will last and can be reused. If you are shooting under tungsten lighting and want to create an overall warmer look to the image, use the "daylight" built-in color correction filter. Conversely, a "tungsten" correction filter can be used when shooting in daylight to give pictures a cold, blue, wintry appearance. To obtain these color changes, the camera operator needs to white-balance under the normal lighting conditions and then add the built-in color correction filter.

11.13 SHOOTING IN DAYLIGHT

Although daylight provides us with a free, convenient light source, it isn't a particularly reliable one. Its intensity and overall quality varies greatly. Clouds pass over the sun, and sharply defined shadows may vanish. Instead we may be left with a much weaker, diffused light. Throughout the day, the color quality and the direction of the light will alter, and the sun that was frontal in the morning will gradually change to side light by the afternoon. All of this may make it difficult to cut together shots that have been taken at different times of the day, where the variations in lighting show in the edited version of the action.

Remember that the effect of light depends on the *position of the camera*. Strong sunlight that offers more than enough illumination from one viewpoint may only give rim lighting to the subject from another angle, leaving the subject in deep shadow. You have a number of options:

- Move around the subject until the sun is roughly behind the camera (but then it may not be the background you want).
- Turn the subject into the light.
- Wait for the sun to move around to a better angle (this is time consuming).
- Add (or reflect) lighting to compensate.

FIGURE 11.10
Light was added to this daylight scene so that the talent had even lighting while shooting a segment for *Access Hollywood*.

11.14 USING REFLECTORS

The easiest and least expensive way to improve a subject's lighting when shooting in sunlight is to use a *reflector*. This is simply a surface, such as a board, screen, cloth, or even a wall, that reflects existing light onto the subject from another angle. The quality of the reflected light depends on the surface you use.

Many commercial reflectors are available such as the one shown in Figures 11.11 and 11.12. These lightweight cloth reflectors, sewn onto a spring-metal frame, can be easily folded and transported. Available surfaces include silver, gold, white, and combination reflectors. A mirror surface, such as metal foil, will reflect a distinct beam of light from a hard light source, creating sharp, well-defined shadows. This light

(A)

(B)

(C)

FIGURE 11.11

Reflectors can be used in many situations with a variety of techniques. (A) The sun provides the key light, and the reflector is the fill light. (B) A reflector is being used to reflect additional light into a building through its window. (C) Two reflectors are being used to increase the illumination. One of the reflectors is silver (the key light), and the other is white (fill light). How effective a reflector is depends on its surface and on its angle to the sun or other light sources. If a reflector is used beside the camera and reflects a source directly ahead of the camera, the intensity and coverage of the reflected light is at its maximum. As the reflector is angled to the source, its output and its coverage fall.

*(Photos by Josh Taber (**A**) and Nathan Waggoner (**B**).)*

FIGURE 11.12
Commercially produced cloth reflectors can be purchased that have a variety of colors. This specific reflector is designed with six different colors, for six different lighting effects.
(Photo courtesy of Wescott.)

travels well, even when the subject is some distance away. (A mirror surface will even reflect soft light to some extent, if placed fairly near the subject.) The angle of a mirror-finish reflector can be critical. When the light shines directly at its surface, the maximum effect is obtained. However, as the surface is angled toward the light, the reflected beam, which only covers a restricted angle anyway, narrows and becomes less effective. In a long shot, its limited coverage appears as a localized patch of light.

If the reflector has a matte-white surface, it will produce a soft, diffused light, which spreads over a wide angle. But this soft, reflected light is much weaker and will only travel a relatively short distance, depending on the intensity and distance of the original light source.

Reflectors can be easily made from a board covered with aluminum foil (smooth or crumpled and flattened) or matte-white painted, according to the type of light reflection required. (A board with a different surface on each side can be useful.) These "boards" can be made of wood, foam core (which is extremely lightweight), or cardboard. The bigger the reflector, the more light that will be reflected over a broad area. Even a large cloth can be used. However, cloth reflectors of this size can be cumbersome to hang and are likely to blow in the wind. Because the only alternative is to use powerful lamps or lights close in to the subject, when desperate, it is certainly worth trying when the sun's direction is appropriate and the tonal contrast is high (Figure 11.13).

Indoors, reflectors can be used to redirect light from windows into shadowy corners or to reflect sunlight as a filler. And when using backlight, a low reflector near the camera will reduce the shadows under people's chins and eyebrows.

Finally, while on the subject of reflection, when shooting in bright sunlight, look out for *accidental colored reflections* from nearby surfaces. Even a bright green shirt may reflect, giving the wearer a green complexion!

11.15 BOUNCE LIGHT

It is a common trick in photography to point the flash at the ceiling or a wall when photographing interiors to give the scene an overall wash of diffused *bounce light*. However, don't use a colored surface, or the reflected light will have a similar hue.

The same idea can be used when shooting video. Just point the light(s) at the nearby surfaces to get a soft "base light" (the amount of light required to obtain a quality video image). However, only a fraction of the light's output will be reflected.

FIGURE 11.13
An umbrella reflector can be attached to a light source to create a soft lighting instrument.
(Photo by Josh Taber.)

11.16 DO WE REALLY NEED TO LIGHT IT?

It is interesting to note that when people look around, their eyes will often pass, without a second glance, over incidental features that seem to stand out in a photograph, film, or video. They overlook the reflections in a shop window and concentrate on the items for sale inside the window. People accept a bright blob of light on a tiled surface without a thought. When they talk to others, they may note their expressions and how they are dressed, but that is usually the end of it.

However, when people look at a video of the same scene, they are likely to react quite differently. The reflections in the window seem to stop them from seeing into the shop. The blob of light on the tiles becomes an annoying distraction. They will tend to look at the people in the picture in a much more detached, critical way than they would if they were viewing them in everyday life. People may be struck by the talent's shadowed eye sockets, how haggard the person looks under the steep lighting, the hot spots on the person's head; they may become aware of ugly neck shadows, bright noses or ears, strongly lit shoulders, and maybe even the long nose shadow that looks like a mustache. What were previously trivial aspects of the everyday scene have a different impact on the screen.

This is why professionals go to so much trouble to readjust and light many scenes when the illumination was obviously insufficient to produce acceptable images. It is not enough, for example, to be able to get shots of an audience at a concert; one wants the images to be attractive too. The available light is often in the wrong direction, or it is too flat or too contrasty, or it only illuminates part of the scene clearly. By adding lighting, the professional seeks to correct these shortcomings.

11.17 LIGHTING OPTIONS

Whatever the type of program being shot, there are basically four choices as far as lighting is concerned:

- Shoot the scene with existing light.

- Increase the intensity of the lighting that is already present. For example, replace the bulbs with others of higher power (check the lamp holder to make sure it can handle a higher-rated bulb).
- Add some lights to the present lighting.
- Remove the existing lighting and bring in television lights.

Then comes the decision as to whether to light the whole action area or restrict the lighting to fit limited action in one small section of the area at a time.

11.18 EXISTING LIGHT

Available light is utilizing whatever lighting already exists at the location. This may include sunlight, recessed lighting, lamps, etc. They may need to be gelled, diffused, or even shut off to work for your production.

By lighting the scene or supplementing the existing lighting, the director has some control over the situation and a far better chance of achieving consistently high-quality pictures. Existing light shooting is a matter of taking advantage of whatever lighting is available to enhance the image (Figure 11.14).

Production personnel begin by asking the following questions:

- Can the scene be shot from the chosen camera position, with the present lighting?
- Is it possible to expose the picture properly?

FIGURE 11.14
While shooting in existing light can create some problems, it also allows the director to capture the mood of the event. No lights were added to this scene.

- Is there good detail and tonal gradation in the subject?
- If part of the subject is in the shadow, does that matter?
- Would some fill light from a reflector or an additional small light beside the camera help to show details in the shadows?
- Are there any distractions in the shot, such as a bright sky?

Perhaps the overall effect would look better if the subject was turned slightly toward the light. Then a fill light may not be needed for the shadows. Would it be better to wait for the sun to come out, or return another day when the light is right?

When shooting an interior and there is daylight around, can the sunlight be used to provide a key light, backlight, or reflected as a fill light for additional light to illuminate the background?

A technique that has been used for years when there is virtually no light or when it's impossible to get good pictures with the video camera is to use a still photographic camera (with a time exposure) to photograph the scene. The image can then be imported into the computer editing system and panned, so that it looks as though it is a video shot of the real scene.

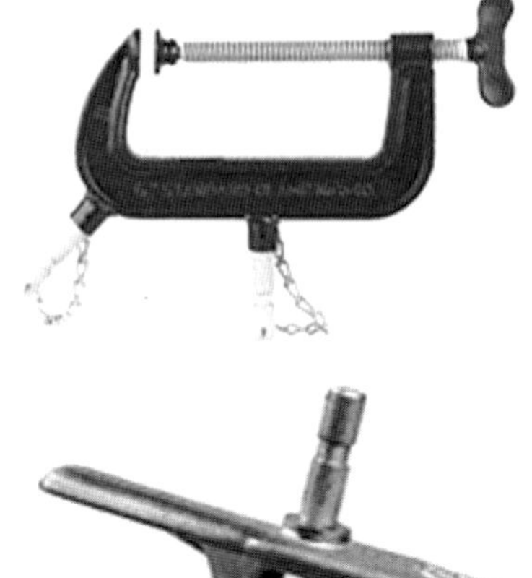

FIGURE 11.15
"Furniture clamps" and "gator" clamps are used to attach a light to anything around the shooting location.
(Photos courtesy of Mole-Richardson.)

LIGHTWEIGHT LIGHT SUPPORTS

11.19 GRIP CLAMPS

A number of different clamps or grips are available on the market in order to hold lights on location or in the studio. All of them include "mounting spuds," where lights can be attached. These clamps clip a light to any firmly based object, such as a door, table, chair, rail, post, window, or ladder. In the studio, they can also be clamped to a light stand and set flat. A clamp can be a useful compact device to secure lamps in out-of-the-way places, especially when space is restricted (Figure 11.15).

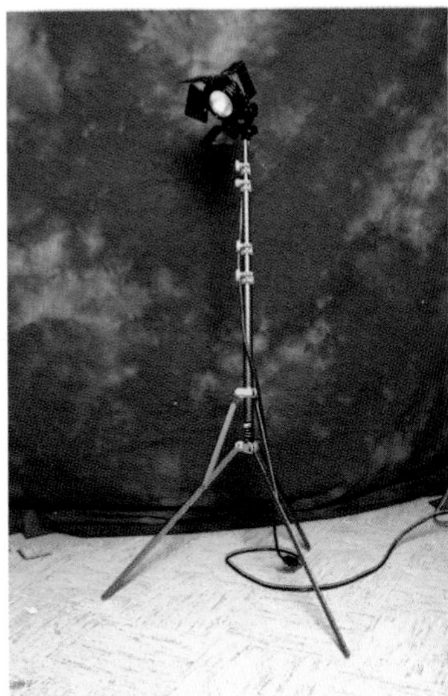

FIGURE 11.16
Light stands can be collapsed and folded into a compact size for storage and transport.
(Photo by Josh Taber.)

11.20 LIGHT STANDS

Light stands come in different sizes and shapes. They can be collapsed, folded, or dismantled into sections for transport. The size of the light will determine how sturdy the light stand needs to be. If the stand is too flimsy, it will be top heavy and easily upset, even by the weight of the light's cable. With more robust types of stands, two or more lights can be attached to a stand when necessary (Figure 11.16).

FIGURE 11.17
Cable trays or "yellow jackets" are used to protect cables and people when in walking paths. These trays can also be driven over by a car, protecting the cables from damage.

LIGHTING SAFETY

When working on the lighting, it is easy to become preoccupied with the effects being created and to overlook some of the practical hazards that can negatively impact the production. A number of issues need to be considered:

Equipment Condition

Check all of the lighting equipment to make sure that it is all in good condition. Lamps should be fitted firmly in sockets (never handle lamps with the bare hands). Check that nothing is coming loose, cables are not frayed or cut, and that the plug and its connections are okay.

Grounding

All electrical equipment should be properly grounded; otherwise there is more of a chance of receiving a severe electric shock under certain conditions.

Electrical Overload

Do not connect too many lamps to one outlet or overload the power supply. There may already be other equipment using the same electrical circuit, making it easy to exceed its capacity. Before connecting to the electrical circuit, find out where the breaker box is located and who is responsible for accessing it.

Hot Lamps

Some types of lamps can get extremely hot, especially quartz lights. Fluorescent and LED lights burn cool. Be careful when working near hot lamps that are lit or were recently switched off. Not only can they burn whatever touches them, but the lamp's filament is fragile when hot and can be destroyed by even a slight hit.

If a hot lamp is within a couple of feet of a surface, there is a chance of scorching or burning that surface. Wood, drapes, paper, and plastic are particularly vulnerable. Cables should not rest against a hot lamp either, because they can melt. Gels attached to the light usually reduce the amount of air ventilation, causing more heat within the lamp. If gels or diffusion material attached to the lighting instrument get too close, they can smell, melt, or even burn when overheated.

Falling Equipment

Lights and light supports can fall down all too easily. Safety wires/chains should always be used when hanging lamps from a ceiling grid. This backup is invaluable if a light falls for some reason. A light on a stand can be hazardous if it is tripped over and knocked down. Whenever using a lighting stand, it is best to place a weight on its base (perhaps a canvas sandbag, a bag of stones, or even a rock) to prevent it from moving or toppling over. Very high lighting stands (taller than six feet) are extremely unstable.

Light Cables

Remember that people trip over cables strewn around the floor, so place the cables as much out of the way as possible. They should be placed near a wall and out of the walking/driving path. Stationary cables in walking locations should be secured with gabby tape/duct tape to keep the cables from moving. People should not be stepping on the cables, so they need to be covered in some way. This could include placing them in a cable tray or covering them with a mat or some type of board.

Cables can also be hung on wall hooks or taped to undecorated walls.

Water

Working with lighting in rain or near water can be very dangerous. If rain falls on a lamp, it is liable to explode or short out the supply, unless the equipment is specifically designed to avoid this. Water on the ground can cause short circuits or electrocute the personnel if it gets in the wrong places.

LIGHTING INSTRUMENTS

11.21 CAMERA LIGHT

A small portable light can be attached to the top of a video camera (Figures 11.18 and 11.19). These camera lights are generally powered by an AC adapter, exterior battery pack, or the camera's battery. Its main advantage is that it always lights whatever the camera is shooting and does not require another pair of hands. Portable lighting of this sort can provide a convenient key light when you are shooting under difficult conditions, especially if you are following someone around. The light

FIGURE 11.18 **On-camera lights can draw their power from an external battery pack, the camera's battery, or an AC power supply.** *(Photo courtesy of Grass Valley/Thomson.)*

can also provide modeling light for close exterior shots on a dull day or fill light for hard shadows when you are shooting someone in sunlight.

While older types of camera lights could be quite heavy, the newer LED lights barely add any weight at all. The disadvantages are that this type of light adds to the camera's overall weight. Also, the light is extremely frontal and so tends to flatten out the subject. The light will reflect in glasses and shiny surfaces near the subject as an intense white blob. People facing the camera may also find the light dazzling.

11.22 SCOOP

The scoop is an inexpensive and simple light instrument that requires little maintenance and works well when a floodlight (fill) is required (Figure 11.20). However, it can be inefficient and bulky. Unfortunately, the light from the scoop spreads uncontrollably, spilling over nearby scenery.

FIGURE 11.19
This LED 6000 K energy-efficient on-camera ring light is designed to provide an overall shadowless shot, or it can utilize individual sections of the ring.
(Photo courtesy of VF Gadgets.)

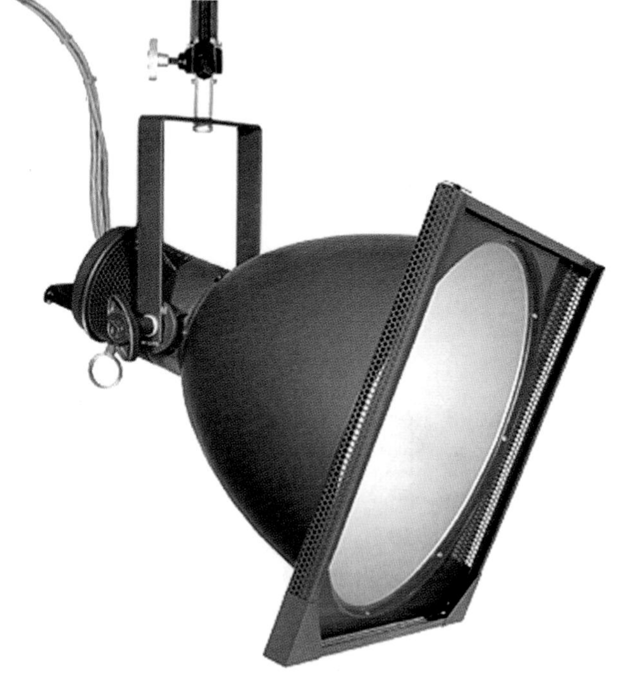

FIGURE 11.20
The scoop is a simple floodlight. It is inexpensive, usually not adjustable, lightweight, and it does not have a sharp outline. The scoop works well as a fill light and is great for lighting large areas on a set.
(Photo courtesy of Mole-Richardson.)

11.23 BROAD

The lightweight broad (broadside) has a short trough containing a reflector and a tubular quartz light of usually 500 to 1,000 W (Figure 11.21).

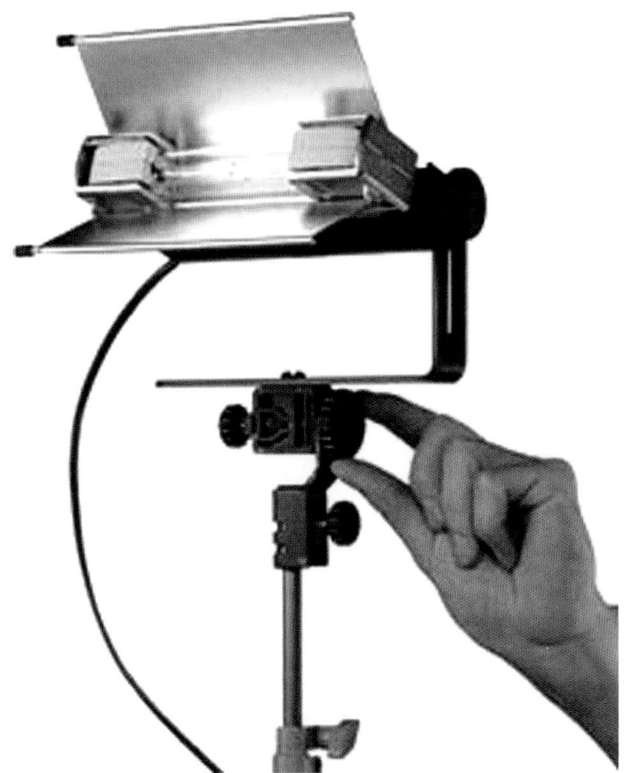

FIGURE 11.21
The V-light, or broad light, is a compact light source. This powerful light source can be used as a key or fill and folds small enough to fit into a camera case.
(Photo courtesy of Lowell.)

The bulb may have a frontal shield to internally reflect the light. Although the broad is widely referred to as a soft light source because of its small area, it produces discernible shadows. Nevertheless, it is an extremely useful wide-angle broad light source that can be hung conveniently in various ways, supported on stands, or laid on the floor. Two-leaf or four-leaf barn door shutters that can be closed to reduce the spread of the light are often fitted to broads.

11.24 THE PORTABLE SOFT LIGHT

The portable soft light is designed to easily be carried into the field. It provides a large amount of soft light (Figure 11.22).

FIGURE 11.22
The portable soft light is lightweight, may work with existing lighting instruments, and provides a large level of soft light.
(Photos by Mole-Richardson and Taylor Vincent.)

The portable soft light is available in different models. Some of these diffusion attachments fit on a standard Fresnel light, while others can be purchased with special lighting instruments. Light from a central lamp is reflected off of the back of the lighting instrument. Although this device spreads its illumination uncontrollably, its portability makes it a handy lighting tool.

11.25 MULTILAMP SOURCES

Several soft light sources use groups of lamps, which combine so that the shadows cast by each are "lit out" by its neighbor's light.

A *strip light* or *cyc light* consists of a row of light units joined in a long trough (Figure 11.23).

FIGURE 11.23
Strip lights or cyc lights are used primarily to light sets from the floor up.
(Photo courtesy of Mole-Richardson.)

Each unit has a bulb with a curved metal reflector. The strip light can be used to illuminate backgrounds or translucent screens from the floor. In a studio, strip or eye lights are often suspended to light backgrounds from above.

Multilamp *banks* are excellent soft light sources. A typical design has multiple panels of grouped PAR internal reflector lamps (Figure 11.24).

FIGURE 11.24
A bank of lamps provides a highly diffused light source and can easily work as a daylight booster. This lighting instrument acts like a series of scoops and houses a series of switchable PAR lamps. Users have little control over the beam coverage.
(Photo courtesy of Mole-Richardson.)

FIGURE 11.25
Fluorescent tube soft lights are often used as a soft light source.
(Photo courtesy of Mole-Richardson.)

Each panel can usually be independently switched and turned to adjust the brightness and spread of the unit. The *floodlight bank* is mainly used as a booster light for exteriors and for large-area illumination. Large side-flaps may be fitted to restrict the light spread. Soft light sources that rely on internal reflection to produce light scatter generate quite diffused light, but they are relatively inefficient.

Some people favor large units fitted with a bank of fluorescent tubes as an inexpensive soft light source (Figure 11.25).

Although these lights can be fragile, one of their main advantages is that they produce little to no heat, use much less energy than a normal television light, and put out a large amount of light.

11.26 OPEN FACE ADJUSTABLE LIGHT

This type of lighting instrument is widely used in the field. It has a variety of names, including lenseless spotlight, open-bulb spot, external reflector spot, and reflector spotlight (Figure 11.26).

Some brands of this light have uneven beams. However, this light has many advantages. It is extremely portable, compact, and efficient, all of which are useful when ventilation and power are limited. Diffuser or corrective color gels are easily clipped to its barn doors.

11.27 FRESNEL SPOTLIGHTS

In television studios, where the lights have to be positioned a fair distance from the subjects, the large heavy-duty Fresnel spotlight is universal, suspended from ceiling bars or battens (Figure 11.27).

It is lighter than the other studio spotlight (the ellipsoidal), sometimes has an adjustable beam, and provides an unfocused spotlight beam. The Fresnel is probably used more in studios than any other light.

FIGURE 11.26
This open face adjustable light unit can be used as a spot or floodlight.
(Photo courtesy of Mole-Richardson.)

FIGURE 11.27
The Fresnel light is a nondefined spotlight. It is lightweight, less expensive than an ellipsoidal, and has an adjustable beam.
(Photo courtesy of Mole-Richardson.)

PRACTICAL LIGHTING

11.28 THE GENERAL APPROACH TO LIGHTING

As discussed earlier, if a light is moved from near the camera's position over to the right, any prominent feature on the subject's surface, such as someone's nose, will cast a shadow to the left. As the lighting angle increases, such shadows spread across the surface, emphasizing its shape and texture. The greater the light's angle, the greater the effect. At the same time, the shadow of the subject itself also moves across the background, growing broader. As the light is moved further around the subject, less and less of the subject is illuminated, until eventually, by the time the lamp has been moved entirely to the right side, only half of the subject is lit. The surface details that are caught by the light stand out prominently, which is a useful technique when lighting low-relief subjects such as coins. As the lamp is raised, shadows grow downward. Similarly, when a lamp is moved upward diagonally, shadows develop downward diagonally in the opposite direction. From these basics, we can see some obvious principles to follow:

- The lamp should not be too close to the lens. This flattens out surface modeling and causes light reflections.
- The angle should not be too steep. It creates crude, gaunt, unattractive top light.
- The lamp should not be too far around to one side, unless the subject is facing that way. This can result in harsh surface modeling and a half-lit effect.

Other lighting tips include the following:

- Choose the light direction that is most appropriate for the subject and its surroundings best. Don't forget to look out for any reflections or shadows that might be distracting.
- The final light position is often a compromise. It depends on what is being lit and what the director wants it to look like. As a general guide, when lighting a person, do not have the lamp flat on, but position it at an angle: a little to one side of the subject's nose direction and a little above the eyes. Clearly, the best position for the light depends on which direction the person is facing. If the subject is going to turn his or her head around between full face and profile, place the key roughly halfway between those two positions.
- A prominent shadow on a light surface behind a subject can seem perfectly natural, or it may cause the picture to look crudely unbalanced. Lightening the shadows with another lamp may cause the background to be overexposed. Instead, either move the subject farther away from the background or raise the lamp a little to push the shadow downward.
- As the light is moved farther away from a subject, the light spreads over a greater area, but its intensity falls.
- If a lamp is placed close to a subject, the light output will be higher. However, its light beam will cover less of the scene.
- Avoid lighting arrangements in which people move in and out of light, unless you are seeking a dramatic effect. Lighting should generally cover the action area, plus a safety region, in case people move beyond their expected positions.
- Find out as much as possible beforehand about what is going to happen. Then set up the lights to specifically cover the action.
- Use the rehearsal as an opportunity to check your lighting treatment on camera. Do not just watch the rehearsal and *then* light the scene. There will probably not be enough time to sufficiently light the scene properly, and you will miss the opportunity to check for lighting defects.

- During rehearsal, look out for hot spots and dark areas, both on people as they move around and on the background. To adjust the lighting *balance* (i.e., the relative intensities of the various lamps), add a scrim to a light to dim it a little, or you may need to increase another light.

11.29 USING ONE LIGHT

Keep in mind that the priorities in lights are as follows: the subject's key light, then a fill light to illuminate its shadows, then a backlight if needed, and finally lighting for the background. However, if you are using a single light and this is the only illumination there is, it will need to be placed relatively frontally.

A single soft light, such as a "V-light," will provide a more attractive effect than a hard light source, particularly if you use a diffuser. This will cut down its light level but improve the pictorial effect. Although this soft light will scatter around, at least it prevents nearby areas from falling into a deep shadow.

If you are using a single hard light source, results can be over-contrasty, leaving the subject unattractively isolated in a pool of light, within dark surroundings, or casting a strong obtrusive shadow.

Depending on how satisfactory the existing lighting is, a single lamp can be used as a key light, fill light, backlight, or background light. It can strengthen the weakest-lit area of the image. A reflector can be used to reflect sunlight or lamplight to reduce shadows.

11.30 USING MULTIPLE LIGHTS

Several lights are usually needed to light the scene in the following situations:

- When lighting has to be provided for a very wide shot, which must be lit evenly.
- When lamps are of low power or have a restricted spread.
- When people and the background need to be lit throughout.
- When a series of subjects are spread around and cannot be lit by one light (each may need its own individual lighting).
- When you want to show detail or modeling in dark background tones.
- When the camera moves around and shows a series of background areas.
- When the subject is to be shot from several different directions.
- When you are attempting to create lighting effects, such as patches of dappled light, light patterns, colored lighting, lighting changes (such as morning to night), or a series of lamps, each lighting a small selected area.
- When you need a considerable depth of field in the shot (i.e., the lens stopped well down).

FIGURE 11.28
With daylight coming in the window from exactly the right direction, the sidelight creates a fine atmospheric effect.

FIGURE 11.29
Waiting for the right light. Sunlight from the side casts attractive shadows and gives dimension and depth.
(Photo by Josh Taber.)

FIGURE 11.30
Rim lighting can reveal outline and texture.
(Photo by Josh Taber.)

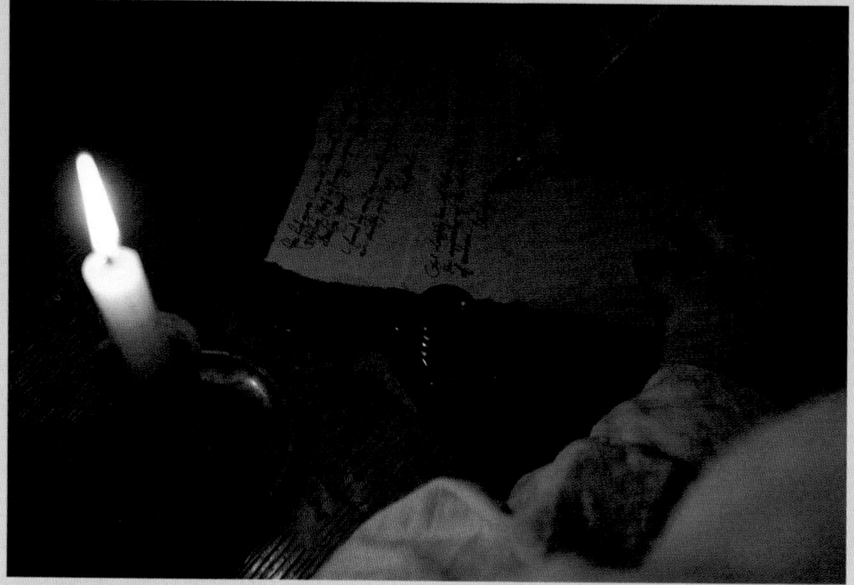

FIGURE 11.31
By keeping the light localized, the attention is concentrated.
(Photo by Josh Taber.)

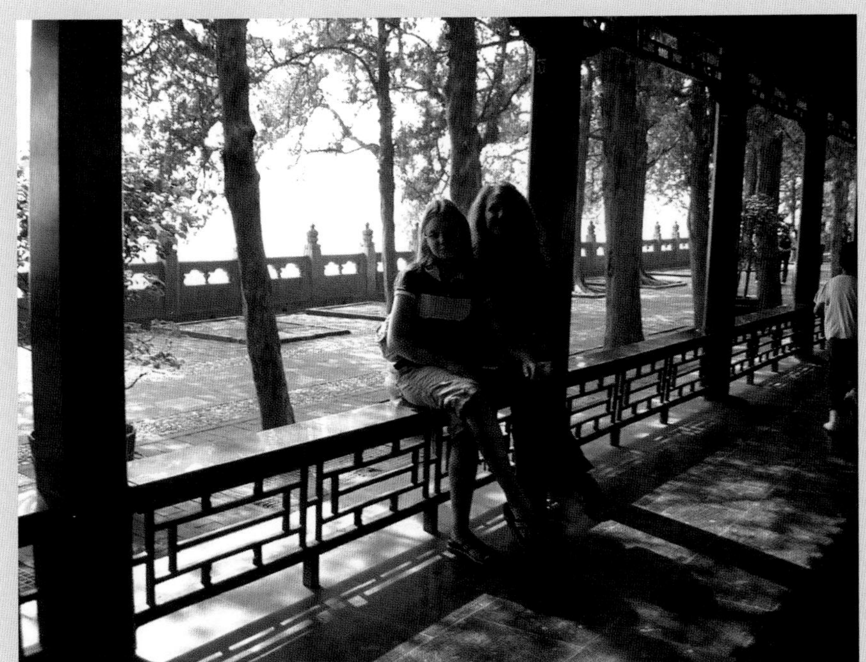

FIGURE 11.32
Where contrast is high, you may not be able to expose the lighter areas and the shadows successfully.

Interview with a Pro

Tommy Brown, Lighting

Tommy Brown, Lighting

Why do you like working with lighting?
I am passionate about lighting because it is fun for me, and I enjoy the challenges of it. When you see what is being accomplished with your light, you feel you are really contributing to the project. I must confess that sometimes it's a little like Christmas morning getting to plug things in and have them work! It's not that I'm surprised when a light comes on; it's that I take great pride in doing the job right.

What makes good lighting?
Experience! Experience! Experience! Knowing what works and what doesn't will save you when there's limited time for lighting! Especially when someone needs that light yesterday! Preproduction is essential. Sitting down with the DP in advance to get his or her vision makes all the difference in the world.

Like acting, lighting can make or break your production. You can have the best script in the world, but if your actors aren't doing their job, good luck getting the project to see the light of day. The same goes for lighting. You can have a vast array of lights at your fingertips, but if you don't know how to use them, you are never going to move beyond the student film level.

What are some of the challenges of lighting?

- Many times the biggest challenge is getting power from one location to another.
- It can be very difficult to stay attentive and not get distracted so that you know what is needed.
- Lighting instruments change. It is tough to quickly learn new lights.

Do you have a favorite light?

I mainly work with ARRI fresnels, but I really enjoy Kinoflo's, and LEDs (1×1-foot panel lights and brick lights).

Where do you see lighting going in the future?

More LEDs.

Tommy Brown has worked on the lighting of corporate videos, network television, and feature films.

CHAPTER 12

The Background

What we are looking for in a dramatic set is an imaginative substitute. Keep in mind, directors produce illusions. However basic the set materials really are, the end result can appear to the audience as the real thing.

—Gerald Millerson, Author

The background is much more than whatever happens to appear behind the subject. It directly affects the success of the program, so it needs to be carefully designed and controlled.

Key Terms

- ***Aspect ratio:*** Televisions have an aspect ratio of 4:3 (SD) or 16:9 (HDTV). It is important to keep the aspect ratio in mind when designing sets so that they fit the screen.
- ***Chroma-key:*** Utilizing a production switcher, the director can replace a specific color (usually blue or green) with another image source (still image, live video, prerecorded material, etc.).
- ***Cyclorama (cyc):*** The cyclorama serves as a general-purpose detail-less background. It can be neutral, colored with lights, or without light (black).
- ***High angle:*** When the camera is positioned higher than the subject.
- ***Low angle:*** When the camera is positioned lower than the subject.
- ***Modular set:*** Usually purchased commercially, modular sets come in a series of components that can be stored and put back together easily.
- ***Open set:*** Created by carefully grouping a few pieces of furniture in front of the wall. Even a small number of items—such as little as a couch, a low table, a table lamp, potted plants, a screen, a chair, and a stand lamp—can suggest a complete room.
- ***Virtual set:*** These sets use a blue or green seamless background, chroma-keying the computer-generated set into the scene. Most virtual sets employ sophisticated tracking computer software that monitors the camera's movements so that as it zooms, tilts, pans, or moves in any other way, the background moves in a corresponding way.

12.1 THE IMPORTANCE OF THE BACKGROUND

Video programs are shot in an extremely wide range of locations: people's homes, offices, factories, rooms, halls, public buildings, studios, out in the streets, and wide-open spaces. Where we shoot the program may be vital (contextually relevant) to what we want to tell our audience, or it can be merely incidental.

To some extent, the importance of the background depends on the director, the way the subject is approached, and the chosen style and form. A dramatic play can be presented successfully in front of black curtains. Shooting the same play on location, or on an appropriately designed set, usually adds to the perceived quality.

Shakespeare's plays were originally performed on an open stage with absolutely no scenery. Everything was left to the imagination of his audience. Today, broadcast documentary programs fly talent around the world, from one exotic background to another. There are times when this kaleidoscope of pictures contributes nothing to our understanding of the subject. It just gets in the way of the words. Effective backgrounds are more a matter of making wise choices than having a big budget.

12.2 THE IMPACT OF THE BACKGROUND

Surroundings have a considerable influence on how we feel about what we are seeing and hearing. It is not just a matter of choosing a background that looks appropriate or attractive. We must determine whether its audience impact is right for the specific points we are making in the program.

The background we choose for our action, and the way we shoot it, can affect how persuasively points are communicated to our audience. It is one thing to see a person standing on a street corner, recommending a type of medicine, and another when we see that same person wearing a white lab coat in a laboratory. The surroundings have swayed our reactions, yet they have nothing to do with the true quality of the product.

The camera cannot avoid being selective. For example, if a video camera is taken to an offshore oil rig, depending on which parts of the structure are shot, a very different view of life on the rig can be expressed. The final emphasis could be on its huge geometric structure, the isolation of this group of workers in treacherous seas, or it might appear as a scene of endless noise and tense activity. In the end, it is the shot selection and editing that will portray the concept of life on a rig to the audience. The result may be a fair cross section of life there, or it could be overselective. Much depends on the point of view the director adopts.

> The detail in HD is remarkable, which has implications for makeup, set design, and lighting. In Hollywood, some major actors are even having it written into their contracts to have their makeup air-brushed because of the detail. On a recent HD project we noticed the slightest scratches or dust on the set. We kept the art department busy between takes just keeping the set wiped off and touched up.
>
> **—Phil Cooke, Director**

BACKGROUNDS (SETS) ARE A MATTER OF TASTE

Television show set designs differ greatly from country to country and even network to network. The following photographs are a study of some of the design choices that were made by two different country's networks who covered the Olympics in Vancouver. These sets were photographed in the main broadcast center during the games (Figure 12.1).

Australian networks

Japanese networks

FIGURE 12.1
Set designs can be incredibly varied.

12.3 REAL AND UNREAL BACKGROUNDS

Most audiences are not concerned about whether the background is real or an illusion. They usually don't care if it is a real location or computer generated. It is the effect that counts. However, it is worth remembering that backgrounds can be derived in a number of ways:

- *Use of actual place.* The action is really shot in the Sahara desert.
- *Use of substitute.* The action is shot in a convenient location that looks sufficiently like part of the Sahara desert.
- *Use of a set.* The action is shot in a studio that has been built to resemble the real thing.

- *Suggested location.* The camera shows location shots of the Eiffel Tower (part of a still photo), intercut with shots of someone standing against a brick wall. Thanks to the sound of traffic and other sound effects, the viewer assumes that the action was shot in Paris.
- *Virtual set.* Using a computer, it is possible to insert the person standing in front of the camera into a separate background image. With care, it can be done absolutely convincingly.

12.4 SET COMPONENTS

There are many different types of set components used for television productions. Here are some of the most common:

FIGURE 12.2
These flats, or standard set units, are the back of the walls of the set.

- *Standard set unit:* Used instead of an interior or exterior walls. A flat is a good example of a standard set unit (Figure 12.2).
- *Hanging unit:* Basically, any background that is supported by hanging on a wall, a lighting grid, or another overhead support. These include curtains, rolls of background paper, and canvas (Figure 12.3).
- *Platforms:* Used to elevate the talent or set
- *Set pieces:* Usually are three-dimensional objects used on a set. Examples of set pieces would include modular set systems, steps, and pillars.
- *Floor treatment:* Includes rugs, wood, rubber tiles, paint, and so on.
- *Stage props:* The furniture on the set. These would include news desks, chairs, couches, and tables.
- *Set dressings:* Set decorations are used to create the character of the set. They can establish the mood and style of the production. The dressings can include fireplaces, lamps, plants, pictures, or draperies (Figures 12.4, 12.5, and 12.6).
- *Hand properties (props):* Any items that are touched and handled by the talent during the production. These could include a pen, dishes, a cell phone, or silverware.

The choices made in each of these component categories fit together to send the audience a specific message about the characters and the time period the story is taking place in.

FIGURE 12.3
A neighborhood hanging unit hanging behind the actual set. This was the view out the window.

FIGURE 12.4
These set dressings will be used to establish the character of the set.

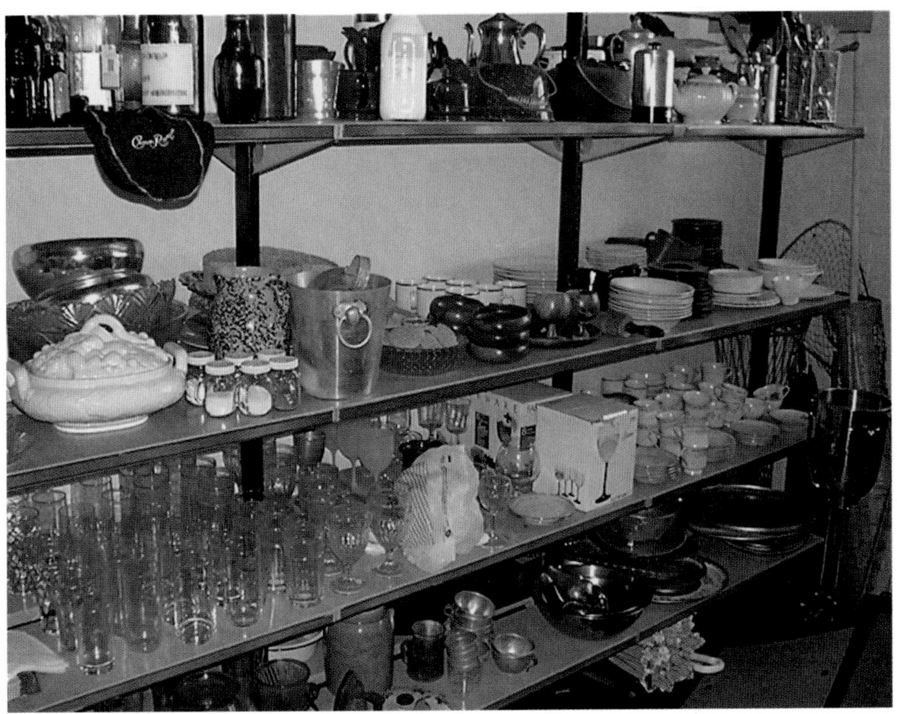

FIGURE 12.5
Prop room showing the various props available for use in a production.

FIGURE 12.6
The set pieces, the dressings, and the props give an authenticity to the time period during which this story takes place.
(Photo by Doug Smart.)

12.5 SET DESIGN FOR 16:9

High-definition television (HDTV) and its 16:9 format create some challenges. Sets that were acceptable on standard definition (SD) television are no longer acceptable because of the high resolution of HDTV. Scratches and dents are much more apparent.

The 16:9 format has also changed the design of the set—and made it more complex, including impacting the locations of the talent. Until the 16:9 format becomes standard, viewers will see more header elements (high sections of the set) because camera operators need to frame by 4:3 as well as 16:9 (Figures 12.7, 12.8, and 12.9).

This is especially true in wide shots. However, once 16:9 framing become the standard, the header elements will be seen much less. It's important to create clean, visually interesting header elements while not dedicating too much of the budget to elements that viewers will see for only a short period.

12.6 THE NEUTRAL BACKGROUND

There are times when we want the background to provide totally *neutral* surroundings for the action. In the extreme, this background could be just a blank white (*limbo*) or black (*cameo*) area, because we are concentrating on the

FIGURE 12.7
Today's sets need to be created with both the 16:9 and the 4:3 formats in mind.
(Photo courtesy of FX Group: www.fxgroup.tv.)

FIGURE 12.8
On all shots, including ones like this, it is important to remember that 4:3 viewers won't see the areas to the far right and left of the screen, so it's important not to put vital scenic elements or graphics in this space. However, 16:9 viewers do expect this area to be filled with visual elements. In this image, the grayed-out areas to the left and right won't be seen by 4:3 viewers; however, 16:9 viewers will see the entire width, including the gray areas.

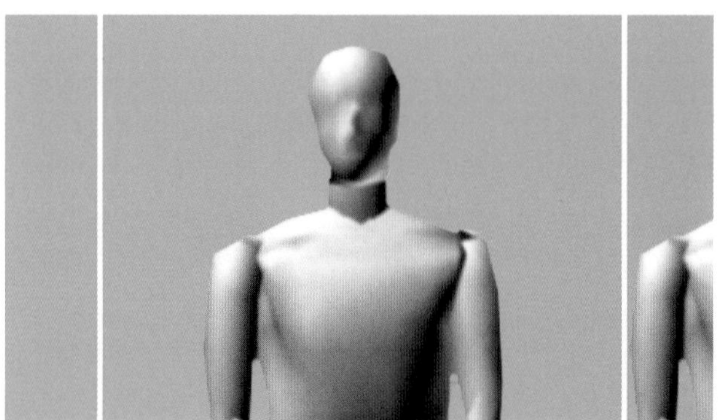

FIGURE 12.9
Whenever two or more talent members appear in one shot, care needs to be taken to make sure anchors don't appear in each other's shots. In this example of a one shot, 4:3 viewers, who only see the area between the white lines, will only see the one anchor. However, 16:9 viewers, who see the entire image, see the co-anchor's shoulder to the right. This issue is particularly important with anchor desks—a set needs to have a desk that seats anchors far enough apart to not encroach on each other's shots while still making anchors not seem too far apart.

performers. However, we usually want something more interesting to look at than a plain area of tone, and TV solved this problem by creating the *neutral setting*, a background that is visually attractive but does not actually remind us of any specific style, period, or place.

Basically, neutral backgrounds are usually made with scenic units, positioned in front of a *cyclorama* or *cyc* (pronounced "sike"). A cyclorama is a curved wall that is used as a background for a television production. This curved wall suggests unlimited space when seen through the camera. The cyc provides an extremely useful general-purpose background surface for studios of all sizes. The cyclorama can be the basis of a wide range of program backgrounds from the mundane to the spectacular. It can be built to fit the project—anything from a few feet long to a complete wall around the studio (Figure 12.10).

Soft cycs are usually made from cloth, and *hard cycs* can be made out of wood, metal, or fiberglass. Soft cycs are typically white and are generally made of scrim. This way, lights can be projected on them from the front or back. Hard cycs are traditionally painted a chroma-key color, green or blue.

12.7 ECONOMICAL SETS

People working on a tight budget and with limited storage facilities will have little opportunity to build much scenery. But that does not need to be a major limitation; it is possible to develop attractive sets, simply and economically, by using just a few multipurpose set units in front of a cyclorama or a background wall.

- Lighting alone can significantly change the appearance of a background, whether it is a plain wall or a cyc. You can light the set evenly, shade it

FIGURE 12.10
The *cyclorama (cyc)* serves as a general-purpose detail-less background. It can be neutral, colored with lights, without light (black), or video can be inserted into a blue cyclorama (like the one pictured), providing a virtual set. Note that it curves between the wall and the floor. Because corners are difficult to light and look like corners, the cyc is used so that it can be effectively treated as a virtual set.

(bottom-lit from a cyc light), light it in blobs or dapples, project shadows or patterns on it, or use plain or blended color areas.

- An *open set* can be created by carefully grouping a few pieces of furniture in front of the wall. Even a few items—such as a couch, a low table, a table lamp, potted plants, a screen, a chair, and a stand lamp—can suggest a complete room.
- *Flats* can be created by stretching cloth or other material over a wood frame.
- *Modular units* can be constructed out of many different materials, from wood products to plastic. The modules can also be purchased commercially in a variety of configurations. The advantage to modular systems is that they can be quickly assembled and disassembled, they are generally designed for optimum storage size, and they can look quite professional (Figure 12.11).

12.8 SEMIPERMANENT SETS

Set design has become more complex over the years. Sets incorporate technology, special lighting, monitors, and areas for keying graphics (Figure 12.12).

FIGURE 12.11
Modular units provide a quick and easy way to build a quick set. They can be constructed or purchased commercially.
(Photos courtesy of Uni-Set.)

Dramatic sets are being built with such detail that they have become incredibly complex. Most complex sets are installed semipermanently (Figure 12.13).

They are complicated enough that it is not worth installing and uninstalling them on a regular basis, until they need to be updated or the show is canceled. This means that they are built into the studio, bolted to the floor, and probably connected to the ceiling. When studio space is available, it saves a lot of time to have a set sitting waiting to be used. A regular show can be shot quickly, without all of the setup time.

A "permanent" or "semipermanent" set has the following advantages:

- Most of the set is assembled, ready to be used.
- The set can be dressed and left in place (various props and furnishings).
- Lamps, both set illumination and on-set lights, usually have already been hung and adjusted and then left in position.

FIGURE 12.12
Sets have become more complex over the years, loaded with technology and multiple surfaces.
(Photos by Jon Greenhoe and Josh Taber.)

When a studio regularly produces a specific program, it may have a permanent set installed, such as a kitchen, a laboratory, an office, a lounge, or a news desk layout, designed to fit the productions.

12.9 CHROMA-KEY

Chroma-keying is one of the most used techniques in television production. It has endless potential in creating backgrounds and as special effects (Figure 12.14).

Wherever a chosen *keying color* (usually green) appears in the shot, it is possible to insert a second source (the *background*), which can be video or a still

FIGURE 12.13
A semipermanent dramatic set being built into the studio.

shot. Chroma-key replaces the blue or green area (determined by the user) with the corresponding section of the second source. This keying technique can be created by using a production switcher in a multicamera production or with a nonlinear editing system equipped with the appropriate software.

Chroma-keying makes it possible for a person to appear as though they are standing in front of a real location such as a castle, a field, the seashore, or a town square—all done inside a studio. If done well, this technique can be convincing and effective with the audience (Figure 12.15).

When utilizing the chroma-key technique, the entire background does not need to be keyed out. Instead, any part of the background or foreground may be chroma-keyed as long as the appropriate keying color is used. Because the image can be as large as the key color, it offers an economical method of providing an impressive giant display screen in a shot (Figure 12.16).

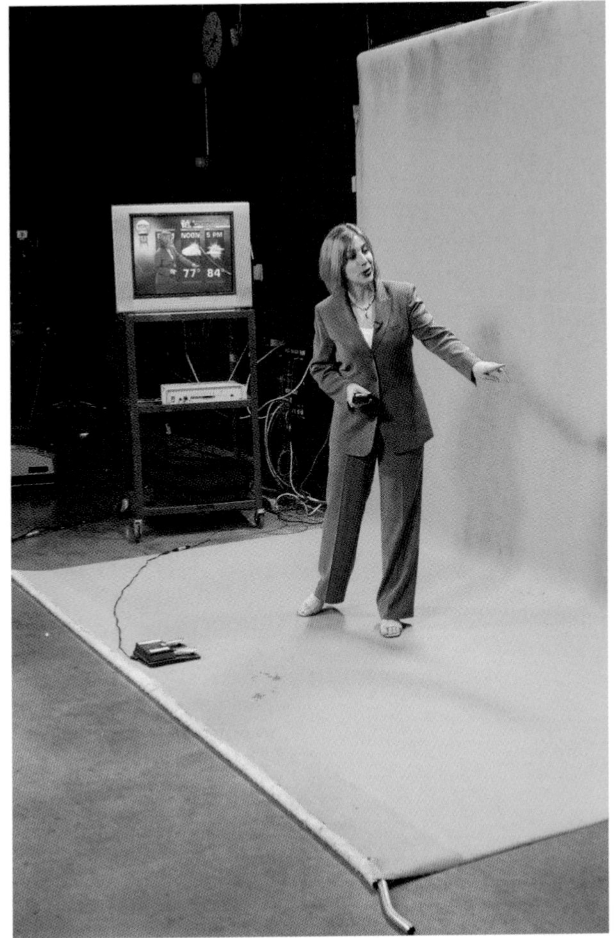

FIGURE 12.14
The television station uses a green chroma-key background for its weather reports. Note the final combined image on the monitor behind the talent. The foot pedal in front of the talent is used to change background images. The talent is looking at another monitor (not shown in the photo) to know where to point.
(Photo by Josh Taber.)

12.10 VIRTUAL SETS

The use of virtual sets continues to grow. This sophisticated type of chroma-key is changing the way sets are designed in many studios (Figures 12.17 and 12.18).

Although in the beginning the cost can be quite significant to set up a virtual set system integrated with cameras, the cost of quickly changing to many different kinds of sets can pay for itself in the long run. Studio space requirements and construction times are reduced with the use of these sets. Virtual sets use a blue or green seamless background and chroma-key the computer-generated

FIGURE 12.15
With the subject sitting in front of a green background, a secondary image (computer-generated news set) was inserted into whatever is green in the camera shot. The combined result makes it look as though the subject is actually in front of the background scene. Subjects within the master shot must not wear or contain the keying color (blue or green), or the secondary background will insert into those areas as well. The secondary background image can be anything: colors, still images, graphics, or recorded or live video images.

set into the scene. Most virtual sets employ sophisticated tracking computer software that monitors the camera's movements so that as it zooms, tilts, pans, or moves in any other way, the background moves in a corresponding way. This system automatically adjusts the background with each shot change, changing the background size and angle to simulate a real set.

FIGURE 12.16
The first image shows the set with a section that can be keyed out in blue. The second image is the external video shot. The third image shows what the viewers would see. Any appropriately colored portion of the set can be chroma-keyed.
(Photos by Tyler Young.)

FIGURE 12.17
The women sitting on the blue cyc are being shot by a camera that is connected to the virtual set computer located in the foreground of this photo. Notice on the middle monitor that the computer-generated set is visible. In the monitor on the right, you can see the combined virtual set and keyed talent.

12.11 OUTSIDE/BACK-LOT SETS

Building an outdoors back-lot set requires quite a financial commitment in both building the set and maintaining it. It is far beyond the small-budget project. However, these sets can be rented and do offer flexibility. The nice thing about them is that, if designed effectively, they can be reused. The outdoor set shown in Figure 12.19 was built decades ago and has been used in

FIGURE 12.18
Some virtual set systems utilize a type of global positioning system (GPS) unit on the camera, combined with a grid system on the blue chroma-key backdrop, to establish the camera's position in order to insert the correct background image.

many different films and television productions. These sets can be decorated to fit the time era, and most viewers do not realize that the set is the same location that was used for earlier shows.

12.12 THE LOCATION

Location backgrounds bring context to the production (Figure 12.20). They help establish the scene for the audience. They can also make the production look real and genuine in a way that it may be hard to imitate in any studio. They usually bring a credibility and urgency to the production. However, anytime the production is moved out of the studio, a little control is lost in audio, lighting, and maybe even camera placement. If it is an outside location, weather may be an issue.

FIGURE 12.19
The buildings and street in the first photograph are part of a set used in a network television production. The second photo shows the back of the same set. Notice that the back has been designed so that actors can appear in windows or move in and out of doors.

However, unless the image on screen is of a famous place, all the audience knows about the location is what they are shown. It is possible to go to an exotic place and shoot someone leaning against a tree that looks just like one back home. If you are on location, make good use of it.

FIGURE 12.20
The makers of this ESPN production wanted to show where it was being shot, so they included the city's skyline in the background.
(Photo by Dennis Baxter.)

12.13 WATCH THE BACKGROUND

In the "busyness" of shooting a production, it is easy to overlook things in the background that can become a distraction in the final image. At the time, they are accepted as part of the scene or not even noticed. In the final production, they distract the audience's attention. Even major films often have a microphone sneaking into the shot at the top of the picture or a shadow of the camera crew or prominent lighting cables, in spite of the filmmakers' vigilance (Figure 12.21).

Here are some reminders of typical gaffes that can spoil the image:

Windows can be the cause of embarrassment when shooting interiors. A large patch of sky in the shot can create problems. Even if the interior is exposed properly, this bright blank area still grabs the audience's attention. Although corrective filters can be used to compensate for the high color temperature of the daylight, its intensity can easily overwhelm the interior illumination and prevent the camera from getting a good tonal balance. In addition, if the audience has a good view of what is going on outside the window, there is always the chance that they will find this more intriguing than the real subject. The simple remedy is to keep the window out of shot, or close the shades.

FIGURE 12.21
Boom pole shadows can be a real challenge on a set.

Reflecting surfaces in the background are difficult to avoid. But glass, plastic, and even highly polished furniture can be troublesome. They can even reflect the camera and its crew. So instead of admiring the gleaming new automobile, the audience watches the interesting reflections in its door panel. Worse still, shiny surfaces reflect lamps. If a camera light is being used, its beam will bounce straight back into the lens. When the camera is moved, the blob of light will move along with the camera.

While low-intensity reflections can give sparkle and life to a surface, strong light reflections are a pain, both technically and artistically. Apart from avoiding shooting straight-on at these surfaces or keeping them out of shot, the quick solution is to change the camera's location, cover up the reflections (position something or someone so that the highlight is not reflected), or angle the surface.

Flashing signs, prominent posters, direction signs, and *billboards* are among the visual diversions that can easily ruin a shot. They are all part of the scene, but if a dramatic situation is taking place anywhere near an animated advertising sign, do not be surprised if part of the audience's attention is elsewhere.

Even if you are shooting in a busy spot, it is often possible to find a quiet corner where there are not too many interruptions. Avoid including a door or busy throughway in the background or similar busy areas with a continually changing stream of people. People staring at the camera and bystanders watching (particularly the hand-waving types) are a regular problem, and there is little you can do except try as much as possible to keep them out of the shot.

12.14 FOREGROUND PIECES

Objects can be *deliberately* positioned in the foreground of an image to improve its composition, to increase the impression of distance, or simply to hide something in the scene.

Many exterior shots have foliage hanging into the top of the frame. It is almost a visual cliché. But the camera operator has done this because the picture looks more complete, and it gives a better sense of scale than if there was just a blank open sky. With this "frame," the picture tends to look more balanced and no longer bottom heavy. When there does not happen to be an overhanging tree to shoot past, a piece of a tree branch can always be held above the lens. If this positively impacts the look of the picture, do it, and your audience will never know.

Although the television's picture itself usually has a fixed horizontal aspect ratio (4:3 or 16:9), a foreground window, an arch, or a similar opening can provide a border that alters the apparent *shape* of the picture.

FIGURE 12.22
Foreground subjects add depth to the images.

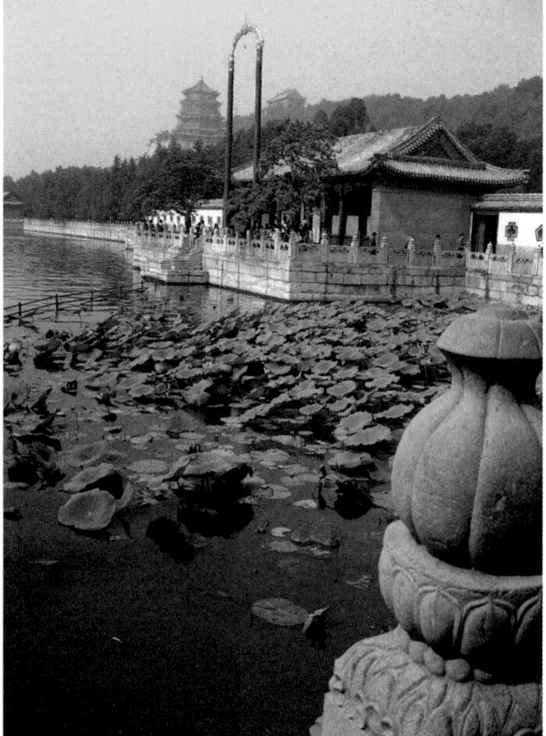

By carefully framing foreground objects, it is possible to hide things in the background that would be distracting to the audience. They might ruin the shot in some other way. For example, if a historical drama is being reenacted, it is convenient, to say the least, if a carefully positioned gatepost, bush, or even a person in the foreground hides the modern signs and power lines. Foreground pieces can also add depth to a limited background (Figure 12.22).

Create depth by shooting through objects, such as a bookshelf, a fence, or flowers. Usually the foreground is kept slightly out of focus to draw the audience's attention to the primary subject. However, the foreground can also help bring context to the image if something in the foreground adds information to the scene.

12.15 VERSIONS OF "REALITY"

The camera does not tell the truth. It *interprets*. Each aspect of the picture and the sound influences how members of the audience respond to what they see and hear. A slight change in the camera position can entirely alter the picture's impact. If the sun comes out, what was once a drab, threatening block of building can transform into an attractive, interesting piece of architecture. In the winter, we see a dull-looking street planted with stark, leafless trees. In spring, it becomes a charming avenue, where sidewalks are dappled with shade.

A location can be shot so that the audience envies its inhabitants or pities them for having to live there. It can appear like a fine place or an eyesore. It's all a matter of what the director chooses to include and omit, what is emphasized, and what is suppressed.

As the camera moves around the scene, it can dwell on busy purposeful bustle as people go to work, or it can linger on those who appear to be lounging around with nothing to do. (In reality, they might be waiting for a bus, but at the moment the camera captures them, they are "aimlessly inactive.") The director can suggest spaciousness by shooting with a wide-angle lens. Use a telephoto (narrow-angle) lens instead, and the same streets can look congested.

In most cities, one can find litter, decay, and graffiti, but conversely, there will be signs of prosperity, attractive buildings, green spaces, fountains, wildlife, things that are amusing, others that are touching. How the images are selected and related will significantly influence how the viewing audience interprets the scene.

12.16 WHAT CAN WE DO ABOUT THE BACKGROUND?

If the director is shooting in a studio and the background is unsatisfactory for any reason, he or she can usually improve it in some way or other. But what can be done when on location, if the background proves to be unworkable?

When you and your production team are guests in someone's home, the answer may be disappointingly little. So much depends on the people involved and the director's diplomacy. If the hosts are not accustomed to appearing on camera, they will probably be disturbed at suggestions that things need to be moved around to any extent.

They may even feel uncomfortable if they are not sitting in their customary chair. There is little point to making suggestions that will jeopardize the interview. However, there are various changes that can be made unobtrusively to improve matters:

- Natural lighting can be used, rather than introducing lights. The person being interviewed will probably feel more at ease. However, it may not be possible to get good images without adding some television lighting.
- Although a room's tones cannot necessarily be changed, it may be possible to shade your lamps off a light-toned surface to prevent them from appearing too bright (by using a barn door, flag, or partial diffuser). Perhaps a little illumination may be added to dark corners.
- If there are reflections in glass-fronted pictures or cabinets, and the lights and camera cannot be moved to avoid them, slightly angling the frame

or furniture may cure the dilemma. A wall picture or mirror can often be tilted up or down by wedging something behind it. To keep the camera from appearing in a glass bookcase behind the talent, it may be possible to slightly open its doors.

- Closing, or partly closing, the room's curtains may help you to adjust the lighting balance in a room.
- If you are shooting a corridor or hallway, it can help if doors in a side wall are opened enough to let extra light in.
- Even if you are shooting in daylight, it may provide more interesting images if the table lamps or other lights in the room are turned on.
- It may even be possible to conceal low-powered lamps behind furniture or wall angles to illuminate distant parts of the room; but be careful that they do not overlight or even burn nearby surfaces.

12.17 REARRANGING THE BACKGROUND

Most of the time, the director will be able to alter the background to achieve the best possible scene. Again, this has to be done diplomatically, but if the director is able to gain the host's confidence, and the director seems to know what he or she is doing, there should be no difficulties. The simplest changes

FIGURE 12.23
People's homes are designed to be comfortable and to be lived in; they are not designed for television. Whenever going into a home with a camera, it is common to have to move some furniture, pictures hanging on the wall, rugs, and knickknacks in order to create an image that works on television.
(Photo by Luke Wertz.)

usually involve moving around what is already there to avoid any unnecessary distractions or unwanted glares in the picture.

It is important to look at the background of any location to make sure that nothing is growing from the talent's head, or balancing on it, and that no vertical or horizontal lines cut through the center of the head or across the shoulders. These visual accidents can make the picture look contrived or comic (Figure 12.23).

There are a number of quick, inexpensive, and simple steps you can take to adjust the background for the camera:

- Rearrange the furniture.
- Replace furniture with other pieces from nearby rooms.
- Add or remove rugs.
- Hide a doorway with a folding screen.
- Attach display posters to the walls.
- Position indoor plants (e.g., ferns) to break up the background.

When shooting outside, there are relatively few things that you can do to cheaply and easily change the background.

12.18 PARTIAL SETTINGS

This is a strategy for convincing your audience that a modest setting is not only the real thing but is much more extensive than it actually is. Yet the cost and effort involved are minimal (Figure 12.24).

FIGURE 12.24
By putting the crowd in just the right place, repositioning the camera so that the crowd is directly behind the batter and catcher, and zooming in the lens to a close-up or medium shot, you will convince viewers that the baseball stadium was filled with a cheering audience.

If the camera does not move, it can only see a limited amount of the scene in a medium or close-up shot. With partial settings, it is important to concentrate on building up a section of the scene that is just large enough to fit the camera's shot and no more. Within the scene, enough features are included to allow the audience to interpret where the action is supposed to be taking place.

Do not underrate this idea. It has been used successfully in film and television for many years. The result does not need to look amateurish. Add the associated sound effects and the combined image can be indistinguishable from the real thing.

12.19 TYPICAL EXAMPLES OF PARTIAL SETTINGS

- An instant store can be created by putting the appropriate type of merchandise on a foreground table (the "counter"), an advertisement or two on the back wall, and a shelf behind the salesperson, who could be holding a product.
- Sometimes even a single feature in the picture can suggest an environment. A stained-glass window and organ music create a church interior. (The window could even be projected.)
- A convincing "room" can be created in a studio with just a couple of flats or screens and a chair. Add an extra item or two, such as a side table with a potted plant and a picture, and the scene begins to take on its own character. If a curtain is hung on one of the walls, a window is assumed to be there. Whether it is interpreted as being someone's home or a waiting room, for instance, largely depends on the way people in the scene behave. If the talent is lying back, casually dressed, reading a paper, it is obviously the person's home. If the talent is wearing outdoor attire, sitting upright, and anxious, he or she is waiting for something.
- Replace the plant with a computer and the picture with a framed certificate and, magically, the setting has become an office.

On location, the same concept is still useful—restrict the shot and change the background. Suppose you are shooting a 19th-century drama in which somebody visits a lawyer. You find a house exterior of about the right time period, but the rest of the street is obviously busy and modern. Fortunately, all you need is a shot of the house doorway with the appropriate business sign attached to it, and the picture will explain itself to the viewing audience. Have the actor go up to the door or pretend to leave the house, and the audience will immediately accept the location as the lawyer's office. You need only to replace the sounds of modern traffic noise with horse-drawn vehicles, and the period illusion is complete. With a little care and imagination, locations can be created from a minimum of scenery and work.

It is incredible how seemingly trivial techniques can give a totally convincing effect on camera:

- The camera rhythmically tilting up and down sells the illusion of a ship at sea.

- The wafting breeze may really be the result of an assistant waving a piece of board.
- The shuddering camera accompanied by things falling to the ground (pulled by unseen fish line) implies an explosion or an earthquake. A hanging lamp swings alarmingly—tugged by an out-of-shot line.
- The flickering flames of a nearby fire come from a stick of cloth strips waved in front of a ground lamp.

These are just a few examples of how a little ingenuity can apparently achieve the impossible and create a strong impression in your audience's minds.

12.20 FACING REALITY

It is one thing to have dreams about creating a program, but it is a different matter to turn them into reality. Among the problems facing all directors are the inevitable limitations of budget and facilities. Some of the things you need may not even be available.

When faced with such problems it is tempting to think small, to cut back on ambition and do a simpler version. Do not immediately abandon your ideas. Instead, ask yourself if there is another way of tackling the situation to get virtually the same effect. How can you get around the difficulty?

Look for *imaginative substitutes*. Keep in mind that directors produce *illusions*. However basic the materials really are, the end result can appear to be the real thing (Figure 12.25).

FIGURE 12.25
Sometimes ingenuity needs to be used instead of reality. A fireplace was desired for the set shown here, but it was impossible to have a working fireplace in the building in this specific situation, and the heat would be a problem. So, an HD monitor (with a video of fire) was used inside the fireplace to substitute for the fire.
(Photo courtesy of LPG/NBC.)

As an example, let's look at an actual scene that was broadcast. The scene was the banquet hall of an ancient castle. The king sat on a throne at one end of a long table, eating from golden dishes. That was the illusion.

What was reality? Two small foreground flags on wooden floor stands masked the edges of the shot so that no one could see the rest of the small studio. The "wooden table" was created from painted boards placed on sawhorses. The far "stone wall" was photographic wallpaper adhered to a flat (slightly sprayed black in order to age it). The "throne" was an old wooden armchair with a red drape thrown over it. The "gold dishes" were sprayed plastic plates. A "window" was painted, black on white, and stuck to the "stone wall." But no one in the audience could recognize all of this in the long shot. Of course, the scene would not have worked for close-up shots, but under patchy lighting, it was perceived as it was intended to be—the banquet hall of an ancient castle.

Interview with a Pro

John DeCuir, Designer

John DeCuir, Designer

Why is design important?
I would like to think that what separates the design professional from other ways of life is that we are constantly on the lookout for the new idea, a better way to, say, package or construct our work. For better or worse, we seem to be dedicated to a life of rolling over those "idea rocks," never too sure what just might crawl out.

Let me suggest that whatever profession you choose, you will inadvertently have to take up the design challenge. Almost everyone does, from the sushi chef arranging slices of raw fish to the architect building his building. Designing is like breathing; we all do it. It is simply that the athlete (the professional designer) works at it a little harder than the rest of us.

Therefore, knowledge of how the design process works will help any young professional. Knowing the fundamentals of design becomes even more critical as your career choices get closer to the applied and media arts, such as film, television, theater, and photojournalism, to mention only a few.

What advice do you have for the beginning designer?

- *Develop a reasoned passion for doing what you do.* Unless you have a reasoned passion for what you do with your life (professionally, of course), chances are you will not be very good at it. So my first suggestion is that the young professional develop a "rationale" for the importance of their work. This work logic, ethic, passion is critical for your own self-respect and self-worth. It is also a vital ingredient to fuel the fire that keeps you on track in times of distress.
- *Skill management*—Develop a working set of professional tools that have proven value. Here are a few of the tools you might wish to consider investing your time in developing.
  a. *Master the technology of your craft.* Whether the task is to make an evening meal, create a video

program, or build a skyscraper, each of these tasks has a sophisticated range of technical skills that must be mastered. It is safe to assume that the technical knowledge we employ can make or break a project. In judging the value of a new idea, always consider the skill level of the person who has created it.

b. *Apply storytelling techniques to your project.* Understanding the narrative of your project will insure you are able to communicate its value both to the client, the world, and, most importantly, to yourself. The professional simply can't design effectively unless he or she can communicate a project's narrative, tell its back-story, and define the theme. All these "story tools"' help establish clear decision-making guideposts for the designer and communicate a project's value to its audience.

c. *Understand and respect the project environment.* You can't design well unless you first understand, then respect, then influence, then reshape the environmental issues surrounding a project. As an example, in a program scene, everything from the religious beliefs of the next-door neighbor, to the objects on the dresser, to the snow falling outside create a contiguous "design biosphere." This biosphere or "story ecosystem" must be allowed to impact each and every choice the designer makes. Essential in this process is how the interaction of two elements creates a third new idea and how the new idea and its component parts all need to exist in a harmonious framework.

What are the challenges that you have to deal with as a designer?

As referenced earlier, the most important challenge you will face is to maintain a high state of energy and enthusiasm for your work. You will make some mistakes with this as your mantra and many times rush in where wise men fear to tread, but most importantly you will never stop looking for a better way. Following this, here are some other challenges to consider:

- *A critical challenge is to eliminate contradictions in the concept phase of a project.* Many times bad ideas lay dormant and hidden in the concept phase of a project. Early on, these bad ideas and misdirected notions have to be eliminated—I emphasize early on. Early conceptual errors inevitably lead to predictable failures.

The challenge is resolved by recycling, refining, and remodeling emerging ideas through a series of tests. Fortunately, only simple tools are needed to do this. They are the sketchpad, pencil (with a very large eraser), spreadsheet, cardboard, knife, and that old dependable pot of rubber cement that holds ideas temporarily together (and I emphasize temporary). Used with skill, the correct application of these simple tools will seriously improve a project's chances of becoming a quality project, on time and on budget.

- *The challenge of maintaining a balanced attack.* To create a quality solution, the designer *must* balance issues of *budget, time, and quality.* As money becomes less available, time may have to expand. If a super emphasis is placed on quality, then perhaps both time and budget will need to expand. When deadlines are shortened, budgets may have to be increased, and perhaps quality (at some acceptable level) will need to be sacrificed. Balancing these three factors at every step in the development process is one of the young professional's great challenges.
- *Managing the client designer relationship*. The designer must earn the client's respect so that he or she can operate in a professional atmosphere. However, this is not a one-way street. The client has equal responsibilities. When a person agrees to go under the knife, they implicitly acknowledge that they have a lot of respect for the skill and the decision-making abilities of the surgeon. The designer's challenge is to earn a similar level of respect in his dealings with the client.

Naturally, an inexperienced designer has a more difficult time in gaining this respect, as it requires an established track record. As such, the portfolio is a critical tool in the young designer's arsenal. While his or her projects may be hypothetical, if they demonstrate skill and good design, many employers will be willing to take a chance with a young professional. In addition to school, one must be apprenticed to a professional. The concept of internship with a practicing professional is essential to building the experience that will eventually earn a client's respect and trust.

John DeCuir designs sets for television series as well as major motion pictures.

CHAPTER 13
Television Graphics

Think clearly about the purpose of the graphic. Ask yourself, what exactly do I want the viewer to learn from this graphic?

—Al Tompkins, The Poynter Institute

The audience's first impression of the program will probably come from the opening graphics. They don't have to be elaborate—they just need to clearly communicate and help grab the audience's attention. However, they do need to be brief, clear, and appropriate in style.

Effective television graphics require the graphic operator or designer to think through a number of stages in the production process:

- How does this graphic help the audience understand the subject or story better?
- What is the purpose or goal of the graphic?
- Would words, illustrations, photographs, or video imagery work best to communicate to this audience?

Key Terms

- ***Character generator:*** Also called CG, this is a generic name for any type of television graphic creation equipment.
- ***Crawl:*** The movement of text horizontally across the television screen.
- ***Credits:*** The text that recognizes those appearing in and contributing to the program.
- ***Lower third (L/3rd):*** A graphic that appears in the lower third of the screen. Traditionally it contains bio information.
- ***Roll:*** The movement of text up or down the video screen.
- ***Safe title area:*** The center 80% of the screen where it is safe to place graphics.
- ***Subtitles:*** Used to identify people and places.

13.1 THE GOALS OF TELEVISION GRAPHICS

The goals for television graphics should be as follows:

- *Convey information clearly and directly.* The graphics should be *prepared for maximum communication impact.* This means that television graphics should be simply created, not elaborate. Because television graphics move quickly and viewers cannot study them for a long period of time, the font should be bold and straightforward.
- *Establish the show's overall mood and tone through the graphic style.* The font and presentation style can do much to advance the story. They can set the scene for the rest of the program (Figures 13.1, 13.2, and 13.3).

FIGURE 13.1
Television graphics can help establish the mood and tone for the whole program.
(Photo courtesy of Compix.)

- *Present facts, concepts, or processes visually so the viewer will understand the program content.* Keep the graphics organized and presented in a way that holds the audience's attention and makes it simple for viewers to follow the process or understand the concept being presented.

> The screen can contain some graphic elements, but the whole focus should be the information, not the pretty background or the design elements.
>
> **—Gerald Millerson, Director**

FIGURE 13.2
Graphics for television often create the look and style of the program. Note that the logo in this photo was used as a set graphic. It is also showing up, probably animated, on the set's video screen in the back and a graphic generator is being used so that it appears as part of the credit design.
(Photo courtesy of KOMU-TV.)

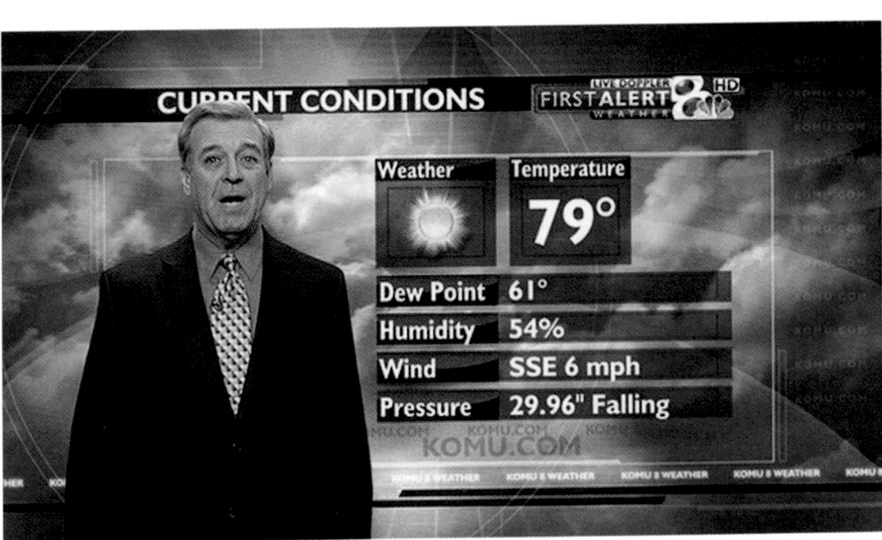

FIGURE 13.3
Graphics need to be organized in a way that can be easily understood by the viewer.
(Photo courtesy of KOMU-TV.)

13.2 TYPES OF GRAPHICS

Graphics add clarity to a show's presentation. They are used *to announce* the place or time, *to identify* a plant, *to display* data, *to clarify* how food should be cooked, and so on. There are a number of different types of graphics:

- *Opening titles* announce the show.
- *Subtitles* identify people and places.
- *Credits* recognize those appearing in and contributing to the program.
- *End titles* draw the program to its conclusion.

> Trendy title styles are often hot today but stone cold tomorrow.
>
> **—Morgan Paar, Producer**

13.3 DESIGNING GRAPHICS

- Video and television productions today may use either of two screen formats. Standard definition has an aspect ratio of 4:3 (4 units across and 3 units high). High definition (HDTV) has an aspect ratio of 16:9 (16 units across and 9 units high). If your audience has viewers using both types of formats, all graphics need to be designed so that they fall into the 4:3 area. Otherwise, viewers using 4:3 screens may not be able to see important graphics (Figure 13.4).

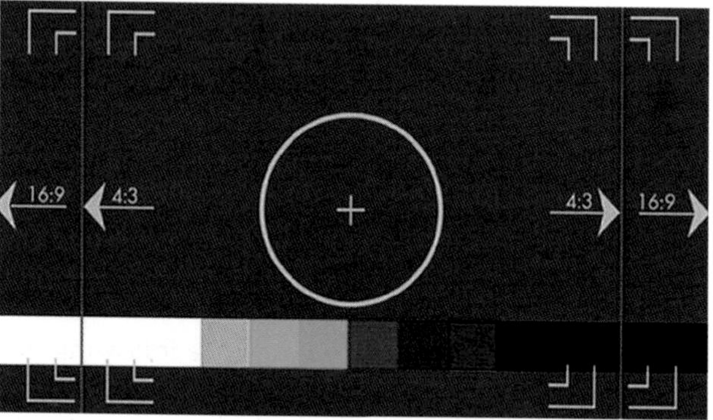

FIGURE 13.4
Today the audience may be viewing a program on 4:3 (SD) or 16:9 (HDTV) television sets. Graphics need to be created so that they work on both formats.

- By titling well away from the edge of the frame, you can avoid edge cutoff. Graphics should be designed so that they fall within the middle 80% of the television's screen area. This center area of the screen is referred to as the *safe title area*.

- Simple, bold typefaces are best. Avoid thin-lined, elaborate lettering. Although HDTV's resolution can handle the thin lines, the majority of the world is still using SD, which struggles with thin lines.
- Limit the number of different fonts within a program.
- Lettering smaller than about one-tenth of the screen height is difficult to read. It is important for directors to determine what media the audience will use to see the final production, or at least what the dominant media will be.
- Avoid placing a black-edged outline around smaller letters because it becomes hard to read. The holes in *B*'s, *O*'s, *A*'s, and *R*'s fill in.
- Outlining and drop shadows often make lettering easier to read by preventing bleeding and providing contrast (Figure 13.5).

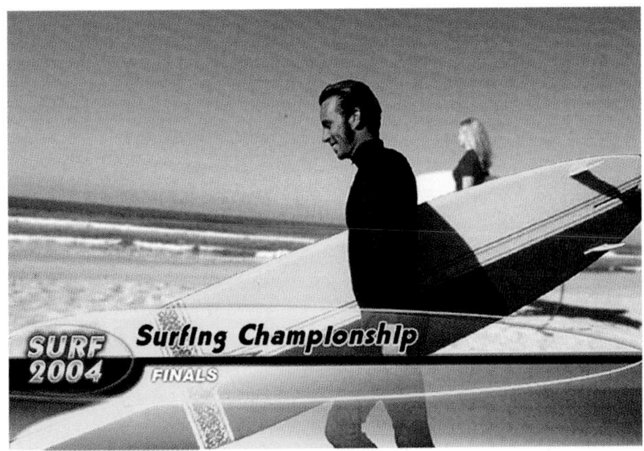

FIGURE 13.5
Outlining the letters often makes them easier to read.
(Photo courtesy of Compix.)

- Punctuation is not normally used, except in the following instances: quotations, hyphens, apostrophes, possessives, and names.
- Abbreviations are never punctuated on television graphics. However, don't be ambiguous; use three lines if necessary.
- Leave a space between title lines of around one-half to two-thirds the height of capital letters.
- Lettering should generally contrast strongly with its background. The lettering is usually much lighter than the background (Figure 13.6).
- Don't fill the screen with too much information at a time. It is often better to use a series of brief frames or to use a *crawl* (continuous information moving vertically into the frame and passing out at the top).
- Warm, bright colors attract the most attention.

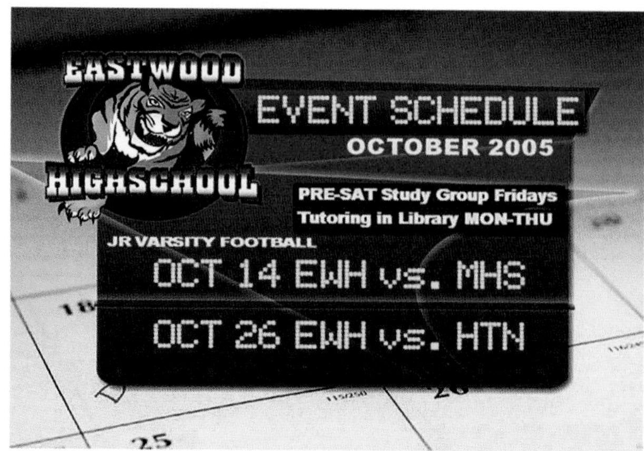

FIGURE 13.6
Letters will be more readable if they contrast with the background.
(Photo courtesy of Compix.)

THE GRAPHIC OPERATOR

The graphic operator is often located behind the director. This provides graphics with the opportunity to see what is currently on screen and what is coming next. In many ways, they need to anticipate where the production is going so that they can already be building (creating) a graphic before the director calls for it (Figure 13.7).

FIGURE 13.7
Graphic operators often sit directly behind the director and technical director in the control room when working on a multicamera production.

13.4 ANIMATED GRAPHICS

Animation can bring a graphic to life. Even the simplest movement, such as panning over it from one detail to another, zooming in/out on details, or cutting between sections of it, can sustain interest in what would otherwise be a static display.

Animation is an effective way to hold the audience's attention, especially in any program that relies heavily on graphics or photographs. Most character generators, the equipment used to make television graphics, can at least animate text (Figure 13.8).

FIGURE 13.8
Animated graphics hold the viewer's attention better than static graphics.
(Photo courtesy of WLEX-TV.)

13.5 BACKGROUNDS FOR GRAPHICS

When creating full-screen graphics, graphic operators need to be careful about how the backgrounds are chosen. If the wrong background is used, it may compete for attention with the graphic. For example, don't use a sharply focused shot of a group of people in the background. Viewers will look through the words and at the people. A number of different strategies can be used successfully for backgrounds:

- Create a simple color background.
- Freeze the video background so that you do not have a moving background.
- De-focus the video image so that it is blurry■ Select a single-color background (grass, water, sky, etc.).

FIGURE 13.9
The background behind the graphics should not compete with the graphics. Note how the graphics operator here blurred and darkened the area behind the text in order to keep the attention on the graphics.
(Photo courtesy of Compix.)

13.6 GRAPHICS EQUIPMENT

Character generator (*CG*) is a generic name for any type of television graphic creation equipment. CGs can change the font, shape, size, color, and design of the lettering. They can make it flash, flip, crawl (move sideways across the screen), roll (move vertically across the screen), and animate. Lettering can be presented as outlines or as solid characters, or it can be given a black border (black edge) or a drop shadow around it. Once the graphic is created, it can be rearranged, stored, and ready to appear on the screen at the press of a button (Figure 13.10).

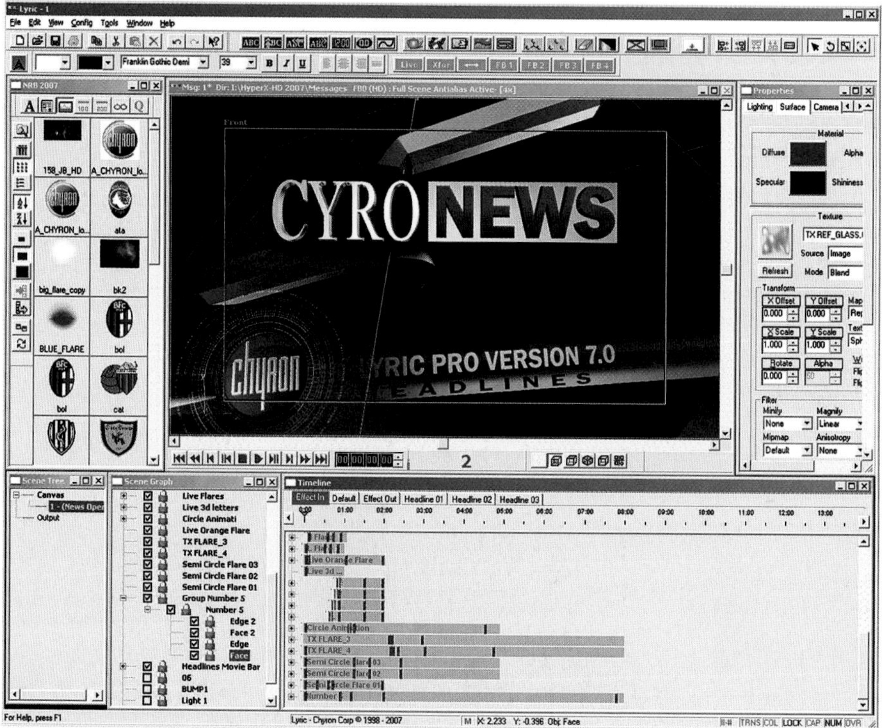

FIGURE 13.10
This is the composition screen of a high-end graphics system. The system allows almost unlimited manipulation of the graphics.
(Photo courtesy of Chyron.)

Stand-alone graphic generator systems used to hold 99% of the market share in professional television. They are still widely popular in larger markets and sports production (Figure 13.11).

However, computers with graphic generation software have significantly entered into the market. Today, computers are used in all markets and provide sophisticated on-screen graphics. Mobile production crews have sometimes moved to laptop systems (Figure 13.12).

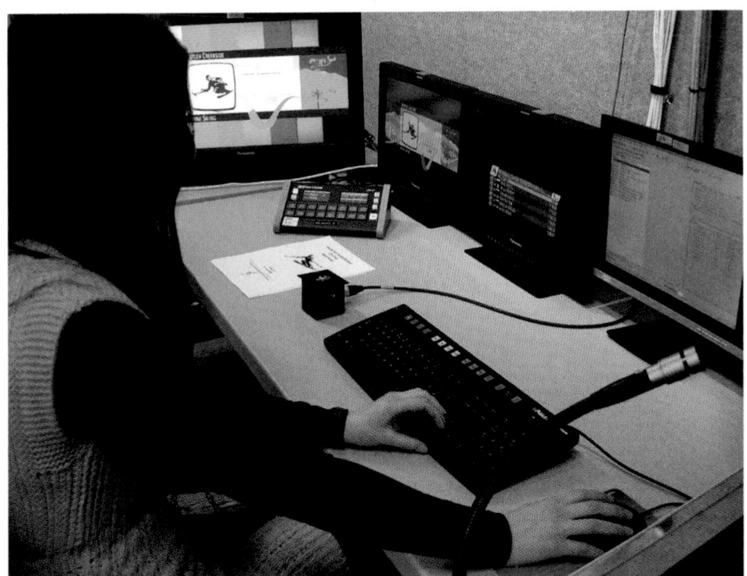

FIGURE 13.11
A stand-alone character generator.

FIGURE 13.12
Laptop character generators have become popular for graphic operators who are on the road a lot.
(Photo courtesy of Compix.)

Interview with a Pro

Lou Moore, Graphic Operator

Lou Moore, Graphic Operator

What is your philosophy about graphics: when do you think they should be used...or not?

- I like using graphics. I have always thought about the guy sitting in a bar where he is watching the TV but cannot hear the audio. It helps keep him informed.
- I am not a big fan of sound on every graphic. I think large graphics or promos can have sound effects. But lower 3rd graphics don't need them.
- I like to follow what the announcers are talking about and augment what they are saying with a graphic. I think it is confusing to the viewer when a graphic is placed on-air that does not follow what the announcers are talking about.
- I think it is always good to build a relationship with the announcer's statistics person. I often ask if he or she has a great stat that I can use with graphics. It's always best if I can be given the stat before giving it to the announcer. If the announcer says the statistic before I can get the graphic built, I have missed the opportunity to use the graphic on air.

What challenges do you have to deal with as a graphics operator?

- The biggest challenge is to keep up with the ever-changing graphic operating systems. Each network has their own favorite graphic machine. While they all have common elements, there are enough differences that you still have to think about what you are doing instead of moving into automatic mode.
- Even the companies that use the same systems set up their shows differently. For example, I might like using a specific graphic in football and I know where things are in the scene graph and can build quickly. When I go to basketball, the same scene graph may be totally reorganized, and it takes a show or two to get used to it.

What changes do you see in the future for television graphics?

- Although the equipment will change and the responsibilities may change, there will always be a need for graphics.
- As technology advances, it is already possible for the show to be in one country and the graphic operator could be at home in another country. I think we will see more of that in the future.
- The equipment continues to get easier to use. In the past I had to create all of the graphics. Today the APs can have the graphic program on their laptops and show up with many of the graphics already built.

Lou Moore works as a graphic operator for news, talk shows, and sports productions.

CHAPTER 14

Recording and Viewing the Video

Formats make a difference, but not as big a difference as we usually think. Image quality is more than pristine pixels. Image quality is about having a picture worth viewing.

—Jim Feeley, Studio Monthly

THE VIDEO IMAGE

There are continual developments in the design and format of video and audio recording systems. Some are mainly used for *acquisition* (shooting original material); others are used for postproduction editing and archiving (storage) work. Video recordings can be done on videotape, hard drive, or a flash memory card. In fact, some of the newest cameras can record on hard disk, and standard definition (SD)—all in one camera. Traditionally, videotape has been the most popular medium. However, with the advent of higher-quality and less-expensive flash memory, most video today is being shot on digital memory. Professionals are also rapidly moving away from tape and into the digital media world as well.

Key Terms

- ***3DTV:*** Televisions that are designed specifically for showing 3D programming. Viewers must watch the images through high-precision 3D glasses, which open and close the left and right shutters in synchronization with the alternating images.
- ***Cathode ray tube (CRT):*** CRT televisions send an electron beam through a vacuum tube to a phosphor-coated screen. These "tube" televisions are large and bulky.
- ***Digital recording:*** The digital system regularly samples the waveforms and converts them into numerical (binary) data. This allows many generations of copies to be made without affecting the quality of the image.
- ***Flash memory:*** Flash cards can store large amounts of digital data without having any moving parts. This makes them durable and able to work in a variety of temperatures, and data can be easily transferred into a nonlinear editor.

- ***HDD:*** Hard disk drives can be used for recording digital video images and can be built into the camera or attached to the outside of the camera.
- ***HDTV:*** The standard high-definition formats currently in use range from 720 to 1,080 lines of resolution.
- ***Interlaced:*** Interlaced television is scanned the same way standard definition television has always been scanned. Alternate lines are displayed.
- ***Liquid crystal display (LCD):*** These flat-screen displays work by sending variable electrical currents through a liquid crystal solution that crystallizes to form a quality image.
- ***Monitor:*** Monitors were designed to provide accurate, stable image quality. They do not include tuners and may not include audio speakers.
- ***Plasma:*** This high-quality, thin flat-panel screen can be viewed from a wide angle.
- ***Progressive:*** The progressive image displays the total picture instead of scanning it using alternate lines.
- ***Television receiver:*** Televisions include a tuner so that they can display broadcast programs with their accompanying sound.

14.1 HIGH-DEFINITION TELEVISION (HDTV OR HD)

> HD is so much sharper than SD that more attention must be given to the small details. Since the flaws in the background, or even makeup, can hold the audience's attention, directors may not need as many close-up shots, which previously was the only way details could be shown.
>
> **—Brian Douglas, Producer and Director**

High-definition television (HDTV) has many more scan lines than standard definition (SD). Generally the lines are between 720 and 1,080, although there is quite a bit of experimentation with more lines. These additional lines, and their scanning strategies, equate to much higher-quality images. For example, a normal consumer cannot see the difference between a 720p (the "p" stands for progressive) and a 1080i image (the "i" stands for interlaced), although a trained eye may be able to do so. Because today's HD has pretty much hit the limits of what normal eyes can discern, going to a higher level of scan lines is not critical.

Two types of HD scanning systems are currently being used: *interlaced* and *progressive:*

- *Interlaced.* Interlaced television is scanned the same way SD television has traditionally been scanned. Interlaced scanning means that the television's electron scans the odd-numbered lines first and then goes back and scans in the remaining even-numbered lines. This methodology can be more prone to artifacts and can be less stable than progressive scanning. However, there can be a noticeable flicker on older large screens. As the technology has advanced, the flicker has disappeared. Current CRT television utilizes interlaced scanning as well as the HDTV 1080i standard.

- *Progressive.* Also called sequential scanning, progressive scanning uses an electron beam that scans or paints each line successively. The HDTV 720p and 1080p system uses progressive scanning. The progressive method can be perceived to have less flicker and more stability than the interlaced system. The progressive image displays the total picture. It has a smoother, more precise picture with limited flicker. However, it uses more bandwidth and can have some motion blur.

Although there are a number of different formats within HD (720p, 1080p, 1080i, etc.), it is difficult for the untrained eye to see the difference between them. There were fairly significant differences when the formats first came out (motion blur, flicker, etc.), but those interferences have mainly been fixed. All of the formats utilize a 16:9 aspect ratio. There are also multiple frame rates to choose from that give a film look, a video look, or something in between. Here are the current HD formats with some data that you can use to compare them:

- *720p.* This is a progressive scanning format that has a pixel aspect ratio of 1,280 × 720 and 921,600 pixels per frame. The progressive scanning gives it a bit of a film look.
- *1080i.* This format utilizes interlaced scanning. It has a pixel aspect ratio of 1,920 × 1,080 and 1,555,200 pixels per frame. 1080i gives a high-quality video look.
- *1080p.* This is the newest progressive scanning format and has a pixel aspect ratio of 1,920 × 1,080 with 2,073,600 pixels per frame. It was designed to compete with high-end film cameras.

There are other resolutions available as well. High-end "film" video cameras can shoot 2K (2,000 lines) and 4K. Japan's NHK has even created an *ultra-high-definition* television system that touts 4,320 scanning lines with 7,680 × 4,320 pixels. Although it is doubtful that this type of system will ever get into the home, it may make it into theaters.

> The *high-definition* of HDTV is currently highly dubious. Depending on the content delivery system, it can look amazing or pitiful. An HD network on some cable systems looks astounding, because network executives cut carriage deals that dictate a minimum bit rate. Many networks don't have the leverage to negotiate the same bit rate.
>
> **—Deborah McAdams, Senior Editor, Television Broadcast**

14.2 VIDEOTAPE

As mentioned earlier, videotape is the most popular professional format. It is popular for the following reasons:

- It is readily available.
- A large number of tape-based cameras have been manufactured.
- The sheer number of tape-based systems already owned by companies is significant.

- Many companies have built a tape-based infrastructure, and it is taking time to make the transition.
- Tapes have the capacity to record the project and then store the raw or finished video.
- Most professionals have a high comfort level with videotape.

However, there are many incompatible videotape formats, and a few obsolescent designs are still in use (Figure 14.1). Although it is not important to worry about design specifics, video producers must realize that there are specific differences between the formats (Figure 14.2). Tapes can only be recorded and reproduced on identical equipment standards.

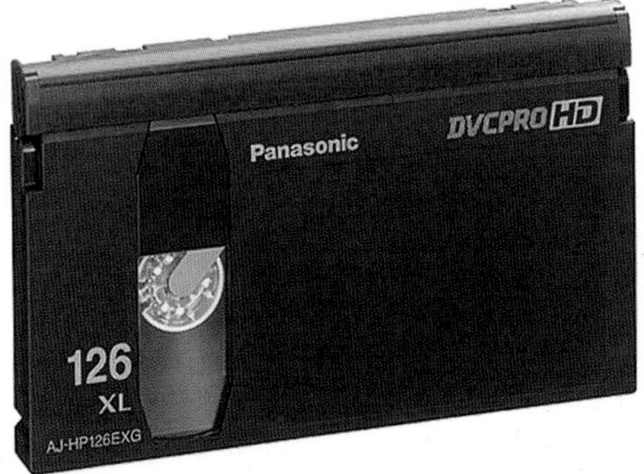

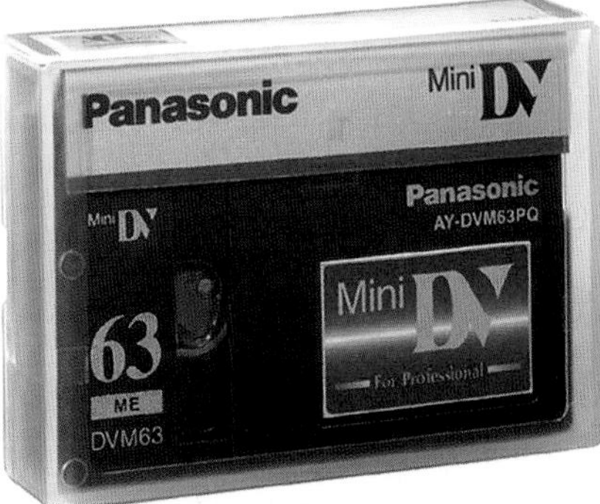

FIGURE 14.1
Videotapes come in many different formats and sizes for professionals and consumers.
(Photos courtesy of Panasonic.)

FIGURE 14.2
Many companies have heavily invested in tape-based infrastructure. Moving toward tapeless production will take time.
(Photo by Jon Greenhoe.)

Design features can vary considerably between video recorders. Here are some of the differences between formats:

- Tapes come in ¼-inch, 8 mm, 1/8-inch, and ½-inch sizes. Cassettes can be different sizes, even within a format, depending on the length of the tape.
- There is a wide range of image quality between the various formats.

With the advent of digital recording, the divisions between consumer and professional formats have significantly blurred. Productions are showing up on networks and film festivals (winning top awards) that were shot on inexpensive digital formats that were primarily touted as a consumer product.

14.3 ANALOG AND DIGITAL

The *analog* system directly records the variations of the video and audio signals. Analog recording has a tendency to deteriorate when copies are dubbed. Only tape can be used to record the signal from analog systems.

The *digital* system regularly samples the waveforms and converts them into numerical (binary) data. This allows many generations of copies to be made without affecting the quality of the image. Digital systems also allow the data to be recorded on media other than tape, such as hard disks or flash memory.

14.4 TAPE FORMATS

Here is a brief summary of some of the most common tape formats used in cameras that are currently produced by manufacturers:

- VHS
  - This format uses 1/2-inch videotape.
  - The VHS deck was the most popular consumer deck ever produced. Until DVDs began to build in popularity, most video rental stores rented out VHS tapes.
  - Cameras are no longer manufactured that utilize VHS tapes.
  - This format has been phased out, although many families still own VHS tapes of films or family footage.
- VHS-C
  - This format uses 1/2-inch videotape.
  - This small tape plays back on a VHS deck and usually requires an adapter. As VHS was the most popular consumer deck, VHS-C gained popularity as a compact camera because its tape could be played on a full-size VHS deck.
  - This format is rapidly being phased out. To our knowledge, only one manufacturer still makes a VHS-C camera.

- Digital8/Hi8
  - This format uses 8-mm videotape.
  - It was highly popular as a subcompact camera but is now rapidly disappearing from the video market.
- MiniDV
  - This was the first digital format available to consumers.
  - Uses 1/4-inch tape.
  - This format is quickly giving way to HD cameras.
  - MiniDV tape will play on DVCPro25/50/HD decks. However, an adapter cassette may be required for them to fit into the larger decks.
- HDV/MIniDV HD
  - A digital HD format that is recorded onto miniDV tapes.
  - The first consumer HD format.
  - The only current manufacturer of HDV is Sony, and they use 1080i when recording in HDV. This format is giving way to the newer HD formats.
  - Many professionals insist that HDV is barely HD because of color and grayscale issues.
- D-9
  - Originally known as D-VHS or Digital-S tape, this system utilizes 1/2-inch metal particle videotape cassettes.
  - This system has not been highly popular and has all but disappeared.
  - A VHS tape can play in the D-9 deck, but the D-9 tape cannot play in the VHS deck.
- DigiBeta
  - This format uses 1/2-inch videotape.
  - It was created especially for companies that had large Betacam archives. Betacam could be played in the DigiBeta deck, although the DigiBeta tape could not be played in the Beta deck. The format gave companies, especially news stations, a way to upgrade without having to change their whole archives.
  - This is another format that is giving way to HD formats.
- HDCAM
  - This format uses 1/2-inch videotape and is the HD version of Digibeta.
  - This metal tape comes in small and large cassettes. The recording time ranges from 50 to 155 minutes.
  - This format has a sampling rate of up to 4:4:4.
- DVCPro25/50
  - This format uses 1/2-inch videotape.
  - DVCPro25 has a sampling rate of 4:1:1, and DVCPro50 has rate of 4:2:2.
  - The DVCPro 50 has lower compression than the DVCPro25, giving a high-quality image.

- A DV tape can be played on a DVCPro25/50 deck, but the DVCPro25/50 tape cannot be played on the DV deck.
- This is another format that is giving way to HD formats.

- DVCProHD
  - This format uses 1/2-inch videotape.
  - DV, DVCPro25/50 tapes can be played on a DVCProHD deck. However, the DVCProHD tape cannot be played on a DV or DVCPro25/50 decks.
  - This is one of the most popular HD formats.

14.5 FLASH MEMORY

Flash memory has become the most popular medium used to record both standard definition and high-definition video. A significant advantage to the flash memory card is that it is easy to transfer files from the card to a nonlinear editor (Figure 14.3).

FIGURE 14.3
A number of very small flash memory cards are available, such as an SD or Pro Duo, that can be used to record video. These cards are currently being used in consumer and semiprofessional cameras.
(Photo courtesy of Panasonic.)

The small size allows the card to be used on compact camcorders. Cameras utilizing flash memory as their medium generally do not have moving parts, which should have less maintenance. Some of the new high-capacity SD cards are as high as 64 GB. As the technology is refined, the capacity of these cards keeps growing.

A number of companies have created professional cameras that utilize large flash memory cards. One of their advantages is that the larger card cameras generally have multiple slots, which are "hot swappable." This means that while one is being recorded onto, an already full card can be removed and replaced with a blank card. This allows uninterrupted recording. Figures 14.4 and 14.5 show the P2 professional flash card system. The P2 card actually includes four SD cards built into it.

FIGURE 14.4
The P2 card is a flash memory card used in some professional cameras. The "player" next to it is really a device that allows up to five cards to be placed in slots and read by a computer, just like any hard drive or memory stick.
(Photos courtesy of Panasonic.)

FIGURE 14.5
This P2 player/recorder can be used to record, edit, play back, and provide slow motion to anything recorded onto a flash card. Note that there are six "hot swappable" slots.
(Photo courtesy of Panasonic.)

14.6 HARD DISK DRIVE (HDD) (INTERNAL HARD DRIVE)

Hard disk drive (HDD) cameras record directly to a hard drive built into the camera. Roughly 4 GB of disk space is required for each hour of video (Figure 14.6).

FIGURE 14.6
This high-end consumer-targeted camcorder utilizes an internal hard disk drive.
(Photo courtesy of JVC.)

HDD cameras have a very high storage capacity. Many of the HDD cameras include an SD slot for video recording to a transportable medium, although it is not required to transfer footage. It is extremely easy to transfer the data to a nonlinear system. Video footage can be transferred directly to a DVD recorder via the camera manufacturer's transfer device, shown in Figure 14.7.

FIGURE 14.7
The HDD camera has the ability to dock to a DVD recorder in order to transfer all footage to an archival medium.
(Photo courtesy of JVC.)

FIGURE 14.8
External drives can be attached to most digital video cameras.
(Photo courtesy of Firestore.)

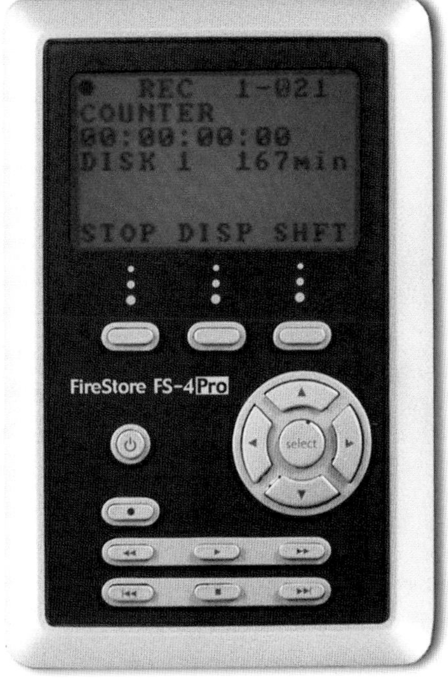

14.7 EXTERNAL CAMERA HARD DRIVES

External camera drives can now be attached to most digital cameras including HD systems (Figure 14.8).

These drives provide extremely long recording times with drives that have an incredibly large capacity. The drives connect directly to nonlinear editing systems, allowing the editor to begin editing the program immediately. Most of these drives attach to the camera via the FireWire port. Audio, time code, video, and control information is passed directly through the FireWire connector. A 160-GB drive will provide roughly 10 hours of DV recording and 5 to 6 hours of HD recording.

14.8 HARD DRIVE SERVER RECORDERS

Stand-alone hard disk recorders are now used to record HD video at a very high quality (Figure 14.9).

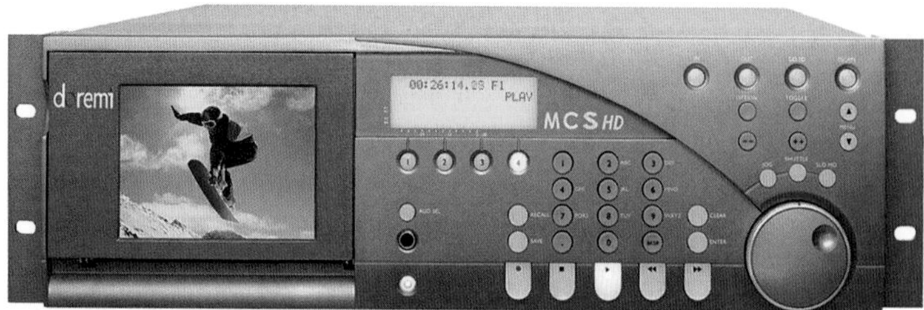

FIGURE 14.9
Hard disk recorders are gaining popularity in the professional video field.
(Photo courtesy of Doremi.)

These real-time recorder/players can be used for SD-SDI or HD-SDI (Serial Digital Interface) recording. Frame accuracy is possible via RS-422 or Ethernet control protocols. They also usually include smooth fast-motion and slow-motion playback (Figure 14.10). These recorders can replace standard tape decks.

FIGURE 14.10
A slow-motion operator utilizes a hard drive server recording/playback system during a sports event.

14.9 RECORDABLE DVD

To this point in time, DVD cameras have been primarily aimed at the consumer market. DVD cameras automatically find a blank section on the disk for recording, so there's no need to rewind or fast-forward. Most of them also use an index screen, which makes it easy to search for a particular scene. When the shooting has been completed, the disk can be taken out of the camcorder and slipped into a DVD player or recorder for immediate playback—there's no need to connect any cables. One of the disadvantages is that disks can be susceptible to scratches. This format is quickly disappearing.

14.10 XDCAM DISK

The XD line of optical disk-based camera systems utilizes blue-violet laser technology to achieve extremely high data transfer rates (Figure 14.11).

This professional camera system can record up to 4 hours of HD on a dual-layer disk, which has a large storage capacity of 50 GB. The disks are rewritable. Sony says that the disk can handle a thousand write and rewrite cycles.

FIGURE 14.11
The XD disk is protected by a case at all times.
(Photo courtesy of Sony.)

14.11 RECORDING MEDIA CARE

It is important to care for recording media. Here are some suggestions for prolonging the life of the various types of recording and storage media:

- Remember that the optimum storage temperature is around 65 degrees. Temperatures above 100 degrees and below 14 degrees can cause problems with some media.
- Avoid rapid temperature/humidity changes (such as moving from a cold exterior to a warm interior), and allow both media and equipment to become acclimatized before use.
- Before loading a medium, check that it has not been protected against recording (if necessary, reposition the safety switch). Make sure it does not contain wanted program material.
- Store media in their protective boxes to avoid damage and dust.
- Make sure that each recorded medium is clearly identified on the label (name, contact information, shot/scene numbers, etc.).

14.12 VIDEO RECORDING SUGGESTIONS

- Use the highest data rate possible on digital media. Although you will not be able to record as many minutes on the medium, this data rate will give you a higher-quality image.
- Watch the elapsed time on the camera to make sure that you know how much memory or tape is left and you know the state of the battery.
- Reset the tape counter whenever you change the tape.
- Review the end of the takes to check that the recording is satisfactory.

- When you remove the medium from the camera, make sure to position the protection device so that no one accidentally records over the original footage.
- Clearly label all media as well as the media container.

VIEWING THE VIDEO

Several types of screen are used to display the video signal's picture. The most common are the *CRT* (*cathode ray tube*), *LCD* (*liquid crystal diode*), and plasma screens:

- *CRT.* This type of monitor has been the standard since it appeared in the 1930s. Historically called "the tube," CRT televisions send an electron beam through a vacuum tube to a phosphor-coated screen. The images are created as the beam hits the screen's surface. Although they have a good-quality image and have become inexpensive, they are large, bulky, and are quickly being replaced by large flat screens (Figure 14.12).

FIGURE 14.12
Although consumer CRTs are quickly being replaced by LCD televisions, many engineers still prefer and trust the CRT as their quality-control monitor.
(Photograph courtesy of Sony.)

- *Plasma.* The plasma television is a high-quality, thin, high-resolution flat-panel screen that can be viewed from a wide angle. The plasma utilizes a matrix of very small cells that become charged by precise electrical voltages to create an image that has a wide range of color and produces deep blacks. The plasma has much higher power consumption and has a limited lifespan (half of the LCD) (Figure 14.13).
- *LCD.* LCD televisions are flat-screen displays that work by sending variable electrical currents through a liquid crystal solution that crystallizes to form a quality image. At this time, LCD screens are more expensive than plasma screens but seem to have a longer life span and have lower power consumption. They work well as smaller-sized televisions and seem to be quickly replacing the CRT technology. Some of the newer LCD televisions use LED lights as the backlight. While they may be referred to by manufacturers as LED televisions, they are actually LCD televisions that use LEDs.

FIGURE 14.13
Plasma screens are considered to be the best at portraying fast motion such as sports.
(Photograph courtesy of Panasonic.)

- *3DTV.* Televisions that are designed specifically for showing 3D programming are designed differently from a normal television. Viewers watch the images through high-precision 3D glasses, which open and close the left and right shutters in synchronization with the alternating images. As a result, a separate HD image is sent to each eye. This addresses the image quality problems and blurring that were common to previous 3D systems, and creates sharp, crisp 3D images. 3D sets that do not require special glasses are being tested in various markets. They use a special lenticular sheet on the screen that gives a 3D view (Figure 14.14).

FIGURE 14.14
3D television sets can show an incredible depth in the video imagery. This photo is an illustration of the 3D. Of course, the images do not really pop out beyond the frame of the television. Note the pair of 3D glasses in the foreground. The highest-quality 3D video images currently require 3D glasses.
(Photo courtesy of Panasonic.)

14.13 HOW WE SEE COLOR

Our eyes contain selective "cones," which detect color by analyzing the visible spectrum into three primary color regions: red to orange, green to yellow, and blue to violet.

Most colored surfaces reflect a color mixture of red, green, and blue light in varying proportions. So, for instance, the various shades of "green" we see in foliage are actually color mixtures reflecting a wide spread of the visible spectrum. Even yellow can be reproduced by adding suitable proportions of red and green light.

HEALTH RISKS AND 3DTV?

Samsung's Australian office issued the following warning about the health risks of watching 3DTV in 2010: "Viewing in 3D mode may cause motion sickness, perceptual aftereffects, disorientation, eye strain, and decreased postural stability. It is recommended that users take frequent breaks to lessen the likelihood of these effects. If you have any of the above symptoms, immediately discontinue use of the 3D device and do not resume until the symptoms have subsided." The advisory also warned that "some viewers may experience an epileptic seizure or stroke when exposed to certain flashing images or lights contained in some television pictures." They recommended that if individuals have a medical history of epilepsy or a stroke, they should consult a medical specialist before trying out 3D television.

14.14 HOW THE CAMERA SEES COLOR

The color video camera, too, relies on this *additive color mixing* process. The light sensors can only respond to the intensity of light. They cannot directly distinguish color. However, by placing red, green, and blue color filters over three light sensors, we can analyze the scene based on its separate color components. If a subject appears to have similar proportions of all three primaries, we see this mixture as white.

In the color video camera, the lens's image of the scene passes through a special prism, which splits it into three identical versions. Three sensors with their respective red, green, and blue color filters provide three *video signals* that correspond to the light and shade of these colors in the scene.

14.15 MONITORS AND RECEIVERS

Although both *television receivers* and *picture monitors* are widely used in video production, they have important differences:

- *Television receivers*. These are designed to display off-air pictures of broadcast programs, with their accompanying sound. A receiver includes a tuner, which allows it to receive television programming. For technical and economic reasons, picture and sound quality are a bit of a compromise, although the performance of top-grade receivers can be extremely good.
- *Monitors*. Monitors were especially designed to provide accurate, stable image quality, and their circuit sophistication is reflected in their higher cost. Picture monitors do not include circuitry to receive off-air programming. These video monitors may or may not include an audio speaker.

Interview with a Pro

Ryan Hammer, Atlas Digital

Ryan Hammer, Atlas Digital

How do you decide what video format to use when working on a production?
Many people look entirely at cost of camera rentals and media cost. I look at it more from a postproduction perspective ... how much is it going to cost to digitize/ingest, are there editing problems with certain video formats, and what issues will we have in the online process?

Do you still use videotape?
Definitely. There's something about having a piece of tape to hold onto that helps me sleep at night. Plus, "tapeless" hasn't been ironed out (in the postprocess), so there are still issues that just *go away* when you use tape instead.

Where do you think editing is headed in the future?
With the competition between Avid and Final Cut Pro, prices are dropping. I personally think that people will be owning their own systems. There will be buildings where bays, storage, and decks are kept and maintained by assistant editors. Editors will primarily work from home—either off their own systems or remotely logging into the edit systems at the facility. Cuts will be streamable to executives for notes, and when they're supposed to be output, they will be emailed to the assistant editor at the facility ... at least, that's what I'm working on. ...

Ryan Hammer is a partner in a major postproduction house in Los Angeles.

CHAPTER 15

Editing

If editing is done well, it will be largely unnoticed by the viewing audience. Editing is both an art and a science; learning some of the rules will enhance your ability to edit, but using editing to tell well-crafted stories takes practice to learn.

—Kathy Bruner, Producer and Teacher

Editing is the process in which the material that has been shot is blended together to tell an effective and engaging story. However, editing has a much more subtle role to play than a simple piecing-together process. It is the technique of selecting and arranging shots; choosing their order, their duration, and the ways in which they are to be joined together. Editing is where graphics, music, sound effects, and special effects are added to the footage shot earlier. It has a significant influence on the viewers' reactions to what they see and hear. Skilled editing makes a major contribution to the effectiveness of any production. Poor editing can leave the audience confused or, worse, bored. The mechanics of editing are simple enough, but the subtle effects of the editor's choices require time and experience to master.

Key Terms

- ***Clip:*** A video segment or shot (usually considered one uninterrupted roll of the camera).
- ***Cover shot:*** A video clip that is used to cover an edit so that the viewers do not know that the edit occurred. The term literally means to "cut away" from the action, and it can be used to cover continuity errors or sometimes show a parallel action.
- ***Coverage:*** The term used by filmmakers that refers to repeating a scene from enough different angles to ensure that a seamless performance can be maintained throughout multiple takes.
- ***Continuity:*** The process that goes hand in hand with coverage, in which attention is paid to the repetition of the visual and aural details within a

scene, to again ensure that that a seamless performance can be maintained throughout multiple takes. For example, at exactly what point in the scene (and with which hand) did the actor take a sip from his coffee cup, or are the burning candles on the table the same height in take six that they were at the same point in the scene in take one? When something in the scene is not consistent, it is called a continuity error.

- ***Cut:*** The "cut" or "take" is the most common transition in editing. It is an instantaneous switch from one shot to the next that implies that the action is taking place in "real time."
- ***Cutaway shot:*** Used to cover edits when the edit being made is likely to result in a "jump cut" or other break in continuity. Generally it is a shot of something outside of the current frame (such as a reaction shot).
- ***Digitize:*** Converting the video and audio signals into the appropriate data files (a process that is necessary only if your original footage was acquired through analog recording).
- ***Dissolve:*** An editing transition effect created by fading out one image while fading in the next image. The dissolve generally implies a passage of time and/or a change in geographic location.
- ***DVE:*** Any effect, such as a dissolve, a fade or wipe, that is created digitally, rather than mechanically.
- ***Fade:*** A gradual change (dissolve) between black and a video image.
- ***FireWire:*** Also known as the IEEE 1394 FireWire is used to connect different pieces of equipment, such as cameras, drives, and computers, so that they can transfer large amounts of data, such as video, quickly and easily.
- ***Jump cut:*** A jarring transition that is created when two shots are cut together that are too similar in size, angle, and subject matter.
- ***Linear editing:*** The copying, or dubbing, segments from the master tape to another tape in sequential order.
- ***Logging:*** Loggers view the footage and write down the scene/take numbers, the length of each shot, the time code, and descriptions of each shot in order for the editor to be able to find the shots quickly and efficiently.
- ***Nonlinear editing:*** The process where the recorded video is stored on a hard drive. Then the footage can be arranged or rearranged, special effects can be added, and the audio and graphics can be adjusted using editing software.
- ***Running order:*** The order that the scenes or shots will be shown in the final project, which often differs greatly from the shooting order. The running order should correspond to the scene numbers in the shooting script.
- ***Shooting order:*** The order in which the scenes or shots are to actually be shot, which almost always will differ greatly from the running order.
- ***Timeline:*** The timeline is the portion of the graphical interface of a nonlinear editing system, which usually appears at the bottom of the computer screen, where the editor will position the program's video segments.
- ***Trim:*** To cut frames off a shot to make it shorter.
- ***Voiceover:*** Commentary or narration over video.
- ***Wipe:*** A novel transition between two video images that can have many different shapes and can have a hard- or soft-edge transition.

15.1 EDITING GOALS

Basically, editing or postproduction is the process of combining individual shots in a specific order. It has several purposes:

- To assemble material in a sequential fashion. Remember, the *shooting order* will almost always differ from the *running order*.
- To correct mistakes by editing them out or by covering them with other footage.
- To create, enhance, embellish, and bring to life images and events that were once captured live. Tools such as visual effects, sound effects, and music can enhance the quality of the storytelling, resulting in a more dynamic impact on the audience.

> While I am cutting a show, I am always trying to determine what was in the director's mind. But if I have been successful, I will be able to present the director with some unexpected surprises. My goal is to make the show better than it was in the script and even better than the director hoped for.
>
> **—Lance Luckey, Emmy-Winning Editor**

15.2 SHOOTING ORDER VERSUS RUNNING ORDER

During the production process, when possible, events are usually shot in the order that is most convenient or practical, and then the takes are joined together during the editing process so that they appear consecutive. The eventual "running order" may be very different from the order in which the scenes were shot (the "shooting order"). Some of the various shooting situations follow:

- Sometimes the action is shot from start to finish, such as might occur if you are shooting someone who is blowing a glass vase. Programs shot in front of an audience, such as a sitcom, are shot in running order so that the audience can follow the plot without becoming confused.
- Only the relevant sections of the total action may be deliberately shot, omitting unwanted action.
- The action or scene may be repeated so that it can be shot from various angles.
- All of the scenes that take place at one location may be shot before going on to the next location, although the script may indicate that there are several other scenes at other locations in between them.
- A series of *similar* subjects may be shot that have reached different stages. For example, shots of various newborn foals, yearlings, colts, and aging horses can be edited together to imply the life cycle of a specific horse.

EDITING IN 3D

Editors should view their dailies in 3D, cut in 2D to tell the best story they can, and then evaluate the work in 3D again.

—Steve Schklair, CEO, 3ality Digital Systems

3D requires a different cadence of editing. Editors should be cautious of extreme fast cuts, excessive camera shake, or jumping from broad wide shots to tight close-ups.

—David Kenneth, President, I.E. Effects

15.3 EDITING VIDEO AND AUDIO

Linear Editing

Linear editing is the process of "dubbing" or copying the master tape to another tape in a sequential order (Figure 15.1).

This worked well for editors until the director or client wanted significant changes to be made in the middle of a tape. With a linear tape, that usually meant that the whole project had to be entirely reedited, which was incredibly time consuming and frustrating. Linear editing also did not work well if

FIGURE 15.1
Linear editing—copying the contents of one tape to another tape, one clip after another linearly—is still used on a limited basis. Although the use of linear editors has been significantly reduced, segments of the industry, such as news, still use them.
(Photo by Jon Greenhoe.)

multiple generations (copies of copies) of the tape had to be made because each generation deteriorated a little more. Linear systems are generally made up of a "playback" and a "record" VCR along with a control console. The original footage is placed into the playback and then is edited to the recorder (Figure 15.2).

FIGURE 15.2
Laptop linear systems have been popular with news and sports crews that are on the road. They also can be used as two separate tape decks when needed.

Although some segments of the television industry (such as news divisions) are still using *linear* editing, the majority of programming today is edited on a *nonlinear* system.

Nonlinear Editing

Today almost all video and television programs are edited on a nonlinear editing system. Nonlinear editing is the process whereby the recorded video is stored on a computer hard drive. Then the footage can be arranged or rearranged, special effects can be added, and the audio and graphics can be adjusted using the computer's editing software. Nonlinear editing systems make it easy to make changes, moving clips around until the director or client is happy. Digital cameras that record to either tape or memory cards have allowed editors to begin editing much faster because they do not need to digitize all of the footage. Nonlinear systems cost a fraction of the price of a professional linear editing system. Once the edited project is complete, it can be exported to whatever medium is desired: tape,

Internet, iPod, CD, DVD, and so on. It is important to note that nonlinear editing may not necessarily be faster than editing on a linear system. Nonlinear systems allow changes to be made and effects to be added so easily that often clients want to see "every possibility," which can be incredibly time consuming and expensive.

15.4 LOGGING

An often-neglected important aspect of the production process is logging the recorded material. Logging saves time during the actual editing process because the logging can be completed before the edit session (Figures 15.3 and 15.4).

FIGURE 15.3
Logging can be done on paper or utilizing software. Here a camera is connected directly into the computer to capture still frames from each clip and automatically import time code ins and outs. The screenshot shows the stored thumbnail frame, duration, and description.
(Photos courtesy of Imagine Products.)

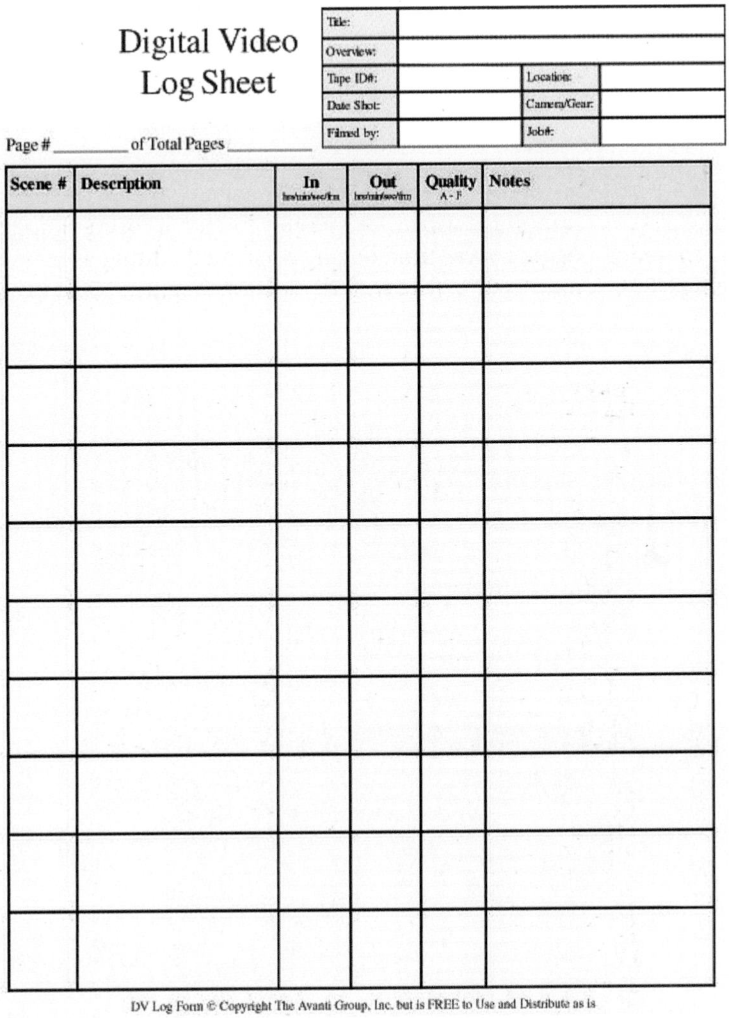

Digital Video Log Sheet

Title:			
Overview:			
Tape ID#:		Location:	
Date Shot:		Camera/Gear:	
Filmed by:		Job#:	

Page # ________ of Total Pages ________

Scene #	Description	In hrs/min/sec/frm	Out hrs/min/sec/frm	Quality A - F	Notes

FIGURE 15.4
Sample of a log sheet.
(Courtesy of the Avanti Group.)

After logging the footage, the editor can then just capture the specific clips that will be used in the program instead of taking time to search through all of the clips. By capturing only the specific clips instead of all of the footage, logging also saves hard drive space. Generally some type of log sheet is used on which notes can be written, including time code (the specific address where the footage is located), scene/take numbers, and the length of each shot. The notes may also include a description of the shot and other comments like "very good," "blurry," and so on. Logging can be simple notes on a piece of paper or can be based on computer logging software. An advantage to some of the logging software is that it can work with the editing software by importing the edit decisions automatically into the computer.

Shots can be identified for the log a number of different ways:

- Visually ("full shot as he gets into the car")
- By shooting a "slate" (clapboard) before each shot, containing the shot number and details (or an inverted board, at the end of shots)
- By *time code*, a continuous time-signal throughout the tape that assigns a unique address to each frame of the recording

15.5 AN OVERVIEW OF THE NONLINEAR PROCESS

- *Step 1.* Capture the footage into the computer.
- *Step 2. Trim* (clean up) each video segment or *clip*, deleting unwanted video frames.
- *Step 3.* Place the clips into the *timeline*. The timeline usually includes multiple tracks of video, audio, and graphics. This timeline allows the editor to view the production and arrange the segments to fit the script's running order (Figure 15.5).

FIGURE 15.5
Screen shot showing the composition page of an editor. The program monitor allows the editor to see the program or to trim a clip to the desired length. The video clip bin is usually where video clips are stored that are to be used in the program. At the bottom is the timeline. This specific editor has two audio tracks and one video track in the timeline.

- *Step 4*. Add video special effects and transitions. Nonlinear edit systems allow all kinds of effects such as ripple, slow/fast motion, and color correction. Transitions include dissolves, cuts, and a variety of wipes.
- *Step 5*. Insert additional audio, if desired, at this point. Audio effects may be used to "sweeten" the sound. Music or voiceovers may be added at different points in the project (Figure 15.6).

FIGURE 15.6
The talent is doing a voiceover in an edit suite for a news story at a local news station.
(Photo by Jon Greenhoe.)

- *Step 6*. Export the final program to the distribution medium.

HABITS OF A HIGHLY EFFECTIVE EDITOR

1. *Schedule enough time to make a good edit.* Quality editing takes time. Be realistic, and then add a little extra pad of time. It is always better to be done a little early than late. Plus, you can always use a little more time to refine the edit.
2. *Get a little distance from the project occasionally.* It is easy to become emotionally involved with a specific element of the project. Take a break from it; when you come back, your perspective may have changed. Ask others for their opinions; there is a good chance that they will see things that you didn't see.
3. *List the issues before fixing them one by one.* It is good to come up with an organized plan for editing the project. Although it takes time to think it through, it is worth it.
4. *Know the priority of your editing elements.* While continuity and the 180-degree rule are important, the most important elements are the emotion and story. If you lose those two elements, you lose the production.

5. *Keep a copy of each edited version.* Each time you make changes to the project, keep the original. That way you have something to go back to if you run into problems.
6. *Focus on the shots you have.* By the time you sit down to edit, it is time to get the best project you can possibly get from the footage you have recorded. You may even have to forget about the script.

(Adapted from Mark Kerin's *Six Habits of Highly Effective Editors*.)

15.6 EDITING EQUIPMENT

FIGURE 15.7
Portable nonlinear equipment makes it easy to edit while on the road.

Editing equipment has drastically changed over the last two decades. Where once a minimal edit system required two editing decks, two monitors, and an edit controller (see Figure 15.1), today the equipment can be as simple as a camcorder (with FireWire) and a computer with one of the editing software packages installed. Even some cell phones include video editing software (Figures 15.7 and 15.9).

Higher-level edit suites may contain multiple types of input devices using a variety of different connectors, such as serial

FIGURE 15.8
Larger edit suites usually offer more options during the editing, a variety of input devices, and multiple screens.
(Photo by Jon Greenhoe.)

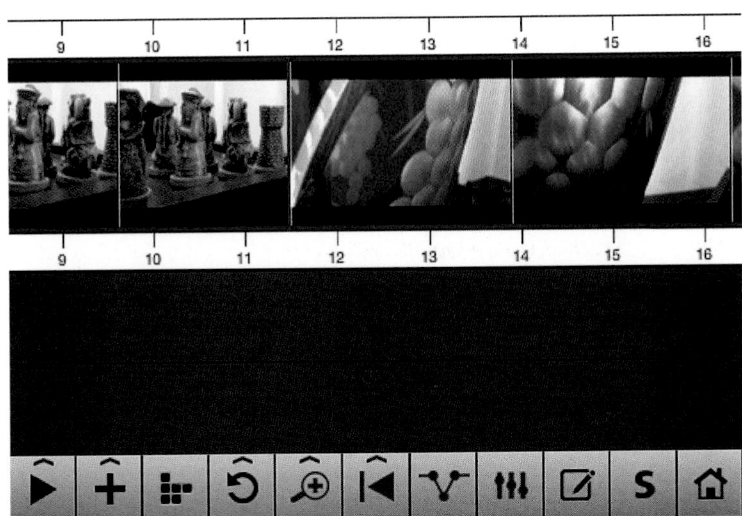

FIGURE 15.9
Simple video editors are available on cell phones such as this system from Vericorder.

digital interface (SDI) to transport the data at a much faster speed. They may also include multiple edit screens, speakers, an audio mixing board, and other tools (Figure 15.8).

Video can be imported into the computer from a camcorder, deck, or a memory storage device (Figure 15.10).

The simplest and most popular connection between the sources is via a FireWire cable. FireWire can move large amounts of data, as well as control signals, through the one cable.

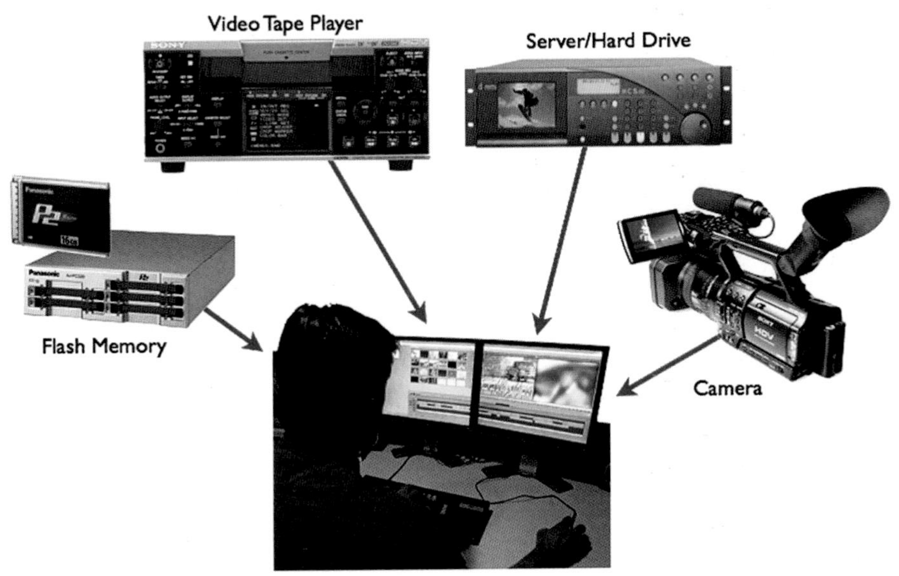

FIGURE 15.10
Many different devices can be used to input video into a nonlinear editor.

15.7 ORGANIZATION

Editing provides ways of correcting and improving the final production:

- Sequences that are uninteresting, irrelevant, or repetitious can be removed or shortened.
- Errors can be corrected by omitting faulty sections and inserting retakes.
- The overall duration of the project can be adjusted.

15.8 EDITING BEGINS

Editing begins with sorting through the available material and doing the following:

1. Selecting the required shots
2. Deciding on the order and duration of each shot
3. Deciding on the edit point (when one shot is to end and the next is to begin)
4. Deciding on the proper type of transition between shots
5. Creating smooth, seamless video and audio continuity

Let's look at these points in more detail.

15.9 SELECTING REQUIRED SECTIONS

It is a normal practice to shoot more than can be used. This is referred to as the "shooting ratio"; only one-tenth or one-twentieth of the total material shot might actually be used in the final edited version. That is partly because they cannot always take the time to check results while shooting and partly to give more choice during editing.

Because the video can be immediately checked for quality, the director usually knows when the needed material has been shot. When the shooting is finally complete, it is time to review the footage. Generally, the following is found:

- Good shots that can easily be used
- Shots that cannot be used because of defects or errors of various types
- Repeated shots (retakes to achieve the best version)
- Redundant shots (too similar to others to use)
- JIC shots (shots taken "just-in-case" they might be useful as cutaways or insert shots/pickups during editing)

So the first stage of editing is to sort out what is available to use and what is not needed. Once the shots are chosen, the next step is to decide on the order in which they will be presented.

15.10 THE ORDER OF SHOTS

To edit successfully, the editor needs to imagine being in the position of the audience. The viewers are seeing a succession of shots, one after another, for the first time. As each shot appears, the viewers must interpret it and relate it to previous shots, progressively building up ideas about what they are seeing.

In most cases, the shots will be shown in chronological order. If the shots jump around in time or place, the result can be extremely confusing. (Even the familiar idea of "flashbacks" only works as long as the audience understands what is going on.)

When series of brief shots are cut together at a fast pace, the program will appear to the audience to be exciting, urgent, or confusing. A slow cutting rhythm using shots of longer duration will appear to be more gentle, restful, thoughtful, sad, and so on.

15.11 WHERE SHOULD THE EDITS BE MADE?

The *moment* chosen to be the edit point can affect how smoothly one shot leads to another. If the first shows a man walking up to a door to open it, and the second shot is a close-up of him grasping the handle, the editor usually has to make sure of the following:

- There is no missing action (his arm hasn't moved yet, but his hand is on the handle in the close-up)
- No action has been duplicated (his hand takes hold of the handle in the first shot, then reaches out and grasps it again in the close-up)
- There is no overextended action (his hand takes the handle in the first shot and holds it and is still seen holding it, waiting to turn it, in the second shot)

Most editors believe that the cut should occur during a movement. The smoothness can vary with the situation, but here we are talking about the finer points of the editing art.

There are occasions when we deliberately "lose time" by omitting part of the action. For instance, a woman gets out of a car, and a moment later we see her coming into a room. We have not watched her through all the irrelevant action of going into the house and climbing the stairs. This technique of *screen time* (*cinematic time*) tightens up the pace of the production and leaves out potentially boring bits or ones that are irrelevant to the story, when the audience's interest could wane. Provided the audience knows what to expect and understands what is going on, this technique is an effective way of getting on with the story without wasting time.

Similarly, it is possible to extend time, creating a dramatic impact. We see someone set the timer on a bomb, cut to people in the next room, cut to the villain's expression, cut to the street outside, cut to him or her looking around, cut back to the timer ticking down, and so on, building up tension in a much longer period of time than it would really have taken for the timer to tick down and explode the bomb.

Again, *cinematic space* can be introduced. We see a person getting into an aircraft and then cut to others at that same moment at the person's destination, preparing to welcome him or her.

SPECIAL EFFECTS

Most nonlinear edit systems include a number of special effects that can be used to enhance the project. However, directors and editors must be careful to use them appropriately. Overuse of special effects is often the sign of an amateur production. Here is a brief list of some typical effects:

Freeze frame. Stopping movement in the picture and holding a still frame.

Strobe. Displaying the action as a series of still images flashed onto the screen at a variable rate.

Reverse action. Running the action in reverse.

Fast or slow motion. Running the action at a faster or slower speed than normal.

Picture in picture. Inserting another picture into the main shot.

Mosaic. Reducing the picture to a pattern of small single-colored squares of adjustable size.

Posterizing. Reducing tonal gradation to a few coarse steps.

Mirror image. Flipping the picture from left to right or providing a symmetrical split screen.

Time lapse. Shooting still frames at regular intervals. When played back at normal speed, the effect is of greatly sped-up motion.

15.12 TRANSITIONS

Figure 15.11 shows the regular methods of changing from one shot to another:

- *Cut*. The *cut* or *take* is the most common, general-purpose transition. It is an instantaneous switch from one shot to another. This powerful dynamic transition is the easiest to make. It is important to note that the cut usually indicates to the audience that the action is taking place in "real time."
- *Dissolve* or a *superimposition*. The dissolve is an effect produced by fading out one picture while fading in another. It is a quiet, restful transition, considered to be "softer" than a cut. A dissolve usually suggests the passing of time or a change of location. One exception to this rule would be the editing of a musical number, in which a dissolve is considered an appropriate "soft transition" between shots, even in real time. If a dissolve is stopped halfway through, the result is a *superimposition* of one image "on top" of the other.
- *Wipe*. The wipe is a stylized transition that can have many different shapes. While it is occasionally effective, it can be easily overused and quickly become the sign of an amateur.

- *Fade*. A *fade* is a gradual change (dissolve) between black and a video image, or vice versa. For example, at the end of a program, there is usually a "fade to black," or if there is a "fade up," it means that the director is transitioning from black to a video image. A slow fade suggests the peaceful end of action. A fast fade is rather like a "gentle cut," used to conclude a scene.

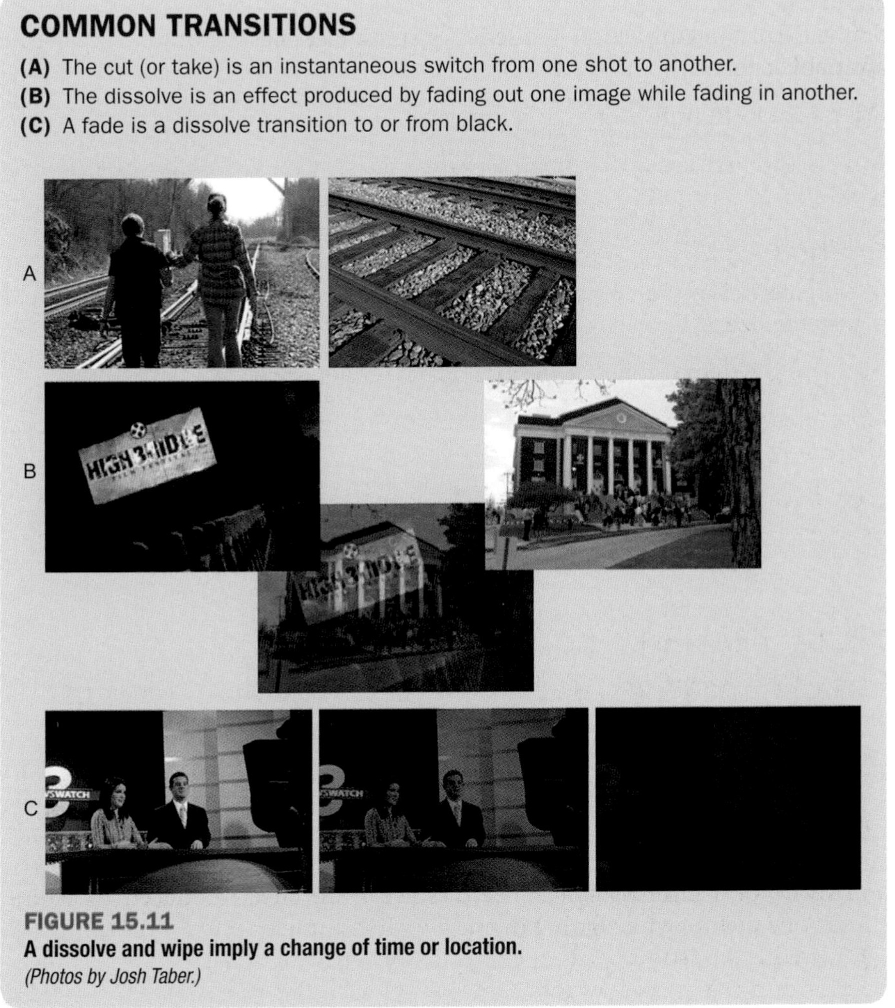

COMMON TRANSITIONS
(A) The cut (or take) is an instantaneous switch from one shot to another.
(B) The dissolve is an effect produced by fading out one image while fading in another.
(C) A fade is a dissolve transition to or from black.
A
B
C

FIGURE 15.11
A dissolve and wipe imply a change of time or location.
(Photos by Josh Taber.)

15.13 GOOD CONTINUITY

Let's say we are watching a dramatic television show. As the director switches from one camera to the next, we notice that in the close-up, the talent's hair is askew, whereas in the second camera's medium shot, the talent's hair is perfect.

Cutting between the two shots in the editing room exposes a *continuity error*. If we see a series of shots that are supposed to show the same action from different angles, we do not expect to see radical changes in the appearance of things in the various images. In other words, we expect *continuity*. *Continuity* in film or video means that during the shooting process, careful attention is given to all the details of a scene, both aural and visual, so that when the different shots from different takes are assembled, the result is a seamless portrayal that appears to have been shot all at the same time.

If a glass is full in one shot and empty in the next, we can accept that if something has happened between the two shots. But if someone in a storm scene appears wet in all the long shots but dry in the close-ups, something is wrong. If the person is standing and smiling with an arm on a chair in one shot but with a hand in a pocket and unsmiling when seen from another angle in the next shot, the sudden change during the cut can be obvious. The sun may be shining in one shot and not in the next. There may be aircraft noises in one but silence in the next. Somebody may be wearing a blue suit in one shot and a gray one in the next. These are all obvious, but they happen. In fact, they are likely to happen whenever action that is to appear continuous in the edited program stops and restarts.

There is an opportunity for a continuity error when the crew does any of the following:

- Stops shooting, moves the camera to another position, and then continues the shoot
- Repeats part of an action (a retake); it may be slightly different the second time, so one cannot edit unobtrusively with the original sequence
- Shoots action over a period of time, such as part of it one day and the rest of the scene on the next day
- Alters how they shoot a scene after part of it was already shot

The only way to achieve good continuity is to pay attention to detail. On most crews this responsibility is often shared between the director and the script supervisor, who functions as a "continuity wrangler" during the shooting of a scene. However, maintaining continuity is ultimately the director's responsibility. Sometimes a continuity error will be much more obvious on the screen than it was during shooting. It is easy to overlook differences when concentrating on the action and the hundred and one other things that arise during production. If there are any doubts, there is a lot to be said for reviewing the recording to look at previous shots of the scene before continuing. Be advised, however, that stopping to review shots before continuing can often result in slowing your shooting schedule to practically a standstill, as everyone will weigh in with an opinion. The most efficient way to "make your day" (finish your day's shooting on time) is to pay close attention to continuity ***while you are shooting the scene***.

15.14 EDITING PRIORITIES

It is worth remembering during the editing phase that either the pictures or the audio may be given *priority*. For example, the dialogue has priority when shooting an important speech. Although the camera needs to focus on the speaker, a single unchanging shot would become visually boring, even with changes in shot size. To make it more interesting, a number of cutaway shots are usually used of the audience, special guests, reactions, and so on. But the dialogue is continuous and unbroken—even when editing the image.

If the speech was too long, it may need to be edited to hold the audience's attention. Generally the most important passages are then edited together. In this situation, because visually it would be easy for the audience to *see* that segments had been removed, shots of the audience may need to be placed over the edits.

There are occasional scenes in which two people are supposed to be speaking to each other, although they were actually shot separately. For instance, all the shots of a boy stranded on a cliff would be taken at the same time (with dialogue). All the shots and comments of his rescuer at the top of the cliff would be shot at another time. During editing, the shots with their respective speeches would be cut together to provide a continuous conversation.

Because it is difficult to get optimal microphone placement in wider shots without the mic being seen on camera, the actual dialogue recording used in wide shots is often that which has been recorded in a close-up when the microphone could be placed much closer to the speaker. Trained actors are fairly accomplished at repeating their dialogue with the same rhythm and energy from take to take, and a skilled editor can take clean dialogue recorded from a close-up and "put it in the actors' mouths" in a wide shot in such a way that the audience is completely unaware that the actors' dialogue is not originating from the actual shot they are seeing on screen.

So there are times when the images have priority, and the sound has to be closely related to what we are seeing. Other times the sound will be the priority, and everything has to be edited to support that sound.

15.15 GOOD EDITING TECHNIQUES

Editing, like so many of the crafts we have examined in earlier pages, is an unobtrusive skill. If it is done well, the audience does not notice it but is absorbed in its *effect*. During an exciting scene, for example, when the duration

FIGURE 15.12
Tension can be increased by quicker cutting. Here an increasing cutting rate is combined with closer and closer shots.

of shots is made shorter and shorter as the tension grows, the audience is only conscious of growing agitation and fast-moving action (Figure 15.12).

There are certain established principles in the way one edits, and although like all "rules" they may be occasionally disregarded, they have been created out of experience. Here are a few of the most common:

- Avoid cutting between shots of extremely different size of the same subject (close-up to long shot). It is jolting for the audience.
- Do not cut between shots that are similar or even matching (frontal close-up of one person to a frontal close-up of a second person); it will look as though person A has "morphed" into person B.
- Do not cut between two shots of the same size (close-up to close-up) of the same subject. This lack of "cutting distance" results in creating a *jump cut*.
- If two subjects are going in the same direction (chasing, following), have them both going across the screen in the same direction. If their screen directions are opposite, it suggests that they are meeting or parting.
- If an object is traveling in one direction (such as left to right) across the screen in a shot, it must continue traveling in the same direction (left to right) in subsequent shots. Otherwise, it will appear that the object has "turned around" and is going back the way it came. If the object exits the screen frame right in the first shot, it must enter the next shot from frame left in order to maintain proper "screen direction."
- Avoid cutting between still (static) shots and moving images (panning, tilting, zooming, etc.), except for a specific purpose.
- Avoid cutting from a shot in which an object is moving to one in which that object is not moving. This is considered a continuity break. The audience needs to see the object stop moving in one of the two shots on either side of the edit. Inexperienced directors make this mistake quite often when they have an actor enter a room and speak in a wide shot but then do not have them reenter for their close-up dialogue. The result is usually a break in continuity in which the director has difficulty making a seamless transition from the wide shot (in which the actor is moving) to the close-up (where he/she is standing flat-footed).
- If you have to break the continuity of action (deliberately or unavoidably), introduce a cutaway shot. But try to ensure that this relates meaningfully to the main action. During a boxing match, a cutaway to an excited spectator can help build the tension. A cutaway to a bored attendant (just because you happen to have the unused shot) would most likely be meaningless, unless you intend it to be used as a comment on the main action.
- Avoid cutting to shots that make a person or object jump from one side of the screen to the other (don't have them frame left in one shot and frame right in the next). This also is considered a *jump cut*.

START HERE

15.16 ANTICIPATING EDITING

It does not matter how good the video images are; if they have not been shot with editing in mind, you may not be able to use them. Here are some of the issues to think about when shooting:

- Include "masters" or *cover* shots (long shots) of action wherever possible to show the overall view of the action.
- Always leave several seconds of *"head"* and*"tail"* at the start and finish of each shot. Do not begin recording just as the action is beginning or the talent is about to speak, and do not stop just as the action finishes. A little extra footage at the beginning and end of each shot will allow more flexible editing (effects such as dissolves and wipes require more frames than simple cuts require, so you'll need that extra footage in post).
- Include potential *cutaway shots* that can be used to cover edits when any sequence is shortened or lengthened. These could include such things as crowd shots, long shots, reaction shots, and people walking by.
- Avoid *reverse-angle shots* unless you need them for a specific reason (such as slow-motion shots of a sports event). If it is unavoidable (such as when crossing the road to shoot a parade from the other side), include head-on (frontal) shots of the same action. These shots break the "axis of action," but when correctly inserted, they can work as transitional shots.
- Keep "cute shots" to a minimum, unless they can really be integrated into the program. These might include subjects such as reflections, silhouettes against the sunset, animals or children at play, and footsteps in the sand. They take up valuable time and may have minimal use in effective storytelling. However, there are times when beauty shots have their place, such as an establishing shot.
- Remember that a dissolve, wipe, or other *digital video effect* (*DVE*) usually indicates a change in location or time.
- Try to anticipate continuity. Every element you include in your frame increases the potential for continuity errors. Do you really need thirty extras in your party scene to tell your story effectively, or can you get the same result with only fifteen?
- Where there is going to be commentary or narration over the video (*voiceover*), allow for this in the length and pace of takes. For example, avoid inappropriately choppy editing that results from shots being too brief. If possible, having your script supervisor read the narration or commentary during the filming of the scene will help ensure that your shots are the proper length for editing.
- Plan to include long shots, medium shots, and close-up shots of action to provide additional editing options (referred to as "coverage"). For example, where the action shows people crossing a bridge, a variety of angles can make a mundane subject visually interesting: a long shot (in which

the subject is walking away from the camera toward a bridge), a medium shot (the subject is walking on the bridge, looking over), a very long shot (the camera is shooting up at the bridge from the river below), a long shot (the subject is walking from the bridge to the camera on the far side), and so on.

- Remember that environmental noises can provide valuable bridging sound between shots when editing. They can be recorded as a wild track (nonsync sound). Always get a minimum of a minute's worth of "location audio" before you wrap your location. This could be the sound of birds in the trees outdoors or simply the "room tone" (all rooms have one) from the interior room in which you are shooting. These recordings will prove to be invaluable in the edit process.
- Where possible, include features in shots that will provide the audience with the context of the event. This helps viewers to identify the specific location (landmarks, street names). Too often, the walls and bushes behind closer shots could be anywhere.
- Wherever possible, use a *slate* at the start of each shot. If this is not possible, the talent or camera operator can do a "voice slate," calling out the shot number on camera so that the editor knows where it goes in the final production.
- Always check what is happening in the background behind the talent or subject. Distractions, such as people waving, trash cans, and signs, can take the audience's attention away from the main subject. When shooting multiple takes of a scene, watch for significant changes in the background that will make it difficult to edit the takes together.
- Remember that edits should be motivated. There should be a reason for the edit. This reason could be physical, such as movement by the talent, or someone new entering the scene, or it could be emotional, such as a moment of high drama, tension, or comedy, but every edit should be motivated by something that helps to tell the story. The fact that "this shot has been on for a few seconds now, so let's change it" is ***NOT*** a valid motivation to make an edit.

Interview with a Pro

Brock Smith, Editor

Brock Smith, Editor

Why do you like editing? What do you like about it?
In essence, it's the biggest payoff. After months of pre-production, preparations, and on-set work, it's the *editor* that gets to see a multitude of talents all converge to form the final product. Not only that, they get to bend and twist scenes ever-so-slightly to push or pull the audience as necessary and drive the story forward.

What do you think makes a good editor (person)?
Editing is one of the rare jobs where being OCD should be on the application. Attention to detail is as crucial as a sense of timing, and you have to be self-motivated. Finally, never get too attached to your ideas, as they will most likely be changed five times before you are finished.

How do you decide where edits are made?
I get asked this a lot, and it's a hard question because there isn't a cut and dried answer like "2.5 seconds into every shot." For a start, aspiring editors may enjoy Walter Murch's book *In the Blink of an Eye*. His theory is that after a person has absorbed a certain amount of information, they blink. In other words, an editor decides how much information to feed a person's mind before "blinking" (cutting) to something else.

How do you organize yourself to edit a program together?

1. Clean and remove all distractions from your workspace.
2. Back up EVERYTHING. Twice.
3. Dissect each scene by camera, reel, take, etc. and place them into appropriate bins or folders.
4. Keep your timelines clean, eliminating all extra sound effects or footage that you are not using.
5. Lots of coffee and patience.

What are some of the challenges you face as an editor ... editing for someone else?
When 8 terabytes of footage and a 6-inch notebook are first dropped off, it's easy to get freaked out. This is where self-motivation comes in; you have to focus on each individual scene rather than the project as a whole until you get past the rough cut. Each scene has to become its own short film in a way, with a beginning, middle, and end.

Editing for someone else is new every time. Each person is different, but you quickly adapt to his or her style and expectations. And, generally, the genre of the film helps determine an edit style.

Brock Smith is the owner of a small postproduction facility. He edits shows for corporate clients as well as short and feature films.

CHAPTER 16

Distributing Your Production

One cell phone can now simultaneously feed real-time video to the entire world. This, quite honestly, blows my mind. There is real opportunity out there and it's available now. Virtually all of the media playing fields have been leveled.

—Frank Beacham, Producer & Writer

Traditionally distribution was not a part of the production personnel's problem. They created the content … and someone else worked to get it out to the audience. However, today distribution often becomes part of the role of the production personnel. Once the production has been completed, production personnel often need to burn it to a DVD or Blu-Ray disc, post it online, or stream it. Distribution depends on where you are sending it since the devices viewers watch their programming on are very varied: traditional televisions, large screens, tablet computers, computers, and cell phones.

Key Terms

- ***IPTV:*** Internet Protocol Television (IPTV) utilizes the Internet to provide programming to its audience instead of broadcast or cable television.
- ***iTV:*** Interactive television, or iTV, refers to online programming that allows the viewer to make choices about how they watch an event.
- ***Streaming:*** Programming that is shown live or transmitted from a video sharing site to a computer.
- ***Video sharing sites:*** Online sites that enable producers to upload programming so that it can be seen by an audience.

16.1 TRADITIONAL BROADCAST DISTRIBUTION

Traditionally it cost thousands of dollars to broadcast your program through a local television station to your local community. If you wanted to transmit your program nationally, it would be very expensive. Transmitting it around the world was almost unheard of unless it was an international event. Transmitting it *live* locally, nationally, and internationally was even more expensive.

The equipment needed to create live broadcasts can be incredibly expensive. Microwave or satellite trucks are used to send the signal back to the station or network (Figure 16.1).

FIGURE 16.1
Traditionally, microwave or satellite trucks were used to send a video program or live feed back to a station or network.

16.2 TRADITIONAL NON-BROADCAST DISTRIBUTION (USUALLY REFERRED TO AS VIDEO)

If you created a production for non-broadcast usage, you had to use videotape or a DVD by snail mail or for sale in stores. There were no other ways to transmit the project.

16.3 DISTRIBUTING HARD COPIES OF THE PRODUCTION

In Chapter 14 we talked about recording and storing your program on a camera device. There were lots of recording media to do that. However, once the program has been edited, if you want to actually hand it to someone, you still need to store it on a medium. While videotape is quickly going away, DVDs and Blu-Ray discs (HD) have become the media of choice for storage and easy hard copy distribution, especially since most people have a DVD player in their home or computer. DVDs are a very economical means of distributing a hard copy. However, with the ability to store large amounts of data and the reduction of cost, USB thumb drives (flash memory) have rapidly become one of the most popular modes of temporary storage. While DVDs are limited to 4.7 GB, Blu-Ray DVDs can hold a maximum of 50 GB, and USB drives currently have a maximum capacity of up to 256 GB. The USB thumb drive can allow you to store entire video files (Figure 16.2).

FIGURE 16.2
Large USB thumb drives are great for storing video files.

When storing the video files during postproduction or for long-term storage, not distribution, hard drives are the most common medium.

16.4 ONLINE DISTRIBUTION

Online distribution allows programming to be distributed worldwide. This has opened up access to people and markets that were unreachable in the past. Online sites provide a variety of opportunities for sharing video. Videos can be distributed to anyone, specific groups, or become part of a channel. It is possible to view SD, HD, and even 3D video on many of these websites. It is possible to upload videos from a computer and cell phones.

Video-sharing websites allow users to upload, share, and view productions. Some of the sites allow commercials, and others don't. Some video-sharing sites are provided by private companies and are aimed at a specific audience. Others, like YouTube, Vimeo, and Facebook, are mass communication websites used by millions around the world (Figure 16.3). Facebook has over 500 million active users around the world, who can upload videos, and YouTube says that over 14 billion videos were viewed on their site in 2010.

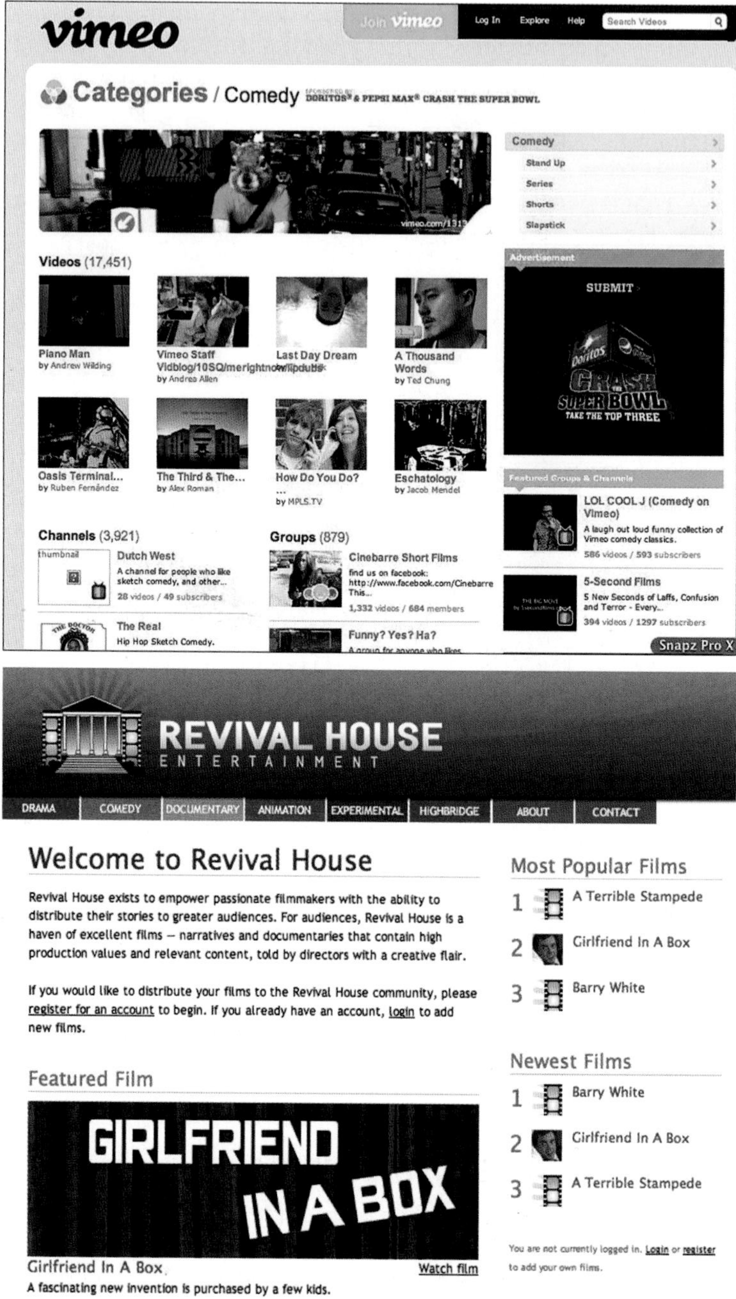

FIGURE 16.3

YouTube and Vimeo are some of the largest video-sharing websites. The second image is of a private website that distributes videos to a specific audience. In this situation it is distributing short films to university students. These video-sharing sites enable producers to distribute their material around the world.

Websites differ greatly on how they manage their content. Some enable producers to upload their programs for free and make it available free to the audience. Other sites may charge a fee to view the video, splitting the fees between the site and the producer (Figure 16.4).

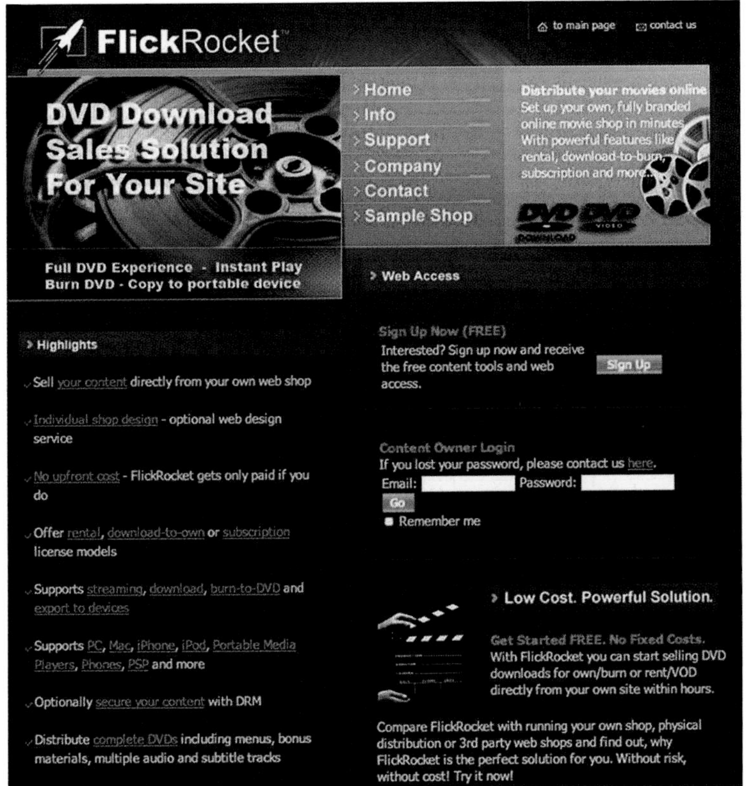

FIGURE 16.4
Some websites provide videos for a fee, splitting the fees between the site and the program's producers.

16.5 LIVE ONLINE DISTRIBUTION

The Internet and mobile phones have incredibly changed the live distribution of content in other ways. In the past there were lots of layers of bureaucracy (gatekeepers) between the producer and the audience. As mentioned earlier, the cost of live transmission gear was also prohibitive. Today you can reach a live audience directly, going around the traditional gatekeepers, by using a computer or some cell phones (Figures 15.5 and 15.6).

As with video-sharing websites, live video streaming of events can be provided to a specific audience or made available to anyone who would like

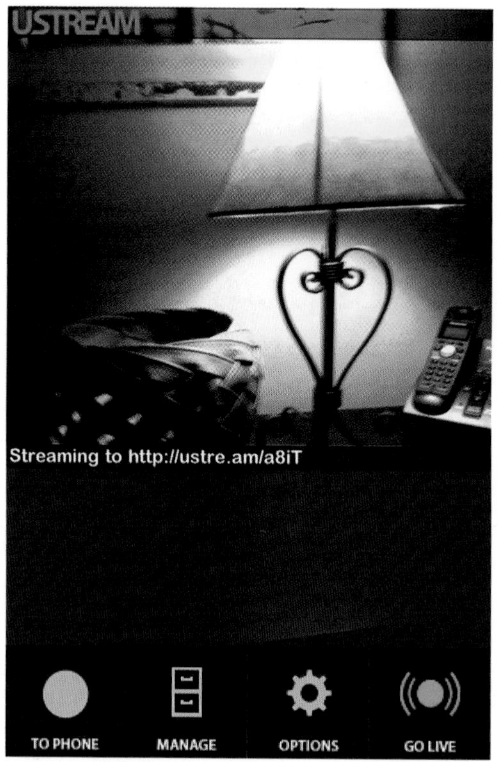

FIGURE 16.5
Some companies, like UStream, provide cell phone apps that enable live video transmission to their website, which then makes the live feed available to an audience. This is a cell phone screen shot of a live video transmission.

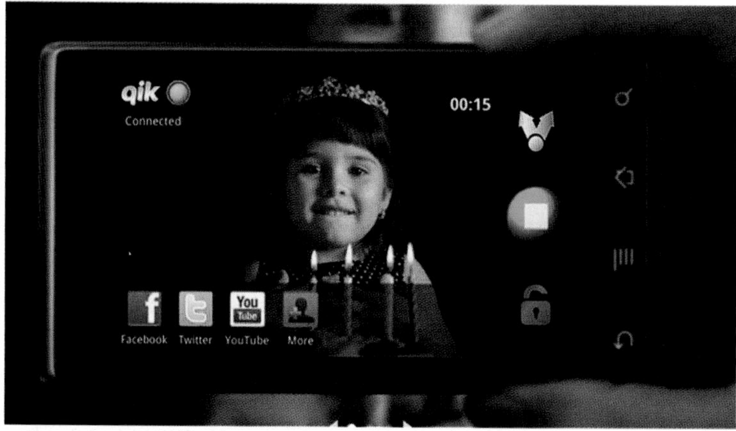

FIGURE 16.6
Apps, such as the one above from qik, allow producers to transmit live or upload directly to facebook, Twitter, or YouTube from a cell phone.
(Photo courtesy of qik.)

to see it. Video streaming requires substantial compression of the data, which often results in a lower-quality image. However, the quality is rapidly improving. Some live streaming sites allow unlimited viewers, while others, such as Apple's Face Time, are currently limited to one-on-one direct video transmissions.

FIGURE 16.7
Slingbox connects television networks and stations to computers, tablets, and cell phones. However, individual programming can be transmitted as well. Slingbox is a one-to-one medium.
(Photos courtesy of Slingbox.)

There are other live online distributors who, like Slingbox, use a box connected to the Internet to stream networks from cable or satellite television (Figure 16.7). However, Slingbox can also be used to stream personal videos to a computer or cell phone type receiver.

16.6 IPTV

Internet Protocol Television (IPTV) utilizes the Internet to provide programming to its audience instead of broadcast or cable television. IPTV is somewhat of a mix of the services by video sharing sites and live streaming sites. Programming can be streamed live, video on demand, or interactive television (iTV). Many times these systems are subscriber-based, which requires the payment of fees in order to access the content.

For example, Major League Baseball began its own IPTV called MLB.com. They provide baseball information, news, sports columns, and statistics. MLB.com also provides games, video and audio streaming of baseball games, official baseball fan products, and ticket sales (Figure 16.8). Some of their information is free, while other material is only available to subscribers. These sites provide an interactivity that gives much more access to the information the audience wants—allowing the viewer to individualize their viewing experience (Figure 16.9).

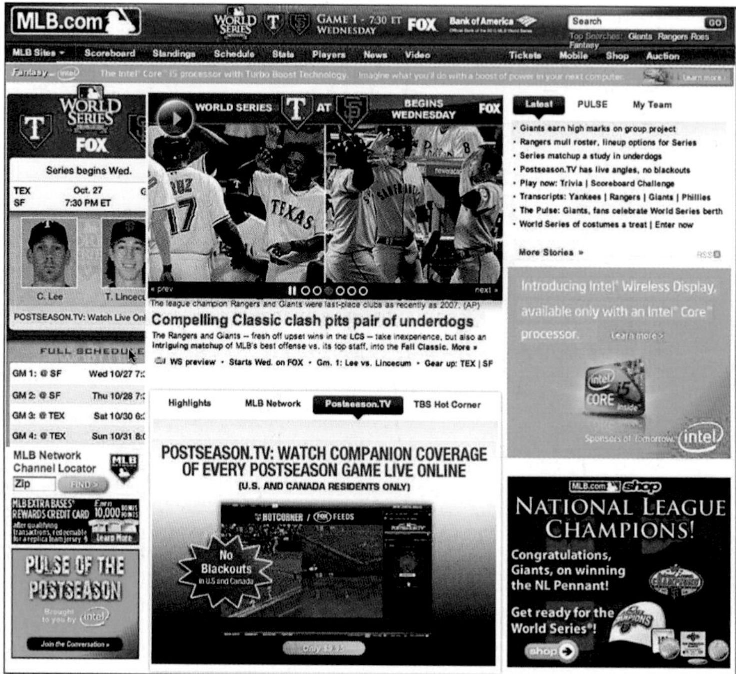

FIGURE 16.8
IPTV channels, like Major League Baseball, provide a wide range of services, often interactive, such as live streaming of games, baseball statistics, merchandise, and baseball news.

16.7 FESTIVALS AND COMPETITIONS

Video competitions and "film" festivals can also be a very productive way of getting your project seen. Productions are often exhibited in front of a live audience, providing a way for general viewers and distributors to see the production.

SUMMARY

Television production personnel are having to learn how to use the new production media as they continue to emerge and converge. Producers need to know how to attract an online audience, including how to use social media to get the word out.

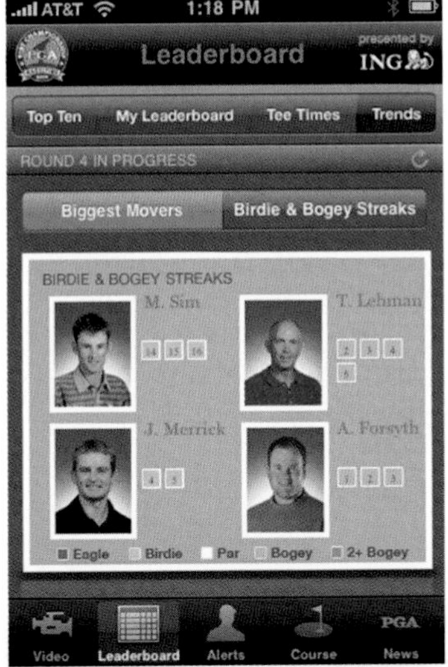

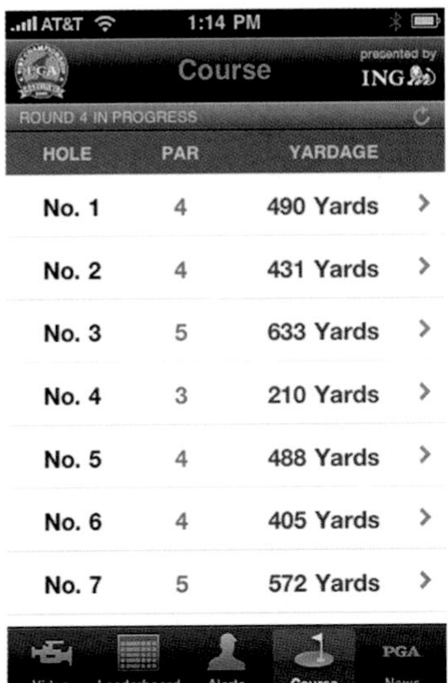

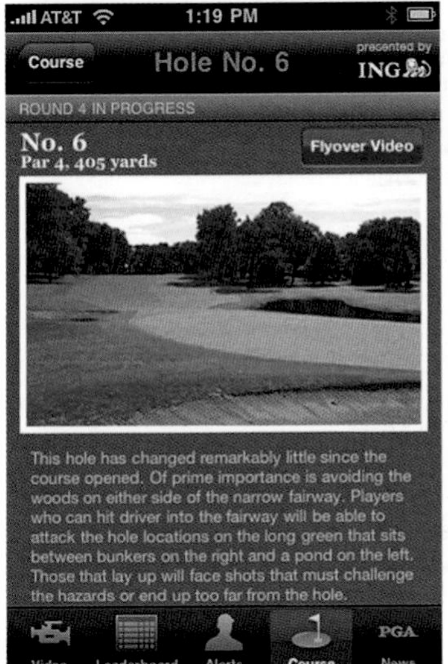

FIGURE 16.9
The Professional Golf Association (PGA) provides an app for cell phones that allows viewers to customize their viewing. This includes receiving alerts when a specific player is at the tee. The apps enable you to follow a specific person without watching everything, as well as provide updated statistics, show the holes, or even watch a specific hole.

Interview with a Pro

Chad Crouch, CEO, The Creative Group

Chad Crouch, CEO, The Creative Group

How do you use online distribution of your videos?
I use the Internet as the main marketing tool for my company. Additionally, many of our clients hire us to help create effective, interactive websites for their organizations and companies. One of our long-term clients has seen significant results, attracting millions of visitors and empowering their political grassroots activism.

Why do you create things for the web?
It is the marketplace for the world. It is the best place to define what makes you unique and valuable.

How have you let your audience know that you put something online?
We use social media tools such as Facebook and Twitter. We have also used traditional advertising, such as postcards or letters.

What changes do you see in the future for online distribution?
Faster connection speeds will allow for higher-quality video files to be downloaded in short periods of time. The Internet will become the main distribution for traditional TV programs and movies. I also think that 3D viewing will become mainstream online within the next two or three years. Additionally, I believe that the traditional "Internet" as we now understand it will be replaced with a new means of transferring data that will move us outside of the current limits. We will be constantly connected, without wires, any place at any time.

What challenges do you have to deal with when putting material online?
People have a very limited attention span when viewing content online. You have to design online content so that it is compelling, informative, and brief. This is a challenge for most organizations and companies. A large part of our relationship with clients is helping them refine their message so that it will communicate effectively online.

Chad Crouch is the CEO of a production and marketing company that works with corporate clients as well as nonprofit organizations.

Glossary

3D Images that appear to have three dimensions: height, width, and depth.

3DTV Televisions that are designed specifically for showing 3D programming. Viewers must watch the images through high-precision 3D glasses, which open and close the left and right shutters in synchronization with the alternating images.

Acoustics Higher-frequency sound waves travel in straight paths and are easily deflected and reflected by hard surfaces. They are also easily absorbed by porous fibrous materials. Lower-frequency sound waves (below 100 Hz) spread widely, so they are not impeded by obstacles and are less readily absorbed. As sound waves meet nearby materials, they are selectively absorbed and reflected; the reflected sound's quality is modified according to the surfaces' nature, structures, and shapes. The acoustic characteristics of scenery, furniture, drapes, and people further modify audio quality.

Action line (line/eye line) The imaginary line along the direction of the action in the scene. Cameras should only shoot from one side of this line.

AGC (Automatic Gain Control) Circuitry in some cameras that automatically adjusts the audio level (higher or lower) to a preset average level.

Analog recording (analogue) Analog systems directly record the variations of the video and audio signals. They have a tendency to deteriorate when dubbing copies and can only be recorded on tape.

Aperture The opening in the lens that lets light into the camera.

Arc A camera move that moves around the subject in a circle, arc, or "horseshoe" path.

Aspect ratio Aspect radio can be defined as the proportion of width to height of the screen. Televisions have an aspect ratio of 4:3 or 16:9. It is important to keep the aspect ratio in mind when designing sets so that they fit the screen.

Audio filters May be used to reduce background noises (traffic, air conditioners, wind), or compensate for boomy surroundings.

Audio mixer A unit used to select, control, and intermix audio sources. It may include filter circuits, reverberation control, and so on. It is usually operated by the *audio mixer* (a job title as well as the name of the board) or *A-1*.

Auto-focus Some lenses are designed to automatically focus on the subject.

Backlight control When there is more light in the background than on the subject, some cameras use a backlight control button, which opens up the iris an arbitrary stop or so above the auto-iris setting to improve the subject's exposure.

Barn doors These metal flaps are usually attached to the top, bottom, and sides of the light in order to shape the beam.

Base light An even lighting covering the area to be shot. This simple light level is enough to create a good video image in the camera. However, it does not create a mood, artistic feel, and so on.

Batten The horizontal ceiling bar that lights are hung onto in a studio. This bar may include electrical receptacles.

Bidirectional microphone This microphone can pick up sounds equally well both in front and in back but is deaf on either side.

Black-stretch control Some cameras include a black-stretch control button that can be adjusted to make shadow detail clearer and improve tonal gradation in darker tones.

Boom pole A pole that is used to hold a microphone close to a subject.

Breakdown sheet An analysis of the script to determine the optimal sequence for shooting the scenes or for analyzing the budget.

Camcorder A camera with a built-in recording device.

Camera control unit (CCU) Equipment that controls the camera from a remote position. The CCU includes setting up and adjusting the camera, luminance, color correction, aperture, and so on.

Camera script Adds full details of the production treatment to the left side of the "rehearsal script" and usually also includes the shot numbers, cameras used, positions of camera, basic shot details, camera moves, and switcher instructions (if used).

Cathode ray tube (CRT) CRT television sets send an electron beam through a vacuum tube to a phosphor-coated screen. These "tube" televisions are large and bulky.

CCD This charged-coupled device is an image sensor used in most video cameras.

Character generator Character generator, or CG, is a generic name for any type of television graphic creation equipment.

Chroma Color.

Chroma-key Utilizing a production switcher, the director can replace a specific color (usually blue or green) with another image source (still image, live video, prerecorded material, etc.).

Clapboard The clapboard (also known as a *clapper* or *slate*) is shot at the beginning of each take to provide information such as film title, names of director and director of photography, scene, take, date, and time. Primarily used in dramatic productions.

Clip A video segment.

Close-up shot Encourages the audience to concentrate on a specific feature. Shows emotion and detail.

CMOS This "complementary metal-oxide semiconductor" image sensor has less power consumption, saving energy for longer shooting times.

Color bar generator Provides a consistent reference pattern that is used for matching the video output of multiple cameras. They are also used to obtain the best-quality image on a video monitor. This test signal is composed of a series of vertical bars of standard colors (white, yellow, cyan (blue-green), green, magenta (red-purple), red, blue, and black). A color bar generator actually creates the pattern electronically. However, it is possible to use a printed color chart as long as it has been cared for and is not faded.

Compressor/expander Deliberately used to reduce or emphasize the audio dynamic range (i.e., the difference between the quietest and loudest sounds).

Condenser microphone A high-quality microphone that can be very small and is generally powered by an inboard battery, phantom power, or a power supply.

Continuity The goal of continuity is to make sure there is consistency from one shot to the next in a scene and from scene to scene. This continuity includes the talent, objects, and sets. An example of a continuity error in a production would be when one shot shows the talent's messy hair combed in one direction and the next shot shows it in perfect condition.

Contrast The difference between the relative brightness of the lightest and darkest areas in the shot.

Convergence In 3D, when a human looks at two overlaid images, one image seen by the left eye and one seen with the right eye, and perceives one image with depth, convergence is when the two images converge on a single point in space.

Coverage The term used by filmmakers that refers to repeating a scene from enough different angles to ensure that a seamless performance can be maintained throughout multiple takes.

Cover shot A video clip that is used to cover an edit so that the viewers do not know that the edit occurred.

Crab See *Truck*.

Crawl The movement of text horizontally across the television screen.

Credit roll Continuous information moving vertically into the frame and passing out at the top.

Credits The text that recognizes those appearing in and contributing to the program.

Cue card The talent may read questions or specific points from a cue card that is positioned near the camera. Generally it is held next to the camera lens.

Cut The "cut" or "take" is the most common transition when editing. It is an instantaneous switch from one shot to the next.

Cutaway shot These shots are used to cover edits when any sequence is shortened or lengthened. Generally it is a shot of something outside of the current frame.

Cyclorama (cyc) A general-purpose detail-less background. It can be neutral, colored with lights, or absent any light (black).

Dead surroundings When area surfaces are very sound absorbent, the direct sound waves strike walls, the floor, the ceiling, and furnishings and are largely lost. The microphone may pick up only a few weak reflections.

Deep focus Deep focus, or large depth of field, is when everything in the shot is clearly in focus.

Depth of field The distance between the nearest and farthest objects in focus.

Diffused light Soft or overcast light.

Diffusion material Material that can be attached to the front of a light to reduce the intensity and soften the light beam.

Digital recording The *digital* system regularly samples the waveforms and converts them into numerical (binary) data. This allows many generations of copies to be made without affecting the quality of the image. Digital systems also allow the data to be recorded on media other than tape, such as hard disks or flash memory.

Digital zoom Zooming is achieved by progressively reading out a smaller and smaller area of the same digitally constructed image. The image progressively deteriorates as the digital zoom is zoomed in.

Digitize Converting the audio and video signals into data files. This term is used when transferring video footage from a camera (or other video source) to a computer.

Directional microphone This type of microphone can pick up sounds directly in front of it.

Dissolve (mix) A gradual transition between two images. A dissolve usually signifies a change time or location.

Dolly (track) (1) The action of moving the whole camera and mount slowly toward or away from the subject. (2) A platform with wheels that is used to smoothly move a camera during a shot.

Drag The variable friction controls located on a tripod head that steady the camera's movements.

DSLR (digital single lens reflex camera) A still camera that shoots video, allowing the photographer to see the image through the lens that will capture the image.

DVE "Digital video effect" equipment, working with the switcher, is used to create special effects between video images. A DVE could also refer to the actual effect.

Dynamic microphone A rugged, low-maintenance, not easily distorted microphone.

Dynamic range The range between the weakest and loudest sounds that can be effectively recorded by a recording device.

EFP An abbreviation for "electronic field production." EFP generally means shooting in the field with one or more cameras.

Ellipsoidal The ellipsoidal light is a sharply focused/defined spotlight.

Empirical production method The method where instinct and opportunity are the guides.

ENG Abbreviation for "electronic news gathering." ENG usually refers to shooting with a single camera outside the studio.

Equalizer An audio filter that can boost or reduce any segment of the audio spectrum.

EXT Exterior location.

Eye line (line) Where people appear to be looking, or line of sight.

Fade A gradual change (dissolve) between black and a video image. Usually defines the beginning or end of a segment or program.

Filmic time This editing technique tightens up the pace of a production by leaving out potentially boring portions of the scene when the audience interest could wane.

Filter wheel Filters may be required to obtain the best color in a video camera. Filters are often fitted inside the video camera, just behind the lens on a filter wheel. Typical correction filters include *daylight, artificial/tungsten light,* and *fluorescent light* (perhaps marked 6000 K, 4700 K, and 3200 K). The filter wheel may also include or combine neutral-density (ND) filters to improve exposure.

FireWire Also known as the IEEE 1394 or iLink, the FireWire is used to connect different pieces of equipment, such as cameras, drives, and computers so that they can transfer large amounts of data, such as video, quickly and easily.

Fish pole See *Microphone boom.*

Flash memory These cards can store large amounts of digital data without having any moving parts. This makes them durable, able to work in a variety of temperatures, and data can be easily transferred into a nonlinear editor.

Flood lighting The light scatters in all directions, providing a broad, nondirectional light.

Focal length Simply an optical measurement—the distance between the optical center of the lens and the image sensor, when you are focused at a great distance such as infinity. It is measured in millimeters (mm) or inches.

Focus zone See *Depth of field.*

Foley Creating sound effects that can be used to replace the original sounds such as hoofbeats, footsteps, and so on.

Follow focus This technique requires the camera operator to continually change the focus as the camera follows the action.

Format The show format lists the items or program segments in a show in the order they are to be shot. The format generally shows the durations of each segment and possibly the camera assignments.

Fresnel The Fresnel is generally an unfocused spotlight (some can be focused). It is lightweight, less expensive than an ellipsoidal, and it has an adjustable beam.

f-stop The f-stop regulates how much light is allowed to pass through the camera lens by varying the size of the hole the light comes through.

FU Fade up.

Full script A fully scripted program includes detailed information on all aspects of the production. This includes the precise words that the talent/actors are to use in the production.

Gaffer The head of the electrical department, many times in charge of lighting on a television set.

Gain (1) (video) Amplification of the camera video signal, usually resulting in some video noise. (2) (audio) Amplification of the audio signal.

Gel Colored flexible plastic filters used to adjust the color of the lights.

Goals Broad concepts of what you want to accomplish with the program.

Graphic equalizer (shaping filter) Graphic equalizers have a series of slider controls, allowing selected parts of the audio spectrum to be boosted or reduced.

Grip clamps These clamps are designed so that a light can easily be attached. The clamp is then used to attach the light to almost anything.

Group shot (GS) A term used by a director when instructing a camera operator to shoot a shot of the whole group.

GS See *Group shot.*

Handheld camera A camera that is held by a person and not supported by any type of camera mount.

Handheld microphone The handheld mic is widely used by news reporters and musicians.

HDD Hard disk drives can be used for recording digital video images and can be built into the camera or attached to the outside of the camera.

HDSLR A high-definition (HD) version of a DSLR. (See DSLR description above.)

HDTV The standard high-definition formats currently in use range from 720 to 1,080 lines of resolution.

Headroom The space from the top of the head to the upper frame.

High angle When the camera is positioned higher than the subject.

Hue Refers to the predominant color—for example, blue, green, and yellow.

I-mag An abbreviation for "image magnification." Refers to large video screen production at events.

INT Interior location.

Intellectual property (IP) Property (music, video, etc.) whose owners have been granted certain legal exclusive rights.

Intercom A wired or wireless communication link between members of the production crew.

Interlaced scanning The television's electron scans the odd-numbered lines first and then goes back and "paints" in the remaining even-numbered lines.

IPTV Internet Protocol Television (IPTV) utilizes the Internet to provide programming to its audience instead of broadcast or cable television.

Iris The diaphragm of the lens that is adjustable. This diaphragm is adjusted open or closed, based on the amount of light needed to capture a quality image.

ISO While all the cameras are connected to the switcher as before, the ISO (or isolated) camera is also continuously recorded on a separate recorder.

iTV Interactive television, or iTV, refers to online programming that allows the viewer to make choices about how they watch an event.

Jib A counterbalanced arm that fits onto a tripod that allows the camera to move up, down, and around.

Jog Playing the video on a recorder/player frame by frame.

Jump cut A jump cut is created when the editor cuts between two similar shots (two close-ups) of the same subject.

Lavaliere microphone These small microphones clip on the clothing of the talent and provide fairly consistent, hands-free, audio pickup of the talent's voice.

LCD These flat-screen displays work by sending variable electrical currents through a liquid crystal solution that crystallizes to form a quality image.

LED light panel A camera or studio light that is made from a series of small LED bulbs.

Limiter A device for preventing loud audio from exceeding the system's upper limit (causing overload distortion), by progressively reducing circuit amplification for louder sounds.

Linear editing The copying, or dubbing, segments from the master tape to another tape in sequential order.

Live surroundings When an area contains predominantly hard surfaces, the sound is strongly reflected. This results in more echo.

Location A place used for shooting outside of the studio.

Logging Loggers view the footage and write down the scene/take numbers, the length of each shot, time code, and descriptions of each shot.

Long shot or wide-angle shot Helps establish the scene for the viewer.

Low angle When the camera is positioned lower than the subject.

Lower third (L/3rd) A graphic that appears in the lower third of screen. Traditionally it contains biographical information.

Luminance The brightness of the image, how dark or light it appears.

Macro Some lenses include a macro setting, a lens capable of extreme close-ups.

Medium shot The medium shot tells the story; it is close enough to show the emotion of the scene but far enough away to show some of the relevant context of the event.

MFD (MOD) The minimum focused distance, or MFD, is the closest distance a lens can get to the subject. With some telephoto lenses, the MFD may be a few yards. Other lenses may be 1/4 of an inch.

Microphone (mic) boom A pole that is used to hold a microphone in order to get the mic close to the action.

Modular set Modular sets are usually purchased commercially and come in a series of components that can be stored and put back together easily.

Monaural (mono) One audio track.

Monitors Monitors were designed to provide accurate, stable image quality. They do not include tuners and may not include audio speakers.

Monopod A camera support with one leg.

Multicamera production Occurs when two or more cameras are used to create a television production. Usually the cameras are switched by a production switcher.

Narrow angle lens See *Telephoto lens.*

NAT See *Natural sound.*

Natural sound (NAT) The recording of ambient or environmental sounds on-location.

ND See *Neutral density filter.*

Neutral density filter (ND) A filter that reduces the amount of light coming into the camera without changing the color of the image.

Nonlinear The process where the recorded video is digitized (copied) onto a computer. Then the footage can be arranged and rearranged, special effects can be added, and the audio and graphics can be adjusted using editing software.

Normal lens The type of lens that portrays the scene approximately the same way a human eye might see it.

Notch filter (parametric amplifier) A filter that produces a steep peak or dip in a selected part of the audio spectrum (e.g., to suppress unavoidable hum, whistle, rumble, etc.).

Objective camera The objective camera role is that of an onlooker, watching the action from the best possible position at each moment.

Objectives Measurable goals. That means something that can be tested for to see that the audience did understand and remember the key points of the program.

Ominidirectional microphone This type of microphone can pick up audio equally well in all directions.

Open set Created by carefully grouping a few pieces of furniture in front of the wall. Even as little as a couch, a low table, a table lamp, potted plants, a screen, chair, and a stand lamp can suggest a complete room.

Optical zoom The optical zoom uses a lens to maintain a high-quality image throughout its zoom range.

Outline script This script usually provides the prepared dialogue for the opening and closing and then lists the order of topics that should be covered. The talent will use the list as he or she improvises throughout the production.

Outside broadcast (OB) Also known as a remote production, an OB takes place outside of the studio.

Pan head The pan head, or tripod head, enables the camera to tilt and pan smoothly. Variable friction controls (drag) steady these movements. The head can also be locked off in a fixed position. Tilt balance adjustments position the camera horizontally to assist in balancing the camera on the mount.

Pan shot When the camera pivots on its mount to the left or right.

Patch panel/jackfield Rows of sockets to which the inputs and outputs of a variety of audio units are permanently wired. Units may be interconnected with a series of plugged cables (patch cords).

Pedestal (1) An adjustable camera support that has wheels. These are normally used in a studio. (2) Can refer to the black level of a video image shown on a waveform monitor. (3) Also can refer to the action of raising a camera higher.

Per diem Refers to a set amount of money paid per day, above the normal pay, to a worker to cover living expenses when traveling.

Photographic lighting See *Three-point lighting.*

Pickup shot If an error is made during the shooting of a scene, a pickup shot is used by changing the camera angle (or shot size) and retaking the action from just before the error was made.

Planned production method The planned method, which organizes and builds a program in carefully arranged steps.

Plasma A high-quality, thin, flat-panel screen that can be viewed from a wide angle.

POV Point-of-view shot. A POV generally shows a person's point of view or is a miniature camera that is positioned to show a unique angle of the subject.

Preamplifier An amplifier used to adjust the strength of audio from one or more audio sources to a standard level (intensity). It may include source switching and basic filtering.

Prime lens A prime lens (primary lens) has a fixed coverage, field of view, or focal length.

Progressive scanning This sequential scanning system uses an electron beam that scans or paints all lines successively, displaying the total picture.

Prop Props, or property, are handled on the set by the talent during a production.

Public domain Music and lyrics published in 1922 or earlier are in the public domain in the United States. No one can claim ownership of a song in the public domain, so anyone may use public domain songs. Sound recordings, however, are protected separately from musical compositions. No sound recordings are in the public domain in the United States. If you need a sound recording—even a recording of a public domain song—you will have to either record it yourself or license one.

Pull focus A person who assists the camera operator by focusing the camera's lens.

Quick-release mount This mount is attached to the camera and fits into a corresponding recessed plate attached to the tripod/pan head. This allows the camera operator to quickly remove or attach the camera to the camera mount.

RAW Uncompressed data from the sensor of a digital camera.

Reaction shot A shot of a person's face that is registering a response to something in the program.

Rehearsal script This script usually includes the cast/character list, production team details, rehearsal arrangements, and so on. There is generally a synopsis of the plot or story line, location, time of day, stage/location instructions, the action, dialogue, effects cues, and audio instructions.

Remote survey (Recce) A preliminary visit to a shooting location.

Remote truck (OB van) A mobile television control room that is taken away from the studio.
Reverberation A device for increasing or adjusting the amount of echo accompanying a sound.
Roll The movement of text up or down the video screen.
Running order The order that the scenes or shots will be shown in the final project, which may differ greatly from the shooting order.
Safe title area The center 80% of the screen where it is safe to place graphics.
Sampling rate Measures how often the values of the analog video signal are converted into a digital code.
Saturation The chroma, purity, and intensity. It affects a color's richness or paleness.
Scene Each scene covers a complete continuous action sequence.
Scoop A simple floodlight. It is inexpensive, usually not adjustable, lightweight, and does not have a sharp outline.
Shooting order The order that the scenes or shots may be recorded using the video camera, which may differ greatly from the running order.
Shotgun microphone A highly directional microphone used to pick up sound from a distance.
Shot sheet (shot card) This sheet, created by the director, is a list of each shot needed from each individual camera operator. The shots are listed in order so that the camera operator can move from shot to shot with little guidance from the director.
Show format The detailed order of the scripted production.
Single-camera production Occurs when one camera is used to shoot the entire segment or show.
Site survey A meeting of the key production personnel at the proposed shooting location. A survey allows them to make sure that the location will meet their production needs.
SMPTE (Society of Motion Picture and Television Engineers) This international professional organization has developed over 400 standards, practices and engineering guidelines for audio, television, and the film industry.
Softlight Provides a large level of diffused light.
Spotlight A highly directional light.
Spreader A base for a tripod that stabilizes the legs and prevents them from spreading.
Stand-by To alert the talent to prepare for a cue.
Stereo Stereo sound uses two audio tracks to create an illusion of space and dimension.
Stereographer A person who operates a stereo, 3D, camera.
Stick mic See *Handheld microphone.*
Storyboard The storyboard is simply a series of rough sketches that help you to visualize and to organize your camera treatment.
Streaming Programming that is shown live or transmitted from a video sharing site to a computer.
Stretch Tell the talent to go more slowly (there is time to spare).
Subjective camera (point of view/POV) The camera represents the talent's point of view, allowing the audience to see through the talent's eyes as the camera moves through a crowd or pushes aside undergrowth.
Subtitles Identify people and places.
Surround sound Surround uses six audio tracks to create a sense of envelopment.
Switcher (vision mixer) A device used to switch between video inputs (cameras, graphics, video players, etc.).
Take See *Cut.*
Talent (performer) Anyone who appears in front of the camera.
Telephoto lens A narrow angle lens that is used to give a magnified view of the scene, making it appear closer. The lens magnifies the scene.
Teleprompter A device that projects computer-generated text on a piece of reflective glass over the lens of the camera. It is designed to allow talent to read a script while looking directly at the camera.
Television receivers Television sets include a tuner so that they can display broadcast programs with their accompanying sound.
Three-point lighting A lighting technique that utilizes three lights (key, fill, and back lights) to illuminate the subject.
Tighten shot Zoom in.

Tilt balance Adjustments located on the pan head of a tripod that position the camera horizontally to assist in balancing it on the mount.

Tilt shot Occurs when the camera moves up or down, pivoting on a camera mount.

Time code A continuous time signal throughout the tape, showing the precise moment of recording.

Timeline Usually includes multiple tracks of video, audio, and graphics in a nonlinear editing system.

Treatment An overview of the video script that usually includes an explanation of the characters and story plot.

Triangle lighting See *Three-point lighting.*

Trim To cut frames off of a shot to make it shorter.

Tripod A camera mount that is a three-legged stand with independently extendable legs.

Tripod arms (pan bars) Handles that attach to the pan head on a tripod or other camera mount to accurately pan, tilt, and control the camera.

Truck (crab) The truck, trucking, or tracking shot is when the camera and mount move sideways (left or right) with the subject.

Underexpose Occurs when the lens lets an insufficient amount of light into the camera. The result is a darker image with a loss of detail.

Vectorscope An oscilloscope that is used to check the color accuracy of each part of the video system (cameras, switcher, recorder, etc.). Incorrect adjustments can create serious problems with the color quality. Ideally, the color responses of all equipment should match. Color bars are usually recorded at the beginning of each videotape to check color accuracy.

Video sharing sites Online sites that enable producers to upload programming so that it can be seen by an audience.

Videotape Tape has been the traditional means of recording video images. However, it is slowly being replaced by hard drives and flash cards.

Viewfinder Monitors the camera's picture. This allows the camera operator to focus, zoom, and frame the image.

Virtual set Uses a blue or green seamless background, chroma-keying the computer-generated set into the scene. Most virtual sets employ sophisticated tracking computer software that monitors the camera's movements so that as the camera zooms, tilts, pans, or moves in any other way, the background moves in a corresponding way.

Voiceover Commentary over video.

VU meter An instrument designed to measure audio levels.

Waveform monitor An oscilloscope that is designed to monitor a video signal. This ensures that all colors will be correctly recorded.

Whip pan (zip pan) A quick pan shot that usually results in the subject being blurred.

White balance The process of calibrating a camera so that the light source will be reproduced accurately as white.

Wide-angle lens Shows us a greater area of the scene than is normal. The subject looks unusually distant.

Wild-track interviews Occurs when images of someone busily occupied (sawing wood, for example) is heard in a nonsynchronous audio wild track of an interview made separately.

Wipe A special-effect transition between two images. Usually shows a change of time, location, or subject. The wipe adds novelty to the transition but can easily be overused.

XLR A professional audio connector. Usually but not limited to three pins.

Zone focus Camera operators are focused on a portion of the scene. Any time the subject comes into that area, the camera has been prefocused to make sure the action is sharp.

Zoom lens A lens that has a variable focal length.

Index

C

G

H

I

T

U

V

W

X

Y

Z